Offshore Attachments

Offshore Attachments

OIL AND INTIMACY IN THE CARIBBEAN

Chelsea Schields

UNIVERSITY OF CALIFORNIA PRESS

University of California Press
Oakland, California

© 2023 by Chelsea Schields

Cataloging-in-Publication Data is on file at the Library of Congress.

ISBN 978-0-520-39080-5 (cloth : alk. paper)
ISBN 978-0-520-39081-2 (pbk. : alk. paper)
ISBN 978-0-520-39082-9 (ebook)

Manufactured in the United States of America

32 31 30 29 28 27 26 25 24 23
10 9 8 7 6 5 4 3 2 1

To my parents, Jacqueline Anderson Schields
and Thomas Freese Schields

Contents

Illustrations

Abbreviations

ABW	Algemene Bijstandswet (General Assistance Act)
AHU	Algemene Haven Unie (General Dockworkers Union)
AVP	Arubaanse Volkspartij (Aruban People's Party)
CBS	Centraal Bureau voor de Statistiek (Central Bureau for Statistics)
CFW	Curaçaose Federatie van Werknemers (Curaçao Federation of Workers)
CPIM	Curaçao Petroleum Industrie Maastchappij (Curaçao Petroleum Industry Company)
EEC	European Economic Community
ERNA	Eilandenregeling Nederlandse Antillen (Island Regulations of the Netherlands Antilles)
FOL	Frente Obrero y Liberashon 30 di Mei (Labor and Liberation Front 30 May)
IPPF	International Planned Parenthood Federation
KVP	Katholieke Volkspartij (Catholic People's Party)

NVP   Nationale Volkspartij (National People's Party)

NVSH   Nederlandse Vereniging voor Seksuele Hervorming (Dutch
            Association for Sexual Reform)

OAPEC   Organization of Arab Petroleum Exporting Countries

OPEC   Organization of Petroleum Exporting Countries

PdVSA   Petróleos de Venezuela, S.A. (Petroleum of Venezuela)

POA   Plataforma di Organisashonan Antiano i Arubano
            (Platform of Antillean and Aruban Organizations)

PWFC   Petroleum Werkers Federatie van Curaçao (Petroleum
            Workers Federation of Curaçao)

RdK   Refineria di Kòrsou (Refinery of Curaçao)

UMA   Union di Muhé Antiano (Union of Antillean Women)

VSAW   Vereniging Surinaamse en Antilliaanse Welzijnwerk(st)ers
            (Association for Surinamese and Antillean Social Workers)

VVD   Volkspartij voor Vrijheid en Democratie (People's Party for
            Freedom and Democracy)

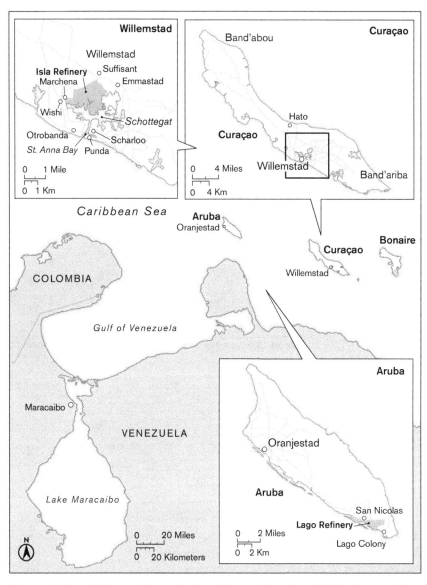

Map 1. Aruba and Curaçao, located a short distance from the oil fields of Venezuela. Map by Ben Pease.

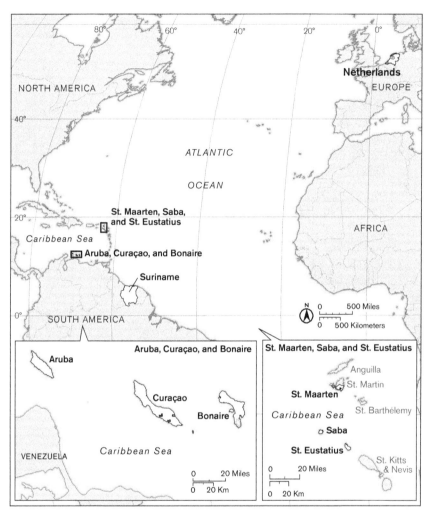

Map 2. The Kingdom of the Netherlands. Inaugurated in 1954, the kingdom had three constituent countries: the Netherlands, the Netherlands Antilles, and Suriname. Suriname became independent in 1975. In 1986, Aruba left the Netherlands Antilles and became a constituent country of the kingdom. In 2010, the Netherlands Antilles dissolved. Curaçao and St. Maarten joined the Netherlands and Aruba as constituent countries. Bonaire, Saba, and St. Eustatius became "special municipalities" of the Netherlands. Map by Ben Pease.

Introduction

"OIL IS THE LUBRICANT"

Pulp fiction author Wenzell Brown liked to tell a lurid tale. But as he arrived from the United States on the arid, wind-swept island of Aruba in 1946, his purpose was ostensibly different. He had come to observe an industrial boom. In the mid-twentieth century, the southerly Dutch Caribbean isles were the center of an emerging global energy system. Aruba, home to the Standard Oil of New Jersey-owned Lago Oil & Transport Company, and Curaçao, site of the equally enormous Royal Dutch Shell plant, housed the largest oil refineries in the world.[1] Stationed at one of the many clapboard saloons erected in the shadow of the Lago refinery, Brown found a lurid tale anyways. In the span of several inebriated hours, he encountered men from nine different Caribbean islands and three countries on the South American main. The men grumbled about wages, working conditions, and political circumstances in their countries of origin. They lamented long, hot hours toiling among the pressure stills while white US Americans occupied comfortable office jobs. They drank, they gambled, and occasionally they fought. And then, before the night was through, they ambled to one of several hotels where Dominican sex workers greeted an impatient line of customers. Together, they made for the rough windward coast of Juana Morto and

1

Smal—a public dump—to copulate among the skeletons of discarded automobiles and trash.[2]

Brown's writing gave personality to the men who turned crude into valuable commodities. He dignified their aspirations at a moment of heady possibility following World War II, even as he also described how race and nation could divide them, grievances spilling over into barroom brawls. Unquestioned by Brown, however, were the other laborers traveling along oil's commodity chain: the sex workers from the Dominican Republic. Brown did not ask about the male desires or the corporate investments that demanded their presence; less still about the longings of the women who labored at the fringes of the oil industry. While attentive to the diverse composition of a migratory male labor force, Brown neglected to see a similar arithmetic at work in the organization of commercial sex. For like many of their clients, the women who sold sex on Aruba were recruited from elsewhere. And like their clients, too, these women formed part of the itinerant and racialized workforce upon which oil companies relied. Indisputable in Brown's account, however, was what drew together these people from distant reaches of the region. Surveying transactional trysts one evening, Brown shrewdly observed that in these encounters, "oil is the lubricant."[3]

By attending to the intimate arrangements thought to facilitate oil's rise and demise in the Caribbean, this book shows that the reverse of Brown's observation is also true. Oil did not simply facilitate sex; sex lubricated the age of oil. *Offshore Attachments* argues that from boom to bust, ideas about sex and race influenced the organization of labor in the peak age of oil and were marshaled again to insulate shocks to the global oil market. Supported by corporate and state leaders, and variously embraced and challenged by Caribbean publics, attempts to shape intimate selves in support of the energy economy were always inseparable from the making and management of race.

Sexual energy and racialized labor were profoundly entangled in the production of energy itself. Often described as global capitalism's most valuable commodity, oil is thought to possess inherent worth.[4] A spate of recent research has shown, however, that oil gained value through the labor that participated in its commodification. In oil camps from Lake Maracaibo to Veracruz, just as on Aruba and Curaçao, women's work of clothing, feeding, and care, often invisible and unwaged, was vital to the sustenance of an exploited, racialized male workforce.[5] But as this book also shows, the kinds of intimate arrangements sought by oil companies and their state protectors overflowed the more visible forms of sexual labor sensationally described by Brown. From efforts to regulate the fertility of Caribbean women as the industry declined to domesticating masculine subjects and encouraging self-sufficient nuclear families, the sites of intimacy deemed pertinent to the oil economy included not just the regulation of sex but the remaking of sensibilities.

This book tracks these projects in two distinct periods on Aruba and Curaçao: the brief boom of the 1930s to the early 1950s, and the bust that followed, through to the sale or shuttering of the refineries in 1985. In each phase, attempts to construct new gender and sexual subjectivities, inseparable from concerns about race, were a primary method for managing the fluctuating demands of the oil economy. Through the boom period spanning the 1930s and early 1950s, Standard Oil and Shell, like other extractive and industrial enterprises in Latin America and the Caribbean, viewed the question of making laborers as a matter of fashioning certain gender and sexual norms.[6] Logics of race and nation also determined the conditions in which men labored and loved. Chemists, engineers, and other managerial staff from Europe and the United States lived in comfortable bungalows with wives and children, solidifying their claims to white respectability.[7] Living downwind of the refinery's toxic emissions, foreign production workers were granted access to women's sexuality on transactional terms. Believing women's proximity to whiteness essential for these men's sexual satisfaction, authorities facilitated the transport of women from the Dominican Republic and Colombia against prevailing colonial law. Local workers, meanwhile, followed a different sexual regime. Company managers offered material supports to incentivize marriage, widely assumed to enhance discipline and performance on the job. The dialectical reasoning connecting "homeplace and workplace" galvanized a renewed civilizing mission in the Caribbean, this time led as much by oil corporations as by state and religious authorities.[8]

From the early 1950s until the shuttering and sale of the Lago and Shell refineries in 1985, automated technologies turned refineries into depopulated industrial landscapes. Price increases following the so-called oil shocks of 1973–74 and 1979–80 spelled further disaster, with reduced demand creating a glut in refinery production. Authorities in Europe and the Netherlands Antilles looked once again to household arrangements and reproductive practices to correct the islands' faltering economy. The next several decades would be spent trying to resuscitate the nuclear family model absent the material incentives that once promoted married life. These interventions denigrated Caribbean repertoires of kinship and intimacy, repeatedly figuring them as lacking while at the same time displacing blame for structural inequality onto individual behaviors. According to family planning campaigners, development experts, and a new cadre of social scientists in Europe and the Caribbean, the collapse of the oil economy would be resolved not through wealth or job creation but by reducing the number of children born to low-income single parents. Intimacy and its racialized regulation, then, facilitated the meteoric rise of the oil industry just as it was imagined to blunt the effects of its equally precipitous decline.

As much as attention to intimacy illuminates the social reproductive foundations of the oil industry, it also highlights other actors and struggles that transformed company practice from the ground up. From Aruban housewives in the 1950s to radical Curaçaoan laborers and activists in the 1960s, popular actors mobilized to challenge oil's peculiar sexual economy. They did so from an array of political and moral positions. Some demanded that oil companies live up to their avowed family values, boldly defending access to middle-class respectability. Others insisted that erotic freedom would be the measure and the guarantor of liberation from corporate interests. Accounting for gender, race, and sexuality in the history of oil does not only tell a fuller story of the labor required to transform oil into wealth. It also expands our understanding of the sites of struggle that arose along the way—struggles that connected the bedroom to the boardroom and the domicile to the distillation towers.

At times, interferences into Caribbean intimate life relied on the stretching and usurping of law, first under Dutch colonial authorities and, after 1948, a democratically elected government operating under Dutch sovereignty. Like other Caribbean islands in the age of decolonization, Curaçao and Aruba opted to retain political ties with the erstwhile metropole. While some European laws remained in the Caribbean in the

postcolonial period, the perceived demands of the oil industry often resulted in the suspension of those statutes regulating marriage and divorce,
sex work, and contraception. The exceptional treatment of intimacy—or,
put another way, the offshoring of sex—thus buttressed a specific capitalist
project in the Caribbean that helped to consolidate a new global energy regime. In this respect, Euro-Caribbean attachments proved consequential.
Unevenly incorporated into the legal order of the erstwhile metropole, the
nonsovereign status of the Dutch islands enabled transnational actors to
intervene in Caribbean intimate lives while also denying the rights and
protections that prevailed onshore.

PETRO-SEXUALITY

This story surprises not just because of the centrality of sex and race to
the hydrocarbon age. That oil has a Caribbean history is itself a neglected
aspect of the region's modern importance. In his 1966 attempt to define
the region, Sidney Mintz noted the Caribbean was "both 'urbanized' and
'westernized' by its plantations, oil refineries, and aluminum mines."[9] That
the plantation helped to inaugurate capitalist modernity is hardly in dispute among scholars today.[10] Perhaps as a consequence of this, we know
more about the plantation than we do about that other paradigmatic site
of global capitalism, the oil refinery.[11] Canonical Dutch-language works
have highlighted the transformations wrought by oil refining in the Dutch
islands, changes so profound that Aruban and Curaçaoan history pivots
on pre- and post-oil axes. Yet, while industrialization changed working
rhythms and commercial tastes, many scholars noted that oil did little to
alter the structural orientation of Caribbean economies.[12] The development of narrowly specialized exports and reliance on a racialized, exploited
workforce echoed uncomfortably with the preindustrial past. As Mintz
reminds us, the plantation and the oil refinery were not on opposite sides
of a tradition/modernity divide.[13] Both reflect the region's fundamentally
modern character, unevenly integrated with but not, because of that, less
central to the global capitalist system.

In the twentieth century, the development of oil refining industries on Aruba and Curaçao linked these southerly isles to ascendant

transnational oil corporations and a burgeoning energy regime. In 1914, major oil deposits were discovered just thirty miles south in Venezuela's Lake Maracaibo region.[14] The following year, Shell broke ground on a transshipment and refinery complex in Willemstad, Curaçao, where Dutch oilmen enjoyed close ties with the colonial government. Shell's Curaçao refinery, known by residents and workers as "Isla" for the peninsula on which the plant was built, became the company's most productive, processing over one-third of Shell's total in 1938.[15] A latecomer to the Venezuelan oilfields, John D. Rockefeller's Standard Oil of New Jersey (since 1926 using its trademark Esso) acquired a small refining and transshipment site on Aruba in 1932 that the company soon expanded into a major refining center. In the decade between 1939 and 1949, Lago's crude runs nearly doubled from 230,000 to 400,000 barrels per day—among the largest throughput of any operating refinery.[16] During the Second World War, the refineries on Aruba and Curaçao supplied the Allies with a staggering 80 percent of their naval and aviation fuel, directly participating in the liberation of Europe from fascism.[17]

Fortuitous proximity to Venezuela's oil reserves was but one factor in the decision to establish refineries on the islands. Shell and Standard Oil also prized the dependent nature of these Dutch colonies. Independent republics and enfranchised laborers, after all, could make costly demands. It was also for this reason that Venezuelan strongman Juan Vicente Gómez outsourced the processing of crude to Aruba and Curaçao rather than risk the effects of labor concentration on his own terrain.[18] The impact of this decision was to be far-reaching. Occupying a combined 250 square miles, Aruba and Curaçao transformed into key nodes in the global energy economy.

The construction of refineries on the Dutch islands presaged the growth of enclave refining sites in the Caribbean region. Apart from abundant oil reserves in the continental shelf stretching across Venezuela and Trinidad and Tobago, much smaller deposits in Cuba and Barbados, and recently discovered hydrocarbons in the Guianas, most Caribbean locales do not possess independent oil reserves.[19] Yet the refineries housed in the Caribbean performed vital tasks, without which oil could not be globally commodified. As David Bond notes, the Panama Canal opened new transoceanic shipping lanes just as Euro-American navies and merchant fleets turned to heavy fuel oil, making the Caribbean a strategic home to new oil depots and refineries. Unlike those built to serve nearby consumer markets in the United States and Europe, Caribbean refineries were "scaled to the oceanic merchant and military networks they supported."[20] It was in these mammoth refineries that oil, of limited use in its crude state, was fractured, cracked, and distilled into an array of petroleum and petrochemical products. From motor gasoline for cars to jet fuel for aircrafts and heavy fuel oil for ocean tankers, these products helped to enable the collapsing of time and space upon which capitalism relies—a fact celebrated by industry executives on Aruba, who boasted of the island's outsized role in fueling global interconnection (figure 1).[21] Just as on Aruba and Curaçao, the dozen or more refineries built throughout the wider Caribbean between 1950 and 1970 were export-oriented, funneling petroleum products to growing markets in the United States and, to a lesser extent, Europe. In this same time period, the Caribbean became the world's largest exporter of refined petroleum products.[22] Together, Caribbean refineries processed over 2.7 million barrels a day in 1975.[23]

In recent years, interdisciplinary energy humanities scholars have drawn attention to the fact that fossil fuels do not simply enable sprawling transnational transport or determine the contours of Great Power politics and geopolitical struggles. They also trickle down, so to speak, shaping individual desires and saturating deeply raced, classed, and gendered notions of the "good life"—often in ways we struggle to recognize because of the very omnipresence of petroleum and petrochemical products in our daily lives.[24] In the twentieth century, the fenced-off vinyl-sided house, connected to work and commerce only by car, became the model of middle-class domesticity.[25] For these reasons, too, oil's heyday is often remembered fondly on Aruba and Curaçao. The age of oil, unlike the era of tourism dependence that followed, was for some a time of reliable wages, expanding employment, and respectable housing. As Cara Daggett has argued, in considering the political economy of fossil fuels, it is important to index their *affective* dimensions, including the ways that collective desires and identities are bound up in the fossil economy.[26] Fossil fuels have also enabled biopolitical projects throughout the twentieth century.[27] In a very literal sense, oil kept the lights on in Curaçao's family planning clinic (the Caribbean, like the Middle East, relies on fuel oil for electricity

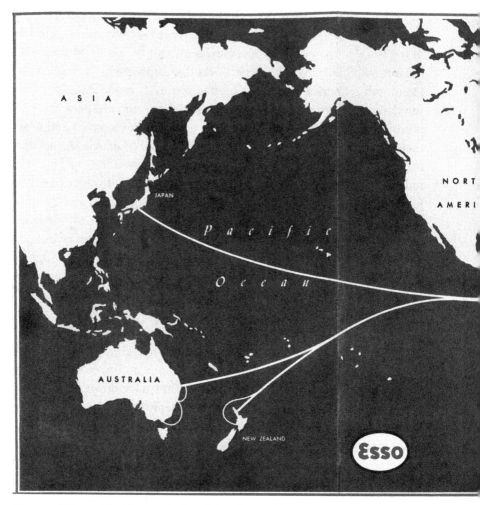

Figure 1. "The world-wide spread of Aruba's influence through the heat, light, and power of its products," 1959. SOURCE: The University of Texas at Austin, Dolph Briscoe Center for American History, Lago Colony, Aruba, Collection, camh-dob-010394. Courtesy ExxonMobil Corporation.

generation) and facilitated the transnational travels of demographic experts, an increasingly common phenomenon as the oil refineries on Aruba and Curaçao reversed fortunes in the 1960s.

What these perspectives bring to the fore is the centrality of oil to the shaping of desires and the regulation of intimacy, a previously unexamined

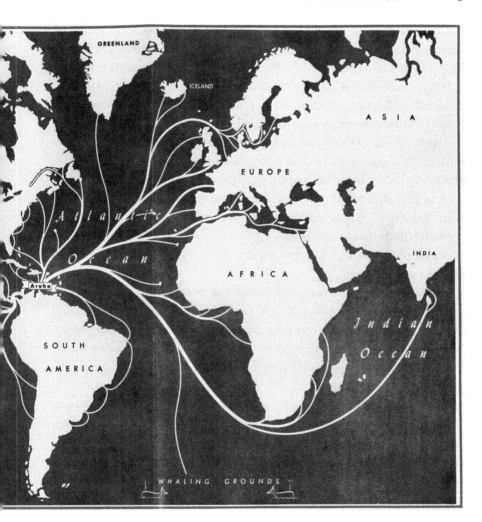

dimension in histories of sexuality and gender. Routinely cited as the "most neglected" among studies of Caribbean sexuality, the Dutch Caribbean thus offers a poignant case study for examining how oil seeped into households and selves as insular societies hosted an immense industrial experiment.[28] In the first half of the twentieth century, industry managers and governing elites on Curaçao and Aruba considered oil a uniquely transformative force both in the organization of its production and in the values allegedly inherent to the commodities derived from it. They placed tremendous faith in the potential of waged industrial labor to discipline what had previously been regarded as ungovernable aspects of Caribbean intimate life. More, the seemingly inexorable appeal of petroleum products was thought to encourage "modern" sensibilities such as acquisitiveness, self-sufficiency, and thrift, values that were imagined to outlive one's tenure in the industry as jobs dwindled with the advent of automation. This process was not always as seamless as refinery managers and political authorities hoped. Oil wealth drove modest mobility and allowed for the reorganization of home life among small sectors of the workforce, but the very targets of these reforms also leveraged the values of domesticity and respectability to gain concessions from the industry. What these sometimes fractious encounters reveal is the unique capacity of oil to find its way into private spaces, aspirations, and yearnings, often in unexpected and contentious ways.

Elites grappling with the destabilizing impact of industrialization held fast to the perceived promise of oil to provide deliverance from the sexual "backwardness" of the slavery past. In this sense, the oil industry more often reinforced and exacerbated existing hierarchies of race, class, and gender. Though European colonists did not succeed in developing quintessential commercial plantations—a fact widely attributed to the arid climate, though countless people survived on these parched but plentiful lands—on both Curaçao and Aruba slavery was nevertheless an important feature. The racial-sexual stereotypes forged in this era profoundly inflected industrial projects. Colonized by the Dutch West India Company in 1634, Curaçao served as a significant transit point for captive Africans arriving in the Americas.[29] As elsewhere in the Atlantic world, racial hierarchies rested on durable notions of inherited moral laxity. The pathbreaking work of Curaçaoan cultural anthropologist Rose Mary Allen has shown that in the decades after abolition in 1863, religious and colonial authorities repeatedly rationalized the subjection of Afro-Curaçaoans in the language of sexual depravity and gender deviance.[30] This devastating common sense persisted into the age of oil, as industry- and state-led reform efforts constructed Blackness as morally lacking and insisted on the heteronormative organization of the Caribbean family. Though less dominant than on other Caribbean islands, African presence also existed in preindustrial Aruba. After the Dutch takeover of the island in 1636,

Aruba was largely closed to colonial settlement and the Dutch West India Company permitted a small number of Indigenous people, likely from northwest Venezuela, to tend cattle in exchange for the right to reside on the island. At the turn of the nineteenth century, the island's population grew as some European colonists and enslaved African laborers moved from Curaçao.[31] At the height of the oil boom, however, mestizo populists defined "real" Aruban heritage as the product of mixed European and Indigenous ancestry, against the perceived sexual, economic, and racial danger of Black West Indian and Afro-Curaçaoan laborers.

Certainly, concern with the containment of racialized sexuality was hardly unique to the Dutch islands. From attempts to incentivize marriage in the long aftermath of slavery to interventions in fertility to meet social and economic objectives, these patterns form an all-too-common Caribbean story, disturbing in its constancy.[32] Taking stock of these projects, one might also ask whether fossil fuels played a role in their design and implementation. Beyond the world's mineral frontiers, labor and sex-worker migration were fundamental to the creation of export enclaves. Across banana plantations, gold mines, and broadened zones of military engagement, sexual energies became enmeshed in globalizing enterprises.[33] No less important were the fossil fuels that facilitated these movements of people and goods. When elites in 1960s Curaçao proposed intervening in women's fertility to mitigate economic decline, they emulated a model of development already underway in places like Barbados and Puerto Rico.[34] Through jet-fueled travel, experts exchanged knowledge across distances, engendering startlingly similar neoliberal schemes in the Caribbean and beyond. High mobility has long been a characteristic of the Caribbean, and though they receive less attention than they are due, the Dutch isles are no exception to this trend.[35] As Wenzell Brown's story suggested, the staggering demand for human labor drew thousands of men and women from Barbados, Grenada, St. Vincent, and beyond to labor among the distillation towers or in the domiciles of elites.[36] What has gone unremarked, however, are the materials that sustained these movements into the twentieth century, and which were produced in the very region that oil now cut new lines of attachment across. Focus on the intimacies imbricated in oil thus opens new views onto otherwise common Caribbean experiences and reveals the crude energies that propelled the region into the hydrocarbon age.

OFFSHORING SEX

On Curaçao and Aruba, interferences in intimate life were supported by a complex legal order that allowed for the stretching and usurping of statutes regulating sexuality and reproduction. The analytic of the "offshore" is useful in understanding this selective application of oversight. A multivalent term characterized by the evasion or minimization of regulatory power, the offshore is most often synonymous with tax havens, "free zones," and flags of convenience that serve as safe havens for capital, or deepwater extraction beyond the reach of drilling codes and environmental regulations.[37] Alluring images of lone oil rigs or isolated tropical islands uphold the misleading view that these sites of legal exception constitute a deviation from the otherwise "normal" business of onshore capitalism. The task, as critical geographers and anthropologists remind us, is to see the offshore as "constitutive of the always uneven and contradictory development of capitalism" itself.[38] Similarly, feminist scholars of the Caribbean have taken aim at the long-standing colonial tropes that cast the region as sexually aberrant vis-à-vis an imagined chaste white European or North American referent.[39] Joining these insights, it becomes clear that, like the seductive imagery of the "offshore," racialized fantasies of the Caribbean as a sexually exceptional space gloss the ways in which transnational oil companies and business-friendly politicians relied upon and carved out distinctive zones of legality to reproduce wealth. On Curaçao and Aruba, this occurred through the repeated circumvention and innovation of laws regulating sexuality and reproduction, which were thought to aid the oil economy in its spectacular growth and to buffer the deleterious effects of its decline.

Importantly, traditional associations of the offshore as a site of minimal financial or labor regulation were equally crucial to managing the "boom" and "bust" of the Caribbean oil refineries. In the early twentieth century, Dutch authorities exempted oil companies from certain taxes to incentivize refinery construction, a pattern replicated in other nonsovereign sites like Puerto Rico and the US Virgin Islands. US and European companies also offshored oil infrastructure to the Caribbean in an effort to circumvent labor guidelines and environmental regulation.[40] Far from an inconvenience, the absence of independent oil reserves in the Caribbean was, for corporate elites, precisely part of the region's allure, mitigating the threat of nationalizing mineral wealth.[41] With the dwindling profits of the refineries in the 1970s and early 1980s, Aruba and Curaçao enticed US and European businesses to funnel money to offshore financial centers and free zones, once again with the promise of sidestepping millions of dollars in taxes. Until the mid-1980s, ties with the Netherlands were imperative in fashioning the islands into safe destinations for capital. As in the US and British Virgin Islands, links with metropolitan governments offered the appearance of legitimacy and helped to secure advantageous tax treaties.[42] Like the treatment of sex, these examples reveal that the offshore "relies on sovereignty to abdicate sovereignty."[43] It is not a ready-made place but a *process* of differentiation, animated by the enduring links between former metropoles and colonies and between spaces of supposed exception and apparent normalcy, which at once accentuates and conceals these very ties.

These hallmarks of the offshore economy underscore the significance of ambiguous integration into the European metropole, the result of a decolonization process that placed Aruba and Curaçao under multiple overlapping layers of authority. In a marked reversal of familiar narratives of decolonization, the end of empire in the Dutch Caribbean resulted not in the severing of transatlantic ties but their revitalization. Fueled in part by the wealth and optimism generated by the wartime oil boom, in 1948 Caribbean subjects became Dutch citizens. Universal adult franchise expanded throughout the islands under Dutch sovereignty, themselves united in a six-island federation known as the Netherlands Antilles (Aruba, Bonaire, and Curaçao—designated as the capital and seat of government—in the southern Caribbean, and the northeastern islands of Saba, St. Maarten, and St. Eustatius).[44] After long-awaited negotiations, in 1954 the Charter of the Kingdom of the Netherlands named the Netherlands, the Netherlands Antilles, and Suriname as constituent countries of a commonwealth polity. Locally elected governments in Suriname and the Netherlands Antilles oversaw laws and affairs deemed internal to these countries (including, quite crucially, national budgets), while the Netherlands retained control over key aspects of kingdom-wide governance, including defense, foreign relations and diplomacy, and the maintenance of citizenship and good governance.[45] The fuzzy demarcation of internal and communal affairs preserved the dominant role of the Netherlands and the Dutch parliament, whose members were not elected by citizens in the Caribbean—a prospect rejected by all parties.[46] The result was a patchwork of member states with differing internal laws and varying resources, bound by Dutch sovereignty and common citizenship.

Like the offshore, the nonsovereign often appears as a profound exception, an anachronistic foil to the modern sovereign nation-state. From the vantage of our present, the decision to maintain imperial ties seems like an exceptional trajectory. But as a growing number of scholars have pointed out, there was nothing at all inevitable about the breakup of empires into sovereign nation-states.[47] The Netherlands, along with France, Britain, and the United States, still encompass numerous nonsovereign territories in the Caribbean and the Pacific and Indian Oceans today.[48] Just as the offshore is not the antithesis of regulatory capitalism, these multiple forms of commonwealths, departments, protectorates, and overseas territories are not the opposites of the territorially bound nation-state. As Yarimar Bonilla has argued, they form a constitutive part of sovereignty itself, enabling the consolidation of the sovereign state through the historical provision of exploitable labor and captive markets.[49]

The offshoring of sex was thought to aid the pursuit of these economic and political objectives. Wenzell Brown's dramatic story of sex workers, laborers, and sailors fornicating on the grounds of a public dump is illustrative of precisely this dynamic. To aid oil companies in maximizing revenue through the suppression of wage expenditures and housing costs, Dutch colonial authorities violated anti-trafficking laws to illegally move sex workers across international boundaries (just as, paradoxically, laws banning brothelkeeping turned unlikely settings into staging grounds for commercial sex).[50] This would be a recurring motif, with European and Antillean authorities taking advantage of the kingdom's blurred spheres of sovereignty to circumvent protections or else to enact more punishing forms of regulation. With the downturn in the Caribbean oil economy in the 1960s, European Dutch development aid supported a family planning campaign on Curaçao and Aruba. Colonial-era laws banning the promotion of contraception were refashioned first in the Caribbean to abate racialized anxieties about the alleged fecundity of Caribbean women. In each instance, the imperative to reproduce wealth furnished the rationale for legal innovation, and in each instance, the complex attachments of the offshore—the demands of an energy economy and association with Europe—came to bear on the peculiar regulation of sex.

The offshore, then, is a categorically entangled space. Thinking along and across these webs of interrelation offers a novel methodological approach for narrating histories of empire's end. In particular, viewing history through the prism of the offshore invites the concurrent analysis of three vectors of influence: global capitalism; lingering ties to Europe; and sexual-racial dynamics internal to insular societies.[51] *Offshore Attachments* holds all three in its gaze. In the movements initiated by US and European petro-capital, racial logics did not always travel neatly. The three-tiered "pigmentocracies" of many Caribbean societies, where light-skinned and mixed-race people of color occupied roles of relative privilege, confounded many US and European sojourners, who repeatedly offended colonial racial sensibilities.[52] Racial antagonism among the islands also mobilized distinct responses to industry practices. Mestizo Aruban women took to the streets in 1951 to demand the expulsion of "foreign" sex workers, including Afro-Curaçaoan women. Their mobilization was successful, halting the development of a state-regulated brothel for refinery workers. In these and other episodes, local understandings of race could shape responses to global petro-capital and European incursion. To go offshore in a methodological sense, then, is to hold in tension transatlantic, global, and local dynamics.

While the oil industry exerted profound pressures on Caribbean subjects, it also fueled defiant responses that could shape industry practices from below.[53] And here, too, sex stood at the center of activism, grievance, and refusal. It is through attention to these pitched debates that we perceive how the ties that bound Aruba and Curaçao, however unevenly, to an international energy system and the European Netherlands also presented various pressure points that Caribbean men and women leveraged quite adroitly. The thousands of Aruban housewives who mobilized in 1951 to prevent the construction of a brothel did so by deploying the rhetoric of domesticity promoted by the oil industry *and* the fragmented sovereignties that proliferated across the kingdom. Rebellion did not always conform to stated corporate values. At the nexus of the sexual revolution and global decolonization, Curaçaoan students and leftist labor leaders in the

1960s denounced the racist assumptions of family planning campaigns, European dominance, and corporate paternalism while reaching out to student movements in the Netherlands, revolutionary Cuba, and the US Black Power movement. In so doing, they arrived at distinct anticolonial arguments that defended women's desire and same-sex love as an insurgent, political act. Much as other scholars have returned to nonsovereignty as a potentially creative political formation in an age of virulent ethnonationalism and right-wing revanchism, this book emphasizes the innovative (if not always defensible) arguments about sex that emerged from these sites of capitalist exploitation and tenuous metropolitan inclusion.[54] Returning to these struggles also serves as a useful reminder that disputes within the oil industry concerned not only wages or working conditions. Popular actors indicted oil's distinct sexual economy.

THE SOURCES AND THE STORY

Like the substance itself, the archive of oil is at once slick and viscous.[55] It is slippery in the sense that corporate archives remain elusive to most researchers. Those approved to work in corporate archives typically must agree to have research vetted prior to publication to prohibit the release of prejudicial information. With the notable exceptions of corporate-commissioned scholars and the Dutch historian Jaap van Soest, who in the 1970s was granted near total access to Shell's records on Curaçao but was asked in 2008 to return or destroy any data in his possession, few scholars have gained meaningful access to these documents.[56] Where corporate records are partially accessible, including the ExxonMobil Historical Collection, these documents bear familiar marks of power that privilege the perspectives of white US actors. This is also true for the resident-organized Lago Colony archive, documenting the enclave community for white US and European managerial staff and their families on Aruba. I dwell on how energy and the segregation of industrial landscapes furnished new ways of articulating whiteness while also elaborating on the fragmentary lives that emerge in the elisions and interstices of the documentary record.[57] Though domestic workers, cooks, and production workers of color appear in the white resident archive as objects of derision and mockery, their ubiquitous presence signals white dependence on a population who actively shaped the conditions of their labor. Occasionally, this ruptured the hierarchical ordering of the archive itself. When workers demanded state intercession in labor conflicts, company records flowed beyond corporate remit and into the hands of state authorities. The limits of corporate authority also became clear when managers approached the state for assistance in disciplining bodies, behaviors, and desires allegedly disruptive to corporate interest, including especially the economic and erotic autonomy of Caribbean women working at the fringes of the oil industry.

Tracking oil outside the corporate archive affords insight into how it affected selves and sensibilities beyond the refinery gates. As oil oozed into intimate spaces, it enveloped actors often illegible in male-dominated histories of labor. This story, by contrast, is populated by production workers and sex workers. It is filled with the voices of housewives, student radicals, and mothers and their children fleeing postindustrial abandonment. Concerns with the perceived "costs" of sexual and reproductive behaviors drew these actors into collaboration and contestation with refinery managers, political and religious leaders, and development experts. Tarred by oil's viscidness, these exchanges exceeded the corporate record. They appear in administrative reports, newspapers, and a diverse array of documents on both sides of the Atlantic that linked the political economy of oil to race and sexuality. In this way, the records of family planning initiatives, the ephemera of protest movements, and the accounts of European Dutch social scientists and development experts all expand oil's historical archive.

As the Caribbean became central to the hydrocarbon age in the twentieth century, different sets of attachments became significant at specific historical moments. The narrative that follows eschews understandings of the transnational as ready-made or constituted simply by bilateral ties between metropole and colony.[58] Instead, it follows the processes whereby transnational configurations came to matter for the organization of the economy and intimate arrangements alike. Going offshore, narratively speaking, also means tracking how, at various times and with varying intensity, the oil economy drew Curaçao and Aruba closer to the oil fields of Venezuela, the transregional participants of the Caribbean Commission, or corporate headquarters in the United States. Likewise, the self-determining actions of Caribbean people forged new attachments. The cultural practice of mobility tethered the southerly Dutch isles to the sending societies of the eastern Caribbean, from which fathers, brothers, and uncles working on Curaçao or Aruba could invite female kin to work in domestic employ. Leftist activists on Curaçao and in the diaspora also reached out across the region, domesticating lessons from the Cuban Revolution and the Black Power movement as radical insurgency rippled across the Global South. And as the Caribbean refineries faced imminent sale or closure in the 1980s, thousands of citizens moved from the Caribbean to Europe, arguably drawing these regions closer together than ever before. Bringing these kaleidoscopic attachments into focus shows how supranational trends reflected in the production plants and domiciles of the Caribbean just as these same sites and the actions of individuals laboring and loving there refracted outward, influencing the circulation of oil and capital.

The chapters assembled here can be read as a series of calls and responses that detail how industrial demands dictated certain ideas about intimacy and how the presumed subjects of these interventions shaped the oil industry and transatlantic connection in turn. They move chronologically from the establishment of the refineries on Curaçao and Aruba in the early twentieth century to the shuttering and sale of the refineries in the mid-1980s, which triggered massive emigration to Europe. In this story, Curaçao looms large. As the center of political authority and the most populous island in the Netherlands Antilles, Curaçao occupied a dominant role in transatlantic relations. But it was also because of specific racialized concerns about the majority Black population that the island's inhabitants often appeared as targets of uplift and reform.

Chapters 1 and 2 examine the provisioning of sexual and reproductive care for refinery workers as oil production reached its zenith in the 1940s and early 1950s. Where chapter 1 focuses on elite-led efforts to develop domesticity among Afro-Curaçaoan men and to arrange transactional sexual encounters for foreign refinery workers on Curaçao, chapter 2 turns to the embrace of corporate domesticity discourse on Aruba. Among the wives and daughters of male laborers on Aruba, sex work was thought to invite new forms of racial danger and sexual competition that threatened the appearance of domestic harmony, a key marker of status in the industry. Chapters 3 and 4 return to Curaçao to explore efforts to manage populations as boom turned to bust in the second half of the 1950s and throughout the 1960s. Chapter 3 considers several initiatives to limit women's fertility and to reeducate Curaçaoan men as they confronted rising unemployment. As chapter 4 shows, however, a younger generation of radical students and disgruntled laborers came to articulate visions of bodily freedom quite distinct from elite actors; they argued that erotic liberation would secure economic and political self-sufficiency. Chapter 5 moves from the Caribbean to the European Netherlands as thousands of Caribbean families fled economic catastrophe during the "oil shocks" of the 1970s and 1980s. By showing how race operated in the European welfare state, this chapter reveals that the process of offshoring was not confined to the literal shores of the Caribbean but constituted a mobile practice of precarious citizenship in the multinational Kingdom of the Netherlands.

In his magnum opus *The Magical State*, the late anthropologist Fernando Coronil wrote, "Oil has helped mold a highly stratified and ecologically unsound world shaped in the image of disconnected peoples and things that have in common their separation from each other and from the history that engendered them."[59] This is the powerful optical effect of oil in the world. But it is my hope that, taken together, the following chapters restore to view a different set of intimate attachments initiated by oil and upon which its global growth relied.

1 Crude Bargains

SEX AND THE MAKING OF AN OIL ECONOMY

The port town of Willemstad brimmed and bristled with sociality on the eve of World War II. Aboard steamers and schooners, thousands of men and women—laborers, domestics, sex workers, seamen, and soldiers—awaited their turn to dock at Curaçao. They had invariably come to staff and serve the Isla refinery, Shell's largest plant. Beyond the brightly colored gabled houses lining the harbor entrance, flare stacks and steel holding tanks cut imposing figures on the rust-colored landscape. These materials of modernity towered over the cacti and divi-divi trees that once marked the plantations surrounding Willemstad's harbor. In the crowded streets of town, scores of sunburned US soldiers and Caribbean workingmen crossed the paths of colonial officials and Latin American sex workers. Clendon H. Mason was one such sojourner. A young man from St. Lucia who had come to work in Shell's HR Department, Mason recalled the "roaring forties" in the oil colony as a time when "life was gay, carefree, exciting, when men worked hard, loved harder."[1] His comments divulged a more fundamental truth: that "loving" and "working" were not discrete but profoundly entangled pursuits. It was in their meeting that the hydrocarbon age began.

Thousands of laborers traveled along the commodity chain of oil in the mid-twentieth century, extending the global power of Shell and securing the transition to a new global energy system. On Curaçao, this labor did not only consist of the racially divided refinery workforce, including white Euro-American managers, chemists, and engineers and the men of color who supervised the gauges, pumps, and furnaces. As Mason's comments suggest, it also involved an equally vital economy of sexual and reproductive care.

The astonishing transformation of Curaçao into a center of bustling cosmopolitanism relied on varied forms of intimacy. From the facilitation of transactional sex for foreign laborers to the enforcement of conjugal domesticity for Afro-Curaçaoan workers, intimate and domestic arrangements carried distinct advantages for the oil company. Focusing on the racialized character of petro-capitalism and the intimate forms of labor that advanced it, this chapter nuances understandings of oil as wealth. It highlights that oil did not merely emerge as "black gold" from the earth. Indeed, truisms that equate oil with wealth "offer ready-made and enduring discourses that constitute oil's power politics as having no social reproductive ground."[2] It was, rather, in very intimate domains that oil transformed into value by widening industry profits and cultivating new sensibilities suited to the industrial environment where crude transmogrified into commodity. If the projects of nationalism and decolonization conscripted specific gendered, raced, and sexed subjects, *work* was also a site where these subjectivities were "enforced, performed, and recreated."[3]

As the Shell refinery grew from the late 1930s to the early 1950s, the company's monumental project relied on the cultivation of a distinctive sexual and racial economy. This chapter chronicles the twin efforts of late-colonial authorities and corporate managers to regulate sex and labor as the Curaçaoan oil economy soared and imperial ties were recast. It begins by surveying the racialized construction of the refinery workforce, which in the twentieth century grafted onto existing colonial prejudices. It then turns to the expansion of the Isla refinery on the eve of World War II. The war would serve as a dramatic turning point. To meet wartime demand for petroleum products and to facilitate Curaçao's transition from a colonial dependency to fledgling democracy, sex and intimacy were offshored. Throughout the 1940s, colonial defenders of corporate interest suspended laws regulating prostitution to pacify an itinerant male labor force. Steeped in racist assumptions about white women's desirability, authorities recruited light-skinned sex workers from the Dominican Republic and Colombia against prevailing Dutch colonial law. Similarly, political and industry elites devised new methods for encouraging marriage and preventing divorce for Afro-Curaçaoan subjects. Sex, then, was neither an afterthought of oil economies nor a mere byproduct of the large concentrations of men in oil camps and company towns. Instead, intimacy and its careful coordination served as the social reproductive grounds of the hydrocarbon age.

RACE AT WORK

When the first wooden barges crossed the brackish waters of the Maracaibo basin to Curaçao's harbor in 1918, important questions remained to be settled. In particular, who would turn thick Venezuelan crude into lucrative petroleum products? The potential for the use of oil as a transportation fuel was just coming into view as World War I drew to a close. The war temporarily halted the construction of the refinery by cutting shipping lines and redirecting steel and iron-ore stocks to the war effort. But with fragile peace restored, and with the war proving the utility of oil over coal-powered energy, pressure mounted to put the refinery's products on stream. Curaçaoans might have seemed an obvious choice to staff the growing refinery. In 1918, only a small portion of the island's 34,639 inhabitants held waged positions as dockhands, in phosphate mining, or in construction. The few profitable industries on the island, including white-controlled shipping and trade, maintained economic privilege in the hands of the few.[4]

Yet Shell would ultimately reject local men as a viable labor source. Repeating long-established tropes about the habitual laziness of African-descended people, in 1918 a report to company headquarters lamented that "Curaçao labour is very unsatisfactory and unreliable. People come to work when they please and good words nor fines can alter them in this respect."[5] The European staff at the helm of the refinery knew little about the rhythms of Caribbean life. These men overlooked the fact that the oil industry held few immediate advantages for Afro-Curaçaoans. Living in the hilly, cactus-flecked countryside of Band'abou to the west and Band'ariba to the east, most Afro-Curaçaoans lived in close-knit communities on plantation properties or government-owned lands. In the early twentieth century, many in these communities preferred the relative autonomy of the seasonal cane harvest in Cuba and the Dominican Republic or temporary work in Willemstad's harbor to the repetition of industrial labor. This arrangement allowed family members to return to their plots of land when the rainy season arrived. The system of sharecropping (*paga-tera*) sustained communities outside of the cash economy while also perpetuating the power of the land-owning aristocracy.[6] It appeared that there was no contingent on Curaçao "patiently awaiting the tides of capital to pull them into wage work," which promised to limit autonomy over one's time and labor.[7] Consequently, Shell employed only three hundred local laborers in 1918.[8]

With many European Dutch employees having first worked in the oil fields of Indonesia (then the Dutch East Indies), the stewards of Shell's operation on Curaçao were no strangers to colonial racism.[9] In colonial Curaçao, perceived sexual respectability cohered hierarchies of color. From the Dutch acquisition of the island from Spain in 1634 to the abolition of slavery in 1863, authorities explained the unfreedom of Afro-Curaçaoans by associating Blackness with irremediable laxity in work as well as sexual life. Abolition did little to alter these racial scripts. With the Dutch Protestant government uninterested in the colonial civilizing mission, Catholic missionaries launched efforts to conform Afro-Curaçaoan families to Western norms, admonishing especially those who lived outside of formal marriage.[10] European Dutch Protestants and Sephardic Jews from the Iberian Peninsula, meanwhile, formed the small core of the colonial elite. These elites sustained their privilege through endogamous marriage practices that maintained white inheritance of legal status and wealth while quietly sanctioning both the consensual and coerced partnering of white men and women of color outside of marriage.[11] Colonial racism accordingly separated women into categories of respectable, white wives and mistresses who were mixed race or Black.[12] Proximity to whiteness conferred some economic advantages not otherwise enjoyed by Afro-Curaçaoans but also stoked fears among white elites that members of the mixed-race middle class would upset colonial racial hierarchies.[13] Despite the evident sexual license of white men in colonial society, it was

African-descended people who were made to bear the stigmatization of sexual profligacy.

As an Anglo-Dutch merger whose burgeoning global power relied on and exploited the already existing inequities in colonial societies, the Royal Dutch Shell Group regarded the moral development of Afro-Curaçaoans as a nearly impossible goal. Colonial elites agreed that local labor was not yet suited to work in an industrial setting, explaining this as an historical failure "to teach the freed slave that labor is a duty and a blessing."[14] Still, authorities insisted that local men should be cajoled to work for the oil company to avoid a large influx of foreigners. Following a number of recruitment drives throughout the Dutch islands and failed efforts to entice Curaçaoan men to return from the cane harvest, Shell professed local manpower to be thoroughly insufficient.[15] Only Dutch subjects from the colony of Suriname were regarded as a reliable labor source given their greater command of the Dutch language in contrast to the Papiamentu-speaking residents of the southerly Antillean islands.

To resolve their perceived shortage of labor, Shell recruited thousands of foreign workers to Curaçao. Such mobility was routine in the Caribbean and circum-Caribbean world, where migrants from Colombia, Dominica, Haiti, and beyond traveled to the cane fields of Cuba and Central American export enclaves to dig canals and labor on banana plantations.[16] In 1924, two thousand laborers from Jamaica, Barbados, and Haiti traveled to Curaçao and the company soon replaced Aruban men who had returned home after a heavy rainfall with Venezuelan workers from Lake Maracaibo.[17] In 1929, British agents recruited workers from the Portuguese islands of Madeira and the Azores. Still others came from Colombia, Cuba, Trinidad, St. Lucia, St. Kitts, St. Vincent, and the Caribbean islands under French control.[18]

In each location, the recruitment process played out similarly. After the company's agents advertised the jobs in the local press, word spread rapidly through small and economically depressed islands like St. Lucia. There, the twenty-two-year-old Joshua Jean Baptiste awoke at three o'clock in the morning to make the journey to Castries, the island's capital, on the day the company's agent was to conduct interviews. Among the roughly one thousand men who appeared before the agent that day, only two hundred were selected after passing a medical examination. Jean Baptiste considered himself lucky to be one of them. On the three-and-a-half-hour plane ride to Curaçao arranged by the oil company, he crossed significant cultural, linguistic, and political borders. Migrant laborers like Jean Baptiste brought with them loyalties and prejudices belied by the corporate category of "British West Indian." Among the migrant community on Curaçao, divisions of language, class, educational background, religion, and belonging within "big" or "small" island societies shaped networks of support.[19]

Shell's growing reliance on itinerant male labor structured corporate practice since the Group's inception. With its origins in the bitterly disputed region of Aceh, Indonesia, the Group honed methods of labor recruitment by targeting nationalities alleged to possess special capacities for strenuous and methodical work.[20] On Curaçao, Shell designated British West Indians for jobs in security, policing, and transport. In contrast, managers regarded Portuguese men as uniquely suited to construction and manual labor.[21] As Shell recruited growing numbers of foreign workers to Curaçao and only reluctantly employed local men, its subsidiary in Venezuela simultaneously enticed Afro-Curaçaoan men to the oil camps of Lake Maracaibo.[22]

This seeming contradiction was, in fact, a careful calculation. For managers of Shell's subsidiary on Curaçao, after 1925 operating as the Curaçao Petroleum Industrie Maastchappij (CPIM), foreign men were imagined as culturally isolated and thus easily controlled.[23] Such workers were thought essential for mitigating threats of unrest that periodically disrupted the supply chain of energy. When the Surinamese Louis Doedel became active in trade unionism while working on Curaçao in the 1930s, authorities simply returned him to Suriname, where the unrepentant radical was eventually forced to live out the remainder of his days in a psychiatric facility.[24] When in 1935 some two hundred Venezuelans agitated for higher wages, they were swiftly replaced by allegedly compliant Portuguese men.[25] Dependence on local workers undermined the perceived benefits of mobility, rendering corporations accountable to the societies in which they operated. Strikes among Curaçaoan dockworkers in 1922 and several hundred local Shell laborers in 1936 seemed to affirm the importance of creating a flexible reserve army of labor, with local workers decrying their low wages and replacement by foreigners.[26] For corporate managers, racist assertions about the alleged unsuitability of local labor couched a

Figure 2. Workers' barracks on Curaçao, ca. 1950. Housing reflected workplace hierarchies, with barracks in the foreground and bungalows beyond. SOURCE: Nationaal Archief Curaçao, Collectie Fischer.

threatening possibility: that workers would make bold political and economic demands.

The rise of the oil industry and the coordinated migrations deemed necessary for its functioning drastically changed life on Curaçao. When construction of the refinery began in 1915, the population of Curaçao numbered 34,000. It would grow 320 percent over the next thirty years, reaching 90,000 in 1947 and 120,000 in 1955.[27] Much of this growth was attributed to the arrival of foreign workers. But the material prosperity brought by Shell was not spread evenly across the island or among the peripatetic men who orbited the industry. After 1929, foreign laborers came to reside in crowded and ethnically segregated barracks north of the refinery (figure 2). A formerly sparse plantation of 150 hectares, the area of Suffisant teemed with activity as thousands of foreign workers like Joshua Jean Baptiste settled in sheet-metal barracks housing eighty men or more.

In these overwhelmingly homosocial environments, men ate, slept, and passed the time together. Mess halls served foods reminiscent of distant homelands and, in segregated social clubs, laborers marked the holidays and traditions of home.[28]

A practice that persisted into the 1950s, the ethnic segregation of worker encampments was designed to amplify divisions among laborers. Fearing mass mobilization and the exchange of radical ideas among workers, in 1935 corporate elites obligated workers to occupy nationally-divided camps with the aim of facilitating oversight by CPIM guards and colonial police. Further restrictions barred workers from entering encampments where they were not resident.[29] When the Venezuelan consul visited the camp of his countrymen in 1943, the official likened the guarded enclosure to the atmosphere of a prison. Venezuelan workers complained to their national press that Portuguese, Colombian, and Surinamese workers had nicer housing, better food, and higher wages.[30] Workers endowed these divisions with their own meaning, arriving on Curaçao with existing assumptions about racial hierarchies. In 1944, a vituperative article appeared in the Colombian periodical *El Siglo* that invoked fears of the violent overturning of white supremacy, claiming that Colombian workers were "under the orders of black foremen who treat them without any regard, some even resorting to violence and punishing our countrymen with a whip."[31] Continuously reproduced in the organization of the workforce and in more mundane exchanges between the company and its employees, racism operated to splinter solidarity among workers whose labor produced enormous profits for Shell.

The deliberate sowing of racial and national divisions also obfuscated more egregious inequities. The white managerial and engineering staff lived at a far remove from the worker encampments and the toxic emissions of the refinery complex, occupying comfortable bungalows in Julianadorp and Emmastad (figure 3). In these gated enclaves, the only Black people permitted entry were local groundskeepers and "sleep-in maids," the female domestics from the British West Indies who sought the limited financial gain of laboring in elite households.[32] The decision to recruit foreign domestics followed a complaint from CPIM management in 1938 about Afro-Curaçaoan women who, in addition to being insufficient in number, were alleged to be "uncontrollable and brutal."[33]

Figure 3. Emmastad, a neighborhood built for European staff and their families, with the Isla refinery and Willemstad harbor in view, ca. 1950. SOURCE: Nationaal Archief Curaçao, Collectie Fischer.

The insult reflected the company's unease with these women's deliberate attempts to control the conditions of their labor. As with industrial work for Afro-Curaçaoan men, cooking, cleaning, and looking after children was not, on its face, an attractive option for many young women. After the abolition of slavery, Afro-Curaçaoan parents often preferred that their daughters enter more autonomous occupations, such as being a seamstress or straw-hat maker, which carried less risk of sexual harassment and invasive scrutiny by employers. With the growth of the refinery in the 1930s, and as demand for domestics increased, the local press reported that Afro-Curaçaoan women were able to demand higher wages—and hence, more respectability—for domestic services.[34] Afro-Curaçaoan women were, it seemed, acutely aware that the respectability of white households depended upon both the material contributions and symbolic capital of their labor.

CPIM met Afro-Curaçaoan women's assertive economic practices with a familiar tactic: outsourcing workers from abroad. To do this, the company relied on colonial authorities to arrange the recruitment and legal migration of domestic workers. Colonial authorities, however, feared the political consequences of women's labor migration. The commander of military police warned that "girls and women recruited abroad will become concubines of foreign and native workers living here."[35] Born on imperial soil, the children of these unions would bear the rights of Dutch subjects and would be allowed to settle permanently on the island, thus undermining the unspoken advantages of a mobile labor force. Eventually, corporate and colonial elites reached a compromise to recruit women above the age of thirty from the surrounding Caribbean islands and Suriname, presumably to limit the childbearing years of women domestics and to increase the likelihood that women would already have families of their own.[36] Although this age limit would later be decreased to twenty (with an upper limit of fifty so that aging women did not become a liability for their employers), the patterns of migration remained.[37] By 1953, 80 percent of the 1,727 foreign domestic workers registered with immigration authorities came from islands under British control. Many were assisted in their migration by fathers, brothers, and other male relatives working for CPIM.[38] And like their male kin, Black West Indian women domestics also sent home wages and goods, linking wider Caribbean economies to the Dutch isles while enhancing women's economic independence through the prized constancy of a predictable wage.

As the above examples make clear, the efficient management of labor included not only the "containment of disruptive intimacy"[39] but also the stifling of worker militancy. Indeed, this was a mobile and lasting feature of multinational oil companies wherever they traveled, from Jakarta and Dhahran to Bakersfield and Veracruz.[40] Like the decision to locate the refinery on Curaçao and not Venezuela, sociality and domesticity were organized with the express purpose of avoiding "a set of *potentialities*," including the prospect of labor unrest and mobilization across ethnic lines.[41] For Shell and colonial authorities, race was at once a tool of division and pacification—a way to fracture solidarity while also, in the incessant production of race through segregated encampments and the ethnicized allocation of work, assuaging elite anxieties about the potentially unsettling

impact of a booming industry in a society long governed by racial prejudice. As the refinery entered a new phase of expansion and as the world
teetered on the precipice of renewed war, the provision of women's sexual
companionship also became a vital ingredient in the management of labor.

LABOR OF LOVE

Across the Atlantic on the morning of May 10, 1940, the Netherlands awoke
to the thunderous roar of aircraft engines flying overhead. After four days
of heavy bombardment, Nazi forces occupied the country and the Dutch
queen and her ministers fled to Great Britain. Once in exile, the crown
struggled to govern its empire amidst expanding global warfare. In March
1942, the colonial army in Indonesia capitulated to Japanese forces. It was
only in the Caribbean that the Dutch flag flew throughout the entirety of
World War II. Despite the outward signs of Dutch sovereignty, the war rendered vulnerable certain aspects of colonial rule. Unable to safeguard the
bauxite and oil refining industries in Suriname, Curaçao, and Aruba, the
Dutch summoned thousands of US troops to defend the Caribbean colonies. In February 1942, 1,400 US soldiers were deployed to Curaçao.[42] Their
mandate there, as elsewhere throughout the oil-producing Caribbean, was
to protect the region's refineries and shipping lines from Nazi attack.

Willemstad's elite residents at first regarded the presence of US soldiers
with enthusiasm and bemused curiosity. Shell hosted parties where white
soldiers and staff fraternized over ping-pong, cards, and beer at the company's social club.[43] But it was not long before US soldiers and other European sailors and marines caused problems for insular authorities. Living
adjacent to the harbor in the neighborhoods of Scharloo and Pietermaai,
Willemstad's elite families now daily encountered the rowdy sojourners
of a new industry. The latter were, it appeared, ignorant of the gradations
of color that assigned status in this Caribbean society. Since the growth of
the refinery in the 1920s, local authorities had allowed between 90 and 150
foreign women to reside on the island for up to one month with the purpose of selling sex. They settled in several hotels in Punda, a neighborhood
east of the harbor entrance abutting Scharloo and Pietermaai.[44] Elites became outraged that the new European and North American visitors were

mistaking the light-skinned wives and daughters of Willemstad's elite for the Latin American sex workers who lived and labored nearby. Worse still, light-skinned Curaçaoan women appeared to welcome these advances. As the writer Jules de Palm recalled, US soldiers were "literally and figuratively received with open arms, to the dismay of young Curaçaoan men who sadly discovered that their charm had been devalued."[45] Elites thus faced a dual challenge to the stability of the colonial order and to their sexual power as men.[46]

In addition to offending the racial sensibilities of colonial society, wartime traffic also highlighted glaring inconsistencies in the Antillean criminal code. Although colonial law tolerated prostitution, it imposed sharp prohibitions on third-party facilitation. Local women worked around these regulations by hosting customers in their homes. For foreign sex workers, however, these statutes forbade the entertaining of customers in the hotels where they resided. Resourceful taxi drivers equipped with makeshift mattress pads instead ferried working women and their clients to Marie Pompoen, a beach east of the harbor. The practice was so routine that US military authorities stationed a patrol car on the beach to dispense prophylactics.[47] In 1949, the police inspector on Curaçao reported that these sojourns had transformed Marie Pompoen into a "veritable open-air brothel." The inspector, M. Gorsira, was anxious that any seeming resolution would breed further complications. Revoking the visas of foreign prostitutes, Gorsira claimed, would increase the number of domestic prostitutes, who were "far less attractive than the foreigners because of their skin color." If men were denied access to white women's sexuality, "opportunity homosexuals" would emerge among the thousands of foreign laborers who settled on the island without their wives or girlfriends. For officials like Gorsira, same-sex desire could only be theorized as an aberrant reaction to the scarcity of putatively "attractive" women. The inspector sympathetically pointed out that white foreigners engaged in public immorality were themselves vulnerable to victimization. Copulating on public grounds and distracted by desire, several sailors had had their wallets stolen "during the act of fornication by unknown persons of black skin color."[48]

For elites, these racialized threats to public order stood alongside ubiquitous concern with the spread of venereal disease that endangered the wartime oil industry. Nearly a year and a half after the arrival of US troops, the US Joint Committee of Medical Officers reported to the head of public health on Curaçao that 154 incidences of venereal disease were recorded in the period between January 1, 1943, and May 31, 1943, resulting in a loss of nine workdays per case. Dutch marines stationed on the island were also contracting venereal diseases in record numbers. The report urged the swift adoption of new measures to defend the oil colony with its large number of transient personnel. Unbeknownst to this US official, in 1942 a government-appointed committee had already been assigned to research potential resolutions to the so-called prostitution question. The committee recommended the sequestration of commercial sex into zones of tolerance and police and medical supervision of sex workers. Above all, the colonial government viewed the adoption of these measures as a profound service to the oil industry. One official stated that CPIM worked hard to provide for the men drawn to Curaçaoan shores. But on the terrain of sexuality the company "simply cannot make provisions. It must leave this to 'private initiative,' subsidized by the government."[49] Warning that "the cleanliness and chastity of many of our girls are in great danger," the committee recommended that the men who staffed and protected the oil refinery be ensured access to light-skinned *foreign* women.[50] In its final report, the committee urged authorities to extend the duration of tourist visas and to license "hotels" where foreign women could lawfully entertain clients. Perhaps most remarkably, two Catholic priests served on the 1942 committee and supported recommendations to recruit and regulate foreign sex workers.[51] The endorsement of the committee's recommendations by the Dutch governor on Curaçao created a peculiar system of recruiting, registering, and surveilling sex workers.

In a landmark study, Kamala Kempadoo described a clear hierarchy drawn in the regulation of sex work between foreign, migrant sex workers and local women on Curaçao. Only the former—light-skinned women from the Dominican Republic, Colombia, Venezuela, and Cuba—would be recruited by colonial authorities and registered to work in designated hotels and, after 1949, in a large, state-facilitated brothel.[52] To be sure, these racial geographies of R&R expanded surveillance of foreign sex workers.[53] At the same time, they also marshaled the power of the state for their protection; for this and for access to light-skinned women's sexuality, customers paid a premium. Afro-Curaçaoan women, meanwhile, worked in the murky interstices of colonial law. After the implementation of new regulations in 1944, the colonial government required both local and foreign sex workers to register with police and medical authorities and to report regularly for medical screening. Barred from zones of tolerance, however, Afro-Curaçaoan women were compelled into clandestine forms of prostitution and subject to harsher penalties for public solicitation. Many of these women worked out of their homes in the growing, working-class neighborhoods west of the refinery.

Tjeerd de Reus, a European Dutch government doctor on Curaçao, wondered whether late-colonial officials had manufactured the demand for light-skinned sex workers. In his view, many white men from the United States "sought out the blackest woman they could find, believing that she would offer better sex." De Reus alleged that men from the US South found this prospect particularly appealing.[54] As Harvey Neptune also observed of US-occupied Trinidad, military excursions in the wartime Caribbean permitted the flouting of taboos otherwise strictly policed in the segregationist environment of the United States. And perhaps because of the potential for soldiers to carry these lessons back to their home country, in 1943 new recruits arrived on Curaçao from Puerto Rico, replacing the primarily white servicemen from the mainland United States.[55] Following de Reus's train of thought here, these officials likely did not respond to a demand for white women but rather sought to guard against the flagrant defiance of racial propriety. The late-colonial government's recruitment of light-skinned foreign women, however, produced the opposite result. Officials had not anticipated that local men of color would also seek out the company of sex workers. As one of de Reus's informants relayed, Campo Alegre was a surprisingly "democratic" place because "here, the white woman is available to everyone."[56]

Prior to 1949, the movements of foreign women to Curaçao resembled other patterns of labor migration in the region. In the early 1940s, women from the Dominican Republic, Venezuela, and Colombia worked with local middlemen such as the owners of schooners and steamboats to submit applications for month-long tourist visas to the Immigration Bureau on Curaçao. After registering with local police and medical authorities, many women would periodically return to Curaçao or neighboring

Aruba, drawn by the availability of work and the opportunity to send wages home.[57]

Like short-term contracts at the Shell refinery, month-long visas were designed to prevent the development of strong ties to the island. Nevertheless, many women attempted to claim residence in Curaçao to provide sustained economic security for their families. In July 1947, the twenty-nine-year-old María Bautista boarded a KLM flight in Santo Domingo along with her sister and three young daughters. Because her name appeared on the registry of sex workers, the Dutch consul in the Dominican Republic requested that María's family be surveilled to verify whether her impending marriage to a Dutch subject was strategic or sincere.[58] Suspicion of "bogus marriages" (*schijnhuwelijken*) could jeopardize a woman's ability to travel to Curaçao. Such was the case with Elba Sánchez who, despite her marriage to the Curaçaoan Willem Eujenio Koolman and Koolman's recognition of her infant child, was denied a transit visa until authorities could verify the legitimacy of their marriage.[59] Colonial authorities and the archives that registered their perspectives regarded these women as the pawns of traffickers or opportunistic criminals. Yet women's repeated efforts to bring kin to a prosperous island trouble their static portrayal in the archival record. Their independent acts of mobility eddied other diasporic circulations that typified the age of oil in the Caribbean.

Colonial authorities had always monitored the movements of sex workers. But in 1949, when local officials and the Dutch metropolitan government agreed to open Campo Alegre, the world's largest open-air brothel, foreign sex workers were subject to more direct forms of oversight. Atop the rocky Hato plain on the island's wind-swept northern coast, Campo Alegre was built in the militarized style of the industry it served. With a mortgage provided by the Dutch National Savings Bank, Campo Alegre offered rooms for 112 women. The familiar rows of barracks-style accommodations were shielded from the main road by a high fence and the sole entrance kept under armed guard. Between six o'clock in the evening and six o'clock in the morning, working women were forbidden to leave the compound.[60]

When viewed alongside the practices of labor recruitment in the oil industry, the state-led facilitation of sex work appears as the norm and not the exception. Just as Shell sought to create a flexible male labor force

divided by ethnicity and race, so too did colonial authorities work to uphold this system by similarly organizing sexual labor. Guided by racist convictions of the inviolability of local white women's honor and the alleged
undesirability of Black women, authorities insisted that light-skinned
women were essential for men's sexual satisfaction. They also defended the
importance of sexual commerce to the maximization of corporate profits.
The 1942 committee tasked with studying prostitution argued that foreign
sex work enabled Shell to avoid the costs associated with family migration, which, "in addition to the capital investment for housing, carries the
consequence of needing to pay higher wages." The committee worried,
too, that family migration would reduce the attractive flexibility of foreign
laborers who "cannot easily be sent back" if accompanied by wives and
children.[61] In an interview with a government committee in 1951, CPIM's
chief of labor relations, Hendrikus Albertus Oetelmans, confirmed that
"we [CPIM] are happy that Campo Alegre has opened" because it allowed
the company to employ thousands of foreign male laborers without paying
for the transit of their kin or the construction of family housing.[62] Petroleum companies needed external help to secure their power over oil and
the labor that produced it.[63] In the Dutch-controlled Caribbean, this help
came in the form of state-provisioned sexual labor.

The seemingly crosscutting imperatives to protect public morality and
satisfy men's erotic yearnings were resolved by facilitating sex worker migration and sequestering commercial sex. Each of these measures was,
however, prohibited by Dutch as well as Antillean colonial law. Articles
259 and 260 of the Antillean criminal code forbade the facilitation of prostitution by a third party and banned brothels. Adapted in 1918, these laws
copied Dutch metropolitan statutes passed during a moment of Christian political revival in 1911.[64] This ironic situation placed the late-colonial
government in the role of pimp, defying the very laws the government was
to enforce.[65] Time and again, oil justified this exceptional state of affairs
on Curaçao, even compelling the Netherlands to pull out of international
anti-trafficking treaties that the country once stridently supported. The
Netherlands was one of the initial twelve signatories of the Paris Convention of 1904 and signed all major international anti-trafficking treaties in
1921, 1923, and 1933. But in 1950, one year after Campo Alegre opened
its doors, the Dutch withheld their signature from the United Nations

anti-trafficking initiative after the Soviet Union petitioned to remove the "colonial application clause." This clause exempted enforcement of anti-prostitution and anti-trafficking measures in European dependencies and mandates. Signing the treaty would put the Netherlands in a troubling legal situation because the treaty forbade state involvement in brothel-keeping.[66] In 1954, the United Nations issued a damning indictment of the regulationist system on Curaçao, claiming that 1,636 foreign prostitutes were "imported through white slave traffic."[67] Owing to this growing pressure both internationally and locally (the subject of chapter 2), in 1953 the late-colonial government acknowledged the illegality of the brothel. Yet this admission did not lead to a change in the law. Authorities insisted on the strategic abeyance of Article 259 to allow the brothel's uninterrupted operation.[68] The distinctive sexual regulations introduced on Curaçao were thought necessary for all aspects of the oil industry, including the pacification and profitability of labor.

In the now voluminous literature on migratory flows in the Greater Caribbean, the most richly documented are those orchestrated by foreign capital in pursuit of male labor. This focus distorts the fact that women also crossed borders. In many cases, they moved to booming port cities to work as domestics and laundresses or to sell food at the fringes of export enclaves.[69] On Curaçao, however, colonial protectors of corporate interest participated in a much more systematic effort to move women to the oil colony. Though women's voices scarcely emerge in the historical record, their sexual and reproductive labor constituted an integral part of the local and transnational economy created by oil refining. As Myrna Santiago has argued, these women were "actors in the metahistorical processes and structural changes in the world's economy" who helped to secure a new global energy regime.[70] The peculiar sexual economy was not an incidental result of the oil industry but a condition that allowed for its global growth.

DOMESTICATING SUBJECTS

In this time of war and oil, the island's looming integration into the Dutch kingdom also entailed its strategic exclusion from the laws that prevailed in the metropole. This became most evident in the deliberate abrogation of statutes prohibiting third-party facilitation and brothelkeeping. But soon other legal precedents would be dubiously reinterpreted, this time to encourage Afro-Curaçaoan men to embrace new conjugal behaviors. The task of recruiting and disciplining Afro-Curaçaoan labor, once regarded by Shell as a futile goal, became a priority during World War II at the confluence of two developments: the expansion of the Isla refinery and the impending absorption of the island in a transatlantic commonwealth under Dutch sovereignty.

The plan to modernize and expand the Isla refinery at last gave the colonial government important leverage to increase the number of local men in the industry. After 1934, the construction of new Trumble and Dubbs crackers, a polymerization unit, and an alkylation plant expanded refinery output by fracturing heavy Venezuelan crude into lighter distillates such as aviation fuel. By 1938, Isla was Shell's largest refinery and the third biggest in the world, after only neighboring Aruba's Esso refinery and the Anglo-Iranian Abadan refinery.[71] Isla's importance would increase with the onset of war, especially as demand for aviation fuel soared.

Reversing prior corporate practice, Shell and the late-colonial government now worked to instill new working rhythms for Afro-Curaçaoans and to guard against the perceived social perils of industrial work. In 1942, Shell offered Curaçaoan laborers a bonus of four hours' wages if they worked for one month without demerits for absence or tardiness.[72] The company also piloted an experiment to transport workers from the outlying districts to Willemstad's harbor. The colonial government declared this effort a success, noting that it was preferable to housing workers in Willemstad itself. Authorities feared that severing family ties and prohibiting the cultivation of one's land would provoke hostility toward the industry and erode the community bonds that encouraged social discipline.[73] Yet, despite the government's warnings, a younger generation of Afro-Curaçaoan men abandoned the countryside for the harbor. For members of the colonial government, this group of wage-earning laborers raised urgent questions: could local men integrate into modern society without disrupting the social stability of the island?

To answer this question in the affirmative, the late-colonial government took an uncharacteristically interventionist approach. Their actions followed a spirit of political reform on Curaçao, a widespread feature of late-colonial rule that saw the limited expansion of rights across the Caribbean and beyond.[74] Chief among these reforms was the creation of an elected council, the Staten of Curaçao, in 1936. Based in Willemstad, the Staten consisted of ten elected officials representing Curaçao and the five remaining Antillean islands.[75] In addition, as an appointee and representative of the Dutch crown, the governor assigned five nonelected members to the Staten. As this measure suggests, the Staten was hardly a representative body. Only men over the age of twenty-five with a certain level of income and education, roughly five percent of the total population, became eligible to vote.[76] Further, the Staten consulted on policy but lacked legislative powers. The governor could override the council's suggestions at will. Though half-hearted, these reforms increased expectations for greater autonomy and brought a group of homegrown elites, most of them light-skinned descendants of established and upper-middle class families, into positions of limited authority. They would prove their preparedness to govern by engaging in a late-blossoming civilizing mission.

For Shell and the Curaçaoan government alike, the key to transforming subjects into citizens and industrious workers lay in conjugal life. On Curaçao, elites understood apathy about marriage to be a unique feature of Afro-Curaçaoan culture inherited from the past. Cohabitation or having children outside of marriage, or so-called visiting relationships wherein the couple did not reside together, were frequently explained as regrettable holdovers from slavery, when formal marriages between enslaved people were forbidden. Rarely were these practices regarded as acceptable or specific to the island's own historical, cultural, and economic conditions. This racialist discourse possessed a long and stinging afterlife. The assumed universality of heterosexual marriage and the nuclear family rationalized a range of incursions into Afro-Curaçaoan households, typically under the supervision of the Catholic Church. It was not until the outbreak of World War II, with the precipitous growth of the oil industry and the perceived crisis of morality that attended it, that the colonial government and Shell began seriously to promote marriage for Afro-Curaçaoans. In some respects these arms of authority were inextricable, with Shell personnel filling various administrative roles within the late-colonial government.[77]

For many in the Staten of Curaçao, the seeming failure of young Afro-Curaçaoan men to adapt to "modern" conjugal norms went together with the island's own lacking infrastructure. Though electricity, paved roads, and potable water served the refinery, few areas beyond Willemstad's harbor boasted similar luxuries. Far from spreading wealth, the wartime oil industry seemed to exacerbate inequality. Local laborers were initially denied even the barracks-style housing of their foreign counterparts. Those workers who left the countryside often settled in the informal *barios* of Wishi and Marchena west of the refinery grounds. Built from industrial scrap and oil drums, these settlements quickly earned a reputation as dens of disease and vice.[78] In a meeting of the Staten in 1942, J. M. P. Kroon, a member of the Katholieke Volkspartij (KVP), drew attention to the shortage of subsidized housing in the city, "which tests hygienic and moral demands."[79] These concerns were affirmed the following year when another member of the Staten claimed that, unable to secure housing, young couples quickly divorced while others were compelled to forego marriage entirely.[80] These associations attached to long-standing white fantasies of Afro-Curaçaoans as sexually promiscuous and unruly, entrenching colonial racial sensibilities in the corporate age.

With the demographic shifts wrought by the oil industry, the Staten now sought to impose conjugal bonds on Afro-Curaçaoans who abandoned the kin networks of the countryside. In particular, the Staten and the governor of Curaçao resorted to new legislative measures designed to "fight the cancer of divorce," which authorities perceived as an unfortunate and increasingly common symptom of unique wartime circumstances and population movements.[81] Members of the Staten acted to avert moral crisis by requiring more stringent evidence of adultery. The debate hinged on whether oral testimony would remain sufficient proof for one of the few legal grounds for divorce in the Caribbean colonies and European metropole alike. It functioned as an open secret on Curaçao that spouses would claim infidelity to escape unhappy marriages, regardless of whether adultery occurred. For the Staten, the resolution to this issue would not be sought by relaxing divorce law, but rather by requiring additional proof beyond verbal confession. All members of the Staten agreed that officials had a duty to defend marriage in a time of war and rapid industrialization. But Lindoro Christoffel Kwartsz, a wealthy Aruban statesman and the attorney general, worried about the unintended effects of exacting standards of proof. If additional witness testimony was needed to verify claims of adultery, it would prevent honest husbands from assuming the blame for cheating wives, sparing the latter public disgrace.[82] Although several members of the Staten questioned this legislative reform, when the Staten voted on the revised divorce law in 1944, only one member of the council abstained. Even critics like Kwartsz ultimately voted to support the new law.[83]

The enterprising efforts of the late-colonial government once again distinguished Antillean from European Dutch law. In the metropole, verbal confession remained sufficient proof of adultery and legal grounds for divorce. Though confident in the moral rightness of their actions, members of the Staten questioned whether this newfangled Antillean divorce law betrayed the principal of concordance that strove to harmonize law across the Netherlands and its empire, especially as plans for commonwealth statehood hung in the balance. The Staten's ability to diverge from European legal norms was a result of democratizing reforms as well as the unique circumstances of the war, which distanced Antillean leadership from metropolitan oversight. The Staten used its newfound power not to reject but rather to reaffirm commitment to a civilizing mission. The majority of the council supporting new divorce legislation pointed out that massive wartime population movements placed the island in a "state of emergency" that warranted the action of Antillean authorities. If the council waited for the restoration of order in the Netherlands, "the legislator would be falling short of his task."[84] One day after the law was approved on August 18, 1944, the local press celebrated the Staten's ambitious program of reform. *Amigoe di Curaçao* reported, "Here it appears that Curaçao is once again paving the path for good morals." Making reference to the Dutch government in exile, the article concluded, "We are sure that in 'London' the important work of our Staten will also be appreciated."[85]

Striking in the council's conversations on morality, marriage, and divorce is the extent to which such discussions functioned to prove and to perform Antillean preparedness to govern Caribbean subjects autonomously.[86] Without prompting from the exiled Dutch government, the colonial governor on Curaçao—a position occupied almost exclusively by European Dutch Catholics—redoubled efforts to incentivize marriage and the recognition of children born out of wedlock. The governor, Piet Kasteel, opened the meeting of the Staten on April 4, 1944 with a bold plan to reverse Curaçao's rate of "illegitimate" births, which accounted for 30 percent of births the previous year.[87] Just before the passage of the divorce law in August 1944, the governor collaborated with an official from the civil registry to promote marriage among unwed couples with children, simultaneously inviting couples to wed easily before the law and to facilitate the legal recognition of their children. According to press reports, 177 children were recognized by a parent during the first two weeks of August.[88] The chairman of the Staten, KVP member John Horris Sprockel, affirmed the importance of the governor's efforts. In his view, the "thorny question of illegitimate children" revealed "an absence of a feeling of responsibility but also laxity and ignorance of the advantages attached to marriage." Sprockel continued that though this situation "may be historically explainable," it now "unnecessarily tarnishes our community and is highly socially undesirable."[89]

Vague allusions to the historical origins of illegitimacy would not have confused members of the Staten. Despite the ubiquity of procreative non-marital relationships among white elites (and including, it was rumored, among members of the Staten itself), these same individuals believed that it was the descendants of racial slavery who lacked enthusiasm for marriage.[90] Such views simultaneously maintained elite sexual privilege *and* presumptions of respectability while equating moral degradation with African descent. Sprockel and Governor Kasteel's references to "laxity" and the absence of a "feeling of responsibility" served as a metalanguage of race, conjuring stereotypes of immaturity, irresponsibility, and sexual danger that had permeated justifications for slavery and remained potent long after abolition.[91] In its new democratizing form, the colonial state would now compel Black subjects to conform to Western ideals of respectability by offering them both the carrot (an easy, expedited marriage process) and the stick (harsher laws that would make divorce all but impossible).

If decolonization represented "a kind of déjà vu akin to abolition from slavery,"[92] then in no arena was this sense of déjà vu more acute than in efforts to manage the sexuality of Curaçaoan subjects. Where after abolition the Catholic Church concerned itself with moral reform, in the years surrounding World War II newly empowered Curaçaoan political elites, many of them also Catholic, now saw interlinked economic and political rationales for joining the cause. Antillean elites were not the only ones to take part in this state-led moralism as global crises weakened or recast European power in the colonies. In the French overseas departments, French officials extolled the importance of paternal duty and marital monogamy, believing Antillean equality to hinge in large measure on assimilation into the allegedly universal values of French culture and family life. After the widespread labor rebellions in the British Caribbean in 1934–39, authorities studying the source of unrest identified "loose" family structures as a primary cause. Interventionist social welfare programs implemented throughout the British Caribbean sought to depoliticize men through industrial employment and "responsible" trade unionism that instilled commitment to family and work.[93] On Curaçao, the advantages of a similar approach were thought to be multifold, transitioning Afro-Curaçaoan men to the industrial environment and proving Curaçao's equality with the Dutch metropole. Like their counterparts in the wider Caribbean, late-colonial officials on Curaçao believed their actions would address the island's inequality at its source: racialized assignations of sexual profligacy would no longer justify Curaçao's political subordination.

THE CORPORATE FAMILY

In the 1940s, the roaring success of the Dutch Caribbean oil refineries lent new credibility to the prospect of autonomous self-governance. Meanwhile, in Suriname, on South America's Caribbean coast, wartime demand for bauxite (a major source of aluminum) generated immense government revenue and enthusiasm for enhanced self-rule.[94] Light-skinned and educated Caribbean politicians championed the cause of equality with and integration into the former metropole. Its vulnerability proven by the Nazi occupation of the Netherlands, the Dutch government also came to embrace visions of commonwealth statehood.[95] In 1942 the Dutch queen announced the state's intent to create "a commonwealth in which the Netherlands, Indonesia, Suriname, and Curaçao will participate, with complete self-reliance and freedom of conduct for each part regarding its internal affairs, but with the readiness to render mutual assistance."[96] This federalist experiment did not play out as the Dutch queen imagined. In 1949, the proverbial crown jewel of the Dutch empire, Indonesia, achieved sovereignty after a series of bloody military engagements. Only in the Caribbean did political attachments remain. On Curaçao, the prospect of commonwealth statehood renewed debates about Curaçaoan subjects' moral preparedness for citizenship. Shell would also be forced to contend with the prospect of a rights-bearing local workforce, deploying new strategies to domesticate and depoliticize Curaçaoan men.

In the run-up to this democratic transition, cleavages had begun to grow between political factions who supported the advancement of democracy and those who hoped to preserve entrenched hierarchies. The charismatic Curaçaoan lawyer Moises Frumencio da Costa Gomez embodied the former, progressive political spirit. Elected to the Staten as a member of the Curaçaosche Roomsch Katholieke Partij in 1936, da Costa Gomez soon found himself at loggerheads with other Catholic-aligned politicians who believed that Afro-Curaçaoans were not yet ready for citizenship. A man of mixed African and European ancestry who was only later inherited by his affluent Jewish father, da Costa Gomez emphasized the latent political consciousness of Afro-Curaçaoans.[97] In his writing and activism, the statesman argued that ordinary people already possessed the sophistication necessary to survive in a modern democracy and developed an extensive network of supporters who aimed to facilitate the empowerment of the Curaçaoan populace.[98] Affectionately known as *Doktór*, da Costa Gomez would become one of the principal architects of the constitution of 1954 that transferred internal governance to democratically elected bodies in the Caribbean. Self-governing in local respects, the Netherlands Antilles would nevertheless remain bonded to the Netherlands as a putatively equal partner state within its commonwealth. The six islands of the Netherlands Antilles would themselves be bound in a federation with Curaçao as its administrative and political center. Da Costa Gomez's vision of decolonization without independence aligned with other federalist experiments playing out both further afield and closer to home. From French West Africa to the British Commonwealth Caribbean, the "federal moment" of the 1940s–50s showed that decolonization could take multiple forms beyond the territorially bound nation-state.[99]

Many in da Costa Gomez's party, which became the KVP in 1938, feared these impending changes to the political order. As Margo Groenewoud

has observed, in the 1940s divisions sharpened between those who believed the majority of Curaçaoans were ready for citizenship and those
who did not. In a 1945 editorial in the Curaçaoan magazine *Lux*, KVP
secretary Michael Möhlmann defended the role of the party as that of
an all-knowing father guiding his children. For Möhlmann, the analogy
between political and paternal authority rationalized a political system
where power rested with ostensibly wiser elites: "Paternal authority is absolute. It does not derive from the will of his children, nor does it fall under
their control. . . . The reason for this is that children are immature and are
therefore not fully formed people."[100] In view of the startlingly opposed
commitments of Möhlmann and da Costa Gomez, the KVP splintered.
During the war years, da Costa Gomez mobilized a grassroots movement
throughout the island, first in secret and later in open rebellion against the
KVP. The *Doktór's* ability to mobilize Afro-Curaçaoans derived from the
expansion of Dutch citizenship and universal adult franchise in 1948, one
of the first truly democratic measures implemented in the colony. To the
great consternation of the party, da Costa Gomez launched his own Nationale Volkspartij (NVP) that year and won half the seats in the Staten
elections of 1949. The party's base lay in the countryside but drew in part
from the new Afro-Curaçaoan proletariat in Willemstad, who supported
the party's defense of local workers against foreign usurpation. Once the
largest party in the Staten, the KVP earned only one seat.[101] As the first
democratic election in the Netherlands Antilles, the outcome of the 1949
election laid bare disenchantment with paternalistic attitudes on Curaçao.

Shell, too, was compelled to respond to these changing political yearnings in an effort to head off potential unrest. As World War II proved the
ascendance of oil over other energy sources, workers exercised circumscribed but no less important agency to halt aspects of energy production.
In the mid-twentieth century, labor struggles in the world's oil-producing
zones often joined with anticolonial and nationalist politics, threatening
the Euro-American stranglehold on global oil wealth. The nationalization
of Mexican oil in 1938 and eruptions of labor unrest in California, Indonesia, and Saudi Arabia all proved that the unequal distribution of profit
according to race and nationality would not go uncontested. In Indonesia,
insurgent nationalists dispossessed Shell of important concessions and,
immediately after World War II, moved to ouster the Dutch entirely. On

Curaçao, the brief strike of 1936 resulted in the creation of the R.K. Arbeiders Unie, which attempted to blend broad social and religious objectives with labor demands. In 1942, a Chinese crew aboard a Shell tanker organized a work stoppage en route to Curaçao. Protesting low pay and the increasingly dangerous nature of their wartime work, over four hundred striking workers were eventually detained in Suffisant. Local police and Shell security shot and killed twelve crewmembers and wounded an additional thirty-eight after several tried to escape arrest.[102] This bloody episode was silenced in the local press and the victims buried in an unmarked grave in Kolebra Bèrdè, a cemetery for criminals and apostates.[103]

In a pattern that prevailed across the world's extractive sites, new corporate schemes emerged to subdue labor unrest that now coincided with the violent overturning of European colonialism. As Robert Vitalis has argued, efforts to defeat unionization and the nationalization of oil industries often resulted in enhanced "welfare work," or paternalistic policies to meet the minimum demands of small segments of laborers, including offering benefits and home loans and building schools, churches, and recreation facilities.[104] Similar arrangements abounded across the Caribbean and Latin America. Colombia's textile mills, Suriname's bauxite mining towns, and Chile's El Teniente copper mine all saw the introduction of "industrial paternalism" in the 1920s–50s. Corporations built homes and constructed spaces of leisure that stretched the company into ever more intimate domains of worker's lives while recasting the corporation itself as an altruistic *paterfamilias*.[105]

On Curaçao, Shell's effort to prevent radical rebellion focused once again on the Afro-Curaçaoan nuclear family. The family was thought to contain within itself a certain degree of welfare work in the provisioning of essential care for which corporations need not bear the costs. It was also believed that duty to work and family would be mutually reinforcing, transitioning Afro-Curaçaoan men to the industrial workplace by binding them to the material welfare of a family and the gendered propriety and masculine duty this was alleged to encourage.

Laborers were keenly aware of the shifting corporate climate and pushed management to make further concessions. They did so by deploying arguments about the family and the defense of morality while also indicting the discrimination operative in the industry. During a public

address of the Dutch governor in 1943, one Curaçaoan laborer successfully passed a handwritten note to the island's highest-ranking official.
Written "in the name of hundreds of workers" who cleaned the refinery's
laboratories and worked in construction, the letter urged the government
to institute a minimum wage because "THERE ARE WORKING PEOPLE
WITH FAMILIES WHO STILL EARN 16.80 FLORINS." More still, the
workers argued, "there should be no distinctions among people whether
they are red, white, or black."[106] That same year, Venezuelan workers
persuasively made the case for improved housing. They argued that the
roughly forty laborers who came to the island with their young children
were routinely exposed to male nudity and immoral acts at the nearby
bachelor encampments.[107] In 1945, the Portuguese press painted a bleak
picture of Madeiran laborers on Curaçao, with some three thousand men
isolated from their families.[108] In response, the attorney general urged
the governor to open talks with CPIM to emulate models of labor recruitment developed in the oil fields of Indonesia. In that ostensibly successful
experiment, Javanese contract workers became "a model of peace and
tranquility" when recruited together with their families.[109] Following the
public relations scandals that emerged whenever foreign workers turned
to their respective national presses, Shell agreed after the war to reverse
prior corporate practice, expanding family housing for some skilled foreign laborers and even subsidizing the cost of family migration. Starting
in 1945, the number of family homes available in Suffisant grew from 40
to 126. As Dutch subjects, Surinamese workers were entitled earlier to
family dwellings, which likewise nearly doubled from 36 family homes in
1938 to 66 the following year.[110]

As workers' awareness of their power increased throughout the war, in
1943 Shell attempted to head off the possibility of unionization by forming an advice committee to appease the demands of Curaçaoan workers.[111]
Corporate management celebrated this step as "proof that we here in Curaçao want to understand the signs of the times."[112] Assuming that married
men with mortgages to pay and mouths to feed would be less likely to join
the picket line, the company expanded family benefits for local workers.
Foremost among these was the pledge to develop family housing for local
laborers. In 1951, Shell built 90 new residences in the neighborhood of Cas
Cora and offered these homes to Curaçaoan laborers on attractive terms.[113]

Though white staff were provided free housing for the duration of their assignment, Curaçaoan workers accepted loans from their employer, funneling wages back into corporate coffers.

The idea that Shell formed a corporate family unto itself was actively promoted through the soft power of company propaganda. At the same time that local men took up refinery jobs in 1942, Shell issued the first edition of its monthly employee publication *De Passaat* (*The Trade Wind*), designed to forge affective ties between the corporation and its workers. The pages of *De Passaat* routinely extolled the virtues of masculine duty. A cover story on "Responsibility" in 1947 connected the cultivation of responsibility in the home to successful performance on the job: "A feeling of responsibility means the fulfilling of one's duty. The greater the sense of responsibility, the higher one climbs the social ladder."[114] Such messaging was designed not only to inculcate a sense of paternal duty among male employees. It also painted the company itself as a model father figure. Trumpeting the beneficence of the corporation, *De Passaat* reported that the oil industry offered Curaçao innumerable material and social benefits, including "wealth for the treasury, buildings, education, relaxation, sport, and hygiene," and that "also of undeniable value is the influence she exercises on her staff, making the latter more methodical and disciplined in their work."[115] Paternalist oversight was also applied in more direct ways. Staff of the personnel department individually addressed every laborer who was known to live in concubinage, exhorting the worker to assume his masculine duty by legitimating family ties and providing for lawfully wedded spouses after death.[116]

Such lessons were thought to be socially exigent and economically expedient. This was not least because Shell's program to enhance workplace and household discipline appeared to produce the desired results. Connecting success on the job to harmony in the home, *De Passaat* regularly publicized the marriages and anniversaries of company employees, celebrating the occasion with photographs of husbands standing alongside smartly dressed spouses and kids (figure 4). In 1947, Shell extended free medical care to workers' wives and children, once again in a bid to transfer the task of reproductive care onto unwaged women's work and to engender higher levels of productivity. These benefits were expanded in 1950 with the creation of widower pensions. Dutch sociologist Eva Abraham-van der

Mark explored the impact of these changes on birthrates and marriages. 183 couples wed in 1915, the year Shell broke ground on the refinery. By 1940, this number had grown substantially: 653 couples married out of a population of 80,112. The sociologist noted, not without a degree of irony, that the power of capital had done more to increase marriages than over a century of moralizing from the Catholic Church.[117] Elsewhere throughout Latin America in the mid-twentieth century, marriage rates were also escalating. In countries like Argentina, Brazil, Chile, and Uruguay, industrial jobs allowed men to materially support wives and children while state-run social insurance schemes enforced legal conjugality by disqualifying informal relations from receiving benefits. Patriarchal families in the region were not "relics of tradition" but "products of modernity, created by economic modernization and the social welfare state."[118] On Curaçao, the corporation took the place of state-sponsored social welfare; its aim was less to shape a national body than a corporate family, with workers—like kin—affectively bound to the workplace.

The expansion of benefits for a now privileged sector of domestic employees heralded Shell's postwar policy of regionalization. Regionalization aimed above all to mollify criticisms of the colonial nature of the industry by appointing local employees to management positions once filled by European staff.[119] In this respect, regionalization mirrored the broader context of decolonization and the incremental transfer of authority then underway on Curaçao. As a result of regionalization, small numbers of local men transitioned into management positions. In 1948, 303 Antillean and 222 Surinamese reached the ranks of salaried staff alongside 804 Dutch or other Euro-American personnel.[120] Regionalization was also implemented in the built environment on Curaçao. Where once the white enclaves of company towns were built to resemble distant European homelands, after World War II management housing conformed to local style. Social clubs, too, were formally desegregated. In 1951, Shell director Henk Bloemgarten even traveled to Curaçao to found a cultural center, once again equating corporate interest with national progress.[121]

These transformations, however, were not as appreciably progressive as outward appearance suggested. As one of the so-called Shell wives—the spouses of the elite class of white workers who moved to sites of extraction and refining—recalled, life in Shell's Curaçao compound was "like the military," with white enclaves "totally shut off—fenced all around with a

E familia grandi cu nos ta mira riba e foto aki, ta pertenecé
na E. S. Apostel, di DA/T, kende ta pará banda di su Señora

Figure 4. De Passaat celebrated the work anniversary of E. S. Apostel, pictured with
wife and children, June 1947. SOURCE: Mongui Maduro Library.

gate to drive in through from the outside world and the only locals were
the maids and gardeners."[122] The attempts to cultivate a corporate family
thus repeatedly ran up against the colonial logics of race, gender, nation,
and class which discourses of corporate paternalism at once glossed and
exacerbated.

· · · · ·

Decolonization on Curaçao had indeed created "new men."[123] Yet quite
unlike in Frantz Fanon's emancipatory vision, Curaçao's "new men"
were incentivized to embrace an emerging corporate culture that valued

industrial competence and its presumed corollary: paternal power.[124] As Afro-Curaçaoan men were encouraged to form families of their own, they were simultaneously urged to ingratiate themselves within the corporate family. The migration of people from countryside to city and into company-built homes in the 1940s and early 1950s further expanded Shell's influence throughout all realms of workers' lives, replacing the communal networks of the countryside with increased corporate surveillance.

Though many foreign laborers and soldiers were excluded from these domestic niceties, their reproductive care was nevertheless a priority for Shell and the late-colonial government. Transactional sex was thought to aid oil revenues by allowing for the maintenance of an ideal, flexible male labor force who, without family, could be easily dismissed and cheaply maintained. This calculus of transience also governed the recruitment of women migrant workers (whether sex workers or domestic workers), which, while beneficial to the bottom line, raised new anxieties about the sexual and economic autonomy of foreign women making a new home on Curaçao. The architects of the age of oil and the end of empire thus created a peculiar offshore sexual economy on Curaçao that relied on the movements of bodies across borders, some of them expressly prohibited by law. These were crude bargains, abrogating newly-won rights on Curaçao in exchange for the modernizing promises of oil and industrial capitalism.

Though oil "intensified modernization like no other raw commodity,"[125] it had other remarkably stubborn effects. In particular, Shell strategically reproduced colonial categories of race, nation, and class precisely as heightened mobility and decolonizing reforms threatened their very stability. Racial division was sown into the built environment, segregating spaces of life, labor, and love. As Hannah Appel writes, the quotidian practices of exclusion and segregation that traveled along with mobile petroleum companies "depended on the reliability of already existing inequalities."[126]

In other ways, however, this sexual and racial economy produced unanticipated results. As oil came to dominate insular life, it simultaneously allowed for the emergence of new political possibilities. The "layered sovereignty"[127] that developed in this time period at once broadened island autonomy and transformed Curaçaoan subjects into Dutch citizens with newfound political and economic leverage. But especially in the treatment of sexuality, Curaçao was not a mirror of the metropole. Soon, the purposeful disregard of Dutch law on commercial sex work drew complaints from newly empowered citizens on the nearby island of Aruba. At the turn of the next decade, the very women who were expected to remain the chaste and dutiful wives of Caribbean laborers rose up in one of the first mass protests of the postcolonial age.

2 Diminishing Returns

DOMESTICITY ON THE EDGE OF WHITENESS

Seventy miles west of Curaçao across a stretch of rough waters, the island of Aruba was set to build a Campo Alegre all its own. There, too, the recent wartime oil boom fueled plans to transnationally recruit and regulate sex workers, a perceived service to the foreign laborers who fractured hydrocarbon molecules at the island's Standard Oil-owned refinery. But in May 1951, an unexpected struggle erupted between "Virtue, cheered on by 3,000 righteous housewives" and "Vice, symbolized by 134 resentful prostitutes." Even a reporter from *Time* magazine chronicled this symbolic confrontation as thousands of indignant Aruban women marched through the streets of San Nicolas and onward to the coastal capital of Oranjestad to register their complaint. Using the vernacular of middle-class respectability, these "Ladies Against Campo Alegre" demanded the termination of plans to open a brothel and the removal of foreign prostitutes. One sex worker from the Dominican Republic, left unnamed by the *Time* reporter, offered a cautious defense: The brothel "would be comfortable," she said; "we could entertain in a room all day long."[1] With this, the two models of reproductive care so prized by oil industries—conjugal domesticity and transactional liaisons –came into stunning conflict.

Though strikes and unrest were not uncommon among men engaged in oil production, the forms of intimacy that the industry relied upon now stoked antagonisms beyond the refinery gates. It was not wages or working conditions in dispute but threats to the idealized domestic lifestyle promoted by the company. And this time, the wives, mothers, daughters, and girlfriends of refinery laborers were the ones to make bold demands. Like its island neighbor, Aruba underwent a profound transformation with the opening of the Standard Oil refinery. While Standard Oil promoted a corporate ethos of family values, transactional relationships played out in the shadows of the refinery compound. Sex workers from the Dominican Republic and Colombia traveled to Aruba to entertain soldiers, laborers, and seamen as the industry swelled during World War II. These familiar circulations were hardly coincidental. Administered from the seat of the Antillean government in Curaçao, Aruba abided by the same laws in force on Curaçao and made the same studied circumventions.

Yet in other crucial respects, oil incited distinct political aspirations on Aruba. In what would become a common Caribbean story, interisland tensions eclipsed even those between metropole and colony.[2] Aruban self-understanding as a white or mestizo island, in contrast to the majority Black population of Curaçao, spurred these separatist ambitions. Hardline separatists like the popular Arubaanse Volkspartij (AVP) fought unsuccessfully to sever ties with Curaçao while strengthening those between Aruba and the European Netherlands. By 1951, however, Dutch authorities had compelled Aruba to remain part of an Antillean federation administered from Curaçao.

The trouble brewing on the political stage also spilled into the insular economy. In 1950, the introduction of automated technologies at the Lago refinery reduced demand for labor. The dismissal of 1,500 foreign workers followed later that year.[3] It was in the context of these political and economic uncertainties that complaints about deteriorating sexual morality and embattled domesticity emerged. Participants in the prostitution debate—including commentators in the press, women of various social classes, and religious leaders—combined previously popularized ideas about the island's distinct racial heritage with new mandates for restrained sexual morality.[4] They called for the spirited defense of a home life under threat from racialized sexual competition and economic danger.

Domesticity attended a multitude of projects in the Caribbean and Latin America in the late nineteenth and early twentieth centuries and featured as a mobilizing ideal among elite reformers and popular figures alike.[5] No less important were efforts to enshrine domesticity as the appropriate form of social organization during export booms that brought transitory populations to emerging urban centers, spurring efforts to fashion class and racial identities apart from the working masses.[6] The oil firm also participated in the popularization of idealized domesticity. As hundreds of white US managerial staff, engineers, and their families took up residence on Aruba, the white middle-class couple became the model of corporate achievement, signaling to local workers how one must organize home life in order to advance in the industry. Aruban men climbing the ladder of corporate mobility in the late 1940s and early 1950s gained access to middle-class luxuries such as housing and higher wages in a bid to pacify small sectors of labor in the industry's host society. The absorption of Arubans into the ranks of skilled labor occurred precisely as, and not least because, imperial governance gave way to democratic transition. The perceived threat of prostitution to new standards of household harmony galvanized thousands of women on Aruba just as authorities were made accountable to democratic processes. At this specific intersection of decolonization and the corporate age, popular mobilization around sexual politics could exercise a profound impact on oil companies and their state protectors. In this case, it successfully thwarted efforts to build an Aruban version of the "Happy Camp."

Recreating the social world in which oil retrenched racial divisions while also engendering new middle-class desires and lifestyles, this chapter moves from the vertiginous growth of the Lago refinery in the 1920s and 1930s to its creeping decline in the early 1950s. It tracks how evolving corporate cultures centering on race, gender, and the family pushed oil-related struggles out of the refinery and into households, church pews, and city streets. In a town where the white middle-class couple embodied industrial achievement and where large numbers of transient personnel were denied access to such repertoires of intimacy, the defense of domesticity that erupted in 1951 channeled multiple longings: from inclusion in the symbolic order of whiteness to the promise of professional success. As the wives and girlfriends of refinery workers marched through the streets of San Nicolas in May, they made clear that ideologies of corporate paternalism and middle-class domesticity were not simply imposed on unwitting subjects. These subjects at turns embraced and weaponized these ideals in an effort to defend the domestic bliss that oil afforded.

SEEING COLOR IN THE COMPANY TOWN

Aruba's oil history began with something of a logistical problem. In July 1922, the Barroso oil gusher exploded in the eastern region of Venezuela's Lake Maracaibo. Flowing at the rate of 100,000 barrels a day, Barroso presented issues in storing and processing the erupting crude that now drenched towns up to three kilometers away.[7] In 1924, the Pan-American Oil Company (Pan-Am) incorporated the Lago Oil & Transport Company, Ltd., to run shallow-lake tankers from Venezuela to Aruba. Crude would then be stored on Aruba and loaded onto large oceangoing tankers destined for refining in the United States. In an effort to bring refining operations closer to the source, in 1928 Pan-Am broke ground on a refinery site in Aruba. The following year, the Standard Oil Company of Indiana acquired Pan-Am, and with it, the Lago Oil & Transport Company and Pan-Am's Venezuelan concessions. In the grips of the Depression in 1932, the refinery and transshipment center were offered for sale. Standard Oil of New Jersey, after 1926 operating as Esso, acquired these holdings along with the concessions in Maracaibo. Lago's new corporate owners reimagined the productive potential of the Aruban refinery, investing 22 million dollars in the expansion of still units, gasoline storage, and docking space in 1938. Within a decade, Aruba boasted the world's largest refinery in terms of crude throughput, operating at 400,000 barrels per day.[8]

The booming economy transformed traditional lifeways across the twenty-mile island, a spit of flat desert rock and coral plateau. Before the arrival of oil in 1922, Aruba was home to some nine thousand souls. The European-descended elite made a living through their exclusive ownership of shops, land, and ships. Residing in the pastel-tinted buildings that dotted the harbor of Oranjestad, this group protected their privilege and wealth through intermarriage. The comparatively larger population that later separatist politicians would define as "real Arubans"—the descendants of European colonists and Amerindian peasants—was, in fact, a nineteenth-century invention. Pervasive poverty pushed poor whites onto government-owned lands and plantations in the desert interior, traditionally populated by Amerindians. In communities of mutual dependence, these groups intermarried. Into the early twentieth century, tending cattle herds and subsistence agriculture were the surest ways to survive in the parched countryside. The division between town and country was also one of religion and color, with European-descended Protestant elites deriving a living from the mestizo Catholics who worked their lands and bought products in their shops.⁹ Oil, and empire's end, would alter these social patterns. A new class of Euro-American oilmen and European Dutch and Curaçaoan bureaucrats displaced the dominance of Aruban elites while the rural mestizo populace increasingly looked to the refinery and not to the island's *shons* (masters) for economic gain.

The oil industry also brought significant population growth. Aruba's population swelled to over fifty thousand by 1948, and represented thirty-eight different nationalities. Reflecting Lago's preference for English-speaking laborers, thousands of migrant workers traveled to Aruba from the British Caribbean, predominantly from Grenada and St. Vincent.¹⁰ These travelers settled west of the refinery in San Nicolas. Once a sparsely populated village centered on fishing and small-scale phosphate mining, San Nicolas now hummed with storefronts and rowdy saloons where workers could procure basic necessities and seek diversion after a long shift. The US author Wenzell Brown, who spent a year traveling the region immediately after World War II, viewed this inter-Caribbean encounter as a consciousness-raising process for the Black Caribbean laborers who "were meeting their fellow islanders for the first time, exchanging ideas, widening their interests, and preparing to return home determined that their particular islands shall provide them with employment."¹¹ Magazines such as *Ebony* and *Negro Digest* appeared on the island, while political pamphlets and radical treatises accompanied laborers on their journeys from Grenada to Aruba.¹²

For many Arubans entering the refinery in the 1930s and 1940s, West Indian migration stoked economic competition. In contrast to the *Inglés* who were recruited on fixed contracts, the several hundred Arubans who worked at the refinery did so primarily as day laborers. Possessing little vocational training or knowledge of the English language, Arubans were, in the eyes of Lago management, an unideal workforce. It would take concerted government pressure to increase the representation of local men as the refinery rebounded from the Depression in the 1930s. The lieutenant governor of Aruba, Isaac Wagemaker, requested that Lago give priority to married men who had experience in Curaçao's oil industry. The number of Aruban employees increased in the years between 1931 and 1936 from 517 to 1,204. But these numbers were soon eclipsed by the arrival of additional foreign recruits. By 1948, when Lago employment reached a historic peak, men from the British Caribbean formed 40 percent of the total workforce. Arubans, by contrast, formed 26 percent.[13] As Brown observed, Aruban men regarded Black foreigners with skepticism and contempt— a rearguard racism borne of stiff economic competition and entrenched colonial prejudice.[14] This would have an unmistakable impact on the posturing of separatist politicians, who defended "real Arubans" against their perceived economic marginalization. Although in public Standard Oil celebrated the diversity of its workforce, in practice the company enforced ethnic and racial division in housing and working units.

As much as racial animus was organized from above, it was also produced from below. In the early phase of the refinery's development, white working-class laborers from the United States and Europe complained bitterly about their proximity to workers of color—complaints that were eventually echoed by Aruban workers. Following W. E. B. Du Bois and David Roediger's important formulation, worker's protestations appealed to the "wages of whiteness," that is, to the psychological pleasures and social privileges of whiteness that compensated for otherwise exploitative class relationships.[15] On February 24, 1928, the first group of roughnecks from oilfields in Wyoming and Texas arrived on Aruba.[16] This was a common practice in refinery construction, including also on Curaçao, as men with experience in the United States and tradesmen from Europe were brought in to prepare the refinery grounds. Felix B. Satter traveled to the US bachelor encampment for this purpose, describing the unforgiving conditions in a 1930 poem entitled "The Arubian [sic] Blues." Satter's lament did not only focus on the crowded, insect-infested barracks and punishing, seven-day shifts. The US American also decried the presence of Chinese cooks and waiters in the mess halls and the supervision of white workers by Black policemen in San Nicolas, where men like Satter spent long hours in the town's saloons.[17]

To some extent, the company relied on racial antagonism as a deliberate managerial strategy. But at times, white workers from the United States and Europe insisted on the maintenance of a rigid color line that corporate management believed imprudent to uphold. In 1934, European Dutch tradesmen summoned colonial authorities to intervene in a dispute with Lago management. In handwritten complaints, dozens of white Dutchmen like Thomas C. Pietersz expressed their dismay that, on payday, white and Black workers stood in line together to receive their paychecks. Seething with racial offense, Pietersz wrote, "You could even say it is pathetic to see a number of white Dutchmen standing among a bunch of negroes."[18] White US American employees also complained to management about drinking from the same water fountain and punching the same time clock as workers of color. Behind closed doors, plant management considered whether such practices could be sufficiently segregated in a place like Aruba. According to Lago's US American general manager, Lloyd G. Smith, to draw the color line "agreeable to American standards" would alienate many Arubans who "have a large admixture of Caucasian blood, and feel that on that basis they are to be classed as white men."[19] Smith's comments reflected the competing notions of whiteness among Aruban and US workers, the latter of whom rejected Aruban belonging in this category.

Yet in this highly racialized corporate landscape, Aruban workers also appealed to the wages of whiteness to demand increased social privileges, such as preferential treatment in the commissary and at the company hospital. In 1934, the Aruban Isaias Oduber complained that Aruban workers were treated "just like the negroes and the Chinese" at the Lago Hospital, grievances that were registered by a handful of other Aruban tradesmen. C. C. Wever, a first-class clerk from Aruba, likewise complained that Arubans performing the same work as Europeans or US Americans would never earn the same salary as the latter.[20] Smith's response to such complaints was cautious. On the one hand, the general manager attempted to assuage white US and European workers by devising subtle segregationist schemes such as assigning different punch-in times for white workers. At the same time, he conceded that white supremacist principles would need to be stretched in order to encourage "harmonious relations" in a society where many inhabitants understood themselves as white.[21]

With racial boundaries muddied by the very ambiguity of race and whiteness itself, in the 1930s Lago turned to domestic arrangements and gendered performance to further demarcate white US Americans from other employees. The bawdy displays of white masculine performance that abounded in the US bachelor encampment—where men drank copiously, gambled, and fought—were now deemed disruptive to corporate interest. In a pattern witnessed across US-dominated oil towns, companies like Lago concluded that they would have a more reliable and stable workforce if their white employees were allowed to reside in the field with family.[22] Nearly two years after Standard Oil's acquisition of the refinery, on July 17, 1934, Lago announced that the company would fund the passage of the wives and children of salaried employees from the United States to Aruba.[23] Throughout the course of the decade, new amenities were constructed to recreate the look and feel of the United States on Aruba.[24] Behind guarded gates lay the Lago Colony, an exclusive enclave for white managerial staff from the United States and Europe. White staff and their families enjoyed exclusive access to private schools and medical facilities. The popular Esso Club boasted a theater and cocktail lounge on the placid waters of Baby Beach. The amenities beyond the Club, from golf courses and tennis courts to private, palm-lined beaches, made "living in the Colony equal to living at many summer resorts."[25] Socializing also occurred in the spacious bungalows and manicured gardens occupied by white residents. Wives were expected to participate in the life of the Colony through various women's associations, company-sponsored recreational events, and the ever-present pressure to entertain colleagues.

The gates surrounding the Lago Colony formed a racial cordon sanitaire designed to regulate the movements of people of color. Some residents expressed ambivalence about the artificiality of this spatial arrangement. Ray Burson, the son of a US chemical engineer who moved to Aruba in 1937, recalled that the Colony was "very artificial," with a strict partition between the white community and "other people" who "lived out in the village," as the San Nicolas neighborhood housing many Black West Indian workers was known.[26] In 1947, Charlotte Warden and her two young sons left the United States to accompany her husband in Aruba. Soon after,

Warden wrote in her diary that the Lagoites were "such a closed" group. Despite frequent social calls, Warden lamented her sense of alienation and domestic ennui. She struggled with her husband's frequent absences and the challenges of childrearing in a community she described as "gossipy and noisy."[27] The separation of these enclaves from the society where the industry operated was not just a question of spatial organization. To distinguish white families from wider society, residents also had to consistently perform raced and gendered expectations that outwardly maintained matrimonial harmony and familial stability. Privately, some residents experienced these expectations as deep hypocrisies.

The separation of white families from an increasingly diverse Caribbean society was, however, always partial. Black West Indian domestic workers cooked and cleaned in the homes of white families like the Wardens. Ann, who was employed by the Warden family, followed a familiar path from the island of Grenada to Aruba. Ann's passage was likely facilitated by a male relative working at Lago, who might share a temporary place to stay upon arrival as well as acquired knowledge about labor laws and the rights of foreigners on Aruba.[28] Beyond the consistency of a wage, other domestic workers were enticed by a feeling of freedom that came with relative anonymity in a new place. Although domestic work drew Black West Indian women into daily contact with white families and colonial and corporate authorities, working for employers to which one had few other societal obligations could also offer treasured independence from social and familial demands.[29]

In the homes of the Lago Colony, however, West Indian women contended with other forms of oversight. Corporate management kept watch over the reproductive lives of West Indian women, who were required to report to the company hospital every three months and promptly deported whenever medical screenings revealed pregnancy.[30] In the 1940s, few prophylactic technologies fit the working rhythms of West Indian women's lives. Cost could be as prohibitive as the time it took to visit a clinic or pharmacy, a facet of fertility control that grew more difficult with frequent labor migration.[31] Given these limitations, it is unsurprising that Ann believed little could be done to avoid pregnancy, yet she hinted to Charlotte Warden that she had on several occasions managed to avoid this fate herself. Was this a frank admission among women who, despite their different social classes, understood all too well the challenges of regulating one's fertility? Or did Warden invent or embellish the exchange in her diary, guided not least by powerful racial fictions of Black women's fecundity? Warden recorded Ann's apparent claim that "she should have 6 [children] by now" with bafflement that the company organized Ann's reproductive and family life so differently from her own.[32] On paper, at least, Warden showed little recognition that this was done in part to ensure West Indian women's availability to assume care burdens in homes like hers.

Such conversations between the white wives of the Colony and Black West Indian women leave only ephemeral traces in the documentary record. More frequent are white women's complaints about West Indian women's desire for autonomy on the job, or the dramas that could result whenever domestics shared household gossip amongst each other. In the kitchen, domestic workers tried to steal moments of solitude, though even this space was prone to intrusion by white women complaining of over-spiced food.[33] Sneaking time to share company and conversation among other West Indian women helped to lighten the weighty expectations that domestics bore the minute they crossed the Colony gates.[34]

Contrary to the messy realities of life in the Colony, Esso promoted the middle-class white married couple as an idealized representation of company values and a marker of one's status in the industry. This served as a ubiquitous reminder to Arubans gaining a foothold in the industry that they must emulate such lifestyles in order to advance. As Miguel Tinker Salas observes of the Venezuelan context, the domesticated middle-class lifestyles of the residential oil camps "altered conceptions of work and time, introduced distinct lifestyles, and promoted new consumer patterns" that profoundly shaped expectations and served as benchmarks against which one would measure their own social status.[35] Colored by the company's desire to promote itself as an unquestioned agent of progress, an employment guide distributed to prospective Lago employees in 1940 claimed that "the Aruban is going through a concentrated course of industrialization" that had resulted in a hardier physical constitution and ambition to attain US-styled clothing, automobiles, and other middle-class luxuries.[36] The historian Johan Hartog registered this same zeitgeist in 1953: "People . . . began to conceive the smooth glossy wonders of technique as the noblest manifestation of culture. Refrigerators, nylon-products, and concrete were defined as marvels of modern times. The electric washer and the pick-up became the attribute of the masses."[37] These oil-drenched commodities (trucks, nylon, and electrified appliances) signaled investment in the waged labor of the fossil economy as well as its derivative products, which projected a classed and gendered claim to whiteness itself.[38]

While many Arubans viewed themselves as far more proximate to whiteness than Black laborers, inside the Colony few Arubans were afforded such status. Some elite Arubans socialized with the Lagoites and held important positions at the refinery. But the shades of color that demarcated privileges in Caribbean colonies frequently confused US visitors. Charlotte Warden severely offended a man from the prominent Aruban Maduro family when she confused him with someone of darker complexion.[39] In 1943, colonial authorities intervened on behalf of a valued European Dutch Lago staff member, D. de Pauw, who threatened to resign after his family was kicked out of their bungalow in the Lago Colony. When de Pauw asked his boss, W. R. C. Miller, why the family could not reside in the Colony, Miller replied using an offensive racial epithet to describe de Pauw's Curaçaoan-born wife.[40] De Pauw defended his wife against perceived racial slander and summoned colonial officials to confirm that she was not Black but "very light skinned (*heel licht gekleurd*)."[41]

At every level of the refinery—from domestic services rendered by women like Ann in the Lago Colony bungalows to daily plant operations—the company relied upon people of color. In a setting where white people depended so substantially on this labor, popular racial dramatizations reproduced the belief that white stewardship of the refinery was necessary. Depictions of people of color as bumbling and baffled in the industrial environment were perhaps most vividly on display in company-organized minstrel shows (figure 5). These racial representations trafficked along the emerging routes of global capitalism in the Caribbean, from banking interests to petroleum production.[42] After the debut of the first minstrel performance on August 20, 1931 at the Pan-Am Club, enthusiasm for the genre increased along with the growth of the Lago Colony. In March 1953, over a hundred members of the Lago community performed the "Cotton Blossom Minstrels" to sold-out audiences at the Esso Club. The show was so popular that, two years later, the crew was asked to entertain an audience of over six hundred US staff and light-skinned island elites at a

Figure 5. A minstrel performance at the Esso Club, ca. 1953–55. SOURCE: The University of Texas at Austin, Dolph Briscoe Center for American History, Lago Colony, Aruba, Collection, camh-dob-009732.

charity dinner for the Rotary Club of Aruba.[43] US Lago engineers performed songs like "Stay in Your Own Backyard," "I'm Going South," and "Are You from Dixie?"[44] These and other racial performances provided powerful scripts that cast the laborers who generated wealth for companies like Standard Oil and Shell as technically incompetent. Such racial dramatizations did not only mirror the inequities of petro-capitalist production; they reproduced and sustained them.

Racial spectacle staged the routine forms of segregation that structured oil towns like San Nicolas. To the west of the refinery lay a world seemingly distinct from the pristine streets of the Lago Colony. "Here," Wenzell Brown asserted, "miles of tumble-down shacks stretch out from the gates of the Standard Oil Company's gigantic refinery."[45] Unlike their US counterparts, who traveled to Aruba with families, the vast majority of contract workers came alone. In 1926, Henry Fujooah bid farewell to his family in Suriname to find employment in the oil refineries. Soon after Standard's acquisition of the Lago refinery in 1929, Fujooah settled in an informal worker encampment, where he lived with several bunkmates under a thatched roof. When the rains arrived, the men would sleep under their cots to stay dry.[46] Fujooah and countless others came alone not by choice but out of necessity. Denied access to conjugal respectability, these workers were thought more beneficial to corporate profit if they traveled as bachelors. The Lago Colony was thus only seemingly removed from the encampments where men like Henry Fujooah lived. It was the exploited labor and substandard housing of the latter that made possible the comparative comforts of the former.

Given Lago's reliance on a mobile male workforce, it is perhaps unsurprising that, just as on Curaçao, men's search for erotic company became a distinct problem for island authorities in the 1940s. Increased wartime traffic to San Nicolas drew tankers from the United States and Europe, and, in February 1942, over one thousand US soldiers arrived to defend the refinery against Nazi attacks.[47] Officials decried the subsequent alarming rise in venereal disease and open and flourishing hedonism in the port environs. In his famous autobiographical novel *To Sir, With Love*, the Guyanese-born author E. R. Braithwaite recalled the throngs of men who waited outside Hija del Día, a hotel that housed foreign sex workers: "Queues of men, old men and young men, white men and dark men, men in clean crisp linen and men soiled from work on a long eight-hour shift, chatting or silent, but all patiently waiting their turn, to get into the big, bright painted building to pay the high prices demanded for the island's most rationed commodity, Women."[48] The pursuit of sex proved to be a strangely democratizing endeavor in this segregated company town—one of the few spaces of sociality where lines of class, race, and ethnicity blurred.

MAKING SEX WORK

As a Dutch territory administered largely from Curaçao, Aruba was beholden to the same regulations set forth there. The 1942 committee tasked

with studying prostitution on Curaçao made a short list of recommendations that was soon implemented on Aruba.[49] The committee called on the
police and health departments to supervise prostitution and endorsed
the recruitment and licensing of foreign sex workers from Colombia and
the Dominican Republic. This system was ultimately introduced on both
Curaçao and Aruba in 1944 as an amendment to the earlier regulation of
contagious diseases.[50] Braithwaite, formerly a technologist at the Standard Oil refinery, recalled how sex workers arrived by the twice-monthly
interisland steamer. As soon as the boat docked, "word went around: 'the
meat boat's in,' [and] the queues of men would begin to form outside its
door, jocularly speeding the tired departees, and eagerly welcoming the
replacements."[51] Three seats were even reserved for sex workers on the
weekly KLM flight from the Dominican Republic to Aruba.[52]

Again as with Curaçao, the regulations of 1944 and contradictory in-
junctions in the Antillean criminal code created a peculiar situation for
foreign sex workers in Aruba. Although authorities permitted foreign
prostitutes to establish temporary residence in the hotels Hija del Día
and Hollywood, the ban on third-party facilitation and brothelkeeping
prohibited sex workers from entertaining clients in hotel chambers
(figure 6).[53] Police surveilled several local bars suspected of letting out
backrooms for erotic encounters. At the Piels Bar in San Nicolas, police
interrupted a Norwegian sailor and Teresa Pérez, a thirty-five-year-old
woman from the Dominican Republic, who were dressing each other in
the bar's backroom. Although mediated by police authorities, Teresa's testimony revealed a boisterous homosocial scene. For European sailors and
soldiers docking at Aruba, patronizing a sex worker was a collective social
activity intended equally for the performance of masculine virility before other men as for erotic satisfaction. A man familiar with the haunts
of San Nicolas might join a newly arrived crew as they ambled between
bars, offering recommendations about where and with whom to have sex.
This was the case the night that local police arrived at Piels Bar. Teresa
had recognized a customer by sight, joining him and several European
sailors as they roamed San Nicolas at midnight. A resident of Hija del
Día, Teresa understood the purpose of their trip to Piels Bar. Yet when
police arrived on the scene, the manager of the bar, a thirty-eight-year-
old man from the Dutch island of Bonaire, denied knowing the sailors

Figure 6. Men queue in front of the Hollywood hotel while sex workers greet them from the balcony, ca. 1938. By L. R. Seekins. SOURCE: The University of Texas at Austin, Dolph Briscoe Center for American History, Lago Colony, Aruba, Collection, camh-dob-009731.

had intended to sleep with Teresa in the bar's backroom, conspicuously outfitted with a simple canvas bed.[54]

As Teresa and other sex workers assumed their nightly stations on the balcony of Hija del Día and negotiated with clients loitering on the street below, a familiar drama unfolded. In a situation virtually identical to that of pre-Campo Curaçao, taxis waited on the street outside the hotel, shuttling sex workers and their customers from San Nicolas to Smal, a public dump, and Juana Morto, an artillery battery perched atop the rugged windward coastline.[55] Local police were hard-pressed to control taxi drivers, who provided a service too valuable to curtail. Edgar Guillaume Gerling, a taxi driver born in Paramaribo, Suriname, brusquely retorted to one officer that he "couldn't give a damn" about persistent police warnings.[56] Gerling walked away with a slap on the wrist. Energy and labor imperatives once again trumped concerns about public immorality or obedience to the law. Most disturbing to insular authorities was the rumored presence of children on the beaches, who came either out of curiosity or to search among the rubbish for money and possessions lost in the act of undressing. Alarming, too, was the precipitous uptick in cases of venereal disease among Lago workers, which increased nearly fivefold, from 52 in 1947 to 249 in 1951.[57]

In view of this developing scandal, some enterprising businessmen on Aruba attempted to remove salacious acts from public view. Inspired by the opening of Campo Alegre on Curaçao, on June 4, 1949, José María Debrot, owner of Hija del Día, requested a permit to build a hotel intended exclusively for a "certain category of women."[58] Debrot's proposed establishment would encompass sixty rooms and a restaurant serving residents and their guests. Unlike Debrot's Hija del Día, this new establishment— also dubbed Campo Alegre by its supporters and eventual detractors— would host paid sexual encounters. In his proposal to Aruban authorities, Debrot strategically emphasized his desire to move clientele concentrated in San Nicolas "beyond the city limit, contributing to the social welfare of the island."[59]

Ironically, it was Debrot's intent to shield the Aruban public from "immoral" acts that triggered popular outcry. In March 1951, as Aruban officials and civil servants repeatedly failed to find a suitable location for Debrot's Campo, several housewives in San Nicolas caught wind of the looming plans. Clarita Villalba and Marianita Chong (née Croes), president and secretary of the Rooms Katholieke Vrouwenbond of San Nicolas, led the charge. Chong was the wife of Chong Hong, a well-known businessman in San Nicolas and owner of Shanghai Store and Shanghai Restaurant, located at 40 Lago Way. A native of Guangzhou, China, who moved to Aruba after the refinery opened in 1929, he was one of the thousands of people who made their living at the periphery of the oil industry.[60] Migrants from China often worked in Lago's mess malls, aboard tanker fleets, or in the laundry. Like Chong, other Chinese migrants joined growing numbers of Lebanese, Syrians, Indians, and Ashkenazi Jews from Europe in opening shops, restaurants, and groceries or working as merchants on Aruba and Curaçao.[61]

Deriving newfound status from these pursuits, the wives of the self-styled protest committee began to draw attention to the troubling specter of a brothel planned just "a short distance from a residential area, very close by the houses of good Aruban families with many children and who deserve to provide those children with a good upbringing."[62] On March 9, 1951, twelve "Aruban mothers" staged a small demonstration outside of Lindoro Christoffel Kwartsz's office in Oranjestad. Kwartsz, now serving as the lieutenant governor, assured the women that he would personally designate a spot for Debrot's "hotel" at a substantial distance from San Nicolas's residential areas. Kwartsz went looking for a suitable location for the brothel several days later. Before long, the lieutenant governor realized he was being trailed. An indignant group of women had followed Kwartsz, insisting at each stop that the official would fail to find a suitable location because brothelkeeping was prohibited by both Dutch and Antillean law.[63] Throughout the spring and summer of 1951, religious women's organizations allied with leaders of the Catholic Church to mobilize thousands of island residents in protest against the island government and its intended Campo Alegre. Their aim was to prevent a brothel from arriving on Aruba and to abolish prevailing systems of regulation. These measures breached the island's Christian values, the women asserted, and brazenly defied both Antillean and Dutch law.

CURAÇAO'S "WORTHLESS EXAMPLE"

Claims to whiteness via the upholding of middle-class gender norms and idealized domesticity inflected the Aruban protest against Campo Alegre. While no doubt informed by the long-standing history of Catholicism on the island, these currents were also shaped by the very industry whose workers were thought to demand distinct forms of reproductive care. Inclusion in the realm of whiteness to which many upwardly mobile Arubans aspired entailed the embrace of marital domesticity, a corporate value that directly corresponded to one's status in the company town. Housing, positions of seniority, and other accolades were bestowed according to marital status and family size. These realities now overlaid another much more local grievance: Aruba's uneven relationship to Curaçao. As the seat of the Antillean government, many Arubans viewed Curaçao as a domineering and corrupt political force. The protest against a copycat Campo Alegre reframed the tensions between the islands, focusing on political and economic grievance as well as racial-sexual threats.

The movement's professed Catholicism and restrained sexual morality became pronounced elements of the protest discourse, intertwining with the defense of hard-won domesticity. The consistently sympathetic *Amigoe di Curaçao*, a widely-read paper established by the Apostolic Vicariate of Curaçao, contrasted the island's dependent status with its autonomous moral spirit: "Aruba lies somewhere on the earth off the coast of Venezuela, a small pile of rocks tossed from God's creating hand. What can we do? . . . Not much. We lie between lands that can trample us. Economically speaking, the question of our survival depends on Lago. We are practically dependent on others for everything." The author asserted that despite these circumstances, "it is a fact that this small, precious, and eternally loved little island has its own mentality and character. We will not discuss Curaçao, which accepted a Campo and foreign prostitutes without protest. . . . Our ideas are different: we do not want a Campo!"[64] For this commentator, Aruba's homegrown moral tradition was all the more remarkable precisely because of the island's political subservience to Curaçao and its dependence on the oil industry. In a curious misplacement of blame, protest leadership and various sympathizers identified neighboring Curaçao, not the oil industry or local elites, as the cause of the present discontent. For many commentators, racialized ascriptions of sexual licentiousness explained Curaçao's acceptance of the original Campo Alegre and the "worthless example" that it now offered to Aruba.[65]

Curaçao loomed large in the protest movement's rhetoric because the island housed the first Campo Alegre. But the opening of the brothel in 1949 and its exclusive admittance of foreign sex workers had also evidently forced some local prostitutes to search for new clientele on Aruba. Police reports from the late 1940s and early 1950s cited the increase in the number of Antillean sex workers on Aruba, among whom the "Curaçaoan element predominated."[66] Forty-four of the island's seventy-five registered prostitutes in 1951 came from Curaçao. Meanwhile, local police reported that, until August 1951, there were "as good as no Aruban prostitutes" on the island.[67] Officials and protesters regarded prostitution as an entirely "foreign" affair. What made the perceived threat of Curaçao so acute was that Curaçao was a *domestic* Other in a position of political authority, unevenly bonded to Aruba through common citizenship and government.

Commentators on all sides of the Campo debate routinely racialized Curaçaoan sex workers and pointed to the alleged undesirability of Afro-Curaçaoan women to justify divergent opinions. In a familiar argument, the Antillean attorney general J. J. A. Ellis defended foreign sex worker recruitment by appealing to the threat to local white womanhood. Dismissing an unusual proposition to "import" exclusively Curaçaoan sex workers, Ellis averred that "these Curaçaoan women would not satisfy the demand and would therefore cause problems for the white women of Aruba. The local [Curaçaoan] prostitutes are black."[68] Members of the protest movement disagreed. One sympathizer argued, "One whispers that the foreign prostitutes must come as the indigenous are not sufficient because of their color. If there are no foreigners then the indigenous will be sufficient; they will only become busier."[69] This argument implied that though light-skinned foreign sex workers made commercial sex more appealing, their absence would not end prostitution but would instead encourage more Black women to find clients on Aruba. Hence, for these commentators, only total abolition would bring the desired resolution. In their shared repudiation of Afro-Curaçaoan sex workers, Campo's detractors echoed the antiblackness of the nineteenth-century Puerto Rican feminists who rejected Afro-Puerto Rican women and sex workers from understandings of "common sisterhood"—a discourse motivated by racial hatred and threat of sexual competition alike.[70] These portable associations between Blackness and deviance in the Americas informed the legal and political treatment of prostitution across various locales.

A minority voice on Aruba also deployed the threat of racial danger, this time as a way to indict the protest movement itself. As protests gained steam in the summer of 1951, the San Nicolas circular *Chuchubi* ran the headline "Curaçao vs. Aruba: *Barbuletas* vs. *Chinchurias*," contrasting "butterflies," a local term for light-skinned Latin American sex workers, with Curaçaoan "whores." The article denounced the island government's decision to deport foreign prostitutes, a victory achieved by the protest movement in August 1951: "Did you all anticipate as you marched through the streets in opposition to the '*barbuletas*' that this situation would cause a migration of prostitutes from Curaçao to Aruba?" Mocking the short-sightedness of local authorities, the author asked, "Did the Island Council consider when they protested against the '*barbuletas*' that Curaçao would remain and give their whores permission to plant themselves on Aruba?"[71] Evidently it was not sufficient for critics of the protest movement to attack the naïve idealism of a strictly abolitionist approach. Instead, these critics invoked racial stereotypes of Black women's sexual danger to argue that the abolition of foreign prostitution had done more to threaten than to protect Aruba.

These comments highlight a central and problematic feature of the Aruban identity popularized in the 1940s: Aruba's whitened racial identity in contrast to that of Curaçao. The formation of the AVP in 1942 did much to popularize notions of a unique Aruban identity that located the nation's founding in the marriage between European colonists and Indigenous Amerindians.[72] In a telegram to the Dutch minister of overseas affairs in 1948, AVP leader Henny Eman pleaded, "We are primarily descended from Hollanders and mixed with Indian blood thus a different race [from Curaçao]. We therefore ask ourselves, why would Holland not want to cooperate with our total separation?"[73] Aruban self-understanding as a "white" or mestizo island in contrast to "Black" Curaçao stimulated separatist ambitions. These actors defined as "real" Arubans the island's large mestizo population, the descendants of early European colonists and Indigenous Caquetio people who likely fled to the island in the seventeenth century as "pacification" wars raged between Spanish colonists and Indigenous communities in Venezuela.[74]

Until the arrival of the oil refining industry, Aruba's population remained relatively homogenous owing to the absence of plantation slavery and various prohibitions on settlement.[75] On Curaçao, by contrast, in the seventeenth century the Dutch West India Company established Willemstad as a center of the Atlantic slave trade. This differed substantially from the historical trajectory of Aruba, where the number of enslaved people at the time of abolition in 1863 totaled 486, roughly one-fifth of the island's population. In the decades before and after abolition, enslaved people and their descendants lived in communities of shared poverty and dependence that led to their assimilation into the dominant population group.[76] By the twentieth century, this erasure of African heritage functioned as a deliberate political strategy, defending "real Arubans" against perceived outsiders.

The popular maxim of separatists like the AVP, "Aruba for Arubans," was as much anti-Curaçaoan as it was anti-immigrant, a fearful expression of one island's subordination to another and a defensive backlash against economic marginalization. At the high point of refinery employment in 1948, roughly 40 percent of Lago's 8,262 employees hailed from the British Caribbean; thousands of predominantly Black Caribbean laborers formed the backbone of the island's most important industry.[77] While the AVP's nativist and xenophobic rhetoric rallied electoral majorities in the days of limited franchise, the broadening of the franchise in 1948 and the organization of migrants in associational clubs and political parties ultimately created increased competition.[78] Although the protest movement did not explicitly align itself with any political party, its equation of outsiders with moral degradation and the concomitant defense of a unique Aruban character in many ways reflected the AVP's rhetorical strategies. Adding to and drawing upon prevailing discourses of Aruban separateness, the protest movement promoted profoundly racialized understandings of sexual virtue.

Such intercolonial antagonisms showed that subalternity was not a fixed but relational category.[79] Indeed, intercolonial contests were not unique to the remnants of the Dutch empire. Other former colonial federations such as the West Indies Federation, a conglomeration of British Caribbean islands, or the Mali Federation in former French West Africa, ultimately dissolved into territorially defined nation-states.[80] Aruban commentators emphasized their own political marginalization vis-à-vis Curaçao using racial idioms and sexual ascriptions that disparaged Afro-Curaçaoan people. Powerful though they were on Aruba, claims to whiteness ultimately did not alter political or social arrangements within spaces of European and US domination. At the insistence of European Dutch administrators, Curaçao maintained its privileged position in the Antillean constellation in which Aruba was obliged to remain a constitutive member. And despite passionate appeals to white belonging, most Arubans were not white enough to pass behind the gates of the Lago Colony. Conditions of common exclusion might have forged alliances across the Dutch-controlled Caribbean, but whiteness remained an aspirational goal and a meaningful marker of difference for many Arubans, spurring resentment not between metropole and colony but across the imagined internal racial frontiers of the latter.

Aruba did not wish to resolve these clashes through the pursuit of national sovereignty. Though "mestizo populism" became broadly popular across Latin American republics in the first half of the twentieth century (including in places like Panama and Costa Rica where foreign corporations also relied on West Indian migrant labor), on Aruba this political movement played out within the geospatial imaginary of the Dutch commonwealth.[81] Separatists sought above all to strengthen and revitalize ties with the erstwhile metropole. In the battle against Campo Alegre, Euro-Caribbean attachments became even more significant as the protest movement leveraged the layers of sovereignty within the Dutch commonwealth. Though the island's complicated legal status had, in fact, created the very conditions against which thousands protested, it was now also thought to hold the key to moral restitution.

LEVERAGING THE COMMONWEALTH

The protest movement modeled the values of chastity and marital monogamy that underpinned white respectability. Yet in other respects, the "housewives" were rebellious actors; they remonstrated loudly in the public sphere and held officials to account. Their effectiveness owed in part to fortuitous timing. Sweeping decolonization policy enacted in 1951 democratized the bodies of Antillean governance and made space for broad participation in civic life. In particular, the protest movement availed itself of new constitutional changes that asserted the authority of kingdom-wide and national governments over local island administrations. Somewhat paradoxically, then, the protest movement exploited Aruba's nonsovereign political status to solicit intervention from authorities in Willemstad and The Hague even as they denounced their dependence on Curaçao. As other scholars have recently pointed out, federated forms of statehood emerged in the 1940s and 1950s as an attractive alternative to revolutionary anticolonial nationalism and territorial sovereignty premised on the national state.[82] While imaginative anticolonial elites and metropolitan officials sketched out the contours of this postcolonial arrangement, in rather unglamorous and quotidian ways others were left to navigate newfangled state structures.

The protest movement's strategy of leveraging the governing bodies of the kingdom was enabled by the introduction of the Interimregeling of February 1951 and the proclamation of the Eilandenregeling Nederlandse

Antillen (ERNA) in March 1951. While earlier regulations in 1939 and 1948 introduced the basic principles of democratic self-governance in the Netherlands Antilles, including freedom of the press, the creation of a national parliament, and the introduction of universal franchise, the Interimregeling and ERNA strengthened the democratic structures of the state. They did so by clarifying the relationships between local island administrators, the national Antillean government, and the Dutch crown. Specifically, the Interimregeling of 1951 increased the authority of the Staten, which assumed responsibility for formulating legislation and governance in the Netherlands Antilles. This changed stripped the governor of the Netherlands Antilles of many executive duties and made the position responsible to an Antillean council of ministers appointed by the Staten. Though the governor no longer exercised any independent authority after 1951, several important functions remained with the governor. As symbolic head of the national government, the governor retained the power to dissolve and hold new elections in parliament. As representative of the kingdom government in the Netherlands Antilles, the governor could reject any ordinance deemed contrary to the mutual interests of the kingdom. Though the national government exercised autonomy in internal affairs, its status within the Kingdom of the Netherlands ensured the ongoing intervention of the Netherlands in issues of mutual interest to kingdom countries.[83]

Quickly following the enactment of the Interimregeling, the royal proclamation of the ERNA on March 14, 1951 expanded the autonomy of each island territory and placed a range of responsibilities under the control of a local island administration. Daily management over the affairs of each island territory rested in the Administrative College, formed by a lieutenant governor who served as chairman and several deputies selected by the Island Council. Members of the Island Council were popularly elected and served four-year terms.[84] Though the autonomy of each island territory certainly expanded through the ERNA, the regulations of national and kingdom governments remained superior. Each island territory was obliged to cooperate in the implementation of national regulations or decrees. The Dutch monarch would appoint the lieutenant governor, whose primary task was to determine whether island regulations came into conflict with national or kingdom-wide agreements.[85]

Island administrators thus answered to the bodies of national and king-dom governance.

The protest movement displayed a sophisticated knowledge of these emerging state structures. Nearly all petitions and declarations issued by the two primary arms of the protest movement—one led by Catho-lic women's organizations and the other by religious leaders—were sent simultaneously to local authorities, national officials in the Antillean capital, and governing bodies in the Netherlands. Initially, protesters addressed their petitions to the lieutenant governor of Aruba, who re-sponded by attempting to relocate the proposed brothel and, at the same time, by quietly accelerating plans to finalize its construction. On May 16, 1951, acting Governor of the Netherlands Antilles F. A. Jas, an unelected official appointed by the Dutch monarch, signed a national decree approv-ing the lease of 17,000 square meters of government land to N. V. Pereira and J. M. Debrot.[86] Although Debrot and his allies in government agreed not to discuss the lease, within ten days word leaked to the public.

The protest movement publicized its cause in the Netherlands and Cu-raçao in the week following this revelation. In a series of telegrams dis-patched on the day of mass demonstrations in Oranjestad, protest leaders Villalba and Chong jettisoned moral arguments and instead emphasized the proposed Campo's infraction of commonwealth laws. Modeled on Eu-ropean Dutch anti-vice laws introduced in the Netherlands in 1911, the An-tillean criminal code prohibited brothels and the facilitation of prostitution by a third party. Two telegrams addressed to the governor of the Nether-lands Antilles in his dual capacity as head of the national government and representative of the kingdom in Curaçao called for the "restoration and en-forcement of Curaçaoan law regarding prostitution," while also requesting that the governor notify "higher authorities in the Netherlands."[87] Villalba and Chong then took matters into their own hands. The two women issued a telegram directly to Queen Juliana of the Netherlands and requested the enforcement of Dutch law to ensure "no tolerance for foreign prostitutes, no tolerance for public lechery."[88] While it is unclear whether protesters expected much from these appeals, the protest movement nevertheless availed itself of the hierarchical structures of the kingdom.

The mass demonstrations against Campo Alegre at the end of May significantly altered local administrators' previously dismissive attitudes

Figure 7. Aruban women protesting Campo Alegre on May 30, 1951. One holds the
Dutch flag. The signs read: "No organized immorality without punishment" and "Our
children deserve the protection of the government." SOURCE: Biblioteca Nacional
Aruba, Departamento Arubiana-Caribiana, Kostbare Collectie (#619).

and compelled a range of elected councilmen to involve themselves in the
Campo debate. On May 30, 1951, thousands of people—the vast majority
of them women—marched to government offices in Oranjestad demanding the reversal of the national decree (figure 7). Sympathetic onlookers
described this event as an unprecedented occasion. While the leadership
of the protest movement included largely middle-class women like Clarita
Villalba and Marianita Chong, mothers and churchwomen living in San
Nicolas, the nearly three thousand protesters in the streets of Oranjestad
and San Nicolas at the end of May drew from a wider cross-section of
society. They included the working-class wives of Aruban refinery workers
and the mothers of young apprentices, who, not unlike the women they
now disavowed, informally contributed to household economies by selling produce, canned meats, and tobacco from their homes. One author

observed, "Old and young, mother, partner, betrothed, from all walks of life, gathered . . . to defend husbands, young men, and fiancés against the attack of money-minded people who make a vile profit by taking away the most precious of what God gave to women in his unending, overflowing love." For some, the protest was a deeply spiritual experience. The same commentator, likely a priest, pointed to the contrast between the protest movement's modest tactics (a hodgepodge of homemade signs attached to broomsticks and riddled with spelling errors, a testament to the humble social status of the protesters) and its sophisticated moral uprightness: "This was the instinctive response of 500 years of Christendom . . . . You looked and you felt a strange lump in your throat: this was the soul of Aruba speaking."[89]

Officials scrambled to respond to the protest. Elected representatives in the Antillean government feared their parties would lose if they did not neutralize the conflict before Aruba's first-ever Island Council election in June. Yet, as politicians competed amongst each other to claim the moral high ground, confusion emerged about the scope of local authority to initiate or to reverse the policy on prostitution. On June 1, 1951, the Staten declared the national decree a "political mistake."[90] Aruban parliamentarians rushed to revise their position on Campo Alegre in view of the fast-approaching Island Council election. AVP leader Henny Eman circulated pamphlets claiming that he had never supported the brothel. Instead, Eman maintained that he had only approved the opening of a cabaret.[91] The minister of justice of the Netherlands Antilles and fellow AVP member W. F. M. Lampe came under heavy criticism after rumors circulated that Debrot funded his political campaign.[92] Lampe swiftly proposed new regulations in the Staten that prohibited the licensing of foreign *and* domestic sex workers.[93] It was the acting Dutch Governor Jas, however, whose dramatic change of heart secured the victory of the protest movement. In a public address on June 19, Jas vowed that no Campo would be built on the island. Additionally, Jas ordered the repeal of licenses for foreign sex workers and prohibited further "importation" of foreign women.[94]

While the protest movement welcomed Jas's measures, colleagues in the Antillean government felt that the acting governor had overstepped his authority and violated the government's democratic principles. In particular, Moises Frumencio da Costa Gomez, now serving as prime minister of the Netherlands Antilles, claimed that Jas's actions showed a "disregard for parliamentary tradition" and faulted the governor's controversial interpretation of the Interimregeling.[95] Lampe likewise challenged Jas's authority and insisted his own regulations should take precedence over those of the acting governor. Indeed, Lampe's measures predated Jas's by two days, but did not reach Oranjestad in time to redeem the minister's tarnished reputation.[96]

Decolonizing democracies were messy. Perhaps because of this, protesters adroitly exploited their blurred spheres of authority. The ungainly responses offered by Antillean authorities can be attributed to the unprecedented nature of this mobilization. Officials were taken by surprise at the appearance of thousands of women demanding a say in the sexual economy of island life. The industry requested the docility of laborers and promised upward mobility and middle-class lifestyles in exchange, yet few anticipated that those same values would be turned against the practices of the industry and its state defenders. Lago records are studiously silent on the topic of the protest. The company did not lend support to the protesters and the ostensibly shared value of marital harmony that it purported to support but in practice also undermined. Foreign workers without local family proved indispensable to Standard Oil's operations—and much cheaper to maintain than the elite white industrial class who publicly represented the company's paternalist ethos. The bifurcated models of reproductive care advanced by the company thus collided spectacularly. The wives of local workers held fast to the image of orderly domestic life in a fierce rejection of the transactional liaisons that were thought to sustain the other half of Lago's workforce. In this exceptional moment as the age of oil met the end of empire, the unwaged spouses orbiting the oil industry acted forcefully to shift policy and practice.

DEFENDING DOMESTICITY

Remarkably, one of the first mass protests of the age of decolonization concerned not rights of citizenship or wages, but the sexual practices cultivated by the state in its support of the oil industry. While neighborhood, familial, and religious networks did much to rally upwards of three thousand island residents against state-regulated prostitution, the protest movement's emphasis on domestic vulnerability also galvanized supporters around the proposed Campo's threat to household harmony and reflected broader ambivalence about the sweeping political and economic changes of the postwar decades. As in Curaçao at this time, local workers on Aruba were in a comparatively more stable position than their foreign counterparts. In what emerged as a well-worn company practice, Aruban workers were granted access to limited benefits in a bid to prevent disruptions in the industry's host society. Aruban men were often more quickly promoted and more likely to retain their jobs. Some with wives and children were offered housing in San Nicolas and the nearby town of Savaneta, prompting many young couples to move away from family homes and plots of land in Noord, on the far western side of the island, and Santa Cruz.[97] Lago provided nearly full male employment on Aruba in the 1940s, and just as with the white managerial staff, for local men, too, marriage was thought to aid discipline and productivity in the workplace.

These commitments were regularly reinforced in Lago's employee publications. In the popular employee periodical *Aruba Esso News*, photographs of men exchanging firm handshakes and small congratulatory gifts announced the engagements of local men like Serafino Geerman, a worker in the instrument shop, and Alex van Gelder of the Payroll and Thrift Accounting Division.[98] Smiling families were pictured enjoying company-sponsored sporting events and holiday parties. Lago's corporate photographer, Nelson Morris, captured Aruban refinery workers in their family homes. Morris pictured Cerilio Feliciano at the head of the dining table with his wife, Rosa, surrounded by their children (figure 8). Their son Raymundo graduated from the Lago Training School in 1947.[99] Photographs of Aruban domiciles bore an anthropological quality, with the US American's photographic gaze highlighting both the unity of the Aruban family and their exotic strangeness. Morris's photographs drew attention to Arubans' large family size, foreign food staples, and the presence of stray pets and farm animals in the home. These same photographs revealed the extraordinary segregation of spaces of work and sociality—but at least in the rituals of marriage and domesticity that bolstered white respectability, Aruban workers moved closer to the periphery of inclusion than most.

Figure 8. Cerilio Feliciano of the Division of Masons and Insulators sits at the head of the table with his wife and children. Feliciano's son Raymundo, pictured left, was an apprentice at the Lago Training School. By Nelson Morris, April/May 1944. SOURCE: Biblioteca Nacional Aruba, Lago Picture Collection, Departamento Arubiana-Caribiana, BNA-LAGO-MORRIS-001-05475.

The halcyon days of full male employment were ultimately to be short-lived. Following the end of World War II, several significant changes in the oil economy decreased the productivity of both Aruban and Curaçaoan re-fineries and resulted in significant layoffs and benefit rollbacks. Under new political leadership, Venezuela reversed course and opened new refineries. Anticipating OPEC's assertion of sovereign rights to oil wealth in the 1970s, Venezuela compelled Standard Oil (and Creole, its subsidiary in Venezuela) and Shell to reduce the processing capacity of the Aruban and Curaçaoan refineries after opening its own plants in 1949 and 1950, a subject explored in chapter 3.[100] Oil production in the Middle East also soon eclipsed that of the circum-Caribbean, flooding the market with cheaper product that, unlike heavy Venezuelan crude, proved easier to refine. New refineries opened in the Netherlands, France, and England in 1950–55 to process the bounty of Middle Eastern feedstock, reinvigorating European economies and consolidating the Middle East as a formidable supplier.[101]

Compounding these shifts, the introduction of automated technologies at Lago and Isla reduced demand for labor in the 1950s. Facing steep competition in nearly all of the refinery's marketing areas, Lago was the first to make the transition to automation in 1950.[102] Increasingly, it seemed, refinery operations could be run from a centralized control room, eliminating the need for men to manually regulate the temperature of a distillation tower. Between Lago's peak employment of 8,262 in 1948 and the protest movement of 1951, over 1,000 people (primarily foreign workers from the eastern Caribbean) lost their jobs. In 1955, the number of Lago employees sank to 6,420.[103]

Contrary to corporate fantasies of a flexible migrant labor force, many men, women, and children stayed in Aruba and Curaçao even as refinery workforces shrank. Until December 1949, Dutch nationality laws extended citizenship to children of nonnationals born on the islands, allowing the children of foreign workers to create the lasting ties that many elites (and local workers) feared. Following complaints from local workers and with the Antillean government also wary of future employment issues, during the 1930s authorities negotiated with Lago to ensure that Arubans and other Dutch subjects held priority in hiring and retention.[104] In part to ease these tensions, in 1949 the Antillean government enacted changes to the citizenship law. After this date, children could only acquire citizenship if the father was a Dutch national. Other men and women married Dutch citizens and obtained permanent residence this way.[105] "Foreign" workers and their descendants thus became permanent members of Aruban and Curaçaoan societies.

With the shrinking job market after 1951, the fissures of race and nation cultivated by the oil industry deepened as many felt their livelihoods threatened. It was in this context that Aruban housewives successfully

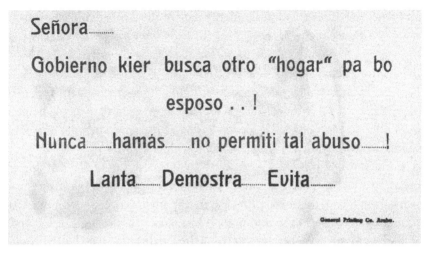

Figure 9. This 1951 protest poster warned women that "the government is looking for another 'home' for your husband!" SOURCE: Biblioteca Nacional Aruba, Departamento Arubiana-Caribiana, Kostbare Collectie (#619).

mobilized against threats to fragile domestic arrangements. When protesters descended on the streets of San Nicolas and Oranjestad at the end of May, posters written predominantly in Papiamento[106] contained messages such as "Women of Aruba! Protest against the danger that awaits your husband or boyfriend!" and "Women of Aruba! Come forth for your family. A Campo Alegre is destructive to your domestic peace" (figure 9).[107] The Antillean press likewise predicted the impending dissolution of household harmony. One fictional story printed in *Amigoe di Curaçao* told of two adolescents who once passed their evenings playing card games on the porch. On the first night the brothel opened, the young men abandoned the porch and did not return until midnight. On the second night, they did not return at all.[108] Echoing this perceived threat to Aruban familial stability, the conservative *Arubaanse Courant* cautioned in an open letter to the "women of Aruba" that a Campo would deliver "great danger to the moral and physical welfare of our homes. A danger to our husbands, sons, fathers, brothers, and boyfriends."[109]

Underlying these arguments was a distinct concern with how intensified sexual rivalry would affect Aruban women. The protest committee affirmed the racialization and heteronormativity of desire in the local press, writing to the *Beurs- en Nieuwsberichten* in November 1951 that the import of "white foreigners" only made "sin more attractive." The committee's leadership, Chong and Villalba, argued that it was absurd to claim, as many officials did, that foreign prostitutes did not threaten the community because of their assumed transience. After all, they opined, foreign sex workers *did* marry Aruban men. Even those that did not assimilate were believed to "spoil the Aruban community" by their very presence on the island.[110] In this way, foreign sex workers were not simply a potential source of corruption for Aruban men. Latin American sex workers, locally racialized as sexually desirable *white* women, also represented racial and sexual competition for Aruban women. Just as many Aruban men feared their usurpation by foreigners behind the refinery gates, some Aruban women worried about their sexual marginalization beyond them.

Perceptions of the vulnerability of Aruban men endured in official response to the protest movement. A committee formed in July 1951 to resolve the "prostitution question" and placate protest demands repeatedly questioned local police and Lago's managerial and medical staff about the vulnerability of young male apprentices. Pupils at the Lago Training School, overwhelmingly young Aruban men aged sixteen to seventeen, were reported to frequent Hija del Día. According to Herre Oppenhuizen, first lieutenant in the Lago Brigade, these young men even succeeded in bringing a sex worker into the barracks, where women's presence was strictly forbidden.[111] Others, however, minimized the sexual dalliances of male Aruban youth. One government doctor favorably compared Aruban to Curaçaoan boys, who "begin to desire women much earlier." In this doctor's view, Arubans were "more sexually serious and stable."[112] These prejudicial assertions once again distinguished light-skinned Arubans from their island neighbors in the racialized idiom of sexuality.

After the mobilization of Aruban women in 1951, many officials cited rising unemployment and worsening economic conditions as primary causes of slackening public morality. This was especially pronounced after a massive wildcat strike at Lago on August 10, 1951, when 6,000 out of a total 7,169 workers went out on strike in a wage dispute. Five days later, after management agreed to implement a modest cost of living adjustment, employees returned to work. Lago management nevertheless rejected the idea that living expenses had risen while wages failed to keep pace. They instead blamed workers for spending beyond their means to acquire middle-class commodities, including cars, homes, refrigerators, home furnishings, and clothing.[113] In meetings of the newly-elected Island Council, officials worried about Aruba's suddenly changing economic fortunes. They decried rising unemployment among Arubans while foreign workers continued to enjoy living standards that were, they alleged, increasingly inaccessible to locals.[114] The strain on male breadwinners imperiled the welfare of the entire family, and officials charted growing unemployment alongside increased incidences of divorce, sexual violence, public drunkenness, theft, and pregnancy out of wedlock. In this way, official anxieties about public morality dovetailed with the protest movement's concerns even as these groups disagreed on how to resolve the crises afflicting Aruban men.

Where once the island's remarkable economic growth legitimated the project of a separate and autonomous Aruba, by the 1950s changes in the economic landscape joined with disappointments on the political stage. The Aruban separatist movement failed to gain traction among European officials while the defeat of proposals to establish equivalence between Aruban and Curaçaoan parliamentary seats heightened the sense of Aruba's marginality and dependence.[115] These setbacks help to explain how several thousand people came to be so convinced of the threat of a Campo Alegre to members of their family and not to the thousands of anonymous sailors and foreign refinery workers whom the brothel was intended to serve.

. . . . .

A number of insights follow from the conflict that unfolded on Aruba in the spring and summer of 1951. The first is that actors on the periphery of the oil industry—in this case, the "housewives" who sustained refinery workers and their families—could exert a profound impact on industry practices. European and Antillean authorities devised systems of international sex worker recruitment and regulation to benefit companies like Standard Oil and Shell. For these companies, high-quality housing and the payment of a family wage were regarded as costly measures only to be enjoyed by small sectors of the workforce. Testing the nascent mechanisms of the decolonizing state, the protest movement compelled public officials to withdraw plans to develop Campo Alegre and, by August 1951, to send away the island's foreign prostitutes. The dramatic mobilization of 1951, among the first popular protests of the postcolonial age, shaped industry practices from the ground up.

These "gains" would be at once durable and short-lived. Though no centralized brothel came to exist on Aruba, by 1954 a significant number of foreign women had entered the island on two-week transit permits designated for "saleswomen." As in prior years, these women headed for the hotels of San Nicolas and clandestinely practiced their trade in the backrooms of bars and clubs.[116] In 1957, the island government of Aruba quietly permitted a number of registered cafés to hire "adult entertainers" from abroad. Though careful never to label these foreign entertainers prostitutes in public, in private correspondence governing officials bluntly conceded that semantic deceptions were necessary for resolving this hot-button and "centuries-old social question."[117] Once again, Aruban officials defended the provisional return of foreign entertainers by claiming that without these women the number of Curaçaoan prostitutes on Aruba would only increase.[118]

A second insight concerns the broadened theaters of oil-related struggles. As the industry permeated all aspects of insular life, and as employees came to live much of their lives *within* the company itself, new and more intimate terrains emerged as unlikely battlegrounds. Not least because of the primacy of family life to constructions of whiteness and the signaling of status in the industry, the domicile emerged as the site of a pitched struggle in 1951. The victory of the protest movement would in many ways be symbolic, for threats to upwardly mobile lifestyles did not derive from sexual competition but from the fundamental fissures in Aruba's economic model. Curaçao also stood to lose from the reorganization of refinery operations. And there, too, market fluctuations mobilized surprising actors and alliances to address the fallout of decreased demand in the 1950s and 1960s. Once again, the solution to exceptional economic crises would be sought in the bedroom.

3 Manufacturing Surplus

POPULATION AND DEVELOPMENT IN THE DOWNSTREAM

Alarming messages saturated Curaçaoan airwaves in the 1960s. Throughout the popular *barios* neighboring the Isla refinery, radio listeners would have been painfully familiar with news of the deepening crisis at the plant. Although refinery output doubled between 1950 and 1970, the total number of employees at Isla fell from its peak of 11,616 in 1953 to around 4,000 in 1969, the effects of automation plunging thousands of households into greater precarity.[1] Radio programs designed by a local family planning initiative, however, proposed new solutions to these dire circumstances. They did not focus on the practices of collectivity and mutual reliance that sustained Willemstad's working-class neighborhoods, where residents were forced to make do with less. Instead, they tied further economic ruin to reproductive behaviors, imploring listeners to exchange libidinal yearnings for the salvation of the national economy. One program in 1968 warned, "Our economy has receded in the last few years and this has resulted in unemployment on a large scale. Looking at our demographic situation and our economic situation we see clearly that it is not responsible to have an unplanned family. We cannot permit ourselves sexual irresponsibility, because that would be prejudicial to our own interests."[2]

Where once refinery workers were implored to reform kinship and re-productive practices to strengthen discipline within the refinery, through-out the latter half of the 1950s and 1960s a new constellation of actors encouraged the redoubling of conjugal responsibility and restrained fertil-ity to buoy those who were increasingly cast out of it. According to propo-nents of family planning in Curaçao, the island faced a perceived surplus not of petroleum products but of people themselves. Worsening economic conditions and the austerity-driven disappearance of Shell's social pro-grams revealed the domestic arrangements once demanded by the indus-try to be altogether contingent and fragile. By 1962, 30 percent of children were born out of wedlock, rising to levels not seen since before the in-troduction of family benefits for refinery workers.[3] Escalating rates of so-called illegitimate births and decreasing rates of marriage between 1957 and 1966 appeared to a growing number of insular elites as a startling reversal of oil's promised development.

Arguments that displaced blame for economic woes onto working class sexual and reproductive behaviors succeeded at a moment of acute crisis. Increasingly throughout the 1950s and 1960s, realignments in the global production of oil and revolutions in industrial technologies turned boom to bust. After the death of General Gómez, who had previously discouraged the construction of refineries in the country, in 1943 Venezuelan officials successfully domesticated downstream operations and negotiated a fifty-fifty split of net profits with foreign oil companies, compelling Shell and Standard Oil to reduce the processing capacity at the Isla and Lago plants.[4] In the 1950s, oil refining was among the first industries to be transformed by automatic control over industrial processes, eliminating the need for the production workers who once monitored the gauges and adjusted the valves.[5] Other oil companies also looked to replicate the achievements of the Dutch Caribbean refineries. In the 1960s, US capital poured into the development of new enclave refining sites like the enormous Amerada Hess refinery on St. Croix.[6] Competition also arose across the Atlantic. The US-directed Marshall Plan financed the purchase of crude oil arriving from the Middle East and indirectly supported the construction of sub-stantial refineries in Europe.[7] In 1959, the operating costs of Shell's newly constructed Pernis plant near Rotterdam were half those of Curaçao's Isla refinery.[8] These trends—cautious attempts to return oil wealth to exporting nations, automation, increased competition, and the location of refineries near consumers and not extraction sites—served to undermine the once towering importance of the refineries on Curaçao and Aruba.

From the late 1950s through the 1960s, this escalating crisis sparked urgent questions about the obstacles to sustained development. This chapter analyzes the shared assumptions of Antillean authorities involved in nascent development bodies like the Caribbean Commission, local Catholic leadership, and proponents of family planning. Though these actors at times disagreed on the severity of Curaçao's economic crisis, nearly all believed that the hope of salvaging oil's promised modernization lay not in the resuscitation of the industry but in strengthening the patriarchal power once thought to bolster its success. As growing numbers of men lost their livelihoods, efforts to address population growth often focused on educating working-class masculinity toward sexual and economic restraint precisely as the horizons for middle-class lifestyles receded. But despite a rhetorical focus on men, it was Afro-Curaçaoan women that bore the brunt of reproductive intervention. Statutes regulating contraception, sterilization, and abortion once again proved fungible according to perceived economic exigency. Redeployed in this era of retrenchment, racialized assumptions of stubborn and "deficient" kinship practices galvanized arguments for enhanced religious discipline, increased parental "responsibility," and incursion into Afro-Curaçaoan reproductive lives.

If these efforts were geared toward distinctly local aims, they were nevertheless imbricated within a range of transnational currents. Conversations about economic development and family planning linked Curaçao to the decolonizing world, where development projects narrowly fixated on the reproductive practices of poor women of color. Amidst growing global concern with population growth in the 1960s, contentious disputes also played out within the Catholic Church about matters of marital sexuality and birth control. Indeed, on Curaçao and elsewhere, many Catholics insisted that nonprocreative sex was an important act of conjugal love. Catholic involvement in Curaçao's family planning campaign thus reveals a more complex history of Catholicism in the global 1960s than that of homogenous conservatism alone.[9] Some Dutch priests brought these seemingly progressive ideals to Curaçao precisely as certain strands of Latin American liberation theology inflected arguments against family planning. For local actors sympathetic to population control, collaborations with transnational aid organizations were paramount. On Curaçao, this intensified reliance on Dutch demographic expertise and economic aid just as the Netherlands became a leading player in the international development project. Efforts to regulate sexuality and reproduction thus entrenched Curaçao in new transnational networks of knowledge and exchange as the oil industry waned.

THE DEMOGRAPHICS OF DEVELOPMENT

The concerns about a demographic crisis swirling on Curaçao in the 1950s had an important precedent in the Caribbean. Regional discussions on demographic growth and the approaches taken to remediate it in earlier decades influenced development discourse on Curaçao. Population politics had lingered on the minds of late-colonial reformers since labor rebellions rocked the region in another era of economic crisis: the aftermath of the Great Depression and the resulting devastation of Caribbean agricultural industries.[10] After labor rebellions swept Britain's West Indian colonies in 1934–39, colonial policy makers targeted the African-Caribbean family as the object of uplift and reform. Previously, authorities viewed kinship patterns that deviated from idealized notions of the restrained, white nuclear family as evidence of the irremediable savagery of people of African descent. But as Deborah Thomas notes, in the aftermath of working-class insurgency, West Indian family formation became a policy concern of the Colonial Office, which established a tendentious link between poverty and what appeared to British middle-class officials and social welfare workers as parental irresponsibility.[11] The British royal commission sent to investigate the challenging conditions in the West Indian colonies in 1938 and 1939 determined that large, mother-centered families strained resources and employment, slackening morale and ultimately fomenting rebellion. These concerns resonated widely; even some nationalist actors like Jamaican politician Norman Manley voiced their support for birth control before the royal commission.[12]

When the findings of the West Indies Royal Commission (popularly known as the Moyne Report) were made public in 1943, the report asserted that overpopulation "ha[d] contributed more than any other single influence to the formidable increase of intermittent employment."[13] While displacing notions of racial inequality rooted in biological fixity, culturalist understandings of poverty rationalized renewed incursion into African-Caribbean family life and explained economic prosperity and peril as the result not of structural patterns but of "cultural" practices. Fixated on family forms and fertility rates, late-colonial efforts to foster economic growth and higher standards of living anticipated the emphasis on development discourse that would characterize the postcolonial era.[14]

Similarly, the specter of potential unrest remained a concern for an emerging cadre of experts from the 1950s on who regarded overpopulation as a serious problem throughout the developing world. This network of development and demographic experts worked to neutralize the threat of the "population bomb."[15] Popularized by Stanford biologist Paul Ehrlich, the nuclear metaphor implied human and atmospheric ruin. Experts like Ehrlich reasoned that the rapid growth of the world's newest, poorest nations would soon overwhelm the resources necessary to sustain human life. In the sharply divided Cold War era, national administrators and transnational NGOs—from the Ford and Carnegie Foundations to the International Planned Parenthood Federation—encouraged low-income women of color to reduce fertility as a solution to the dual dangers of underdevelopment and political radicalism.[16]

Motivated by the memory of recent unrest and the spirit of colonial reform, the United States and the United Kingdom founded the Caribbean Commission on March 9, 1942, to exchange expertise and inform social and economic policy across the region. These goals remained pressing in the era of decolonization. As empires reformed into commonwealths, kingdoms, and other forms of extended statehood in the 1950s, the commission redoubled its study of demographic bottlenecks to advance economic and political development. At the meeting of the preparatory committee in Trinidad in August 1956, a now enlarged commission joined by France and the Netherlands called for a regional conference to address "the demographic problem" in the Caribbean. In the run-up to this conference, held in July and August 1957 in Port of Spain, Trinidad, participating countries appointed committees to study the demographic situation in their jurisdictions. The Dutch Antillean committee included a number of island elites, doctors, and politicians under the chairship of Dr. William Charles de la Try Ellis, a jurist born on Curaçao who remained politically active until his death in 1977. The committee's work commenced at a pivotal moment for the Antillean capital. Though employment at the Shell refinery had decreased slowly since its 1953 peak, these developments accelerated after 1957 owing to the effects of automation. Following the dismissal of large numbers of foreign workers, between 1957 and 1966 the number of local workers employed by Shell fell from 4,896 to 3,314.[17] It was no secret that Curaçao's prosperity relied on oil refining and some feared the consequences of this for population growth. Already in 1953, the European Dutch governor of the Netherlands Antilles, Teun Struycken, cautioned that with any retrenchment in the oil industry, "the whole matter of overpopulation will be let loose."[18]

Contrary to the predictions of the governor, the Antillean delegation to the Caribbean Commission doubted the very existence of a "demographic problem." Instead, the delegation minimized the island's changing economic fortunes and challenged the commission's faith in technocratic knowledge to address thorny social problems. This reflected the attitude of many Antillean authorities, who, several years prior, were unalarmed at the dismissal of 1,700 foreign laborers from the British West Indies and Portugal. Following this mass layoff in 1953, the Antillean minister of economic affairs averred that Shell's failure to forewarn the Antillean government proved the oil companies were themselves unconcerned. As the historian Jaap van Soest described, the massive layoffs that followed after 1957 thus "contained an element of surprise" for many Antillean leaders.[19] The delegation subsequently maintained that if foreign workers were employed in the oil industry, albeit in dwindling numbers, one could assume that jobs exceeded the number of local individuals available to fill them. Serious economic problems, they reasoned, would be avoided by simply replacing foreign with domestic laborers.[20]

This optimistic outlook elided the growing impact of automation. Prior to the implementation of computerized control systems in petroleum refineries and electrical power plants in the 1950s, open-loop analogue computer systems monitored and measured output but required human operators to implement corrections. Increasingly throughout the 1950s, closed feedback loop control systems were introduced in energy plants. In this system, a controlling device monitored and measured output. The resulting data would then be fed back to the controller to make the indicated adjustments. These new devices did not require an operator to adjust pressure valves or regulate the temperature of a still. In the 1950s, oil, electricity, and chemical plants were among the first industries transformed by the introduction of highly automated production processes. Unlike the conveyor-belt system, which required human labor to transport products from one to another workstation, energy production now required minimal human intervention as computerized processes moved liquid or vaporized molecules through pipelines to boilers, distillation towers, and cracking units.[21] Refining plants could increasingly be run almost entirely by a handful of technicians located in a control room.[22]

Automated technologies were introduced at the Isla refinery in the early 1950s and became operational by the end of the decade. This development resulted from an agreement among CPIM management to diversify the refinery's products and to produce them as cheaply as possible, a response to the glut in refinery production and the decreasing price of heating oil—one of the refinery's most competitive products—in the United States. In 1953, CPIM management decided to construct a catalytic cracker, which was more effective than thermal and other cracking technologies at fracturing heavy Venezuelan crude into lighter molecular-weight distillates. With the construction of the catalytic cracker complete in 1958, the need for manual operators was all but eliminated. Anticipating this outcome in 1953, CPIM ceased to recruit foreign contract workers.[23] Initially, local laborers benefited from the opportunities to install computerized systems. But after 1957, increasing numbers of Curaçaoan workers were let go and unemployment soared to over 20 percent.[24] At the same time, the company increasingly subcontracted with other agencies to undertake construction projects at the refinery. Although subcontracted agencies could partially absorb laborers who had lost jobs at the refinery, these companies typically paid lower wages for the same work.[25] The effects of these seismic shifts in industrial organization were coming into full force as the Antillean delegation traveled to Trinidad in 1957.

Although the Antillean delegates dutifully provided statistical data on rates of natural increase and migration, they questioned whether demographic expertise could resolve what was in their view a thoroughly

cultural phenomenon. "By means of a stringent limitations [sic] to numbers, formulae, and graphs we cannot arrive at an acceptable and correct
analysis of the present picture of the Netherlands Antilles," the committee argued, "nor at a notion or conception about the future, because cultural life will not stand to be expressed in or squeezed into mathematical
formulae."[26] Addressing Curaçao's "population problem"—if such a thing
even existed—required a robust treatment of cultural and moral factors,
factors that were expressly excluded from the commission's mandate.[27] In
the committee's view, economic determinants would not ensure the island's
prosperous future. Instead, the cultivation of responsible, hardworking,
and self-sustaining individuals would be paramount. The national priority
should thus be "to strengthen a moral base as a foundation to construct
further upon in the interest of character-formation and cultivation and
strengthening of sense of duty and sense of responsibility." Only a profound "psychological adjustment" could help to instill these values, which
included "will power and self control to accept marriage-life also in another
sense than responding to exclusively materialistic and sensual motivates
[sic]."[28] These moral inclinations, paired with thrift and hard work, would
allow "a well-balanced person" facing the prospect of unemployment
to "not consider himself as a sinking wreck or a shipwrecked person in
society." Rather, "he will be able to obtain from his education, his experience, his achievements, moral courage as to look for a decent job abroad
if there is no other way out."[29] This was complex circumlocution. Antillean delegates denied the existence of an economic crisis while affirming
that revitalized family life and individual resolve—possibly to move off the
island—would furnish the solution.

When delegations from across the Caribbean gathered in Port of
Spain in 1957, the Netherlands Antillean delegation stated their official
recommendation that no measures be implemented to influence population patterns. They maintained that "on moral and practical grounds
the Netherlands Antilles reject birth control by use of mechanical and
chemical contraception, and do not consider any measure to promote
this practice."[30] French officials shared this sentiment, rejecting contraceptives on religious and legal grounds. Chastened by growing criticism
of the racialist overtones of family planning campaigns throughout the
British empire, the delegation from the British Caribbean expressed some

support for family planning programs but doubted their effective implementation given the divergence of opinions on the topic. Although in 1955 the government of Barbados joined a handful of countries worldwide in offering state support for family planning—a trend that would gain steam throughout the former British Caribbean islands in the mid-1960s—the report produced by the commission instead emphasized economic development, especially in education and housing.[31]

Not all Antillean authorities agreed with the decision to forego population management projects. Prior to the Caribbean Commission conference, the Antillean minister of finance cautioned that with the advent of automation, the oil industry's inability to absorb local labor "menaces us like the Sword of Damocles over our heads" and urged intervention "if within a few years we are not going to face an eventual catastrophe."[32] Another commentator criticized the vague answers offered by the Antillean delegation and their unwillingness to confront what some foresaw as an imminent demographic disaster.[33]

Although the Antillean delegates rejected family planning, their diagnosis of the issues facing Curaçao proved consequential to later discussions. First, citing moral considerations undoubtedly influenced by the prominent role of the Catholic Church and the devotion of the delegation's chairman, de la Try Ellis, to local Catholic leadership, the Antillean delegation urged the adoption of a moral and cultural approach to what nascent development and demographic experts regarded as a matter of technocratic expertise.[34] The Antillean committee insisted, "Rational scientific thinking cannot penetrate to the very root of culture-problematic. It is not possible nor desirable to control the delicate organism of cultural [sic] from above."[35] In the aftermath of the Caribbean Commission conference, family planning advocates would largely concede to these terms of debate, agreeing that scientific intervention would prove futile without cultural transformation. Secondly, though the Antillean delegation challenged as dubious any attempt to study demographic patterns according to race, citing what was in their view a thoroughly mixed society, they nevertheless offered numerous theories about the sexual dynamics of the slavery past to explain demographic trends.[36] Though the oil industry's impact on the regulation of family life scarcely warranted mention, the more durable legacy, it seemed, was that bestowed by racial slavery:

"Wrenched away from their country, their family, and popular customs," enslaved people were forbidden from marrying and unions (whether of a long-lasting or ephemeral nature) were "encouraged, favored, or enforced, because children bron [sic] from female slaves, pertained to the owner of the female slave." For the Antillean delegation, the inheritance of slavery was not only of an intimate nature. The committee continued, "And as the slave could not possess anything by rights, nor hold any property, every incentive to be active or gainfully occupied was absent."[37] From this perspective, the slavery past also bore on contemporary questions of labor and productivity.

These assertions echoed uncomfortably with arguments once deployed by colonial elites about the "failure of emancipation" in the 1920s. As discussed in chapter 1, colonial officials alleged that Afro-Curaçaoans were poorly suited for industrial employment because slavery and its aftermath had inadequately instilled labor and familial discipline. By the late 1950s, and failing to account for the conjunctural causes of rising unemployment, Antillean authorities once again turned to these durable racial scripts. Even though Afro-Curaçaoans had successfully integrated into the industrial economy and their increasingly bleak economic prospects resulted not from lack of individual initiative but deliberate corporate practice, Antillean delegates held fast to the understanding that the problem Curaçao faced was not, in fact, a dwindling job market, but an abiding issue of human resources. Foremost among these were racialized assignations of wasted productivity and anomalous family forms.

Though the idea that slavery exerted a lasting impact on Caribbean kinship had circulated in social science and common sense thinking prior to the collapse of the oil industry, it was redeployed with new explanatory power in an age of economic decline.[38] The urgency to secure future economic development prompted new theorizations about potential obstacles, which focused overwhelmingly on Afro-Curaçaoan gender and sexual norms. The role of the Catholic Church was unavoidable in these discussions, for until the arrival of Shell nearly all Afro-Curaçaoans relied on the Church for spiritual instruction and practical needs such as education and medical care.[39] Eventually, these discussions would lay bare stark divides among Catholic leaders about the precise nature of Curaçao's "crisis" and the role of the Church in resolving its putatively cultural origins.

REFORMING CULTURE AND CATHOLICISM

In the 1950s, the Catholic Church on Curaçao reached an inflection point. Since the nineteenth century, the Church had attempted to carry out a civilizing mission on the island under the supervision of the Dutch province of the Dominican order.[40] Education, health care, and spiritual instruction were important venues for cultivating *drecha bida*, the Papiamentu term for bettering one's life through marital monogamy.[41] But in the 1950s and 1960s, the social controls that the Church once exercised through these very institutions were no longer enforceable. With the availability of public schooling, children born to unmarried parents were at last allowed to attend the same institutions as peers born within wedlock. Similarly, with the creation of secular health care facilities, single mothers gained entry to the same maternity wards as their married counterparts.[42] Structural unemployment and increasing poverty further estranged the Church from its parishioners, and the reassertion of Catholic social control thus became a top priority for the Curaçaoan Church in the 1950s. Hardening divisions among Catholics on the topics of personal faith and sexual and reproductive autonomy, however, muddied consensus about how best to achieve this rapprochement. By the turn of the decade, a younger generation of priests once again insisted that the uplift of Afro-Curaçaoan men would be essential for reviving Catholicism and Curaçaoan society.

Church leaders and Catholic politicians called for a new pastoral approach to address what they viewed as a worsening spiritual situation. Following the appointment of the European Dutchman Michael Holterman as apostolic vicar on Curaçao in 1956, the Curaçaoan Church increased the recruitment of a new generation of primarily European-born priests trained in theology and humanistic pursuits such as journalism and social work. Though Holterman was not a reformist in all respects, he called for an end to "authoritarian behavior" within the Catholic Church.[43] Following from this, in 1958 the provincial father of the Dominican order in the Netherlands sent a young but highly respected European Dutch priest to assess the spiritual situation on Curaçao. It is unclear what motivated the provincial father to commission the study. The decision might have arisen from the deepening sense of crisis on Curaçao or else from the movement of theological renewal already underway in the Netherlands, where many priests and clergy were beginning to anticipate the issues that would dominate the Second Vatican Council by emphasizing deeper bonds with parishioners as well as personal faith and closeness to God.[44] Whatever the reason for his visit, Wim van der Marck spent nine months assessing the spiritual and moral situation on Curaçao. In 1959, he produced a controversial seventy-seven-page report of his findings. Having received his doctorate in theology at Fribourg in Switzerland—an institution known for its modernizing orientation—van der Marck criticized "traditional" methods of Catholic instruction and looked for social and historical explanations for the seemingly inadequate absorption of Catholic values in Curaçaoan society.[45] For van der Marck, the evidence of this "dangerous superficiality" of faith was to be found above all in the bonds and structures of the Afro-Curaçaoan household.[46]

Van der Marck did not simply attack Afro-Curaçaoans for deviating from Catholic convention. He instead criticized the leaders of the Catholic Church on Curaçao for their insufficient attention to the spiritual and moral health of men. Van der Marck claimed that priests and other religious figures on the island were excessively focused on administering sacraments to the neglect of the substance of their parishioners' faith. According to the Dutch priest, evidence of this could be found in the Church's lackadaisical attitude toward the "'remarkable' conjugal and family situation" and in the Church's superficial "grip on the male population."[47] Defending these controversial views in a series of exchanges with the provincial father in the Netherlands in 1959, the priest reinforced the acute crisis of masculinity, writing, "Especially for the men, *marital fidelity* is hardly mentionable. In broad segments of the population, *sexual activity before marriage* increases the social prestige of boys and men." Also shocking to this observer was the purportedly *"abnormally* high measure" of male same-sex relationships on the island. The priest found this astonishing given that Campo Alegre provided men on-demand access to women's sexuality.[48]

Van der Marck weighed what he viewed as the persistence of anomalous masculine behavior against the long-standing presence of the Church on Curaçao. While blaming local Catholic leadership for neglecting the substantive cultivation of faith, the priest also proffered another historical explanation. In his view, disregard for marriage among Afro-Curaçaoans was "determined by a number of historical factors, including slavery and the behavior of the elite of society."[49] Echoing the Antillean delegation and other Antillean politicians, van der Marck conceded that slavery, which forcibly dissolved family ties, exerted a lasting influence on the descendants of the enslaved. But the priest ascribed the practice of "concubinage," or cohabitation without marriage, to Black male mimicry of white colonial elites.[50] With this transparent recognition of white sexual license, van der Marck diverged from the rhetoric of the late-colonial regime and Shell, which equated whiteness with sexual virtue, even as he continued to uphold the nuclear family as the unquestioned ideal.

In order to encourage Afro-Curaçaoans to maintain church teachings on marriage, van der Marck exhorted religious leaders to embrace new standards for guiding parishioners. The priest advocated that clergy devote "extensive care to the development of women and girls, who in the current situation scarcely know a function apart from bearing children or, more important still, being a physical-sexual partner for the man." Changing this dynamic would require improved instruction on marriage and a broader program of empowerment so that women could assume social roles alongside and equal to men. Enhanced information on birth control would be vital to this social transformation; the priest noted, "The growing population of Curaçao increasingly demands the provision of detailed and systematic information, including consultations about birth control (*geboorteregeling*), etc., if one does not want to be faced with surprises."[51]

The explicit endorsement of birth control and recommendations for spiritual revitalization mirrored other Catholic movements developing across the European continent. After Pope Pius XII announced in a 1951 speech before the Italian Catholic Society of Midwives that periodic abstinence might be acceptable under certain circumstances, a growing number of Catholics argued in favor of changing traditional Church teachings on marriage and sexuality. Indeed, with declining European birthrates in the first half of the twentieth century, it was evident that many Catholics had already begun practicing contraception.[52] In the Netherlands and Belgium, where support for a liberalizing approach was particularly strong, many Catholics believed that change would be inevitable in the secularizing climate of the postwar years. They argued that Catholics should be empowered to adjudicate moral decisions about sexuality on the basis of their own conscience.[53] Prior to the conservative backlash against this majoritarian movement, which culminated in the 1968 promulgation of the encyclical *Humanae Vitae* reaffirming the prohibition on artificial birth control, van der Marck's recommendations would not have been altogether controversial in some European circles.

Similarly, when Church leaders on Curaçao reviewed van der Marck's report, it was not his apparent progressivism that sparked critical rejoinders. Though sympathetic to van der Marck's observation that the Curaçaoan Church was very traditional, Holterman took offense at the priest's suggestion that clerical authorities had been negligent in their duties. Other Catholics rebuked van der Marck's naiveté, drawing attention to the Church's repeated efforts to address the "male problem, which makes many of us hopeless and melancholic." One priest mocked, "If [van der Marck] knows novel methods for dealing with this problem, do not let him hesitate—we are waiting on him and still know no solution."[54] Thus, as Curaçao's economy plunged further into crisis, two certainties cohered among Antillean authorities and Church leadership: first, that cultural rather than structural factors explained Afro-Curaçaoan family forms, and, second and relatedly, that men were desperately in need of a revamped moral program to strengthen virtue and industriousness as employment prospects shrank.

"RESPONSIBLE PARENTHOOD"

By the turn of the next decade, van der Marck's proposal to introduce family planning on Curaçao would gain new backers within and beyond the Church. In 1963 Ewald Ong-a-Kwie, the general secretary of the Petroleum Werkers Federatie van Curaçao (PWFC), approached a physician at Shell's hospital, the Sanatorium het Groene Kruis, about establishing family planning services for refinery workers.[55] Born in 1929 in the Dutch colony of Suriname, Ong-a-Kwie worked at the Shell refinery from 1948 to 1975 and remained a stalwart leader of the labor movement. His organizational acumen and reputation for securing deals between company management and PWFC workers made him a well-known figure on the island. This notoriety would only increase after 1969, when Ong-a-Kwie, then chairman of the Curaçaosche Federatie van Werknemers (CFW), called for a strike among subcontracted refinery workers. The strike precipitated an explosive revolt among the working class and urban poor, a transformative moment in Curaçaoan history explored in chapter 4. With the erosion of Shell's social programs in the late 1950s, including widower pensions, company-built homes, and free health care for spouses and dependents, Curaçao witnessed an uptick in births outside of formal marriage and decreasing marital rates. These figures seemed to correspond with growing unemployment and the liquidation of family services. In 1960, 28 percent of children were born out of wedlock, increasing 4 percent from the historic low of 1952.[56] Ong-a-Kwie approached Dr. Sergio Leon to determine, if robust benefits were not to return, whether workers themselves might embrace contraceptive methods.

The son of an elite plantation-owning family on Curaçao, Leon had recently returned to his native island after completing his medical training in obstetrics and gynecology in the United States. Arriving on Curaçao in 1962, the doctor was appalled by the dismal medical facilities and what he identified as pervasive ignorance among the island's population. After joining the Sanatorium het Groene Kruis in 1963, Leon agreed that Ong-a-Kwie's proposal would be an ideal opportunity to educate Curaçao's citizenry on "responsible parenthood." The physician quickly contacted the International Planned Parenthood Federation (IPPF), who sent coordinator Ofelia Mendoza from Guatemala to Curaçao to assist in the establishment of family planning services. On October 1, 1965, Leon's Stichting tot Bevordering van Verantwoord Ouderschap (Foundation for the Promotion of Responsible Parenthood) was officially registered with island authorities. A year later, the foundation, locally known as Famía Planiá, opened a clinic on the Abraham de Veerstraat in downtown Willemstad (figure 10). Although Ong-a-Kwie hoped Leon would establish an office at Shell, the doctor insisted that family planning services—the first offered in Curaçao—be made available to the island's population writ large.[57]

Securing support for Famía Planiá, however, was no easy task. To overcome the stated opposition to family planning by the Antillean government and others within the Catholic Church, Leon emphasized that his primary purpose would be "to promote the idea of responsible parenthood among the people in the broadest sense of the term, and taking into account the official standpoints of the churches and the cultural and religious convictions in our society."[58] Like the arguments of the Antillean

Figure 10. The Foundation for the Promotion of Responsible Parenthood occupied the second floor of Abraham de Veerstraat 7a in Willemstad. SOURCE: *Amigoe di Curaçao*, October 1, 1966. Koninklijke Bibliotheek.

delegation at the Caribbean Commission, the promotion of "responsible parenthood" spoke directly to the putatively moral and cultural causes of demographic crisis on Curaçao, promising redress through a vigorous educative program. The message featured everywhere in the foundation's activities and outreach, including in lectures, advertisements, television and radio programs, roadside billboards, private client consultations, and even participation at popular public festivals such as Carnival. With promises not to undermine religious teachings, within Famía Planiá's first year Leon secured the support of representatives from the Diocese of Willemstad, the council of Protestant Churches, the Jewish synagogue Mikvé Israel, the Association of Physicians, the Rotary Club, and the Credit Union, a lay Catholic savings and credit union that aimed to cultivate spiritual and social self-sufficiency.[59]

Shell played an important role in the establishment of the foundation. The PWFC joined the aforementioned religious and social institutions as a member of the foundation's board of creators. A union representative from the PWFC, Hans Jannsen Steenberg, even served as Famía Planiá's first director. Shell also provided material support in the form of office furnishings, medical instruments, and use of the company's printing services. Finally, the company offered periodic cash contributions to offset the foundation's operating costs.[60] For Shell, the message of "responsible parenthood" resonated with the company's own efforts to cultivate paternal duty. Now, however, island elites hoped to marshal this value less to encourage productivity within the refinery setting and more to manage the crisis of its waning economic importance.

Next to Curaçao, Famía Planiá found its greatest success on Aruba, where changes in the global oil economy had taken a similar toll on insular employment. Famía Planiá participated in the opening of a new health center in a residential neighborhood near the Lago refinery in San Nicolas. With the closure of the Lago Hospital in 1973, another casualty of retrenchment in the industry, the community health center assumed responsibility for providing medical services to workers and residents. Officials lauded Famía Planiá's "important results" in San Nicolas, evident in the "very sharp decline in the birthrate" since the foundation's establishment on Aruba in 1969.[61]

Famía Planiá was not the first organization concerned with family planning on Aruba. Over a decade earlier, the white US women of the Lago Colony had collaborated in the Marital Guidance Foundation. White US women viewed their participation in this organization as an important act of charity that affirmed their position as arbiters of raced and gendered propriety. From this standpoint Claire Burson, the wife of a US chemical engineer, attempted to educate Aruban women about planning their families "so that each child is a wanted child." While the Marital Guidance Foundation worked to popularize the idea that family planning "contribut[ed] to the welfare of the community by curbing overpopulation with its consequent unemployment, poor living conditions, low social standards, and juvenile delinquency,"[62] inside the Lago Hospital more direct reproductive interventions were sought—seemingly both by Lago staff eager to reduce the birthrate and by Aruban men and women seeking more reliable forms of birth control. The medical director recalled in the early 1970s how he had performed hundreds of vasectomies and tubal ligations on Aruban men and women starting in the late 1940s. He was compelled to halt tubal ligation procedures in the mid-1950s following opposition from the prior medical director. At least according to this account, Aruban women had enthusiastically embraced the operation in past decades. But in the 1960s, when tubal ligations resumed, impetus slowed with the opening of government-supported clinics like Famía Planía.[63]

Although Lago employees of West Indian origin could visit the Lago Hospital, the medical director contended that they were, for unspecified reasons, not offered these services. It was in clinics like Famía Planía or among local doctors that West Indian men and women could seek similar procedures. According to one 1994 study of former migrant domestic workers on Aruba, eighteen of the twenty-six women interviewed had undergone hysterectomies—a decision shaped also by the stringent terms of domestic employment, wherein women who became pregnant were deported to their islands of origin.[64] On Aruba, Famía Planiá did not invent but rather elaborated on existing assumptions that it was overpopulation that exacerbated unemployment and not, in the first instance, the changing organization of labor within oil refineries. Individual reproductive choices, however, were motivated by distinct concerns. Some Aruban women viewed tubal ligation as a reliable form of birth control that was quietly condoned by local Catholic clergy. Some Aruban men, meanwhile, hoped to spare their wives a serious medical procedure by undergoing a vasectomy. Others, it seemed, enjoyed the ability to have extramarital relationships without risk of pregnancy. At least one researcher saw a correlation between the availability of vasectomy procedures and Aruban men's increased patronage of San Nicolas's crib saloons.[65] For migrant domestic workers, a more permanent resolution to one's fertility could help to secure employment in an industry where pregnancy carried the probability of deportation.

Across the Atlantic, Famía Planiá also received substantial support. After the transfer of sovereignty in Indonesia in 1949, the Netherlands increasingly directed money and expertise to the international development project. That same year, the Netherlands made its first contribution to the United Nations aid program: a sum of 1.5 million guilders. By 1975, the Netherlands would become one of the largest providers of development aid in the Western world, increasing aid contributions to

1.5 billion guilders. Researchers once active in Indonesia and Dutch New Guinea, the latter relinquished by the Dutch in 1962, increasingly joined UN aid organizations.[66] The country's postcolonial pivot from a defeated empire to a major player in international development helped to fuel the country's self-representation as a bastion of postwar progressivism. Also within the Kingdom of the Netherlands, development emerged as a top priority as the returns of the Caribbean oil boom diminished. Between 1960 and 1975, development aid to the Netherlands Antilles increased ten-fold to 200 million guilders.[67] By 1969, the European Dutch government provided 197,200 guilders (roughly equivalent to 104,000 US dollars) of Famía Planiá's operating budget. By contrast, the IPPF and the Antillean government each contributed 5,000 guilders annually.[68]

European Dutch interest in family planning was at least partially self-serving. In the 1960s, European officials fretted over the prospect of Caribbean migration to the Netherlands as refinery jobs disappeared and the Antillean birthrate increased.[69] With financing from The Hague, Famía Planiá established a new outpatient unit to professionalize obstetrical and gynecological training.[70] The foundation also capitalized on enduring Euro-Caribbean ties to forge partnerships with institutions in the Netherlands, calling on the Nederlandse Vereniging voor Seksuele Hervorming (NVSH) to provide Dutch-language sex education materials for use in Antillean schools. Doctors from Curaçao traveled to the Netherlands to receive advanced instruction in performing medical procedures and utilizing new reproductive technologies.[71] Lingering postcolonial attachments and the zeitgeist of development thus offered new opportunities for investment, exchange, and collaboration across former metropole and colony.

These ties were also plainly evident in the legal inheritance of Dutch colonialism. In this respect, the rhetoric of "responsible parenthood" also served strategic importance, allowing the foundation to promote family planning without running afoul of legal conventions established under colonial rule. When in 1918 the colonial government implemented a new criminal code in the Caribbean that directly mirrored Dutch anti-vice legislation, statutes went into force banning the advertisement of contraceptives to any person below the age of eighteen (Article 246) and the public advertisement or promotion of methods to prevent (Article 472) or disrupt (Article 473) pregnancy. Article 262 criminalized abortions and strengthened penalties for individuals who performed them.[72] In the Netherlands, too, it took decades to reverse these statutes. Owing to the allegedly exceptional problem of the "illegitimate" birthrate on Curaçao, the ban on contraceptive advertisements was in fact lifted in the Netherlands Antilles one year before the repeal of the Dutch equivalent in 1970.[73] Antillean legislators rationalized the law's removal by underscoring the threat of overpopulation.[74] These signal moves of what would later be known as the sexual revolution were first anticipated in the former colonies and tied to racial anxieties about the fertility of poor women of color. Gender and sexual liberalization thus did not drive all legal reversals in the globally radical climate of the 1960s. Once again, the perceived exigencies of the Caribbean oil economy were thought to demand legal innovation.

"MOMMY, WHO IS MY DADDY?"

Like van der Marck and the Antillean delegation to the Caribbean Commission, supporters of Famía Planiá believed the crisis of unemployment and overpopulation to be symptomatic of a larger problem afflicting working class masculinity. What became clear through Famía Planiá's radio and television programs and correspondence was the extraordinary fragility of Shell as both an economic project and a transformative social force. It seemed that male refinery workers had shrewdly capitalized on corporate incentives to marry, including the allocation of housing, health care, and access to promotions, without transforming their desires or intimate behaviors. As Eva Abraham-van der Mark's interviews among the children of refinery workers in the late 1990s often attested, "the marriage certificate had little impact on people's behavior."[75] Some men continued to have extra-marital relationships and children outside of legal partnerships. According to the foundation, the alleged absence of paternal responsibility now imperiled the entire insular economy. Hans Jannsen Steenberg, a representative of the PWFC, bitterly rebuked men's unwillingness to uphold what was in his view sexually responsible behavior. In a 1967 report on the foundation's annual activities, he wrote: "The most irresponsibly proliferating group of the weakly intelligent appear to be so indolent that they no longer experience their misery as misery. They do not wish to exchange laziness and carelessness for greater knowledge of birth control." According to Steenberg, "This aversion to accepting responsibility seems to manifest more frequently in men than in women."[76] Dr. Leon shared these frustrations. According to a former internist, the doctor's anger about perceived paternal absence and irresponsibility was the "galvanizing force behind Famía Planiá."[77]

At least in Famía Planiá's view, the stakes of male behavior were extraordinarily high. The entire economy was imagined to hang in the balance. Rectifying the island's economic future would require men's willingness to legally recognize and provide for their children. One radio broadcast in 1968 asserted: "About 35 percent of the children born do not bear their father's name. This human irresponsibility goes hand in glove with a lack of knowledge of the possibilities to prevent pregnancy. As a consequence of the irresponsibility of many men and women, many of the children born out of wedlock become a burden on the whole community."[78] Repeatedly, Famía Planiá emphasized that it was men whose neglect of their children strained diminishing public resources and bred miserable and tortured children. One program, "Mommy, Who is My Daddy?," aired several times on television and radio. As images of crying, neglected babies flashed across the screen, a young boy inquired about his father's identity. Pausing for dramatic effect, the show's host repeated the boy's question: "Yes, who might his father be?"[79]

On radio as on television, men were instructed in reproductive restraint and in practical tasks like financial management and coping with the growing likelihood of unemployment. Collaborations with the Rotary Club and local Credit Union offered short lessons in the management of household finances, which Famía Planiá deemed an indispensable skill of the responsible patriarch. "Build a Dam and Wait for the Rain," a television program that aired on October 3, 1968, brought together Adgil Henriquez, a working father, and host Ronnie Martina from the Credit Union. Both men agreed that financial planning allowed fathers to fulfill their paternal duty by providing their children with education, health care, and the observation of religious sacraments like holy communion and baptism, each of which carried monetary costs. More still, maintaining a household budget would allow families to prepare for unexpected events, including the loss of a job that was, both men agreed, an unfortunate but increasingly commonplace occurrence.[80] Male members of the Credit Union also featured on radio programs to explain how fathers could develop their own household budgets by itemizing recurring monthly expenses and setting aside savings for unexpected costs.[81]

Holding fast to the notion of the wage-earning patriarch, Famía Planiá urged Curaçaoans to embrace a future whose horizon had already receded. An appeal to the orderly domiciles of the 1940s, home to the acquisitive couple with their traditionally bounded gendered roles, accompanied lessons on financial planning. Part of what made middle-class belonging so desirable in terms of wealth and sensibility was the ability to uphold the ostensibly natural division of the sexes. Mr. H. van Delden from the Minor's Protection Board and Jossy Martina, a Curaçaoan theater actor, explained to one television host the advantages of marriage:

> Many times a child without a father cannot receive a good education. His mother has to go out to work in order to support him. . . . Sometimes the mother finds herself forced to start an affair with another man, just to improve her financial situation . . . but the result is, that she finds herself with more children . . . and more misery!! When mother and father are married and live together more often this family can count on a fixed sum of money for the maintenance of the family. And there is no need for the mother to go out to work.[82]

The reassertion of patriarchal power thus carried the perceived advantage of curbing women's social and sexual autonomy. While women had long supplemented household incomes, layoffs at the refinery sent many women looking for regular wages. New opportunities emerged as the Antillean government tried to attract export-oriented industries to Curaçao promising generous tax exemptions and minimal labor regulations, particularly in the form of low-waged women's work during long overnight shifts. Throughout the late 1960s, the creation of foreign-owned assembly plants run by Texas Instruments, Schlumberger, and Rockwell turned a growing number of women on Curaçao into waged industrial workers.[83] Famía Planiá presented this response to economic hardship as an affront to women's natural role within the domicile. Appealing to aspirations for class mobility and the domesticated gender roles of the middle class, Famía Planiá reasoned that a "planned family was a happy family" not least because planned families could maintain the proper division of duties between husband and wife (figure 11).

No ta tur dia ta PASKU pero..............
Por tin PASKU pa nos TUR, si tin di
nos ku NO tin:

TRABOW, KAS, PANYA NI BASTANTE KUMINDA ?

pa nos por yega na dianan di Pasku kontentu

pa un i tur nos MESTER bira mas responsable

pa ku nos mes i nos famia.

PLANEA FAMIA ADELANTA !

Figure 11. Around Christmas, Famía Planiá promised those who planned their families a happier holiday along with work, housing, and enough to eat. Note the abundance of gifts in the couple's arms. SOURCE: *Vitó*, December 24, 1970. Internationaal Instituut voor Sociale Geschiedenis.

RACE AND RESPONSIBILITY

Famía Planiá's repeated suggestion that men and women regulate fertility for the sake of the national economy bespeaks an important paradigm shift in the postcolonial world. Feminist theorist Michelle Murphy has called this the "economization of life," a distinct move away from a eugenic program that sought to improve racial fitness to one primarily focused on regulating reproductive sex for the betterment of the economy. Yet as Murphy contends, even within this reformulation, racial logics did not disappear.[84] The presumed subjects of family planning efforts were not the island's light-skinned elites, for whom marriage was an affordable and attainable goal, but rather low-income Afro-Curaçaoan men and women. On Curaçao as in other post-slavery societies, elites understood Caribbean families by analogy alone. They identified Western and middle-class conjugal norms as the only respectable way to organize a family, even as light-skinned elites were rumored to maintain numerous informal relationships with women of color. Although the birthrate did not rise uniformly on Curaçao after 1960, the number of children born to unwed parents did. According to proponents of family planning, then, it was not overpopulation that threatened Antillean society but reproduction within single-parent families—a phenomenon they believed to be exclusive to the Afro-Curaçaoan community.[85]

While many family planning campaigns employed the language of "responsible parenthood," on Curaçao the concept of "responsibility" had long assumed a racial valence. As chapter 1 explored, the promotion of "responsibility" saturated late-colonial and corporate-led efforts to integrate Afro-Curaçaoans into the workforce and citizenry through the embrace of nuclear family values and industrial discipline. As racialized development schemes and international population control movements were implemented throughout the former colonial world in the 1960s, language that focused on individual reproductive behavior facilitated "the eclipse of structural causes of national ills and obviated alternative, less coercive pathways to personal and national well-being."[86] Responsibility, a catchphrase of racialized common sense on Curaçao, guided Famía Planiá's proposed solution to growing inequality in the 1960s.

Despite the foundation's attempts to encourage productive and conjugal masculinity, it was in fact Afro-Curaçaoan women whose bodies were most vulnerable to reproductive intervention. In an interview with the author Jeannette van Ditzhuijzen, one physician's assistant at Famía Planiá recalled that some doctors would perform a partial or total hysterectomy on a patient, seemingly without advanced warning or consent, if doctors deemed it "(medically) irresponsible" for the woman to have additional pregnancies. Removal of the uterus might also attend the routine treatment of uterine fibroids, a condition that overwhelmingly affected Afro-Curaçaoan women.[87] In regions marked by racialized health disparities and racially coded anxieties about reproductive excess, sterilization procedures persisted despite the existence of other, less invasive, techniques to remove fibroids. In Puerto Rico and the mainland United States, too, fibroid tumors were a common pretense for performing hysterectomies on women of color. African American women were twice as likely as white women to have had a hysterectomy because of fibroids.[88] Physicians on Curaçao justified the procedure by pointing to various legal restrictions in the Netherlands Antilles. The public medical insurance utilized by many patients at the Famía Planiá clinic did not cover medical expenses related to sterilization but would cover the cost of a hysterectomy if performed for medical reasons. Doctors loosely interpreted medical necessity, determining medical need based on whether a patient already had a "complete family." Dr. Leon felt that such curtailments on women's reproductive self-determination were necessary in a society that restricted or forbade other methods of birth control and abortion.[89]

Though colonial-era laws criminalizing abortion remained on the books after the consolidation of political autonomy in 1954, in 1970 the Sint Elisabeth Hospital—a Roman Catholic institution where Dr. Leon also worked—created a committee to approve abortion on medical indication. Formed jointly by the medical director of the hospital, the general practitioner for women, a social worker, and a psychiatrist, the committee convened to address the outbreak of a rubella epidemic in 1970–72 that heightened the risk of congenital disorders. Although Famía Planiá officially held that "the Foundation for Responsible Parenthood is there to help people plan their family, not to help them get rid of their pregnancy," the reality was more complex.[90] Some doctors who cooperated with Famía Planiá interpreted the medical indication quite broadly. They considered social factors such as a woman's class and marital status and existing family size. Former clinic director Sietze Friese recalled, "Look, there were lots of single-parent families. A mother with a child could only survive if she had a man in the house, and would then get pregnant again. . . . That's why we were rather liberal with abortions."[91] In 1970, Famía Planiá reported that 101 "therapeutic abortions" were performed at the foundation's family planning centers.[92] One physician's assistant recounted that many women who had an abortion on grounds of medical indication were also simultaneously sterilized. Dr. Leon remembered these events differently, claiming that many women preferred sterilization to other contraceptives like condoms or the pill so that they would not raise the suspicion of male partners hoping to prove their virility through procreation.[93]

The sterilization abuse of overwhelmingly poor women of color in the twentieth century is undisputed.[94] But research has also shown the operation to be considerably more complicated. As Nicole Bourbonnais has shown for Bermuda and Trinidad and Laura Briggs and Iris López for Puerto Rico, some women elected to undergo sterilization when access to other contraceptive methods was limited.[95] Women in Peru and North Carolina at times requested eugenic sterilizations as this was the only way to safely access the procedure.[96] These histories do not minimize the coercive context in which predominantly low-income women of color were subjected to sterilization abuse. Rather, and as Iris López has argued, they highlight the limitations of binary understandings of reproductive agency *or* victimization in contexts of severe constraint.[97]

While it may be true that not all women who underwent sterilizations on Curaçao did so as victims, most women made reproductive decisions within vastly restricted parameters shaped by medical and economic pressures and social prejudices. Public insurance and legal restrictions narrowed women's access to alternate methods of birth control. Without access to patient files, it is difficult to assess whether women were advised about the consequences of sterilization and if they knowingly chose this permanent method to regulate their fertility.[98] What is clear, however, is the absence of what feminist activist and scholar Sonia Corrêa has called "enabling conditions," or conditions that allow people who can get pregnant to decide to have a child or not in social, political, and material conditions that guarantee their thriving.[99] As the legal scholar Dorothy Roberts has argued, racialized development and family planning initiatives that ignored these enabling conditions perpetuated the view "that racial inequality is caused by Black people themselves and not by an unjust social order."[100] Based on a similar belief that reproductive choices underlay national prosperity and peril in the aftermath of oil, Famía Planiá promoted reproductive intervention in a context of material deprivation.

PIETY AND PROGRESS

Women were also a focus of Famía Planiá's outreach—not only in the sus-pect regulation of their fertility to buffer fluctuations in the oil market, but also to inform new gender norms to stimulate economic development. Strikingly, some of the most outspoken promoters of liberalized views on women's sexual agency and reproductive choice came from Catholic allies of the foundation. In fact, in 1965 the Roman Catholic Diocese of Willem-stad provided Famía Planiá's first cash donation of 300 guilders to regis-ter the foundation with the notary.[101] Though not all among the Catholic establishment endorsed Famía Planiá, the support of some prominent Catholics reflected the progressive movement represented by van der Marck and a growing cohort of Catholics in the Netherlands and glob-ally who demanded reformed approaches to gender roles, sexuality, and family planning. On Curaçao as in other parts of the Global South, de-mands for sexual *aggiornamento* were not always easy to disentangle from mounting concerns about overpopulation.[102] In the course of the 1960s and in the wake of the Second Vatican Council (1962–65), this progressive movement seemed to gain powerful institutional backing as the Pontifi-cal Study Group on Population overwhelmingly voted to relax doctrine to facilitate sex as a positive expression of marital love and to provide relief to Catholics in the Global South faced with poverty and population pres-sures. Met with opposition from some conservative factions, Pope Paul VI overruled the will of this majority in the 1968 encyclical *Humanae Vitae*, a crushing blow to the reformist movement.[103] Given the fast-changing ecclesiastical views on family planning and birth control, Famía Planiá called on representatives from the Diocese of Willemstad to explain the Church's official position.

Soon after the promulgation of *Humanae Vitae*, in October 1968 Famía Planiá hosted a question-and-answer session on local television. One in-credulous viewer asked: "How is it possible . . . that the Diocese of Willem-stad continues to give its cooperation in the Foundation for Responsible Parenthood, after the publication of the encyclical *Humanae Vitae*?"[104] The question prompted the foundation to host a television program solely de-voted to the topic. On November 11, 1968, Father Cees Streefkerk, a pro-gressive Dutch priest on Curaçao and member of Famía Planiá's advisory board, appeared on "The Encyclical Letter and Family Planning." The priest argued that *Humanae Vitae* did not call for an absolute ban on birth control. Defending the encyclical while also creatively interpreting its meaning, Streefkerk insisted, "The Pope is not against Family Planning, for we bear responsibility. . . . He takes the problems and ideas of our modern time into consideration: population explosion, emancipation of women, the idea that procreation is not the only purpose of marriage." When the program's host urged Streefkerk to address whether observant Catholics could use only the rhythm method despite its inefficacy, Streefkerk responded that "those Catholics who can keep to the words of the Pope" should do so, but "those who, for serious reasons, cannot, let them look for another way!" Streefkerk continued that couples could use "artificial" contraception "for serious reasons . . . if the rhythm method is not good for them. And such persons must not think themselves less Catholic or outside of the Church." Streefkerk's insistence that, above all, the encyclical encouraged couples to be "conscious of their responsibility" allowed the priest to defend the Church's continued collaboration with Famía Planiá.[105] Similar arguments about the primacy of individual responsibility prevailed among many Catholics in the Netherlands who continued to promote family planning services in the wake of *Humanae Vitae*. Famía Planiá maintained contact with one such organization, the Katholiek Nationaal Bureau voor Geestelijke Gezondheidszorg (National Catholic Bureau for Spiritual Health), which shared materials related to sexual and reproductive advice.[106]

Unsurprisingly, Streefkerk's views were not universally shared among Catholics on Curaçao. Amado Römer—a progressive and immensely popular Curaçaoan diocesan priest—was skeptical of Famía Planiá. In Römer's view, the language of "responsible parenthood" masked the foundation's focus on limiting fertility among the poor and working class. More still, Römer viewed the discourse of overpopulation as itself entirely incoherent. While Canada and Australia "call[ed] out for more people," other regions of the Global South, including Africa and Latin America, were implored to decrease their populations without attention to "other factors that determine quality of life," such as economic conditions.[107] Römer's putatively conservative stance on birth control was not rooted in a Catholic rejection of family planning but in an anti-imperial ethos that underscored the reductive and unevenly applied assumptions of development discourse, a familiar argument among some liberation theologians in Latin America.[108] Indeed, in the previous decade, Römer's nationalist and anti-imperial orientation had sparked anxiety among his colleagues, who unsuccessfully attempted to relocate him to Rome.[109]

At least on paper, Famía Planiá's collaborators did not support family planning for the sake of population management alone. They also paid attention to shifting norms of companionate marriage and gender equality. Various television and radio spots affirmed the view that women as well as men should receive sex education. A radio program in 1968 promised liberating payoffs for women exposed to early instruction, asserting, "A girl who respects herself and who has received a good sex education does not allow any man to use her as a doll and to put her aside later on, when he has had enough of her!"[110]

While confirming the importance of sex and reproduction within wedlock, commentators also opened up taboo discussions on nonmarital sex. In another radio broadcast that year, a nurse discussed whether nonmarital sex itself constituted "a lack of responsibility." The nurse reasoned, "This is a question, which, in my opinion, cannot be answered just with a simple yes or no: A large group of people . . . are of the opinion that sexual intercourse is only permitted in marriage . . . and there is also a group of people who want more liberty in this field."[111] Streefkerk did not publicly challenge these views on nonmarital sex, stating only that it was the duty of cooperating parties in Famía Planiá not to criticize claims made by another religious or social organization. Though he admitted to feeling "not very happy" after the promulgation of *Humanae Vitae*, the priest said that a closer reading of the encyclical letter revealed the Pope's admirable preoccupation with the character of marital love and the topic of women's emancipation, the realization of which demanded "a well-instructed and educated conscience."[112]

This attention to women's sexual agency and reproductive choice eventually gave way to a topic of long-standing importance to the Church: the question of children born outside of formal marriage. Some actors in Famía Planiá urged the adoption of new social attitudes. Kicking off a radio program in 1968, one discussant claimed, "What we must not forget is, that a child whether it is born in a complete family, which means, to a married couple—or in an incomplete family, which means that his mother is not married to his father and father and mother do not live together, either of these children have the same right to a future and to the same chance in life." The commentator lamented the fact that "in the past the community did mark these children." Indeed, until 1951 the Church prohibited children born to unmarried parents from being baptized during the daytime, earning those children the moniker *yunan di skuridat,* or children of darkness.[113] Famía Planiá supporters now insisted that these children, historically subjected to a range of discriminatory practices, not bear the blame for parental indiscretion.

For Leon, the resolution to this issue lay in holding men to legal account for their reproductive behaviors. In the 1960s, Leon even proposed the introduction of a paternity law that would make biological fathers financially responsible for children regardless of the child's legal status. The doctor recalled that the Antillean governor, Efraïn Jonckheer, laughed heartily at this suggestion, claiming no member of the Antillean parliament—many of whom were alleged to father children out of wedlock—would support such a measure.[114] Though legal pressure might have failed, Famía Planiá repeatedly warned men that "times have changed. There is no need anymore for a man to be boasting about the amount of children he has, like in the old days! Nowadays only shame is left for such men."[115] At the same time that Famía Planiá collaborators contradictorily sought to empower women's sexual and reproductive choices while rendering women's bodies sites of dubious medical intervention, they also attempted to inculcate new paternal attitudes among working-class men.

·   ·   ·   ·   ·

In 1970, contemporaries credited Famía Planiá with the salubrious decline in fertility on the island. The birthrate fell from 35 to 23 per 1,000 residents that year. According to the IPPF, the foundation's television and radio series had succeeding in doubling the number of visitors to Famía Planiá clinics.[116] Writing in 1979, the Curaçaoan sociologist René Römer hypothesized that the foundation's promotion of the planned, nuclear family would not have succeeded without the prior saturation of "modern Western conceptions of marriage and reproduction" in Curaçaoan society.[117] Indeed, Famía Planiá was not the first to endorse the family as an important economic actor, though the foundation now encouraged its revitalization for very different ends. Unlike the administrators and corporate elites who upheld paternal duty and domestic life as bedrocks of achievement within the refinery, Famía Planiá advocated for these values as the answer to an uncertain post-oil future.

Despite the reported decline in birthrates, the foundation cast doubt on its own supposed accomplishments. In light of the continued prevalence of bearing children out of wedlock, Dr. Leon feared that it was the middle class who planned their families, and not, as he had initially hoped, the working class and urban poor. Famía Planiá and other concerned individuals had sought to transform working-class men into what Carla Freeman, building on the ideas of Michel Foucault, termed "entrepreneurial selves," a subjectivity driven to industriousness, flexibility, and adaptability in the realm of work and self-improvement in the context of family and intimate partnership.[118] But detached from the material incentives that once propelled higher rates of marriage, state, religious, and medical actors now appeared quite ineffectual in regulating populations, practices and, ultimately, desires.

Though the discourse surrounding family planning most often focused on the economic and social value of limiting fertility, proponents of family planning also intimated that men and women might utilize contraception for other reasons. Some birth control advocates cautiously waded into discussion of women's sexual empowerment *even as* some physicians intervened in women's reproductive autonomy by performing sterilizations seemingly without consent. Leaders associated with Curaçao's family planning campaign also argued for the destigmatization of children born outside of wedlock, even as they affirmed the importance of marriage and distinct spheres for men and women. Eugenic argumentation to uplift the Afro-Curaçaoan working class thus appeared alongside new and seemingly progressive incitements to form mutually pleasurable relationships and liberal social ties. Eugenic concerns, in other words, were not only highly compatible with but in fact made much more persuasive by their entanglement with the liberalizing promises of development discourse.

If sexual restraint and binary gender roles were thought to be the guarantor and measure of postcolonial development in the wake of oil, then, according to Famía Planiá's founder, Curaçao's outlook appeared grim.

By the close of the decade, as thousands of refinery workers, youth, and other discontented Afro-Curaçaoans took to the streets in a fiery reproach of the deteriorating economic situation, it appeared that the foundation's efforts had also failed in that other vital task of Cold War development: to curb population growth to keep radicalism at bay.

4 "Sexuality, Yes! Slavery, No!"

EROTIC REBELLION AND ECONOMIC FREEDOM

Early on the morning of May 30, 1969, around four thousand men gathered at Post V, one of the large, gated entrances to the Shell refinery on Curaçao. The men congregated in a solidarity strike with the Curaçaose Federatie van Werknemers (CFW), a union of subcontracted laborers who handled steel construction for Shell.[1] Prominent labor leaders like Wilson "Papa" Godett and Amador Nita of the radical dockworkers union summoned the growing crowd to march along the outer edges of the Schottegat Bay, through the narrow streets of Punda, and onward to Fort Amsterdam to register the CFW's protest with the government. What had begun as a wage dispute among the employees of Werkspoor Caribbean, the subcontracted agency locally known as Wescar that employed CFW workers, transformed along this seven-mile route into an ever-larger movement. As the strike progressed to the seat of government, other discontented individuals, primarily young men, joined the protest. An upswell of discontent over mounting poverty, the hegemony of foreign oil interests, and abiding racialized inequity manifested in the streets of Willemstad that day. Chanting "we will teach them to respect us" (*nos lo siñan respeta nos*) and "these are the possessions of capitalists, just destroy them" (*ta kos di kapitalista, kibra nan numa*), protesters overturned and set fire to cars, smashed windows, and looted businesses.[2]

This outpouring of frustration, coupled with the carnivalesque suspension of social norms, only intensified when police fired upon the crowd, wounding Godett and killing two demonstrators. Local police called on the Netherlands to request the mutual assistance promised by the kingdom's constitution. The next day, three hundred European Dutch marines arrived on the island. With the streets cleared following the arrival of reinforcements, leftist pamphlets explained the causes of this abortive uprising: "The people have become fed up! The workers have become fed up!" "Now that we have burned everything down," the leaflet continued, "there is new room to start building again."[3]

These calls to rebuild society from the ashes of destruction included not only mandates to redistribute corporate wealth and to democratize labor relations. From the mid-1960s to the early 1970s, Caribbean intellectuals—many recently returned from university in the Netherlands—also reflected on the sexual reforms initiated by and for the oil industry in its phases of growth and decline. They shared concerns about overpopulation while criticizing the racist assumptions of overpopulation discourse; they wrestled with the legacy of regulated prostitution and brothelkeeping; they called on women to militate against sexism and men to find emotional closeness with partners; and, more still, they demanded erotic liberation as an integral part of economic and political self-determination. May 30, 1969, has been variously understood as a coordinated labor movement and an unplanned "riot," but the leftist intellectual production that helped to stimulate this event was also concerned with the creation of a distinctly *sexual* revolution.[4] In this sense, the May 30 uprising is not the only story to tell about the radicalism of this era. While this day served as a watershed moment in the history of the kingdom, initiating urgent political and labor reform and sparking new attention to Afro-Curaçaoan culture, it was also dominated primarily by men. This fact obscures leftists' nuanced attention to revolutionary gender and sexual norms and the participation of women in this intellectual production.[5]

Considering leftist agitation in the run-up to and aftermath of the uprising thus reveals new actors, preoccupations, and transnational exchanges. In articulating demands for sexual emancipation, young progressives in the Dutch Caribbean drew lessons from other Atlantic currents, including the radical climate of Dutch universities in the 1960s, the Cuban Revolution, and the Black Power movement. Socialism's purported ability to eradicate prostitution, an accomplishment that Fidel Castro celebrated in 1966, inspired some to theorize sex and desire beyond the bounds of capitalism.[6] Radical activists likewise embraced Black Power's exaltation of Blackness and its potential to revitalize romantic love among and between Black men and women. Their articulation of a revolutionary masculinity premised not on a "vigorous revindication of black manhood" but rather on emotional availability, respect, and mutuality for straight and same-sex-desiring men alike is perhaps one of the most remarkable features of the movement's professed gender and sexual politics.[7]

Illuminating the transmission of these ideas across the Atlantic world reconceives both the substance and geography of the sexual revolution. Until very recently, this history has largely been told from the vantage of Europe and North America and featured an overwhelmingly white cast of characters.[8] Returning to the creative invocation of sexual liberation within postcolonial struggles broadens the scholarly view of the many ways in which sex became politicized in the 1960s. It also draws vital attention to the formation of what Christopher Lee has termed the *communitas* or imagined "community of feeling" that could bind nonstate actors across the Global South in their efforts to realize and anticipate new worlds.[9] It was the promise of liberated sexuality that inspired activists in Curaçao and the diaspora to combine and adapt revolutionary Atlantic movements as they fought stridently to build their own.

Netherlands Antillean and European Dutch authorities registered this strengthening leftist momentum with some anxiety, but it was not until May 30, 1969, now commemorated as the *Trinta di mei* uprising, that officials were compelled to seriously consider the political demands of the working class and urban poor. Some of the effects of this reckoning are well known. Antilleans of African descent occupied government posts never before held by Black individuals. In 1970, the Dutch government appointed Bernadito Leito as the first Black governor of the Netherlands Antilles and Ernesto Petronia became the country's first Black prime minister.[10] Once denigrated Afro-Curaçaoan cultural expressions moved from the margins to the mainstream in a celebration of the island's previously suppressed African heritage. While yearnings for change were widely shared among working people, not all of these aspirations took the form of independence from the Netherlands promoted by some leftists. Eventually, prominent leftist leaders also dispensed with calls for sovereignty.[11] But off the island, demands for independence grew louder. Following strong assertions by the Black working class on Curaçao, Aruban politicians revived the project of a *status aparte*, or separate status, to untether Aruba from its island neighbor. And in a clear reversal of dominant postcolonial narratives, Dutch authorities smarted over their obligation to deploy what could be perceived as colonial force and actively moved to encourage the eventual independence of the Caribbean countries of the kingdom.[12] Eager to shed its blighted colonial image, the Dutch government quietly suspended development aid for family planning on Curaçao. In a transparent recognition of the intimate interventions that defined the age of oil as it reached its seemingly explosive end, Dutch authorities retreated from the very project once thought to ensure the island's postpetroleum future.

BUILDING THE LEFT

In the 1960s, several local, regional, and global currents served as important vectors of radicalization on Curaçao. The most immediate were the cutbacks at the oil refinery. In the decade between 1957 and 1967, the oil industry's share of the gross national product decreased from 40 to 22 percent. The number of unemployed rose from five to eight thousand between 1961 and 1966, increasing total unemployment to 20 percent.[13] This uncertainty devastated communities, with some individuals developing stomach ulcers and chronic nightmares from the stress. Afro-Curaçaoans were particularly impacted by these changes. With decreased demand for unskilled labor, individuals who had left the countryside hoping to find employment in the city now confronted bleak prospects. The ripple effects were enormous. With many family members often depending on a single wage, entire households were quickly plunged into economic despair. And with foreign workers dismissed in growing numbers after 1953, many of the Curaçaoan women who had fallen in love and begun families with migrant men were now forced to fend for themselves.[14] In part to address global criticisms of the company's paternalistic oversight of labor, Shell suspended the construction of homes and sold most of its residential properties directly to employees. The culture and amenities of the company town diminished as a result.

Efforts to obscure the centrality of Shell to seemingly all insular operations also carried substantial cost-saving benefits for the company. Though subcontracted firms had operated in limited fashion in the Caribbean oil industry from the start, in the 1950s and 1960s this process intensified. In this period, Shell increasingly put out to contract subsidiary tasks such as shipping, maintenance, repair, and construction. People who lost their jobs at Shell might be hired by subcontracted agencies paying lower wages for the same work. As Hannah Appel observes, subcontracting practices in the oil production process anticipated by several decades the commodity chain organization that came to typify other transnational industries in the 1980s and 1990s.[15] On Curaçao as elsewhere, subcontracting practices deepened inequalities by providing benefits such as higher wages and insurance to a reduced segment of workers in the industry. Indeed, this was the grievance registered by CFW laborers in their wage dispute with Wescar. While workers saw diminished returns on their earning power, oil production temporarily rebounded. In 1961, the Netherlands Antilles formalized a treaty with the European Economic Community (EEC). Petroleum products from juridically Dutch territories in the Caribbean could be imported duty-free into the member nations of the EEC Common Market.[16] In 1962, production reached another peak. By 1966, the Isla refinery processed 300,000 barrels of crude oil per day.[17] These developments generated continued profits for Shell, but not for the workers whose labor was increasingly marginal to production.

The global trend toward specialization and international contracting-out in the oil industry reverberated in the development of Curaçao's offshore economy. In 1956 Schlumberger, a firm specializing in geologic exploration and drilling services, incorporated the firm in Curaçao for tax purposes.[18] This was part of a larger move to diversify sources of public revenue in the 1950s by establishing Curaçao as an attractive offshore financial center. Low taxation, lax corporate regulation, and the promise of client confidentiality drew investors from abroad, by 1969 resulting in the creation of 1,350 shell companies.[19] Yet the proliferation of financial services had a negligible impact on insular employment, generating no more than 3 percent of total employment at its peak.[20]

Changes in the labor market served to politicize and occasionally to unify fragmented labor unions on Curaçao, which had steadily increased in number and size since the decolonization reforms of 1954. Though in the 1940s some political parties formed labor organizations in an effort to attract the votes of the working class, by the 1950s these organizations were largely dissolved. In their place grew a number of independent labor unions led by workers themselves.[21] Shell assiduously sought to prevent this development by forming a management-appointed Werknemers Advies Comissie in the wake of a 1936 dockworkers strike.[22] After the removal of legal prohibitions on union activities in 1956, only fear and intimidation remained as union-busting tactics.[23] Around this same time, the leaders of the Democratische Partij—since 1954, the dominant political party on Curaçao—established the Petroleum Werkers Federatie van Curaçao (PWFC) with financial assistance from the International Federation of Petroleum and Chemical Workers in Denver and advisory support from the Puerto Rican section of the American Federation of Labor and Congress of Industrial Organizations (AFL-CIO).[24] In December 1957, Shell Curaçao and the PWFC, a union representing some 2,300 members, reached their first collective agreement.[25] Also important was the prominent role played by immigrant workers, especially those from the British Caribbean, in the local labor movement. Since the 1930s, economic crisis had spurred labor activism and unionism in the British Caribbean, meaning that some migrant workers brought crucial experience and know-how to the Dutch islands. For others, such as Theophilus Albert Marryshow, Maurice Bishop, and Eric Gairy of Grenada, the oil refineries on Aruba and Curaçao served as important "schools of unionism," with lessons later exported to their countries of origin.[26]

Perhaps because of its members' privileged position as employees of Shell, the PWFC earned a reputation as a moderate union willing to take the side of its employer. It was a historic occasion, then, when in May 1969 PWFC leadership agreed to join a solidarity strike alongside subcontracted workers. PWFC contracts often served as aspirational models for subcontracted workers, especially among moderate unions favoring a gradualist approach. Among these groups was the CFW, a general union that represented workers from numerous businesses and industries on Curaçao. Included in its membership were construction workers employed by the Dutch construction company Wescar, one of several companies under contract by Shell.[27]

Other unions departed from the tendency of groups like the PWFC and CFW to be moderate and nonpolitical. The most well-known of these militant unions was the Algemene Haven Unie (AHU) led by two prominent labor leaders, Papa Godett and Amador Nita. Hailing from St. Eustatius, Godett's parents came along with hundreds of others from the Dutch-controlled island to find employment in the oil industry, a migration that began in the 1920s following pressure from colonial authorities to improve the economic position of the northeastern islands.[28] Godett was born in the vibrant working-class neighborhood of Otrobanda in 1932. As a young man, he was a successful boxer before finding employment as a longshoreman in the 1950s. Contemporaries like René Römer described Godett as providing the power and Nita the brains behind the AHU.[29] Nita was born in Willemstad in 1921, the son of a shipyard worker and straw-hat maker. After completing law school, in 1952 Nita wrote a short pamphlet criticizing major foreign companies like Shell for their unequal treatment of European and Antillean workers. He argued that Antilleans should have the same pay, pension, and benefits as the white "expatriate" class living in the plush neighborhoods of Julianadorp and Rio Canario, a criticism that would remain high on the agenda in 1969.[30] These views galvanized AHU's rank and file and earned Nita and Godett considerable admiration. Despite the different ideological orientations of these fragmented unions, the increased strain on workers and the unifying impulse of charismatic labor leaders would help to pull the labor movement to the left.

A second vector of radicalization was the experience of migration to the Netherlands. With the advent of autonomy in 1954, the Netherlands Antilles needed highly educated individuals to take part in administration and civic life. To fill this demand for educated administrators, the popular politician Moises Frumencio da Costa Gomez developed a program to grant scholarships to low-income students to study in the Netherlands. A small but not insignificant number of Caribbean students landed in major university cities like Amsterdam and Leiden in the 1950s and 1960s, where they encountered students from other parts of the colonial world. These included Surinamese students in contact with the radical Black internationalist Otto Huiswoud. Studying Marxism and Maoism, they followed liberation struggles from Cuba to Vietnam, Algeria to the United States.[31] From the mid-1960s Dutch universities and cities were also sites of radical protest and sexual rebellion. Engaged in their own struggle against the social and political conservatism that dominated the postwar Netherlands, the anarchist Provo movement captured the imagination of many student radicals after its formation in Amsterdam in 1965. The Provos waged public protest in often absurdist "happenings" against state and police violence, private property, and sexual conservatism.[32] But perhaps most politicizing of all was the experience of racism in the Netherlands. Light-skinned individuals who benefited from ascriptions of white respectability in the Netherlands Antilles became racialized as Black in Europe. Despite their Dutch citizenship, Caribbean students in the Netherlands were increasingly bound together by their common status as "outsiders."[33]

Among the first leftist student groups formed by Antilleans in the Netherlands was *Kambio* (*Change*). Antillean students spread across the major university cities of Leiden, Utrecht, Amsterdam, and Nijmegen founded *Kambio* in 1964. Under the editorship of Harold Hollander, Harold Arends, and Marlène Eustatia, the group began publishing a journal of the same name a year later. In anonymously authored articles covering topics from anticolonial movements to Marxist ideology, *Kambio* criticized lingering colonial forces in the Netherlands Antilles and debated the prospects of a working-class revolution there. Active for just two years, *Kambio* circulated in the Netherlands and Curaçao, where it printed a thousand copies of each issue.[34] As other progressives entered the fray in the mid-1960s, *Kambio* became known as an excessively ideological paper written for an educated Dutch-speaking intelligentsia. Its critics, many of whom were fellow leftists and former collaborators, dismissed as "romantic Marxism"[35] the paper's academic treatment of leftist thought and its seeming estrangement from laborers, an issue that *Kambio* acknowledged and struggled to resolve.[36] Though *Kambio*'s reach may have been limited, its arrival on the political scene opened new space for trenchant critiques of local and kingdom-wide governance, foreign capital, and social conservatism.

Vitó (*The Overseer*) occupied and enlarged this space. Now practically synonymous with the May 30 movement, *Vitó* was launched on Curaçao in

Figure 12. Stanley Brown embraces a supporter wearing a shirt that says, "Make Love, Not War." Quoting Brown, the caption reads: "Women's emancipation is now one of the most important things." SOURCE: *Amigoe di Curaçao*, September 30, 1969, 9. Koninklijke Bibliotheek.

1966 by recently returned graduates. In pithy and anonymously authored articles and editorials, *Vitó* attacked the corruption of dominant players on the island. In particular, *Vitó* upbraided the Democratische Partij for representing the interests of Shell and local white elites against the Afro-Curaçaoan majority. Formed in 1944, the party rose to prominence in 1954 in part through courting the industrial working class. But after fifteen years in power, radical laborers and the intelligentsia criticized the party for its increasingly oligarchic tendencies.[37] Shell was also a frequent target of condemnation in the pages of *Vitó*. While the Black underclass confronted unrelenting insecurity, white managers and technicians from Europe and North America continued to live in sequestered comfort.[38]

The most visible leader of the *Vitó* movement was the schoolteacher Stanley Brown (figure 12). Born in the neighborhood of Groot Kwartier to a white mother from the binational Dutch and French island of St. Maarten/St. Martin and a Black refinery guard from St. Lucia, Brown's radicalism appeared to manifest the anxieties of an earlier generation of colonial officials who feared that migrant workers and their offspring would establish a permanent presence on the island. In 1961, Brown returned to Curaçao after completing university in the Netherlands and soon attracted the ire of Antillean authorities. Together with a multiracial and mixed-gender group of former students, fellow schoolteachers, and workers, Brown organized Provo-inspired "happenings" in Willemstad's Gomezplein. Each Saturday afternoon, as many as several hundred protesters gathered to mock the ruling Democratische Partij in demonstrations that mirrored the humor and absurdism of the Dutch anarchists, with whom Brown maintained direct contact.[39] Though militant activity was not a new feature of Curaçaoan society, the demonstrations of the 1960s marked something of a turning point. Characteristic of other New Left movements, these protests moved beyond the industrial workplace to demand not only political change and economic equality but also the reimagining of social relationships. In a small society where one could not hide behind a veil of anonymity, taking part in these demonstrations carried tremendous risk of police intervention and social ostracization.[40]

In 1967, Brown became editor-in-chief of *Vitó* and soon began publishing in Papiamentu to attract readership and stoke political consciousness among the industrial working class. This goal brought Brown into collaboration with labor leaders like Godett and Nita. *Vitó* supported demands for higher wages and assisted in militant strike activities by producing pamphlets for striking workers. The trio celebrated this partnership between labor and the intelligentsia as a rare achievement. Soon after the May 30 uprising, Brown quipped, "It would have been great if Nita was a woman, then it would have been done, perfectly complete. The laborer, the intellectual, the emancipation of the woman; but we are already very content with two laborers."[41] The bond between labor leaders Nita and Godett and the intellectual Brown drew the struggles of the working class to the fore of *Vitó*'s pages while broadening the labor movement's interests beyond the workplace.[42] With its wide-ranging attention to political, economic, and social issues, at its peak *Vitó* printed fifteen thousand copies of each issue that circulated across Curaçao, the wider Netherlands Antilles, and even

Figure 13. Emmy Henriquez.
SOURCE: *Amigoe di Curaçao,*
April 4, 1970, 9. Koninklijke
Bibliotheek.

to the Netherlands and Cuba.[43] The group's acerbic indictments of the political and economic situation on Curaçao, its demands for a cultural revolution representing the Black underclass, and its provocative public presence helped to secure a broad readership until the paper folded in 1971.

Two women, the Curaçaoan-born Emmy Henriquez and Yellie Alkema from the rural Dutch province of Friesland, amplified attention to women's emancipation in *Vitó.* Moving to the Netherlands to attend boarding school at age fourteen, Henriquez became radicalized through her involvement in the 1960s student movement in Amsterdam, eventually choosing to return to her natal island to fight injustice (figure 13).[44] Henriquez briefly assumed editorship of the paper in 1970 after Brown resigned and devoted himself to the creation of a socialist worker's party, the Frente Obrero y Liberashon 30 di Mei (FOL). It was under Henriquez's direction that the recurring column "Open Letter to Women" appeared. Alkema also drew attention to women's issues in *Vitó*. In Alkema's own words, her task was to publish a story in each edition "about a family where the woman was completely alone while the man went around seeking sexual pleasures." These stories were drawn from Alkema's observations as a social worker on the island, where she arrived in 1967. Then twenty-two years old, Alkema met Brown while organizing recreational activities for impoverished youth. This partnership eventually brought Alkema into conflict with the Reformed Church that employed her, resulting in the social worker's forced return to the Netherlands just two days before the May uprising.[45]

Other progressive groups formed in the wake of May 30, 1969. This included, among others, a younger generation of Caribbean diaspora students in the Netherlands. After the deployment of the Dutch marines to Curaçao, an estimated three to five hundred Antillean students in the Netherlands protested the use of military force. *Kontakto Antiano* appeared soon after this demonstration. In addition to reporting on events organized or attended by students from the Netherlands Antilles, this bimonthly publication featured reader-submitted pieces including poetry, practical tips for navigating Dutch bureaucracies, and meditations on metropolitan life. *Kontako Antiano* also shared content with *Vitó*; in November 1969 *Vitó* reported on a two-day workshop on the topic of sexuality organized by *Kontakto Antiano*. Convening in Amsterdam, participants discussed persistent problems in their sexual lives, including mistreatment from men and the need for greater education around and access to contraceptives.[46] All three leftist publications took up questions of sexual morality and gender discrimination, a fact that Antillean authorities attributed to the liberal climate of the 1960s Netherlands. But elite fears that "the island stood defenseless against Dutch-imported moral decay"[47] minimized the other radicalizing forces, both homegrown and transnational, then shaping radical imaginaries.

THE PROBLEM WITH OVERPOPULATION

One of the foremost debates on sexual and reproductive politics taken up by the growing left was the matter of overpopulation. As the previous chapter showed, on Curaçao and globally in the 1960s, overpopulation discourse had become the preserve of middle-class actors advocating the idea that familial poverty was caused by an abundance of children. For this reason, anticolonial critics often rejected the idea of overpopulation all together, claiming, as did the Egyptian Marxist theorist Samir Amin or the Ugandan scholar Mahmood Mamdani, that overpopulation was a "myth," a misleading premise that blamed poverty on the alleged ignorance and sexual promiscuity of individuals while conveniently obscuring the colonial roots of inequality.[48] Yet on Curaçao, leftist intellectuals and laborers agreed with more conservative actors that overpopulation posed an enormous threat to Curaçaoan society. Groups like *Vitó*, the PWFC, and CFW even worked together with Famía Planiá to support family planning services among the working class. General secretary of the PWFC and CFW chairman Ewald Ong-a-Kwie, who had initially approached Sergio Leon about family planning for refinery workers, continued to represent the PWFC on Famía Planiá's board and deliver public talks on the theme of responsible parenthood.[49] Advertisements for Famía Planiá also regularly featured in *Vitó*, *Petrolero* (the periodical of the PWFC), and the *Voz di CFW*. Indeed, the CFW adopted a resolution in 1971 endorsing "the general lawful application of birth control" and obligatory instruction on birth control in schools.[50] Yvonne Damasco, the second secretary of the CFW, proudly reminded listeners of the radio program "Voz di Obrero" that the labor unions were the first to insist on the creation of Famía Planiá against conservative opposition.[51]

Though the radical intelligentsia in Curaçao shared the concerns of conservative actors and moderate labor leaders about overpopulation, they departed from these groups in some significant ways. Radicals posited that population growth would undermine the ability to realize economic independence and eventual separation from the Netherlands. In a climate where the very concept of overpopulation was, for many on the global left, synonymous with neoimperial aims, Curaçaoan intellectuals devised clever *anti*-imperial arguments to stem population growth. In a 1970 edition of the regularly recurring "Open Letter to Women," the author claimed:

> The majority of the 3,000 children born on Curaçao will not be able to be cared for. *IT IS IN OUR HANDS TO DRAMATICALLY CHANGE THIS SITUATION. YOU, ME, WE ALL MUST COOPERATE.* Vitó *will work all week*

to loudly proclaim our revolution, which will give us back our rights to be human, which will give us back our LIBERTY.[52]

Vitó proposed "fertility control" not as a method to stifle political radicalism across the world's developing nations, as was so often the case, but precisely as a revolutionary strategy to advance self-determination.[53] In the view of this unnamed commentator, curbing population growth promised a more capacious understanding of freedom than political arrangements alone. Acting as a sovereign public to address population growth and the care and education of children would also restore full personhood and human rights.

Crucially for these commentators, the embrace of widespread projects to control fertility did not have to neglect the structural origins of poverty. Leftists on Curaçao and in the Caribbean diaspora in the Netherlands were deeply skeptical that birth control offered a simple antidote to structural issues. The author of *Vitó's* "Open Letter to Women," most likely Emmy Henriquez, insisted that modernization would require a "large project to control fertility" in addition to total social equality for women and robust social welfare programs.[54] In less ambiguous terms, a contributor to *Kontakto Antiano* criticized the underlying assumptions of the family planning campaign in the Netherlands Antilles. According to this commentator, the myopic focus on reproduction misidentified the true source of the problem, which owed not to "the increase in children but the increase of the richness of the rich. The few rich ones become richer and instead of investing in the stagnating economy prefer to hang on to their money or put it in foreign banks."[55] Without the redistribution of wealth, prosperity would remain concentrated in a few elite hands. Importantly, then, leftists endorsed broader economic transformation alongside population management efforts and the expansion of women's rights. Only by reorganizing the economic foundations of the island—a program viewed as inseparable from demands for women's social and reproductive freedom—could Curaçao achieve greater autonomy from foreign interests, both colonial and corporate.

Elaborating on this anti-imperial argument in defense of population control, leftists decentered the conventional emphasis on individual sexual and reproductive practices. Instead, they located the rising birthrate in the persistence of colonial attitudes and institutions. Specifically and also somewhat ironically, many commentators indicted the domineering role of the Catholic Church. In one of the inaugural issues of *Kambio* in 1965, an anonymous author claimed, "The overpopulation with which the Antilles must now cope is the direct consequence of the conservative, bigoted politics of the Catholic Church in general and her representatives on the Antilles in particular." While this commentator pilloried Catholic leadership for silencing discussions on sex, they did not spare the Antillean government, which they accused of failing "to formulate new insights towards a progressive approach to the overpopulation problem."[56] The conservatism of the Church and inaction of political elites, rather than individual reproductive choices, were thought to be the primary culprits of rising birthrates and staggering unemployment. Writing prior to the emergence of Famía Planiá, which was in part supported by the very institutions that leftist commentators now assailed, *Kambio* authors fit their pleas for progressive population policy into attacks on Catholicism and local governance.

Conservative attitudes and institutions did not simply hinder population policy. According to leftists, they also stymied erotic expression. Calls to address overpopulation were thus at once demands for sexual as well as economic and political liberation. Given the involvement of Brown and Henriquez, among others, with radical European student movements, where the works of Wilhelm Reich, Herbert Marcuse, and Guy Debord were wielded to defend the social and political import of unbridled eroticism, it is perhaps unsurprising that these Curaçaoan leftists affirmed that repressed libidinal longings led to damaging social effects.[57] In a lengthy article on "safe sex" in *Vitó* in 1967, one commentator sought to destigmatize sexual pleasure:

> The sex drive remains an almost primal human need. Hunger, thirst, heat, and bowel movements are primal human needs. . . . The sense of sexual satisfaction is not entirely primal: total abstinence does not lead to death. However, abstinence can be detrimental to health: long-term feelings of unhappiness, dejection, nervous spells (women), aggressiveness (men). . . . However, a large part of the sexual energy can be converted to other energy (sublimation). Such as labor, sports, games. But the sex drive is almost never completely sublimated. And that's where the problem lies.[58]

In advocating for the broad acceptance of sexual gratification, leftists expected the benefits to extend far beyond the bedroom. That same year, authors in *Kambio* lamented the "fear and prejudice" that dominated sexual attitudes in Curaçao. They blamed "social conformism" on Catholic indoctrination and challenged the Church's teachings on sexual abstinence, which, they claimed, left many sexually ignorant and perennially unsatisfied.[59] Such argumentation defended sex not only as natural and healthy but also as an intrinsically political act thought to remedy conservative attitudes.[60] For some intellectuals, then, *more* sex was the necessary riposte to reactionary political and religious beliefs.

Similarly, commentators in *Vitó* largely replaced rhetoric on "responsible parenthood" with a critique of lingering colonial influence. *Vitó* reminded its readers of the colonial-era laws that prevented sexual education or the advertisement of contraceptives to persons below the age of eighteen: "Something to 'add' to the long list of legal measures waiting to be changed," one author caustically remarked.[61] Two years before the repeal of Article 240, which banned public displays of contraception, *Vitó*'s 1967 cover depicted various forms of birth control—from condoms to diaphragms, from the pill to vinegar—and featured a lengthy report on contraceptive methods (figure 14). Whereas Famía Planiá sought to avoid public discussion of abortion, *Vitó* loudly proclaimed support for its unrestricted decriminalization.[62] Though generally supportive of Famía Planiá, *Vitó* nevertheless denounced unequal access to family planning services that cleaved closely to class divides. Published in December 1970, an article on "Illegitimate Children" highlighted the curious statistic that though the birthrate overall fell between 1960 and 1968, in the same time period children born outside legal marriage increased from 28 to 35 percent. The authors ascribed this phenomenon to the more "favorable response" to birth control among middle-class women and argued, "This means that the more educated the woman, the higher she is on the social ladder, the better she is able to 'plan' her family." Calling this inequity a "social crime," *Vitó* insisted that access to birth control be radically democratized: "The chance must be the same for every woman. For Maira the nurse, but also for Marie, the maid or shop girl. For Sonja, the wife of a teacher, but also for Sonda, the dockworker's wife."[63]

Port Betaald

Int Instituut
Soc Geschiedenis
Keizersgracht 264
Amsterdam-C.

Uitgevers-Stichting Vitó.
Hoofdredacteur: Stanley Brown.

Aztekenweg 10 — Tel. 43280,

Gironummer: 561010

VITÓ

LOSSE NUMMERS ƒ 0,50
Hollandse Boekhandel
Boekhandel Salas - Boekhandel Van Dorp
Boekhandel Samen - El Chico
De Wit Stores N.V. - Boekhandel Mariska
Kees Grocery

Cur. Courant N.V.   JAARGANG III No. 2

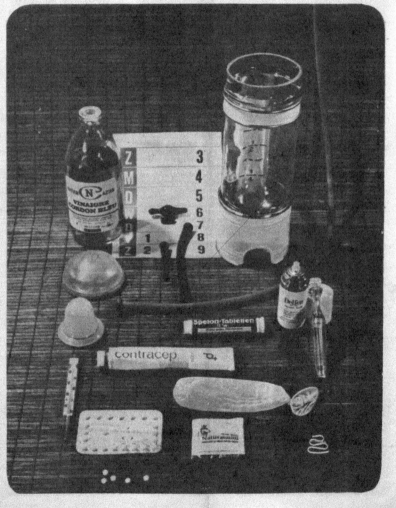

Figure 14. An array of contraceptives on the cover of *Vitó* 3, no. 2 (1967).
SOURCE: Internationaal Instituut voor Sociale Geschiedenis.

Sergio Leon even sat for an extended interview with *Vitó* after Famía Planiá opened its first clinic in 1966. The interviewer questioned Leon's belief that the systemic issues facing the oil industry could be resolved by individual initiative alone. At this point, the physician interrupted the interviewer. Drawing upon an emerging stereotype of the Portuguese worker, who in the 1950s suffered mass layoffs from the refinery, Leon insisted: "There is no unemployment on Curaçao as long as a Portuguese walks around with an ice cream cart."[64] Interacting with society outside of the segregated ethnic enclaves of the refinery, the Portuguese ice-cream seller became the stereotypical representative of someone hardworking, enterprising, and willing to perform undesirable jobs.[65] Although *Vitó* mocked Leon's naïve assessment of the relationship between population and economic growth, this skepticism did not prevent leftists from forming pragmatic partnerships with individual family planning advocates and organizations. The benefits of this approach were thought to be multifold. For leftists, addressing overpopulation was not simply a way to ensure economic and political autonomy. It was also an opportunity to challenge laws and social conventions that prohibited free sexual expression.

"WHAT FIDEL CASTRO HAS ACHIEVED"

Many leftists on Curaçao and in the diaspora looked to the Cuban Revolution to inspire new economic, political, and even sexual models. Commentators in *Kambio* and *Vitó* agreed that Cuba's socialist experiment had fruitfully dissolved the island's former dependence on US tourism and the moral baggage that came with it. These issues were pressing for leftists for two reasons. First, with ongoing retrenchment at the Shell refinery, Antillean policy makers insisted that tourism would protect against further shocks to insular economies. Already in 1953, the Antillean parliament approved a law for the "Promotion of Industrial Establishments and Hotel Construction." Much like the efforts to attract international investors to participate in Curaçao's offshore financial sector, the bid to encourage foreign investment in Curaçao's tourism industry also relied on generous tax incentives.[66] Hilton, Holiday Inn, and others accepted these tax concessions and in the course of the 1960s constructed new hotels and casinos in Willemstad.

   Leftists feared that tourism reliance would simply invite new forms of dependence, as was evident in prerevolutionary Cuba. And ironically, as leftists looked to Cuba, Curaçao's own tourism industry grew as a result of Cuba closing its borders to US tourists. Minor gains in the tourism industry, however, were not enough to compensate for the losses in oil refining. Tourism increased from just 4 to 12 percent of the national GDP between 1957 and 1966, while oil refining decreased from 40 to 22 percent in the same period.[67] In a prophetic article entitled "Where will the first fire begin?," *Vitó* interviewed a thirty-year-old man laid off from the Shell refinery in 1962. He stated: "Every day I ask myself, when will I see some of the millions that Curaçao earns on the thousands of tourists. When will my brother and I find work? . . . In my opinion, the Hilton can go up in flames. The Holiday Inn can burn down. Maybe then I could find work cleaning up the mess."[68]

   Secondly, leftists also looked to Cuba to resolve the thorny question of commercial sex work on Curaçao. If tourism were to replace oil refining as the island's economic backbone, leftists feared that Curaçao would resemble the hedonism of prerevolutionary Havana—or else the roaring 1940s of Curaçao's oil boom. Because of the historic precedent established during World War II, when light-skinned foreign women were recruited to Campo Alegre to serve an itinerant group of soldiers and refinery workers, in the 1960s the renewed influx of "Yankee dollars" sent the left searching for answers to this particular vestige of petro-capitalism. After 1966, some Curaçaoan leftists seized on Cuban leader Fidel Castro's declaration that the Cuban Revolution had "nearly eliminated" prostitution. Castro's announcement came at the end of a six-year campaign to rehabilitate an estimated thirty to forty thousand sex workers. According to Rachel Hynson, the revolutionary regime initially treated sex workers as victims of capitalist exploitation. By 1962, however, Cuban authorities viewed the persistence of prostitution as an affront to the revolution's success and sent sex workers to toil on collective farms. Although commercial sex persisted underground, Castro's 1966 statement signaled the supposed success of the campaign to reeducate sex workers.[69] As evidence of this reputed achievement, in the 1960s Cuban women—long outnumbered by sex workers from the Dominican Republic and Colombia—were no longer licensed to work at Curaçao's Campo Alegre brothel.[70]

Leftists on Curaçao and in the diaspora applauded the alleged disappearance of commercial sex work in Cuba. In 1967, an author in *Kambio* proclaimed, "Before Castro, Havana, the cheerful tourist city, counted hundreds of brothels for 12- and 14-year-old daughters of the poor." The article attributed the disappearance of prostitution to the revolution's victory over US imperialism. Without a similar revolution in the Netherlands Antilles, however, there would be no defense against the corrupting influences of foreign capital. The article opined, "A government faced with serious economic downturn and that clings to tourism as a singular solution . . . must fully realize the consequences and develop guarantees to protect the community from the possible excesses inherent in flourishing tourism."[71] Several months later, another article in *Kambio* warned that the intrusion of US capital in prerevolutionary Cuba had led to an increase in prostitution as well as "sharpening discrimination" and "the loss of national identity."[72] Cuba's socialist experiment, it seemed, could help islanders to resolve precisely the sexual, social, and political issues that rankled the Netherlands Antilles.

Within the dual imperatives of socialist revolution and sexual liberation, leftists struggled to determine if prostitution was the ultimate form of exploitation or perfectly acceptable within a sexually liberated society. Writing in 1971, an anonymously authored piece in *Vitó* exclaimed, "What Fidel Castro has achieved, and what we also hope to achieve on Curaçao, is to be able to end the exploitation of people. . . . The system of prostitution here on Curaçao . . . is a form of exploitation that does not fit with our socialist system."[73] Elsewhere, however, *Vitó* offered a flexible appraisal that differed markedly from Castro's own approach. A cover story on Campo Alegre contended, "*Vitó* is not against prostitution in general" because voluntary sexual relationships between adults, single or married, or "whether between people of the same sex," should be protected by the law.[74] The debate even surfaced in Frank Martinus Arion's *Dubbelspel (Double Play)*, one of the most acclaimed works of Curaçaoan literature. In a discussion on the merits of communism between two male protagonists, one—a frequent visitor of Campo Alegre—disparaged Castro's seeming affront to men's sexual license: "They made whores drive buses. Buses!"[75] Indeed, support for commercial sex among leftist men could function to uphold their sexual privilege, but in this debate sex workers were not silent. Repeating the popular demands of protesters on May 30, 1969, Marlene, a seventeen-year-old sex worker interviewed by *Vitó*, requested the same treatment afforded to industrial workers as a means for ending exploitation: "Give us respect (*respet*). Give us recognition (*rekonosementu*) so what we can get our freedom back. Otherwise we are not free."[76] As Michelle Chase and Isabella Cosse have suggested, such creative interpretations of the Cuban Revolution reveals that it was not only guerrilla warfare and armed insurgency that established Cuba as a model across the Third World. The revolution's espoused gender and sexual politics were also vital to its internationalist appeal, even as these liberatory ideals were unevenly applied in practice.[77] As leftists looked to Cuba to redress Curaçao's crumbling economy, they simultaneously stretched the revolution's professed egalitarianism to ever greater inclusivity, reinterpreting its lessons to serve distinct sexual and political aims.

While male leftists on Curaçao self-consciously styled themselves in the image of the Cuban *barbudo*, donning the iconic dress of the heroic, bearded, and gun-toting guerilla warrior who helped to secure the success of the Twenty-Sixth of July Movement, they also espoused views that diverged from this masculinist revolutionary figure.[78] *Vitó* in particular committed to destabilizing the prevailing order by all possible means. Incorporating those deemed marginal to society was one of the primary ways *Vitó* activists hoped to accomplish this. In April 1969 *Vitó* featured an "Interview with a Homosexual" as its centerfold story. The author lambasted the hypocrisy of Antillean politicians who, this article alleged, sought sex with men in private while denouncing homosexuality in public. *Vitó* defended its ability to uplift these marginalized voices, claiming theirs was a "vanguard movement . . . for the groups who are abused, whether black people, the laborer, the homosexual, youth, or women."[79] Leftist groups in the Netherlands also sought solidarity with Antillean men who identified and organized as homosexuals. In 1971, *Kontakto Antiano* wrote about the formation of an Antillean group to "bring emancipation to our people, using homosexuality as our point of action." These activists asked how organizing around homosexuality could "change the antiquated structures, colonial and capitalist, that exist in the Antilles."[80] Similarly, for self-identified "homophile" groups formed from anticolonial student movements on Curaçao in the 1970s, including the Sociedad Homosexual

Antiyano and the Grupo Homofilia Antiyano, social acceptance of male same-sex eroticism would help to challenge the attitudes and institutions that collaborated in the oppression of same-sex-desiring individuals and Antillean society broadly.[81]

Such an approach diverged from 1960s Cuba, where the government increasingly viewed those who did not conform to revolutionary standards of appropriate masculinity and femininity as counterrevolutionaries, interning suspected sex workers and same-sex-desiring men in reeducative labor camps.[82] Though generally inspired by the egalitarianism of the Cuban Revolution, some Curaçaoan leftists nevertheless saw socialism as a chance not to eradicate but rather to redeem multiple forms of intimacy. In this way, efforts to locate struggles for sexual freedom within an anti-imperial and anticapitalist frame dovetailed with emerging homosexual rights movements in South America, including the Frente de Liberación Homosexual.[83] Yet, in other crucial respects, the stated support of same-sex desiring men served as a distinctive feature of the leftist movement in Curaçao and the diaspora in the Netherlands. With several exceptions— including the diasporic Puerto Rican Young Lords and, after 1970, the Black Panther Party—anti-imperial and antiracist movements in the 1960s Caribbean and beyond most often reaffirmed the importance of normative desire to the restoration of Black manhood.[84]

Despite the inclusivity of leftists' professed politics, some silences remained. Women's same-sex desire was not a topic of discussion in radical periodicals, even as commentators vigorously defended the autonomous erotic longings of presumably heterosexual Antillean women. There are, however, other ways to interpret this omission. Leftists might have acknowledged alternate notions of women's same-sex eroticism that did not align with the New Left's emphasis on sexual orientation as a fundamental marker of one's identity. As Wigbertson Julian Isenia has shown, the Afro-Curaçaoan practice of *kambrada*, wherein women entered erotic or platonic relationships with other women, shared resonances with Afro-Surinamese conceptions of *mati* or the English Caribbean *zami*. In these expressions, sexuality was understood not as an identity to be announced but as a practice that one lived, something one *does* versus something one *is*.[85]

Whether focused on male same-sex eroticism or commercial sex work, radicals in Curaçao and the diaspora assigned capacious political importance to transgressive acts of intimacy. They did so at a time of crisis in the oil industry. These conditions proved fertile ground for questioning social values and rethinking intimate arrangements. Though leftist intellectuals agreed, at least on paper, about the need for sexual liberation, they at times disagreed on the specific contours of that freedom. Not unlike in other liberationist and women's movements, this was especially true about the topic of commercial sex work. But in the process of debate, Caribbean radicals arrived at ideas about gender norms and sexual freedoms that were distinct from those that shaped emancipatory struggles elsewhere.

BLACK POWER IN THE BEDROOM

The increased international influence of the US Black Power movement shaped the tenor of leftist activism in Curaçao and the diaspora. Soon after Stokely Carmichael popularized the slogan "Black Power" in a 1966 speech, *Kambio* ran a story favorably profiling Carmichael and the radicalization of the US civil rights movement.[86] After 1968, when the Mexico City Olympics broadcast the elan and iconography of the Black Power movement into Curaçaoan living rooms, *Vitó* featured a regularly recurring "Black Panther" column, renamed "Black Power" in 1970. As Stanley Brown recalled thirty years after the 1969 uprising, "The unions were influenced just as much as I was by Fidel Castro and Che Guevara, Black Power and Black Panther."[87] Throughout the Caribbean, Black Power, "inspired though not guided by the North American movement,"[88] found wide resonance in societies where decolonization resulted in only partial relief from historic inequities. Black Power-inspired demonstrations and strikes swept numerous Caribbean locales in the late 1960s, the most dramatic of which occurred in the 1968 Rodney Riots in Jamaica and the 1970 February Revolution in Trinidad and Tobago, which culminated in massive street demonstrations and a failed coup against Prime Minister Eric Williams.

Certainly, economic precarity and disillusionment with the political status quo made Curaçao ripe for a Black Power movement of its own. But the racial politics of the leftist movement were complex and historically changing. Several white and light-skinned individuals (like Brown and *Vitó's* founding editor-in-chief, Erich Zielenski, who resigned after one year) became prominent intellectual leaders on the left. Brown even claimed responsibility for the recurring "Black Panther" column. Perhaps because of the multiracial composition of the early leftist movement, Black Power did not emerge as a primary organizing principle. It was after May 30, 1969, that the alliance between intellectuals and laborers broke down, a fact that Brown and Hollander, also light-skinned, attributed to rising Black nationalist sentiments among labor leaders like Godett.[89] Though leftists did not uniformly label theirs a Black Power movement (nor did they initially shun alliances with white or light-skinned individuals), they found in Black Power's language and imagery a way to critique sexism within the ranks of the leftist movement itself.

Here, too, activists insisted that the rewards of antiracist activism would be experienced in the bedroom. It was through the language of Black Power that leftist women rebuked male comrades and brought the movement toward consensus on the topic of women's social and sexual equality. Several commentators railed against the hypocrisy of Curaçaoan men who "yell all day about BLACK POWER" but "jump at the chance to sleep with a white woman." This anonymous author offered a loosely psychoanalytic theory to explain Black men's abiding desire for white women:

> The black mother, with her prominent role, dominates the child. Dominates his emotions, his feelings. Dominates his sexual urges. These things are necessary here in order to maintain the community of Curaçao, which is ruled by the customs, cultures, and laws of the white man. The result of this domination is that the black child becomes a black man with a lot of aggression toward the person who dominates his emotions: THE BLACK WOMAN.[90]

In a paradoxical argument, the very single-parent families that conservative elites identified as the largest obstacle to development emerged here as both the strongest defense against white hegemony and the explanation for internalized racism. According to this author, long-standing perceptions about white femininity and desire even resulted in higher prices paid to light-skinned sex workers at Campo Alegre.[91] In the pages of other radical periodicals and pamphlets, Antillean women were summoned to reject this mistreatment. A pamphlet distributed on Curaçao and reprinted in *Kontakto Antiano* in 1970 rallied Black women to "think black, be black, feel proud." "Wear a shorter miniskirt," the article continued, "show your liberated black thighs, let go of your shame. The Black Panthers can prove to you: THE BLACKER THE BERRY, THE SWEETER THE JUICE."[92]

Of course, the celebration of Black women's sexual power risked their reobjectification by men. Left-feminists were keenly aware of this danger. Gladys do Rego-Kuster was one among a number of Curaçaoan women radicalized by the events of May 30, 1969, and the transnational reverberations of the "Black is Beautiful" movement. At the age of sixteen, do Rego-Kuster left her family's home in Marchena, west of Isla, to pursue an education in the Dutch city of Tilburg. The daughter of working-class parents—her father had been sent from Suriname to work as a mechanical fitter (*bankwerker*) for CPIM—do Rego-Kuster considered herself among the "privileged generation" of Antillean students to receive government scholarships in the 1960s. But within several years of her arrival in Europe, Willemstad was engulfed in flames and Dutch troops arrived to forcibly subdue them. Observing these events from across the Atlantic was the catalyst of a profound political awakening, alerting do Rego-Kuster to the abiding importance of colonial structures in Curaçaoan society. A disenchantment with European feminist movements also influenced her later activism. Her upbringing in a strict but egalitarian household where boys and girls had equal rights, and the dramatic events unfolding on her natal island, spurred a critical sense that European Dutch feminist movements could not adequately address the triple burdens of capitalism, colonialism, and women's oppression in the Caribbean. By 1970, do Rego-Kuster had returned to Curaçao and devoted herself to the struggle for independence from a feminist perspective.[93] In 1975 she formed the island's first explicitly feminist organization, the Union di Muhé Antiano (UMA). Active into the 1990s, UMA would become the locus of the largest anticolonial movement long after some leftist revolutionaries of the *Vitó* generation abandoned their radical aspirations. In the group's voluminous production of pamphlets and radio programs, UMA was highly attentive to the ambivalences of women's erotic liberation, stressing the importance of women's sexual expression *and* the perpetual risk of their sexual objectification under enduring capitalist and colonial relations.[94] More than the previous generation of leftist revolutionaries before them, left-feminists also attacked the colonial-era laws that maintained women's servitude, leading successful struggles against legislation that forced women employed in the public sector to abandon their jobs after marrying, for instance.[95]

At least on paper, many male leftists were persuaded by arguments to reformulate revolutionary gender roles and even sought to reeducate male readership. Like the family planning advocates discussed in the previous chapter, many leftists agreed that masculinity stood at a critical juncture of reinvention. And in some respects, the visions among these groups were not totally distinct. Leftists urged men to play a greater role in the household. But instead of emphasizing a return to patriarchal power vested in the nuclear home, leftist men argued that women's social and sexual emancipation would deepen intimate ties and romantic affection among couples. In a 1970 article titled "Attractive Masculinity" in *Kontakto Antiano*, the author outlined defining characteristics of attractive manhood, including patience, responsibility, and the free expression of emotions with one's intimate partner.[96] Still others longed for closer intimacy premised on equality. In *Kontakto Antiano*, the celebrated Curaçaoan poet Guillermo Rosario dedicated the poem "Women's Emancipation" to "Antillean women in Holland." It read,

> Never trust the one
> Who wants to keep you in servitude
> Whether as property inside the bedroom
> Or in the kitchen like a queen of beans
>
> I want to love you without domination
> On a foundation of greater tolerance
> For you to be a friend, with an equal role
> Contributing and sharing equally.[97]

Although it is difficult to discern whether these ideas touched the intimate corners of people's romantic lives, this vision of revolutionary gender roles is nevertheless noteworthy in its departure from then contemporary leftist movements. In the 1960s, Black Power-inspired movements spread throughout the region. From Jamaica to Bermuda, Belize to Trinidad, Black Power "found wings in the Caribbean."[98] Yet these Caribbean-born Black Power movements overwhelmingly emphasized the recuperation of Black manhood through male leadership in the revolutionary struggle.[99]

The radical Jamaican journal *Abeng* devoted precisely one article to the topic of women's oppression.[100] Though male revolutionaries in Belize's Black Power-inspired United Black Association for Development recognized women as "sisters," they regarded women's liberation as a particularist issue incapable of winning liberation for all.[101] In a striking reversal, in the pages of Antillean radical publications it was women who were enlisted to act with greater militancy and men who were called on to reflect and defer. These ideas also shaped leftist leadership. Upon relinquishing his position as editor-in-chief of *Vitó* in October 1969, Stanley Brown insisted a woman take over the role to further advance the cause of women's emancipation. Brown insisted that the paper remain the mouthpiece of "the workers, the youth and, not to be forgotten, the woman."[102] Soon after, Emmy Henriquez's name appeared on the masthead.

Through discussions of racialized desire, radical intellectuals also explored the legacies of racial slavery. Just as family planning advocates and Antillean politicians had done before them, leftists looked to the intimate dynamics of slavery to explain contemporary situations. They did this, however, with the explicit aim of exploding long-standing inequities through erotic liberation. One editorial written by a twenty-six-year-old woman titled "Which one of us is the whore?" attacked male sexual privilege and called on women to reject "living like slaves."[103] An "open letter to women" appearing in *Vitó* offered similar advice: "REMEMBER NOT TO HAVE SEXUAL RELATIONS WITH A MAN WHO TREATS YOU LIKE A SLAVE."[104] Deanna Amzand, an Antillean student in the Netherlands and frequent contributor to *Kontako Antiano*, authored an editorial in 1971 later reprinted in *Amigoe*. Amzand argued that women as well as men needed to be educated on the importance of female sexual pleasure "and that sexuality is one of the few pleasures in life, for both rich and poor." The author insisted that it was "high time that the Antillean woman realize that the great struggle for INDEPENDENCE, mental and sexual, will take place in large part in the bedroom." Amzand's editorial defended women's sexual pleasure as a liberatory goal. She closed her article with an inspirational cry for women to embrace sexual pleasure and reject oppression: "Sexuality, Yes! Slavery, No!"[105]

Others connected the legacy of racial-sexual violence to contemporary manifestations of racism, which stood to be exacerbated by the unfolding economic crisis. In a special English-language edition of *Vitó* addressed to "yankee" tourists visiting "our golden island in the Caribbean, where only the labourers go hungry," one author discussed the changing social consciousness of the "Curaçao white." The light-skinned progeny of European men and women of African descent, the Curaçao white was "not American white or real-white"; the Curaçao white was "the result of a lot of free and forceful fucking by white men and their black slaves. My grandmother and her mother."[106] Far from being reductive or hyperbolic, statements such as these reflected the very real ways in which intimacy and power were profoundly interlinked during the slavery and colonial past—histories that wove through genealogies and family trees. For this commentator, the servitude and docility that once defined the consciousness of the "Curaçao white" were beginning to change as Curaçaoan society came to recognize its suppressed African heritage. These reflections on slavery in a pamphlet written for "yankee tourists" might be read as an allegorical repudiation of the tourist economy with its reliance on submissive, racialized labor and compliant bodies. At the same time, though, slavery functioned as more than mere metaphor in leftist writings. It also offered a powerful historical explanation for present dynamics. And if slavery was maintained at the site of the bedroom, as this commentator suggested, then leftists like Amzand insisted that liberation would take place there, too. Women's sexual pleasure was thus endowed with revolutionary potential precisely because of the legacies of sexual subjugation that characterized racial slavery and its afterlife. These arguments gained new popular currency as one model of economic dependency threatened to replace another.

Such unabashedly politicized discussions about sex emphasize that the sexual revolutionaries of the 1960s were not just white Euro-Americans who believed making love and waging war to be incompatible. Whereas European New Left movements connected sexual repression, or the absence of sex and pleasure, to fascism and militarism, in the Caribbean it was not the absence of sex but its abusive prevalence that explained numerous problems.[107] For this reason, intimacy needed urgently to be reimagined. Such perspectives rhyme with later feminist theorizations of "erotic autonomy" or "erotic agency," concepts that ask how Caribbean people use "the energy of sexuality, spirituality, and investments of eroticism not just to reclaim their citizenship, but also to assert their humanity in, sadly, all-too-frequent contexts of dehumanization and physical violence."[108] In the case of Curaçao, leftists invoked an at times irreverent erotic politics to target multiple injustices: from lingering colonial institutions and attitudes to the deepening inequities of the island's oil industry. Because control over sexuality was instrumental first to the exercise of Dutch colonial control and racial slavery and second to labor practices in the oil industry, sexual revolutionaries in Curaçao identified the intimate as a locus of power *and*, in the words of M. Jacqui Alexander, "a site of its own instability."[109] It was these historical legacies that would make sex an imaginative site for political transformation in the global 1960s.

DEFUNDING FAMILY PLANNING

When the fires of rebellion prophesied by *Vitó* leapt from the pages of this periodical and into the streets of Willemstad in May 1969, authorities in the European Netherlands did not only deploy the marines to subdue the unrest. The Ministry of Defense pored over issues of *Vitó* and translated from Papiamentu to Dutch articles especially searching in their critique, including those denouncing the racist and classist dimensions of gender inequality and family planning.[110] Prior to the 1969 uprising and under the auspices of the Long-term Development Plan for the Netherlands Antilles, the Dutch government had provided substantial aid to Famía Planiá. But by 1970, Dutch authorities announced that they would gradually reduce and eliminate this funding over a four-year period.

This unexpected decision imperiled the survival of the foundation and mobilized a small army of its supporters to plead with the Dutch government to reconsider. When pressed by Antillean authorities, Dutch officials offered no explanation for their decision. They stated only that, as an autonomous country in charge of its own budget, the Antillean government must invest more in Famía Planiá if population control was truly important to the country's future. Other considerations surfaced, however, in the internal memos and reports of the Dutch Ministry for Kingdom Affairs. One report circulated among public administrators soon after the May uprising. Twice underlined in red ink was its concluding line: "The rising tide of nationalism in most developing countries makes external advice increasingly less welcome on all issues and especially so on such sensitive matters as population polices."[111] Funding for Famía Planiá was cut at the start of the fiscal year following the revolt.

Another indication that the uprising influenced aid allocation is the Dutch government's paradoxical decision to defund Famía Planiá against the unambiguous recommendation of the government's own appointed expert. One month before the uprising in April 1969, Dutch officials in the cabinet of the deputy prime minister arranged for Arie Andries Haspels to visit the Netherlands Antilles.[112] Haspels, a professor at the Royal Tropical Institute renowned for his research on emergency contraception, visited the Caribbean in 1970 to advise on Dutch collaboration in population management efforts. In his final report, Haspels echoed the commission appointed by the Antillean government to study the causes of the May 30 uprising. Headed by René Römer, the commission concluded in May 1970 that overpopulation significantly contributed to the growing appeal of radicalism.[113] Writing his report in September 1970, Haspels agreed with the commission that family planning and birth control would be crucial for preventing future instability. Haspels thus recommended that the Dutch government continue its "energetic support" of Famía Planiá. "Along with vital support for the existing initiatives on the terrain of family planning," Haspels concluded, "measures will need to be adopted for planned emigration."[114]

When the Dutch government commissioned Haspel's report in the spring of 1969, it stated that the continued allocation of development aid for Famía Planiá would be contingent on the doctor's recommendations. But when the report was delivered in 1970, Dutch administrators abruptly announced that aid would instead be terminated. In ultimately unsuccessful pleas to the Dutch government published in the Antillean press, family planning advocates pointed out the irony that a country fast establishing a reputation for international largesse was suspending financial assistance to its own overseas territories. The anonymous commentator wrote that setting aside arguments about "moral guilt," The Hague should continue to finance Famía Planiá as an *investment*: "After all, this prevents the need to donate much larger amounts or to borrow hard or soft loans to finance education, housing, and social services, not to mention creating jobs."[115] This assertion was, of course, a far cry from the robust social programs envisioned by leftist intellectuals and union leaders who promoted family planning as a complement to and not a replacement of welfare and job creation. But leftist agitation had evidently struck a chord across the Atlantic. Suddenly, Dutch authorities rejected collaboration in what had been a historically important and long-standing project: the differential regulation of intimacy offshore.

.   .   .   .   .

The events of May 30 proved once again that laborers and protesters could transform industry practices and transatlantic ties from the ground up, albeit in ways not wholly anticipated by those actors themselves. Late in the afternoon on May 30, Ong-a-Kwie, the head of the CFW, announced in a public radio address that the strike had ended. The union had reached a one-year agreement with Wescar honoring the principle of equal pay for equal work on Shell terrain. The solidarity strike initiated by the PWFC, the typically moderate union representing laborers employed by Shell, thus ended as well.[116] Beyond the wage dispute, new protections for labor became enshrined in law and governing institutions. A new department of labor was created to address the grievances put forward by unions during the May protest.[117] After May 30, the government routinely asked unions to advise on economic policy. Some were even invited to serve on civic boards. Union membership skyrocketed, giving unions new leveraging power. The CFW counted 1,200 members prior to May 30. By July 1970, their membership more than doubled to nearly 3,500 members. Shell attempted to address criticisms of the company's privileged managerial class by installing more Antilleans in technical and supervisory positions. The company also began offering non-Antillean employees courses in Papiamentu and both Shell and Wescar implemented sensitivity training for foreign staff.[118]

The grievances of the May movement also extended beyond the economic realm. The leaders of the May uprising called for the resignation of the Antillean government, a demand that was eventually met. In addition to the appointments of Black political leaders in top roles, the Antillean parliament held special elections in September 1969. Radicals hoped to dislodge the fifteen-year hegemony of the Democratische Partij.

Running on a "law and order" platform, the party retained nearly all of its parliamentary seats. Yet, in a surprise victory, the newly formed socialist worker's party, the FOL, garnered 22 percent of the popular vote and won three of the parliament's twenty-two seats, ending the majority once enjoyed by the Democratische Partij block.[119]

This short version of the cause-and-effect of *Trinta di mei* is well known to scholars of the Dutch Caribbean. But the centrality of sexual and gender politics to the May movement—arguably one of its most creative and distinctive features—remains underexplored. This is not least because of the overwhelming optics of the day. Without a doubt, the majority of street protesters on May 30 were men. Participants vividly recalled these gender dynamics, and the day's arrests records also testified to this divide: 308 men were arrested compared with just 14 women.[120] But as Aisha Leer has pointed out, women participated in *Trinta di mei* in less visible but no less important roles. Women supported men in the strike and protest process; they cared for children while men took to the streets; and, as this chapter has shown, some also partook in the vital task of imagining a society free from gender, sexual, and racial domination.[121] In a robust written record spanning both sides of the Atlantic, activists looked abroad to revolutionary Cuba, Black struggle in the United States, and student movements in the Netherlands to inspire a freedom at once sexual, political, and economic. These circuits of exchange included but were not confined to Europe or North America, revealing that arguments about revolutionary sex and gender norms emerged simultaneously in the Global North and the Global South.[122] These arguments succeeded at a critical conjuncture. Hardship in the oil refining industry spurred creative critique of a society forged through centuries of colonialism and dominated in the twentieth century by corporate interests. Many leftists believed that meaningful social renewal would begin at the very site where colonists and capitalists had elaborated their own visions for a racially hierarchic, profitable, and compliant society: in the bedroom.

What became of the demands for erotic rebellion, for the reclamation of sexuality as an integral part of self-determination, in the aftermath of May 30? Two years after the FOL entered parliament, the party successfully pressured the Antillean executive to study laws that upheld gender-based discrimination.[123] It would, however, take at least another decade and the emergence of renewed feminist activism to abolish many of these discriminatory statutes. These included colonial-era laws mandating that women resign positions in public administration after marriage; laws barring women from serving as the executor of estates or to sign legal agreements or contracts; and discriminatory public housing practices that adversely affected single mothers.[124] As former revolutionaries joined Antillean politics, many abandoned demands for total independence from the Netherlands, a change widely attributed to these actors' absorption into the political class and their desire to preserve the resulting privileges.[125] Even as some of the participants of the May uprising dispensed with their revolutionary commitments, the insurgency inspired a later generation of left-feminists like Gladys do Rego-Kuster.[126] As the Curaçaoan feminist scholar and activist Jeanne Henriquez recalled, "May 30 initiated a consciousness-raising process among women."[127] It is no accident, then, that the next large movement in support of independence was led by Curaçaoan women, who imagined their liberation as indistinguishable from the goals of anticolonial and anticapitalist freedom.[128]

The ironic outcome of the May movement, an explosive rebuke of dependency in economic as in political forms, was that Europe and the Caribbean did not become increasingly disentangled as leftists on both sides of the Atlantic hoped. Even as the Netherlands looked to cut ties with their Caribbean territories, the very same structural issues that drove unrest there would, from the 1970s, propel a growing number of individuals and families to move from Curaçao and Aruba to the Netherlands. Haspels's recommendation for a "planned emigration" to alleviate population pressures proved prescient. Yet it was not Dutch authorities but ordinary women and men who made plans to pursue a life that was increasingly unavailable in the Caribbean as oil companies moved to suspend operations. In a cruel twist, tens of thousands of Caribbean families arrived in the Netherlands just as that country entered the throes of its own energy-related crisis.

5 Dutch Diseases

RACE, WELFARE, AND THE QUANTIFICATION OF KINSHIP

The same spirit of anti-imperialism that infused *Trinta di mei* on Curaçao would profoundly reorganize the world oil economy in the following two decades. From the nationalization of crude and other natural resources in Latin America and the Middle East to the increasingly assertive use of the "oil weapon" as a geopolitical tool, oil-producing nations began forcefully to demand a greater share of oil wealth.[1] Though parallel visions of Global South resurgence united Curaçaoan workers and nationalist elites in places like Algeria and Saudi Arabia, the decisions of the latter produced some inadvertently disastrous effects for the former. The successive "oil shocks" of 1973–74 and 1979–80 resulted in skyrocketing fuel prices and decreasing demand, leading to a glut in refinery capacity further aggravated by the opening of new refineries in the Middle East. By the turn of the 1970s, multinational oil companies like Exxon (formerly Standard Oil of New Jersey/Esso) and Shell saw declining profits.[2] Venezuela, a founding member of the Organization of Petroleum Exporting Countries (OPEC), asserted its sovereignty over oil wealth by ending the preferential pricing of crude sold to the refineries on Aruba and Curaçao. And as oil prices reversed direction and plunged on the world market in the 1980s, the unthinkable happened: Exxon announced in 1984 that the company would close the Lago plant. Unless Venezuela rescheduled the crude once destined for Aruba to Curaçao, the closure of Shell's refinery appeared imminent as well. No matter how beleaguered these enterprises often seemed, it was for many inconceivable to imagine an Aruba without Lago or a Curaçao without Shell. As one reporter in the *Washington Post* noted, for residents of the refinery-dependent Dutch islands, "immigration to the Netherlands may be the only way out."[3]

The reporter's comment was less a prediction than an observation of fact. As in the wider Caribbean, intraregional migration among the Dutch islands had long been a strategy of survival and savvy cultural practice.[4] But it was only with the deepening economic crisis of the 1970s and the 1985 shuttering of Lago that large numbers of Caribbean Dutch citizens began to make their way to Europe. Tens of thousands of women and men crossed the Atlantic in pursuit of economic and educational opportunities that had been foreclosed in the islands, unevenly integrated with Europe and deliberately developed toward the overseas export of wealth. This was, after all, their right as Dutch citizens.

The unfettered access of Caribbean Dutch citizens to the European welfare state came under fire soon after their arrival. In the Netherlands, state spending was being rethought in the wake of the 1973–74 "oil shock" and the effects of so-called Dutch disease. The discovery of natural gas fields in the northeastern province of Groningen in 1959 helped to underwrite the Netherlands' transformation from one of Europe's smallest social safety nets to one of its largest.[5] But resource wealth overvalued the domestic currency, hampered the export of industrial goods, and undermined manufacturing sectors. The trifecta of spiraling hard currency, weakening industrial growth, and rising unemployment typified what became known as "Dutch disease"—a peculiar name, as Fernando Coronil noted, for a condition that only occasionally afflicts the resilient, diversified economies of the Global North but is endemic to the Global South, where narrowly specialized monocrop and primary product exporters are vulnerable to violent cycles of boom and bust.[6] Curaçaoans and Arubans fled precisely this scenario in the Caribbean only to be greeted by its appearance in Europe.

In the Netherlands, the migration of Dutch citizens from the Caribbean was perceived as a crisis, colliding with the end of postwar economic prosperity. At the behest of the Dutch government, a new generation of social scientists translated this perception of crisis into hard data by indexing the organization of Caribbean households and tabulating use of public services. The hunger for knowledge of an "inventorying character" was immense.[7] For as European Dutch civil servants repeatedly bemoaned, families from the Netherlands Antilles and Suriname entered the Dutch welfare state not as foreign nationals but as Dutch citizens, obscuring what many suspected were uniquely Caribbean trajectories through the welfare system. Through charts, graphs, and tables depicting Caribbean interactions with the welfare state, the hallmarks of an "uncomfortable mathematics" that had long fashioned Black intimate life into a matter of state intervention, state-subsidized research conjured the paradigmatic figure of the Caribbean migrant crisis: the single mother.[8]

No topic featured more prominently in state-funded studies of Caribbean communities in the Netherlands than that of the "matrifocal" or mother-centered family, imagined as fundamentally heterosexual if not properly heteronormative.[9] Though concerns about Caribbean kinship and reproductive practices were not new, in the 1970s these concerns shifted to the European Netherlands and involved actors with ascendant importance in postwar European society, including bureaucrats, state-funded researchers, and social workers.[10] This chapter explores the state subsidization of social scientific research from the 1970s to the mid-1990s and the material supports that were institutionalized and imperiled as a result of this knowledge production. In the 1970s, perceptions of energy crisis and accelerated migration catalyzed state investment in research on migrant groups. By the mid-1990s, this research had created a racial group defined according to its putatively essential matrifocal quality and the Dutch state abandoned its social obligation as a result. Though Dutch authorities no longer used "race" as an administrative category after World War II, in publicly-funded research the consolidation of group identities based on kinship offers powerful evidence of the process by which "family [became] racial ontology," ushering in racist essentialisms through the backdoor of culturalist arguments about family life.[11] Ultimately, knowledge production participated in the reimagination of public responsibility, resulting in contested schemes to restrict Dutch citizenship to the European continent, the reduction of social assistance, and the termination of programs for migrant welfare that, at least in the minds of their fiercest European critics, epitomized the "tragedy" of multiculturalism.[12] The offshore—a process, not a place—thus became visible in the erstwhile metropole.

Knowledge production and its consequences did not go uncontested. Caribbean activist groups organized to defend the welfare state and its promise of economic equality. In contrast to the radical student activists of the 1960s, these organizations sought to effect a wholesale transformation of Dutch belonging to include the Caribbean and its diaspora in Europe. Social welfare organizations established by Caribbean Dutch citizens in the 1970s and 1980s identified state-funded knowledge production as uniquely harmful, concretizing stereotypes of dependency while weakening institutional support for Caribbean families in Europe. Activists thus attempted to seize the means of knowledge production, forging their own collaborations with scholars and defending access to public services like childcare, community centers, and family allowances. Activist efforts to claim emancipation through the welfare state, however, ultimately ran aground on the erosion of social spending by 1996. Dutch authorities reduced social assistance for single parents, fearing increased fraud and welfare dependency—thus linking the histories of the Caribbean, oil markets, and the decline of the European welfare state.

MOBILITY UNDER EMBARGO

The vicissitudes of the global oil economy at once enabled and endangered multiple migration streams to the postwar Netherlands. Between the onset of nationalist insurgency in Indonesia in 1945 and the eventual relinquishing of Dutch New Guinea in 1962, nearly three hundred thousand people had emigrated from the former Dutch colonies in Southeast Asia to the Netherlands. Comprised primarily of individuals of mixed Asian and European ancestry, this stream of postcolonial migration, unlike its later Caribbean counterpart, occurred at a time of rapid postwar economic expansion. Fueled by the abundance of cheap fossil fuels, the Netherlands' postwar industrial boom also drew thousands of "guest workers" from Italy, Spain, Portugal, Greece, Yugoslavia, Turkey, and Morocco. Even a small number of people from the Netherlands Antilles, primarily male industrial laborers and female health care workers, participated in these recruitment drives.[13]

Guest workers arrived in the Netherlands to work in labor-intensive sectors such as coal mining and the steel, textile, shipbuilding, and meat-packing industries.[14] Growing levels of education among European Dutch citizens caused shortages in low-waged labor, and so foreign guest workers helped to fuel the country's extraordinary economic rebound after World War II. The newfound prosperity of European Dutch people rested, too, on the highly profitable exploitation of the Slochteren gas fields in Groningen.

Although the Netherlands produced some 58 million cubic meters of natural gas in 1973, a growing percentage of the country and the European continent's energy needs were met by oil from the Middle East. In 1955, 78 percent of Western Europe's energy demands were met from within the continent, largely through provision of coal. In 1972, this number decreased to just 35 percent. Dependence on oil imports from the Middle East, meanwhile, rose: this source supplied 13.4 percent of Western Europe's total energy requirements in 1956 but 45 percent in 1973.[15]

The Netherlands played a primary role in Europe's growing petro-dependence. In 1972, about 70 percent of Europe's oil supply came from the Organization of Arab Petroleum Exporting Countries (OAPEC), a quarter of which was delivered through Rotterdam's oil terminals. Rotterdam housed five oil refineries, including Shell's Pernis plant, that together comprised 10 percent of Europe's refining capacity. Oil refining was itself a thriving industry in the 1960s, employing some twenty thousand people, including foreign guest workers. In 1972, an astonishing 149 million tons of oil passed through Dutch ports.[16]

The optimism generated by cheap energy began to wane in late 1973. What is widely known as the "energy crisis" of 1973–74 was, in fact, a more complex series of tangentially related events. OPEC states meeting in Kuwait in October 1973 decided, after a month-long negotiation with oil companies, to unilaterally raise the posted price of oil, which was the basis for calculating the tax rate that ensured producing states—not just oil companies—also pocketed the windfall of rising prices.[17] At the end of this same meeting, oil ministers from Arab producing states (OAPEC) reconvened to address events unfolding earlier that month, when on October 6, 1973, Egyptian and Syrian troops attempted to regain the lands illegally occupied by Israel since the Six Day War of 1967. Dutch support of Israel put the country into an escalating confrontation with the states

that supplied Europe's oil. Meeting in Kuwait on October 17, OAPEC announced a minimum 5 percent reduction in crude exports. Four days later,
Iraq nationalized Shell's share of the Basra Petroleum Company. That
same day, Syria called for a general boycott of the Netherlands, which six
countries joined in the days that followed. On November 2 Saudi Arabia,
the Netherlands' largest supplier, also joined the boycott, now threatening
some 40 percent of the Netherlands' oil supply.[18] While many associate the
"oil shock" with the ultimately ineffectual embargo of the United States,
the Netherlands, and other countries supporting Israel, it was OPEC's
actions in Tehran in December 1973 that seemed to cause real pain for
Western nations. As Giuliano Garavini writes, the decision to once again
double the posted price of crude "triggered one of the most rapid transfers
in wealth from one part of the globe to the other in world history."[19]

These events had an ambivalent impact in the Netherlands. Though
intended to hurt countries supporting Israel, the OAPEC embargo did not
seriously endanger energy supply in the Netherlands, which could also rely
on its abundant gas reserves. In fact, the surging price of crude oil lifted
the cost of natural gas and produced enormous revenues in the Netherlands. Eventually, however, this led to the overvaluation of Dutch currency
despite slowdowns in productive sectors—the onset of "Dutch disease."
Migrants were among the first to feel shocks generated by perceptions of
energy scarcity (more myth than reality) and rising fuel costs. In 1973, the
Netherlands terminated guest worker recruitment agreements and closed
the country's borders to labor migrants. While most guest workers from
southern Europe returned to their home countries, Turkish and Moroc-
can populations grew in the Netherlands as family reunification policies
facilitated the migration of spouses and children.[20]

Major changes were also afoot on the other side of the kingdom. In
May 1973, the newly elected cabinet of Dutch Prime Minister Joop den
Uyl of the Partij van de Arbeid announced that it would begin talks with
Suriname and the Netherlands Antilles about the future independence
of the Caribbean territories. Dutch progressives had grown especially
weary of maintaining transatlantic ties after the deployment of military
force to Curaçao in May 1969. Leftist and progressive political parties in
Den Uyl's coalition, including the Democraten 66 and the Politieke Partij
Radikalen, supported the liberation of the Caribbean countries from what

they viewed as an antiquated colonial relationship. Widely shared concerns about potential Caribbean migration to Europe also exacerbated the perceived urgency of this goal. At least initially, neither Suriname nor the Netherlands Antilles appeared willing to cooperate with the rushed deadline of 1976 for the transfer of sovereignty.[21] But with a change of political leadership in Suriname in February 1974, the small country became the first in the kingdom to announce its imminent departure. Suriname would become independent before the end of 1975.[22]

European Dutch attempts to confine citizenship to the continent had the opposite of its intended effect. By 1980, one-third of Suriname's population—over 160,000 people—had left to claim citizenship in the former metropole. Independence had never been put to a popular referendum and, troubled by the rapid decolonization process, many residents voted "with their feet against the transfer of sovereignty."[23] Residents of the Netherlands Antilles watched skeptically as the fragile gains of sovereignty in Suriname resulted first in the exodus of the country's population and, by 1980, in the violent consolidation of a military dictatorship.[24] Concerns about the eventual loss of citizenship and worsening economic circumstances accelerated migration from Curaçao and Aruba to Europe in the 1970s. In contrast to the limited migration of Caribbean students and laborers in the 1960s, the 1970s saw a rise in the migration of thousands of people from the most vulnerable socioeconomic circumstances. Family rather than individual migration brought with it a concomitant increase in migrating women, who outnumbered men after 1973.[25]

It was not until the shuttering of the Lago refinery on Aruba in 1985 that migration from the Dutch islands reached its own exodus level. With declining production after 1971 and burdened by billions of dollars in foreign debt, Venezuela was struggling to supply crude to corporate clients on Aruba and Curaçao. By 1983, Venezuela had reduced the amount of crude it sent to Lago to 180,000 barrels a day, under half the refinery's capacity. Lago posted 50 million dollars in losses, and Exxon announced at the end of October 1984 that it would close the facility by March. Although the refinery's workforce had shrunk steadily since the 1950s, on the eve of its closure Lago still supplied some 30 percent of the island's real income and the Aruban government with 50 percent of its revenue.[26] In 1984, Lago employed nine hundred individuals and an additional thousand worked for agencies subcontracted by Exxon. The Aruban Chamber of Commerce estimated that Lago's closure would affect an additional eight thousand jobs in adjacent industries, driving unemployment from 19 to 40 percent.[27] The prospect of this economic and political calamity caused tense negotiations between Aruba, Exxon, and Venezuela. Fearing political instability in the region, Venezuela even requested the intervention of US President Ronald Reagan to keep Lago afloat. The US-led invasion of Grenada the previous year weighed on the minds of political and business leaders.[28] Exxon and Aruba hoped to pressure Venezuela to reconsider the end of its "netback" pricing system, which sold heavy crude to Exxon at preferential rates based on the market value of refined products rather than on the world price of crude.[29] But Venezuelan officials insisted that they could make an additional 25 million dollars by processing crude once destined for Aruba through Venezuela's own underutilized refineries and selling the rest at market rates.[30]

After protracted negotiations, Lago agreed to sell the refinery, transshipment facilities, and the grounds of the former Lago Colony (renamed Seroe Colorado in 1958 to diminish the imperial overtones of the appellation) to the Aruban government for one US dollar. Aruban politicians had failed to persuade Exxon's negotiating team that, after decades of touting the corporation's commitment to insular welfare, Exxon owed a "moral obligation" to the island that far exceeded the value of the aging refinery and the toxic grounds upon which it sat. Industry representatives clarified the nature of a relationship that had become blurred over decades of entanglement between the oil industry and Aruba: "We are here as businessmen," they retorted, "not as a charity organization."[31] The nominal sale price of the refinery was contingent upon Lago's release from all liabilities or claims resulting from past operations.[32]

Shell's refinery on Curaçao faced similar troubles. Since 1981, the Isla refinery had been losing an average 75 million dollars per year. In 1985, Shell sold its dangerously outdated refinery to the Curaçaoan government for the equally symbolic sum of one guilder.[33] Like Aruba, Curaçao paid a high price for this dubious act of corporate largesse. The Curaçaoan government waived present claims against Shell companies and agreed to indemnify Shell against future claims for demolition, pollution, environmental degradation, and past taxes.[34] Only through massive layoffs and wage cuts did the refinery remain open. On October 1, 1985, the Venezuelan state oil company, Petróleos de Venezuela, S.A. (PdVSA), nationalized in 1976, took over its management and that of the Curaçao Oil Terminal at Bullenbaai. Once again citing fears of political unrest, the Venezuelan government pressured PdVSA into signing a lease agreement through 1994. Venezuelan President Jaime Lusinchi warned that if the refinery closed, Curaçao would face a communist infiltration akin to Cuba or Nicaragua.[35] The government thus preferred to maintain the unprofitable refinery rather than close or sell it to a new foreign oil company.

Although Curaçaoans welcomed news of the refinery's continued operation, the island nevertheless took a severe economic hit. PdVSA had agreed to lease the refinery under conditions of a tax holiday, causing a substantial loss of government income. The 1,400 employees that remained at the refinery were forced to take a 15 percent pay cut.[36] To compensate for these losses, the Curaçaoan government turned to two familiar enterprises: tourism and offshore banking. After 1985, the Curaçaoan government made large investments in the development of new tourist destinations. To the east of Willemstad, the Sonesta Hotel and the Marriott were built out of view of the distillation towers and gas flares that dotted the city's skyline.[37] And as the offshore financial sector reached its peak in the mid-1980s, ever more financial companies arose on Curaçao that enabled US corporations to borrow billions of dollars in Europe and avoid US taxes, although these companies provided only 3 percent of the Curaçaoan workforce with jobs.[38] Henceforth, the refinery's importance as the gravitational center of the Curaçaoan economy would diminish.

The downward spiraling of the Caribbean oil industry led to a sharp increase in emigration from Curaçao and Aruba. From 1984 to 1999, the number of Caribbean Dutch citizens living in the Netherlands tripled to nearly 106,000. This group constituted a very small portion of the total population of the Netherlands, which was 15.81 million in 1999—a fact belied by the outsized and often negative attention they received. But it was a significant number in the context of the Netherlands Antilles, equaling one-third of the country's total population.[39] Oil companies shrewdly capitalized on the benefits of Dutch citizenship to stanch the effects of their sudden retreat from the Caribbean. During a layoff program at Lago following the first oil shock, the company paid for the relocation of former employees to the Netherlands. The idea was floated again in the early 1980s as closure loomed, with management explaining that "emigration during times of duress can be extremely attractive as the emigrees immediately receive financial assistance from the Dutch government with the amount depending on the size of the family, housing, etc. No financial assistance exists for unemployed people resident in the Netherlands Antilles."[40] After the announcement of closure in 1984, Lago earmarked an estimated 1 million dollars for relocation assistance, based on the cost of travel from Aruba to Amsterdam.[41]

The fact that migration was required to access the full economic benefits of Dutch citizenship points to the uneven reach of welfare within the kingdom. The architects of this transatlantic state opted against a French model of departmentalization, which integrated the French Antillean islands into the nascent social security system of France. Instead, leaders like da Costa Gomez prioritized self-determination over budgets and domestic laws, believing that enhanced insular autonomy would facilitate equality among partner states and put to an end to the oversight that characterized colonialism.[42] For this reason, though Dutch citizenship reached across the Atlantic, its material rewards did not do so uniformly. As the refineries shuttered and shrank, Dutch citizens in the narrowly specialized and strategically underdeveloped economies of the Caribbean were left with few options besides those available through freedom of movement.

INVENTORYING THE CARIBBEAN FAMILY

While Dutch citizenship facilitated access to certain rights, state bureaucrats and welfare providers argued that common citizenship prevented public servants from assessing the ostensibly unique needs of Caribbean families in the Netherlands. Civil servants repeatedly complained that among the many problems resulting from Caribbean migration to the Netherlands, "the most important is that Surinamese and Antilleans are, rightly, not separately registered in the Regional Labor Office or the Municipal Housing Services, nor in municipal Social Service departments or schools."[43] In their view, this situation warranted devoted study of citizens arriving from the Caribbean. This initial interest in tabulating Caribbean interactions with the Dutch welfare state arose just as the Netherlands felt the economic effects of the first and second oil shocks in 1973–74 and 1979–80.

Home to the largest number of overseas nationals in the 1970s, the municipality of Amsterdam spearheaded initial efforts to track Caribbean-born Dutch citizens in the Netherlands. This emerged in connection with heightened demand on public housing, under strain because of the city's aging urban center and the virtual monopoly of private corporations in the residential market. Many Caribbean families lived in overcrowded hotels and boarding homes intended for temporary residence while awaiting an offer of permanent housing. Securing even these accommodations required laborious negotiations with social workers. In 1977, two women from Suriname landed in a group home run by a charitable organization on the Plantage Middenlaan in Amsterdam. Though the organization received a substantial daily subsidy from the municipality, residents like Tine Westhout and Helia Morman, each with young children, lived in a decrepit three-story building that lacked regular trash pickup and natural daylight. Westhout complained about the ubiquitous presence of cockroaches and mice, while Morman lamented the confining nature of the bedrooms.[44]

Tine Westhout and others might wait on the public housing list for years. Those who eventually received accommodation were frequently directed to isolated suburbs lacking critical infrastructure and connectivity to employment and schools, such as the Bijlmermeer in Amsterdam Southeast. Initially built as a modernist haven for the white middle class, the Bijlmer project failed to attract its intended demographic and its characteristic high-rise apartment buildings sat empty in the 1960s and early 1970s. Owing in part to the availability of space, many families from Suriname and the Netherlands Antilles came to live in the Bijlmermeer.[45] But housing options were also powerfully determined by European Dutch landlords and housing providers, who refused accommodations to people of color in major Dutch cities and other predominantly white suburbs. At the end of 1978 Welsuria, an organization established in the late 1960s to provide for the Surinamese community in the Netherlands, publicized the banning of residents born outside the European Netherlands in at least eight Amsterdam neighborhoods. Public servants confirmed before an audience of 150 protesters that the municipal housing service did in fact try to limit the number of non-European Dutch families to one per floor.[46]

White city residents also made plain their antipathy. In 1974, a white European Dutchman circulated racist pamphlets to his neighbors, proclaiming, "The Hague must remain white and safe. Away with the Surinamers and Antilleans who parasite off our labor and welfare."[47] Activist groups like *Kontakto Antiano* documented these injustices, warning Caribbean communities in the Netherlands to "be on your pease [sic] and queues" as the pamphleteer received only a fine and pledged in court to continue distributing his racist screeds.[48] It was not uncommon for municipal authorities to field angry letters from white European Dutch property owners denouncing allegedly absent fathers, unruly children, and the pungent smell of Caribbean cooking.[49]

Officials agreed with white city residents that accepted norms in Caribbean family life clashed with those of European Dutch society, noting that the "very large families" of the former were ill suited to the housing styles of the latter.[50] At the behest of the Municipal Bureau of Statistics, in 1979 city authorities in Amsterdam established a special "working group for very large families" to address the demand for public housing.[51] One representative from the Municipal Relocation Services contended that it was "nearly impossible" to provide information on those families currently in need of housing since no distinction could be made among Dutch citizens. Despite this lack of clarity, the representative stated confidently that "there are 344 urgent cases registered for dwellings of six or more rooms, from which it can be assumed that these people belong to an ethnic minority."[52] In an effort to clarify these suppositions, in the spring and summer of 1979 the working group produced an inventory of Surinamese and Antillean families with four or more children to determine options for their accommodation.

Similar efforts to index Caribbean families emerged at the start of the 1970s in connection with another social program: the Algemene Bijstandswet (ABW). Established in 1965, the ABW transformed the Dutch welfare state by entrusting the provision of social assistance to the government and not, as previously, to religious and other charitable organizations. This social insurance legislation was initially intended to strengthen the financial position of the nuclear family by offering the presumed male breadwinner unemployment assistance, child stipends, and widower pensions. But the implementation of the ABW actually undermined the importance of marriage by extending economic security to single parents, a phenomenon accelerated by the relaxation of divorce law six years later.[53] Under the ABW's social insurance provisions, single parents with dependent children under the age of sixteen were entitled to 87.5 percent of the minimum income.[54]

At the end of 1971, the Ministry of Social Work requested detailed information about "the extent to which migrating kingdom partners appeal to the ABW."[55] The social service departments of Amsterdam, Rotterdam, The Hague, and Utrecht were asked to participate in the study, though only Amsterdam had sufficient resources to employ sociologists and anthropologists to review the department's case files.[56] Circulated internally in 1972, the report asked, "Why do these roughly six hundred parties require assistance?" The answer was conclusive: "The family situation" of Dutch nationals from the Caribbean was the most important predictor of demand on social services.[57] According to the report, at least half of the Caribbean-born clients seeking relief through the ABW were "female heads of household." In total, Caribbean-born ABW clients constituted 1,028 out of a total 26,527 in Amsterdam, a mere 3.8 percent.[58] Yet, despite their statistically small size, Amsterdam's report concluded that this contingent of Caribbean-born mothers formed the largest group of clients not registered for unemployment assistance, which required active solicitation of work. According to these bureaucrats, the caretaking duties of single mothers prevented their entry into the workforce, causing "structural" dependence on welfare.[59]

In this decade of increased movement across the kingdom, European Dutch authorities conceived of single motherhood as a problem of welfare reliance. What is more, they identified single motherhood as the essential framework by which Caribbean populations (otherwise indistinguishable from European Dutch in official records) could be defined and made legible in administrative accounting. For Caribbean communities in the Netherlands, the authorities' fixation on conjugal arrangements and welfare use became part of the everyday experience of racialization, feeding into the allocation of public housing and lending a false legitimacy to white resentment toward Dutch citizens of color "parasiting" off the labor and welfare of Europeans—a characterization that, as activists would later assert, more accurately described the Netherlands' relationship with its former Caribbean colonies than the reverse. Early "inventories" of Caribbean populations and their interactions with public services created categorical separation between Dutch citizens while at the same time eliding the heterogeneity within Caribbean communities. This proved instrumental in establishing the perceived legitimacy of welfare dependence and carved a path for subsequent research on the Caribbean family.

REACTIVATING RACIAL KNOWLEDGE

At the start of the 1980s, the growing recognition that the Netherlands would be a permanent rather than temporary home to migrants increased state investment in migration research and resulted in an unusually close relationship between social science and state policy.[60] Under the auspices of the Ministry of Social Work, the Dutch government became the primary sponsor of social scientific research on migrant groups. Created in 1965, the ministry was initially charged with reorienting European Dutch families to urban and industrialized milieus through the expansion of social work and the introduction of nationally organized social insurance legislation that same year.[61] Similar concerns would guide the ministry's funding of research on migrant communities. Beginning in 1981, the government annually earmarked the equivalent of 28 million euros for research on migrant groups.[62] This body of state-funded research grew precipitously. Between 1980 and 1985, the government funded nearly 800 studies, more than doubling a bibliography produced in 1978 that documented 350 government-sponsored studies since World War II.[63]

Paradoxically, this investment in knowledge production came just as the Dutch government handed down other spending cuts. Though panic followed the first oil shock of 1973–74, Dutch authorities believed its economic effects to be temporary. Contributing to this optimistic outlook was the rising price of natural gas, which was tethered to the price of crude. Popular social policies that had transformed the Netherlands into one of the most expansive welfare states—including a universal pension plan, disability insurance, social assistance, and insurance for special health care costs—were not fundamentally rethought until the end of the decade, when oil prices soared to 39.50 dollars per barrel in 1979. The immediate cause was the drop in oil production caused by the Iranian Revolution. The following year, the Iran-Iraq War led to further cutbacks in production, triggering worldwide economic recession, including in the Netherlands. The country also confronted the effects of "Dutch disease." Between 1970 and 1985, labor force participation dropped from 57 to 48 percent, and the number of social security benefit recipients per 100 workers rose from 44 to 85. Unemployment tripled between 1975 and 1985 alone.[64] At the same time, conversations began across Dutch society about the social and economic cost of the welfare state, which accounted for one quarter of the GDP. Public debt rose to unforeseen levels, from 150 billion guilders (68 million euros) in 1982 to 339 billion guilders (approximately 154 billion euros) in 1991.[65] In the course of the 1980s, government spending cuts also impacted the national university system, making academics further reliant on the Ministry of Social Work for funding. Eligibility for public research funding narrowed after 1984, when the Dutch government made policy relevance an explicit requirement for research support.[66] In this context, "policy relevant" research on Caribbean migrants focused almost exclusively on their interactions with the embattled welfare state.

The state's enlistment of sociologists and anthropologists for research on Caribbean communities proved particularly consequential, galvanizing a near obsession with the concept of the matrifocal household that had deep roots in both disciplinary traditions.[67] In the mid-twentieth century, social scientists in the United States and the Caribbean had become increasingly fixated on defining the contours of working-class Black family life in societies cleaved by racial inequality and rocked by radical rebellion. In the era of the Great Migration, which saw millions of African Americans leave the US South for northern metropolises between 1910 and 1930, and in the aftermath of labor rebellions in the British Caribbean in the late 1930s, sociological literature drew a link between poverty and conjugal patterns. As Deborah Thomas writes, it was these patterns that "ultimately became proxies for race, . . . constitut[ing] poor black people as unassimilable to the national mainstream and therefore exclud[ing] them from the normative categories of citizenship."[68] Such arguments were, of course, familiar to development projects on Curaçao and Aruba. But in the European Netherlands, state-funded social scientists now redeployed colonial knowledge toward a new end: the integration of Caribbean families in the European welfare state.

In this process, researchers embraced the explanatory arguments of an earlier generation of scholars debating the origins of the mother-centered family. They referenced in particular the debate between US anthropologist Melville Herskovits and sociologist E. Franklin Frazier that captivated early scholars of the African diaspora in the 1930s and 1940s.[69] Though Herskovits and Frazier disagreed on the origins of matrifocality, both dispensed with views of biological racial determinism and instead sought to illustrate how Black kinship stemmed from complex historical and cultural processes. A celebrated Black intellectual and student of the Chicago School, Frazier argued that many working-class Black households were durably shaped by the violent inheritance of slavery, which prevented lasting bonds between enslaved men and women.[70] Herskovits, however, refuted the idea that the Middle Passage initiated new familial forms. The anthropologist argued that the diaspora retained African cultural practices. West African polygynous arrangements, with husbands taking multiple wives and fathering offspring with each, habituated children to closer maternal bonds.[71] This cultural pattern, Herkovits claimed, persisted in the Americas through the formation of strong ties between mother and child and the peripheral position of the biological father.

In the 1970s and 1980s, this debate was restaged in Dutch social science research. European Dutch researchers found in it tools for anticipating future demands on social assistance. Researchers predicted that single parenthood would persist among subsequent generations of Caribbean families in the Netherlands if, in fact, the matrifocal family owed its origins to deeply rooted West African cultural practices. Many researchers supplemented Herskovits's theory with that of US anthropologist Oscar Lewis, who concluded that matrifocality responded to the economically precarious positions of both biological parents while also creating a cyclical "culture of poverty" that could sustain itself even in changing economic circumstances.[72] Alternatively, if single parenthood and nonmarital reproductive relationships turned out to be economically determined, then access to social assistance and improved educational and job opportunities would likely lead to an increase in formal marriages among Caribbean

Dutch citizens and their descendants in the Netherlands.[73] Writing in the early years of Caribbean migration, University of Amsterdam-trained sociologist Ineke Gooskens initially predicted that economic prosperity would witness the rise in "legal relationships" among "Creole" populations in the Netherlands. By the turn of the decade, however, researchers like Maria Lenders and Marjolein van Vlijman-van de Rhoer offered new theories. Funded by the Ministry of Social Work, their coauthored dissertation, "'My God, How Will I Manage?': The Position of Creole Single Mothers in Amsterdam," contended that cultural patterns would override economics and lead to the endurance of single motherhood.[74] Such predictions were not left to speculation alone. As immigration continued into the 1980s, demographers housed at the Centraal Bureau voor de Statistiek (CBS) tracked marriage rates and fertility levels among Dutch citizens of Caribbean origin. The annual reports published by the CBS and other demographic institutes continued to separate Caribbean-born Dutch citizens and their descendants from their European-born counterparts.[75]

The Dutch government was certainly not the first to turn social science into a handmaiden of public policy. Closely informed by social scientific research, mid-twentieth century development imperatives repeatedly cast working-class Black family life as the primary cause of economic suffering and a matter of urgent state intervention. French civil servants in the 1940s and 1950s turned to the very same social scientific studies of Black family life circulating in the United States and the British Caribbean (notably, the work of E. Franklin Frazier) as the French Antillean islands were remade from colonial dependencies into overseas *départements*.[76] With growing migration from Puerto Rico to the mainland United States from the late 1940s through the 1960s, social scientists at leading universities collaborated with policymakers to address the seemingly exceptional nature of the Puerto Rican family, described as large, chaotic, and mother-centered—an argument that drew extensively on the Black family studies program of the 1930s.[77] Perhaps no study represents the disastrous entanglement of racial knowledge and social policy more than the so-called Moynihan Report of 1965. Authored by US Assistant Secretary of Labor Daniel Patrick Moynihan, this document represented less a novel argument about Black family life than an affirmation of prior sociological convictions about the "cultural" rather than structural determinants of racial inequality. In Moynihan's view, male marginality and maternal dominance conscripted African Americans in the cyclical reproduction of their own immiseration.[78] Moynihan's "report" also drew on knowledge produced by the likes of E. Franklin Frazier. And so, in a painful irony, the circulation of these studies reinforced precisely the racial determinism that social scientists like Herskovits and Frazier sought to contest. For although family forms could be studied as a cultural practice, they were, like biological difference, anxiously alleged to be unchanging.

The delayed reception of US social scientific paradigms in the Netherlands disrupted prior consensus on the origins of the matrifocal family. A previous generation of European Dutch sociologists living and working in the Caribbean had arrived at markedly different conclusions than Frazier or Herskovits. Harry Hoetink, a European Dutch sociologist who helped to introduce the comparative study of race and ethnicity in Caribbean societies,[79] argued in his 1958 study of preindustrial Curaçao that matrifocal families stemmed from Black imitation of elite *white* male behavior during and after slavery. In this "seigniorial behavior pattern," extramarital relationships between white Dutch Protestant and Sephardic Jewish men and women of color were routine and, at least in Hoetink's view, frequently amorous.[80] Afro-Curaçaoan men merely mimicked the sexual behaviors of white male elites in an effort to approximate the latter's social status. Rooted in the island's specific history, Hoetink's theory of matrifocal origins was proposed as an historical corrective to the "a-historical structural functionalistic analysis of Afro-American" kinship.[81] Though in this account the originary figure of the absent white father was not seen as particularly controversial, by the late 1970s in Europe, the historically specific theory of Hoetink and his supporters was replaced by abstract explanations of matrifocality that glossed any discernably Dutch role in the histories of racial slavery and colonialism.

Efforts to fix and typologize the seemingly diverse ways that Caribbean women organized their romantic lives attended the redeployment of racial knowledge in the Dutch welfare state. This, too, drew from earlier anthropological studies which shaped a heteronormative conception of the family in the Caribbean.[82] European Dutch researchers employed similar schemas to classify family forms by conjugal union type and household composition. They were particularly interested in identifying the prevalence of "concubinage," defined as a nonmarital cohabiting relationship between a man and woman of varying length, or the "visiting relationship," a non-monogamous sexual relationship of short duration that did not involve co-habitation. As feminist legal scholar Tracy Robinson observed, this system of categorization fixed women in one category while men were imagined to "transcend them as sexual agents."[83] More still, the very category of "single mother," as Curaçaoan scholar and activist Jeanne Henriquez pointed out, elided wider familial networks (mothers, siblings, female friends and relatives) that provided critical moral and financial support.[84] Nevertheless, the Dutch welfare state deemed these taxonomies important for its effective administration. In 1979, sociologists employed by Amsterdam's Department of Social Services made a case for correct classification: "Because only legal relationships are registered, concubines without children are, for example, registered as two single people, while a concubine relationship with children is registered as a single-parent household with an additional single resident. Illegitimate children and foster children are not registered as children living at home, but as singles."[85] They reasoned that this categorical confusion might entitle some to claim benefits based on the incorrect registration of familial relationships.

The steady accrual of statistics on household composition, conjugal norms, and welfare use throughout the 1970s and 1980s laid the groundwork for the racialization of social assistance. For state- and municipally-funded social scientists, it was precisely the perceived similarities in family structures that cohered so-called ethnic groups despite their immense heterogeneity. The authors of *Surinamese and Antilleans in Amsterdam*, a report commissioned by the Ministry of Social Work in 1979, contended that the key differences between Surinamese, Antillean, and "other Dutch" families lay in the "composition of families and households." Even on this terrain, the report argued, there was a "big difference between Creoles and Hindustanis," by which they meant Surinamese of South Asian ancestry, who also moved to the Netherlands but featured less frequently as subjects of state concern.[86] Though the term "Creole" was not used to describe people of African descent in the Netherlands Antilles as it was in Suriname, the authors nevertheless slotted Antilleans into this deracinated category and argued that "Antilleans belong almost exclusively to the Creole population group." Warranting Antillean inclusion in this designation was the alleged ubiquity of single motherhood: "It is generally accepted in Suriname and the Netherlands Antilles that a Creole woman is the head of the household."[87] Just as Antilleans and Surinamese were increasingly collapsed together on the basis of kinship and race, so, too, were differences among "Antilleans" effaced, with islanders from Curaçao and Aruba (as well as those from Bonaire, St. Maarten, Saba, and St. Eustatius, who moved to the Netherlands in much smaller numbers) corralled into a category long accused of reflecting administrative convenience rather than meaningful cultural unity.

Though "race" as a term all but disappeared in the postwar Netherlands, social scientific fixation on putatively Black family forms promoted the view that cultural difference, like biology, would prove equally fixed and immutable.[88] Assuming the transportability of research on Black families in distant times and places, European Dutch bureaucrats and the researchers that they commissioned brought race into the heart of the welfare state. Though family practices were explained in decidedly culturalist terms, they were nevertheless viewed as unyielding problems on the path toward liberal subjecthood. In the wake of the 1973–74 and 1979–80 oil shocks, economic self-sufficiency and notions of individual rather than collective responsibility became vaunted ideals in the Netherlands. European Dutch research thus problematized certain forms of kinship as obstructive to an emerging neoliberal ethos. Though Dutch bureaucrats refrained from naming race, they repeated its essentializing logic by indexing family forms that were imagined as atavistic and injurious to individual enterprise. Étienne Balibar described this phenomenon as "neo-racism," or a racism without races, where "culture," regarded as archaic and unchanging, also came to "function like a nature."[89] This preoccupation with kinship as *the* defining "cultural" feature of Blackness was not arbitrarily chosen. It stemmed from a longer and globally itinerant methodology of producing the Black family as an object of knowledge and a problem for national welfare.[90] At the same time, concerns in the Netherlands differed from those that prevailed in the Dutch Caribbean. While the crisis of refinery employment caused elites in prior decades to concentrate on the reeducation and remaking of men, in Europe it was the Caribbean woman who emerged as the focus of research and surveillance.

REDEFINING FAMILY

In the late 1980s and early 1990s, the preoccupations of European Dutch researchers evolved in step with changes in the kingdom and European Dutch society. The profound irony was that as citizens from the former colonies brought with them multiple repertoires of kinship, European Dutch women also increasingly uncoupled marriage and reproduction. With the relaxation of divorce laws and growing institutional recognition of nonmarital partnerships, European and Caribbean families came to resemble each other. But it was also at this time that tremendous intellectual energy went into quantifying their differences. This was not lost on some contemporaries. European Dutch sociologist R. A. de Moor's 1985 volume *Marriage and Family: What is their Future in Western Europe?* contended that, in the aftermath of the sexual revolution (here imagined as an exclusively white European phenomenon), growing acceptance of nonmarital, nonreproductive intimacies would lead to increased tolerance of migrants and their plural notions of kinship.[91] Even the 1979 report by Amsterdam's Department of Social Services proposed a "new definition of family" in view of the changes in Dutch society that had diminished "the differences in family composition between Surinamese and indigenous Dutch people."[92] Although European Dutch researchers regarded Caribbean families as diverse, they nevertheless assumed that this diversity existed exclusively within heterosexual arrangements.

Yet these seemingly progressive invitations to redefine the family more often aided the erosion of social spending and tightening restrictions on immigration. Into the 1980s, individuals in the Netherlands were increasingly free to organize their households as they wished, but the state no longer held itself accountable for their well-being. As the Dutch state moved away from policies that enforced the gendered institution of marriage as the exclusive site for reproducing citizenship, it also shifted social policies to encourage the self-sufficient and responsible individual as the prototypical citizen. In the late 1980s and early 1990s, Dutch authorities responded to economic recession by dismantling and reducing social programs. With the Welfare Laws of 1987 and 1994, which reduced child stipends, unemployment support, and incentives for women to balance part-time employment with childcare, issues once regarded as public duties were increasingly figured as private responsibilities. Dutch immigration policy was brought in line with this changing definition of citizenship, with new integration requirements introduced to ensure that migrants would not become a burden to the state and would smoothly adapt to the competitive lifestyle of the Netherlands.[93] Though nonnationals could be expelled or rejected on this basis, Dutch citizens from the Netherlands Antilles and, until 1980, Suriname, could not.

Dutch citizenship, however, proved to be an unreliable assurance of equality. After 1980, the Netherlands enacted a visa requirement for Suriname, ending the unrestricted right of abode in the former metropole. While this act seemed to finalize Suriname's decolonization process, in the Netherlands Antilles the Netherlands was compelled to abandon its efforts to decolonize the islands according to nationalist models. Dutch politicians in the late 1980s accepted that they could not thrust independence on islanders who rejected national sovereignty as the only rightful state formation. This was a welcome development on Aruba. In 1983 Aruban politicians reluctantly agreed to accept eventual independence in exchange for the island's separation from Curaçao and the Netherlands Antilles, a goal initially held by populist leaders in the 1940s and 1950s and revived again in the 1970s by Betico Croes's Movimiento Electoral di Pueblo.[94] Yet by 1986, when Aruba achieved what was to be a preparatory ten-year stage of autonomous statehood within the kingdom, the rights of Dutch citizenship had become all the more valuable for many Arubans as the Lago refinery closed and unemployment skyrocketed.

In Curaçao, structural adjustment policies and austerity measures implemented with the guidance of the International Monetary Fund made circumstances still more challenging in the 1990s, reducing already meager social assistance programs.[95] The flight of foreign-owned companies like Texas Instruments, which established a production center on Curaçao in 1968 and relied on generous tax holidays and low-waged work largely performed by women, further weakened the economic position of Curaçaoan women.[96] By the end of the decade, many women sought relief from economic hardship through migration.[97] Given the seeming permanence of transatlantic ties and the inability of Dutch politicians to restrict the right of abode, government-funded research now assisted new policy objectives by addressing the perceived problems of Caribbean-born Dutch citizens *before* they arrived in the Netherlands and by discouraging migration altogether. In the 1990s, the Dutch government devoted the equivalent of 1 million dollars to informational campaigns to dissuade Caribbean migration to Europe.[98]

Once again, the Dutch state found useful ever more intimate domains of knowledge as it crafted policy for an enduring kingdom. Some researchers contended, not without a degree of anxiety, that the surge in the Netherlands' historically low rate of teen pregnancy and abortion owed exclusively to the influx of Caribbean-born young women in the 1980s.[99] A government-funded project led by Humphrey Lamur, a Surinamese-Dutch sociologist known for his studies of enslaved families and reproduction on Surinamese plantations, compared the uses of contraceptive methods among Antillean and Aruban and European Dutch women. Lamur was alarmed by the "high frequency" and "high recidivism" of abortion rates among the former.[100] Using interviews and survey data, Lamur's research team solicited information about Caribbean women's experiences with sex education and contraceptive methods as well as their sexual and reproductive histories. By making this knowledge available to European policymakers and social workers, researchers hoped to strengthen the effective use of contraceptives among women from the insular Dutch Caribbean. The authors of these reports often recommended mandatory educational sessions before moving to the Netherlands, suggesting for example that "better information and orientation about what Antilleans and Arubans can expect to find in the Netherlands is also important . . . because it appears that those who had clear expectations for the future applied contraceptives more consistently."[101] The interventionist aims of research in this period marked a significant departure from Dutch policy since 1969, when in the aftermath of the May 30 uprising the Dutch government had halted all funding for family planning. By the 1990s, the Netherlands directed increased funding to nongovernmental organizations working with single mothers in the Netherlands Antilles and Aruba, with the ultimate goal of preventing the mobility protected by their rights of citizenship.[102]

CRITIQUE AND COMPROMISE

While the production of knowledge helped to solidify notions of difference between European and Caribbean Dutch, state focus on single motherhood opened circumscribed if also overdetermined avenues for diasporic activists to make claims on the Dutch welfare state. Beginning in 1974, the Dutch government subsidized the formation of Surinamese and Antillean social welfare organizations.[103] "Categorical work," as this unique policy was termed, attempted to streamline contact between the national government and various migrant groups by creating separate organizations for each "category" of migrants in the Netherlands. The reasons for funding these self-organizations varied over time. In the 1970s, the Dutch government expected migrants to return to their countries of origin, necessitating the preservation of cultural identities. In 1983, the Dutch government issued its first Minderhedennota (Memorandum on Minorities), which recognized that migrants would remain in the Netherlands as permanent "ethnic minorities." Policymakers now affirmed that the preservation of cultural identities would encourage integration into European Dutch society.[104] Yet, by the start of the following year, decentralization and "decategorialization" measures devolved federal funding to municipal governments, who subsequently directed constituents not to categorical organizations but to general municipal social services.[105] By 1987, with growing political and popular ambivalence about "ethnic minorities" policy and pervasive public spending cutbacks, funding for categorical organizations dwindled.[106] As one Antillean organization lamented, "The government stopped where it needed to begin."[107]

In the twilight of funding for categorical work, activists of Caribbean descent devised clever arguments to defend notions of state and communal obligation. Activists joined their defense of the welfare state with the goal of building an antiracist society. This effort would demand the reimagination of the terms of inclusion in Dutch society and the recovery of histories otherwise silenced in dominant social science research. Activists scaled this critique up and down. They targeted the inequality institutionalized as a result of colonial histories as well as the routine, interpersonal exchanges that perpetuated racism. The Plataforma di Organisashonan Antiano i Arubano (POA) formed in 1983 as an umbrella organization for Antillean categorical groups, asserted that "in part because of riches accumulated in the overseas territories, people in the Netherlands were in a position to develop robust collective provisions through which the less productive Dutch citizen could be insured and cared for by the state."[108]

The inequality resulting from the uneven allocation of resources in the kingdom also manifested in the paternalism of European Dutch service providers and bureaucrats. For activists, reckoning with inequality meant reckoning with racism—a term otherwise shunned in state policy and research. The leftist Vereniging Surinaamse en Antilliaanse Welzijnwerk(st)ers (VSAW), formed in 1981 by six social workers born in Suriname and the Netherlands Antilles, relayed in Fanonian fashion a typical exchange between a white bureaucrat and a Black activist:

> He encounters resistances, obstacles in his negotiations with (white) policy makers on the Dutch government side in order to obtain accommodations or resources for the interests of the Antillean community. He experiences difficulties with those same policy makers to gain recognition of his 'Antillean' identity. This evokes contempt, anger, and aggression. But . . . he realizes very well that this sick policymaker is also a representative of the same repressive apparatus that he is dependent on for the subsidy (alms) he needs to keep his 'Categorical Welfare Foundation' up and running.[109]

Writing in the *VSAW Bulletin*, social worker Lina Elodie claimed, "In my opinion every white Dutch service provider that works or wants to work with foreigners must begin to work on their own internalized sense of superiority, their ethnocentrism and racism."[110] Some activist organizations even instructed European Dutch social workers on the endurance of colonial ideologies and their palpable psychological effects. Addressing an audience of primarily European Dutch social workers in The Hague in 1988, POA member Mary Aitatus encouraged social workers to regard their clients' reticence to discuss personal issues, which many identified as an obstacle to delivering care, not as an individual failure of Caribbean-born women. Instead, Aitatus argued, "slavery was a time where the slave had nothing to say" and the impact of this disavowed personhood "still affects many Antillean women today."[111]

If historical argumentation proved central to activist efforts to transform the welfare state, it was because dominant social scientific research offered little to no account of Dutch connections to the Caribbean, rendering Caribbean-born Dutch citizens undeserving recipients of state benevolence. A topic of recurrent criticism, state-funded research featured regularly in activist critique (figures 15a and 15b). The POA encouraged

Figures 15a and 15b. Activist organizations criticized European Dutch knowledge production. Top: Women hold a sign reading: "We are not objects of research!" SOURCE: *Bosero*, August–September 1980, 9. Nationaal Archief Curaçao, Union di Muhé Antiano, 210, box 15. Right: A bespectacled white man named "Dr. Book" creates, through a magical incantation, an "allochthonous problematic criminal," depicted as a stereotypical Black man SOURCE: *Kontakto Antiano*, December 1971. Internationaal Instituut voor Sociale Geschiedenis.

European Dutch researchers to study racism in the Netherlands and not racialized minorities themselves. Under the headline "Research on minorities: in whose interest?" the POA insisted that "ethnic groups are too often considered at a distance" and that, despite claims to expertise, European Dutch researchers lacked sufficient familiarity with immigrant experiences. Still, the POA maintained that white researchers and their traditional research subjects both had important roles to play in a progressive intellectual agenda. European Dutch researchers could be made useful by turning their social capital against the state, uncovering and eradicating institutional racism.[112] As lay experts, Caribbean-born Dutch citizens could assume responsibility for research on their communities. VSAW, meanwhile, disputed the state's overreliance on academic research altogether, claiming that Black people in the Netherlands did not need scientific reports to confirm the existence of racism though "whites apparently do."[113] Social welfare activists thus challenged the state's definition of expertise as well as its focus on problems pertaining only to migrant groups and not wider European Dutch society.

Calls to investigate racism in Dutch society were ignored in state-funded social science research, but they were taken seriously by some scholars of color in the Netherlands.[114] Originally published in Dutch in 1984, Philomena Essed's *Everyday Racism* offered a powerful framework for apprehending racism in an age when many Europeans insisted that race and racism were no longer operable in Dutch society.[115] Essed, a Surinamese-Dutch sociologist, conducted interviews with Black women in the Netherlands and the United States to analyze the quotidian ways that assumptions of white superiority and its entanglements with sexism pervaded Euro-American societies. Essed wrote that biologically-determined views of racism were increasingly being transmuted into "cultural beliefs" portraying Black people as "people who refuse to adapt to Dutch culture while abusing the benefits of the Dutch welfare system." Contributing to this transformed racism was the fact that "some publications overemphasize the situation of Black 'single' mothers, which may pathologize the Black family."[116] Essed's study was pathbreaking in academia, introducing racism as a topic of serious theoretical consideration. But few contemporary European Dutch academics agreed with its interventions. Rinus Penninx, a European Dutch civil servant who later became a key figure in migration research, accused Essed of introducing US notions of "race rela-tions" into a foreign context. Penninx instead referred to the "open situa-tion" in the Netherlands after World War II where racial categories were unsettled and eventually eliminated.[117] Though Essed's detractors were quick to point out the specificity of race (or its absence) in Europe, they did not take issue with the reliance of European Dutch researchers on US-based studies of Black family life. Categorical organizations, meanwhile, found Essed's framework compelling and circulated discussion about "everyday racism" in their publications.[118]

Throughout the 1980s, activists increasingly aligned knowledge pro-duction with the goal of emancipation, working to contest the "negative stereotypes of Antillean women in media and in education" by comman-deering the state's research agenda.[119] The Dutch government saw an ad-vantageous opportunity to enlist categorical organizations in research on single mothers given the latter's proximity to the target demographic.[120] With funding from the newly renamed Ministry of Welfare, Public Health, and Culture (formerly the Ministry of Social Work), researchers partnered with categorical organizations to publish several studies on single mother-hood. In 1984, the categorical organization Kibra Hacha worked with doc-toral candidate Monique Haveman to publish 'Here I'm on My Own,' an "inventorying research on Antillean women" in Utrecht.[121] In 1990, POA collaborated with several researchers to write Mama Soltera, a book-length study of working-class Curaçaoan and Aruban single mothers in the Netherlands. Here, too, the dictates of state funding left research-ers in a tough bind.[122] While the authors of 'Here I'm on My Own' and Mama Soltera sought to portray the rich texture of Caribbean women's lives, including their achievement of greater financial autonomy in the Netherlands and the valued sense of freedom that attended the deliberate rejection of heteronormative relationships, they also needed to make con-vincing arguments to compel government funders to strengthen material supports.[123] There were thus certain limits to the emancipatory portrayal of alternate family forms in state-subsidized research.

Far from refusing the "single mother" as an object of state knowledge production, then, activist organizations like the POA argued that single mothers emblematized the struggle for emancipation in the Netherlands. In 1985, POA circulated a statement by an anonymous "single mother with two growing children." Providing a snapshot of her daily budget, this mother asserted, "I spend practically nothing on entertainment, going out, etcetera. My expenses include primarily living essentials. I'm glad to receive a child stipend every quarter, but what a shame that, with all of these budget cuts, the government keeps reducing it."[124] As the Dutch government reduced social spending in the 1980s, categorical organizations took up discussion of single mothers to remind the Dutch state and those who staffed its institutions that "a strong economic position is, without exception, necessary to achieve emancipation."[125] Such attempts to meet the state on its own terms sat uneasily alongside activist demands for the robust and transformative inclusion of Caribbean territories and people in notions of European belonging. Ultimately, neither strategy proved persuasive. The evaporation of state funding for categorical work in the late 1980s shunted the majority of activist efforts toward the pursuit of new funding streams. Though the efforts of enterprising members kept a handful of organizations operating into the 1990s, the horizons of what they might accomplish receded along with state investment.

. . . . .

Spending cuts did not merely affect state funding for migrant welfare. With the reformulation of social obligation following successive energy crises, in the early 1990s the Dutch parliament launched an inquiry into the cornerstones of the Netherlands' progressive social welfare policy, including social security and disability insurance. The broad provisions of the ABW also came under parliamentary scrutiny. Once again, the government commissioned research examining the use and implied abuse of social welfare. In a 1992 report on Surinamese, Antillean, Aruban, and Moluccan welfare clients, authors R. A. Wong and J. Arends concluded, "Antilleans form the migrant group with the most problems."[126] Wong and Arends argued that these problems stemmed from the changing demographic profile of Antillean and Aruban migrants after 1985, when mothers and their children formed over 80 percent of those moving to the Netherlands, primarily from Curaçao. With popular and political discussion urging reform of the ABW to encourage workforce participation and to reduce the fraudulent collection of social assistance, researchers studying welfare reliance now made bold recommendations to assist these objectives. Wong and Arends recommended reducing financial payouts to single parents and enhancing childcare services and education on pregnancy prevention for Antillean and Aruban women.[127]

In 1996, the ABW was overhauled in line with these recommendations. Single parents with children over age five would now be required to work in order to access assistance through the Act. Assistance payments were simultaneously decreased by 20 percent to incentivize parental participation in the labor market. Women born outside of the European Netherlands were particularly impacted by these changes, hampered by the initial lack of state-subsidized childcare and the absence of supplemental care networks among family, friends, or neighbors.[128] Economists have often dubbed the reduction of social spending in the 1980s and 1990s Netherlands as the "Dutch miracle"—a swift and stunning recovery from a putatively "Dutch disease." Its miraculous quality owed to the alleged social consensus that underwrote spending and wage cuts, resulting in impressive wealth and job creation. But the widely held perception that welfare retrenchment was especially benign and immune to racist manipulation (in marked contrast to the United States' "War on Welfare") appears dubious when considering how the welfare state and its scientists responded to internal migration across the Kingdom of the Netherlands.[129] If, as many economists suggest, broad social agreement ushered in the "workfare" legislation of the 1990s, then that consensus stemmed at least in part from racialized assumptions about the undeserving poor. As this chapter has shown, Dutch policymakers singled out citizens from Curaçao, Aruba, and Suriname as unique among other "migrant" groups, insisting that Caribbean cultural practices placed singular burdens on social services. They based this contention on the corpus of state-funded research undertaken throughout the 1970s–90s that explored the connection between single motherhood and welfare reliance. By the end of the twentieth century, this knowledge production created an atmosphere conducive to the retrenchment of the welfare state.

At a moment of crisis in the global oil economy, the creation of European expertise on the transplanted Caribbean household consolidated notions of difference between ostensibly equal Dutch citizens. In this case, difference cohered around forms of kinship alleged to be specific to Black families—even as white women increasingly uncoupled marriage and reproduction. And though the word "race" all but disappeared from the Dutch language, it was European Dutch actors at the helm of the welfare state who disaggregated Dutch citizens by birthplace and family structure, which functioned as "substitutes for race" that significantly shaped prospects in locating housing and social services for citizens from the Caribbean.[130] As Hazel Carby writes, race "is a verb not a noun," a process of calculating and assigning differential value to human life.[131] Though European Dutch researchers found new ways to elaborate difference absent the terminology of race, the *work* of race was accomplished through heightened expert interest in Caribbean family forms and welfare dependence. This knowledge assisted in the reformulation of social policy in the wake of energy crises and economic recessions, revealing that fluctuations in the oil market would once again be met with efforts to differentially regulate intimacy.

Conclusion

ACTS OF ATTACHMENT

Lured by images of azure seas and palm-lined beaches, visitors to Aruba—one of the most popular tourist destinations in the Caribbean—are often surprised to discover the ruins of an oil refinery towering over Rodger's Beach on the island's southeastern shore. Once an exclusive retreat for residents of the Lago Colony, Rodger's Beach is now publicly accessible and routinely promoted to a new group of US visitors as a quiet escape from the crowded western hotel district.[1] Departing the hotel zone on Lloyd G. Smith Boulevard, a thoroughfare named for the US American who managed the refinery at its zenith, tourists will eventually drive past the concrete walls surrounding the now-defunct plant. Those who reach the serene waters lying on the opposite side might wade in hesitantly, wondering whether the sea is so warm, so blue, despite or because of the toxicity emanating from the eerie industrial silhouette. Others will step confidently, recalling the wisdom of a hotel concierge who has reassured them the refinery has been idle for years. In this scene, the past persists as an eyesore in the present. The remnants of a bygone era of petro-dependence haunt the waveless waters and white sands that have given a new era of tourism its power.

The seductive images that sell the Caribbean as an attractive tourist paradise render such relics of heavy industry anomalous. Yet while this particular refinery is no longer operational, the age of oil that it helped to fuel is not over, nor is that epoch distinct from the era of mass tourism that now supports much of the region, including Aruba and Curaçao. Today, oil refineries form essential parts of the energy infrastructure that make possible jet travel and large air-conditioned hotels. Fossil fuels and tourist amenities also sustain new iterations of the offshore economy in the Caribbean, facilitating the circulation of visitors and capital primarily from the Global North through an archipelago of free trade zones, tourist enclaves, and offshore financial centers—a license to mobility that rarely extends to those residing in the region.[2] Also like their industrial predecessor, the industries that now dominate Caribbean economies rely upon foreign investment and demand, as well as on distorted, racialized assumptions about Caribbean people and landscapes.[3] The intertwining of race and capitalism is an old script in Caribbean history. Though not in historically or culturally congruent ways, it threads through the decimation of Indigenous people and the despoiling of nature by the first European conquerors as it does racial slavery and mass tourism. The age of oil is no exception.[4] But as this book has also shown, equally indispensable for understanding this history on Aruba and Curaçao are the intimacies that nurtured, sustained, and at times contested the terms of an emerging global energy system.

Offshore Attachments has illuminated the neglected energies that go into the production of energy itself. Such an approach reminds us that oil's value is not inherent in its materiality but is, in fact, produced. It is produced in the diverse forms of labor that transform crude into profitable commodities and it is forged culturally in the gendered, raced, and classed ideals alleged to attend the industry. Looking to these zones of value production relocates oil histories. Typically, two narratives reign: the eulogizing of Euro-American company men engaged in daring pursuit of world's most valuable commodity—a narrative genre that Robert Vitalis called "mythmaking"—and the heroic, male-dominated stories of labor.[5] But disputes over the functioning of the oil economy did not just transpire in corporate headquarters or among the distillation plants and dockyards. They also reached into households, bedrooms, and the backrooms of bars. In elaborating the "political economy of intimacies," this book has shown how the perceived demands of an energy system differentially organized intimacies according to race, rank, and status in the industry.[6] In the "boom" phase of the Dutch Caribbean refineries, these practices ranged from facilitating transactional sex for migrant production workers to encouraging marital domesticity for local laborers and for a small, elite sector of the white managerial class—a practice that continues to govern contemporary oil and gas frontiers.[7] The common pursuit of the prolonged "bust" period was to refashion the sexual and reproductive behaviors of the Caribbean working class, not to aid productivity within the oil industry but to encourage entrepreneurship and industriousness without. In each instance, it was deeply etched assumptions about race, forged long before oil industries arrived and revitalized again as the import of that industry waned, that underwrote acts of heightened control or else purposeful neglect.

In the transatlantic kingdom that bound the Caribbean to Europe's continental core, the plasticity of laws and regulations was an attractive draw for oil companies like Shell and Standard Oil. Late-colonial authorities welcomed these industries not only for their promised wealth and industrial modernization. The appeal lay, too, in the opportunity to shape souls and selves. To aid in this pursuit and to maximize profit, laws were conveniently circumvented or rewritten. Authorities illegally moved sex workers across state boundaries and crafted disjointed statutes (or simply ignored existing ones) to regulate divorce, contraception, and welfare. With oil refining one of the first industries to become thoroughly automated, the enclave refinery sites on Aruba and Curaçao anticipated the developments that would later beset the entire region. As men's jobs in oil refining, bauxite mining, and commercial sugar production became increasingly mechanized, women entered the tourism economy as housekeepers and wait staff and took on low-paying jobs in export processing zones and assembly and data processing centers offshored from the Global North.[8] These hallmarks of the offshore economy also relied on gendered assumptions, this time concerning women's historically lower pay and presumed passivity.[9] Like the mechanization of labor in the oil industry that preceded it, more recent iterations of offshoring and automation required a steady rise in nonhuman energy inputs to secure economic growth for foreign-owned enterprises.[10]

Caribbean people did not passively confront the forces of global capitalism and empire that connected them to newfangled commonwealth polities and the global energy economy. Leveraging the fragmented sovereignty of the islands where they resided, Caribbean people forged attachments of their own. In asserting rights to the orderly domestic lifestyles of the middle class, Aruban women in the 1950s turned ideologies of corporate paternalism back on the corporation itself and enlisted the overlaying tiers of kingdom authority in their defense. In the following decade, Curaçaoan activists forged common cause with radical Atlantic movements to re-create social bonds at a moment of economic crisis. They imagined bodily freedom and pleasure as vital to overcoming colonial conservatism and corporate interest alike. And facing what appeared to be the terminal decline of the Dutch Caribbean refineries in the 1980s, many asserted their rights as Dutch citizens through the emancipatory practice of migration.[11] This, too, constituted a popular mobilization, a self-organized movement of people that became possible with the concomitant ubiquity of air travel in the 1970s. These acts of negotiation and contestation could shape industry practices and the contours of transnational attachment, both real and imagined.

Considering together the histories of sexuality and oil does not only invite scholars of energy to think about the multiple actors who participated in the production of petroleum products. It also invites historians of sexuality to account for that which, in its ubiquity, hides in plain sight: fossil fuels. Interdisciplinary energy humanities scholars have urged us to consider the reciprocal development of energy economies and selfhood, to see energy not just as a physical thing but a social relation that shapes values and desires.[12] As we linger at a profound impasse regarding anthropogenic climate change, historians have a role to play in imagining a world beyond oil. Scholars attentive to the intersections of sexuality, race, and class can account for how oil has shaped and fulfilled certain desires while painfully blocking the realization of others, a first step in envisioning an energy transition that will involve not only matters of technology and alternative energy sources but also the reimagination of social values embedded in the fossil economy.[13] As one example, we might take a diary entry penned by Lago Colony resident Charlotte Warden in 1948, recounting her wistful observation of a young woman of color transiting solo at the Oranjestad airport. Dressed up, drinking beer, and laughing flirtatiously with male sojourners, the unnamed woman's fossil-fueled mode of transport and paraffin-laden makeup bespoke a sense of autonomy and litheness that Warden, alienated within the Lago Colony, admired.[14] What did petroleum products mean for intimate self-expression and embodiment among those who appear only as fragmentary figures in oil's historical archive? And what did they mean for Warden, who more often lamented her overwhelming isolation in the communities that oil had created? Such a candid reckoning of the opportunities, precarity, and pain engendered in the age of oil is urgent if we dare to imagine a more just and equitable world to come after it.

ENERGY TRANSITIONS

Periodically, the refineries on Aruba and Curaçao emerge as objects of international speculation that lay bare the links between global capital and the Caribbean, where alleged exceptionality has become vital to the operation of capitalism writ large. After Exxon began dismantling the Lago refinery in 1985, the Aruban government took over the plant and sold it in 1989 to the now defunct Texas-based Coastal Corporation.[15] Drawn by the lack of environmental regulations on Aruba, in 2004 a larger Texas outfit, the Valero Energy Corporation, purchased the aging refinery under conditions of a tax holiday and injected 640 million dollars into its revivification.[16] Declining profits caused by falling prices for gasoline, heating oil, and feedstock, however, led to Valero halting production in 2009, 2011, and 2012. The refinery sat idle again until 2016, when the Aruban government reached a deal with Citgo, a subsidiary of PdVSA, to once again refurbish and reopen it.[17] In 2019, Citgo reneged on the proposed 1.1 billion dollar project following the imposition of US sanctions on Citgo's parent company.[18] In a supremely ironic twist, as the global COVID-19 pandemic ground tourism to a halt in 2020 and 2021, the Aruban government renewed efforts to reopen the refinery in order to ease reliance on tourism. From Jamaica to the Dominican Republic and the US Virgin Islands, many Caribbean islands faced with declining tourism angled to "reinvent downstream relics."[19]

In recent years, Curaçao's refinery faced similar uncertainty as its southern neighbor, Venezuela, plunged into economic turmoil. In 2019, Curaçao's state-owned refining company Refineria di Kòrsou (RdK) allowed the lease established with PdVSA in the mid-1980s to lapse. The Venezuelan state oil company had struggled to continue operations due to aging equipment and shortage of crude. In recent years, several ambitious bids to reopen the plant failed. In 2018, a 5.5 billion dollar agreement with Guangdong Zhenrong Energy, a Chinese state-owned energy company, collapsed amid allegations of corruption. Saudi and German companies also entertained the project.[20] At the time of writing in early summer 2022, new US and Brazilian investors were being courted after an agreement with the Curaçao Oil Refinery Complex, a company based on the island, fell through.[21]

Opinions about the future of the refinery are mixed. Some have pleaded for a wholesale reimagining of Willemstad's harbor area to focus on sustainable energy and the retraining of skilled labor. Numerous lawsuits have decried the toxic body burdens borne primarily in the low-income neighborhoods that sit downwind of the plant, where pollution and particulate matter—one study reported levels of atmospheric polycylic aromatic hydrocarbons (PAHs) to be among the highest globally—contribute to cancer, asthma, and other chronic health issues.[22] Before the plant was idled in 2018, Curaçao had the highest carbon dioxide emissions per capita (52.1 metric tons) of any country in Latin America and the Caribbean and the third largest in the world. The energy industry accounted for nearly 30 percent of these emissions, the largest share among all social and industrial sectors.[23] Yet, as Rivke Jaffe has noted, for many living in the *barios* that arose in coevolution with the refinery, Isla is thought to be something "permanent and unalterable." Especially among an older generation of residents, the refinery holds an emotional importance and economic significance that outweigh its potential hazards.[24]

The toxicity engendered by the oil refining industry is not new, nor should it distract us from the fact that larger, wealthier nations like the United States, the Netherlands, and other European countries are more substantial emitters of greenhouse gases and bear historical responsibility for the ever-more horrifying climate catastrophes witnessed in the Caribbean today, including the category five Hurricane Irma that devastated St. Maarten in 2017 and the sea level rise that threatens low-lying Caribbean islands like Bonaire.[25] Since the founding of the refineries in the colonial era, harmful practices (for instance, the wartime dumping of an estimated 1.5 million tons of asphalt—the residue of benzene and aircraft fuel—into a chemical waste lake on Curaçao, or the one million barrels of hydrocarbons found in the groundwater at the Lago refinery site in 1985) amassed vast profits for oil companies and, by extension, the Netherlands.[26] The advantage of the offshore legal regime ensured that Isla would not be subject to environmental regulations until 1997, after which point Shell had successfully negotiated the company's indemnification against future claims for pollution or environmental damage. Relatedly, the fragmented sovereignties of the Kingdom of the Netherlands and that *other* supranational organization to which the Netherlands belongs—the European Union—mean that the Dutch Caribbean islands are not included under the Paris Climate Accords, nor entitled to the significant financing to combat climate change that comes with it.[27] In view of the racial and colonial histories that render Caribbean people and environments more vulnerable to the effects of climactic and ecological catastrophe, Yarimar Bonilla has invited us to dwell on the "coloniality of disaster," seeing both the spectacular and slow forms of climate violence and environmental ruin as outgrowths of a particular racio-colonial capitalism in the Caribbean.[28] Offshoring has helped to ensure the unequal distribution of the resulting harm.

These processes play out not only in landscapes but on much smaller scales: at the molecular level of the body and between and among individuals.[29] In this way, as the machinery of oil refineries sits idled on Curaçao and Aruba, the intimacies initiated by the industry endure. This is evident in the nostalgia of some residents for the "good life" that the industry provided or promoted as an aspirational ideal, a time when the oil refinery was synonymous with national progress and when cars and modern housing designed for the cohabitation of the nuclear family hitched the desires of workers to wage labor and the energy that made possible these domestic arrangements.[30] Perhaps the most visible testament exists in the treatment of regulated prostitution. Just three miles north of the Isla refinery lies Campo Alegre. Until COVID-19 forced its closing in 2020, the world's largest open-air brothel had operated continuously on the initial site designated by the late-colonial government in 1949.[31] Over the last several years, the economic crisis caused by declining oil prices in Venezuela has compelled thousands of women to flee to the nearby Dutch islands. On Curaçao, many are filling the "gap" caused by Campo's closure by working in roadside snacks (small restaurants with beer licenses) and selling sexual services to supply families back home with money and essential goods. Because for nearly a century authorities encouraged the migration of light-complexioned sex workers, Venezuelan women enter highly racialized landscapes where Latin American women are perceived as sexually available and attractive.[32] On Aruba, the competing demands of the oil industry and the "housewives" who orbited it reverberate in the contemporary management of sex work. No centralized brothel came to exist in Aruba. But after tensions from the 1951 protest cooled, in 1957 Aruban officials established a "zone of tolerance" in San Nicolas, which continues to serve as a destination for foreign tourists and Aruban men alike. Here, sex work remains legal, regulated, and reliant upon the labor of women largely from Venezuela and Colombia. Certain desires and mobilities animated by the oil industry have long outlived its decline.

EUROPE AS AN ISLAND

Linked to concerns about the oil economy, intimate politics crisscrossed the Atlantic and bound the kingdom's constituent pieces in ever-intensifying exchange. Owing to these heightened ties, Caribbean commentators placed the European continent within their own archipelagic frameworks, dubbing the Netherlands the "seventh island," as the activists of *Kontakto Antiano* maintained, or claiming as did the Curaçaoan author Tip Marugg that "Europe is very a big island where rich people live."[33] The more than four-hundred-year history of Euro-Caribbean ties renders it impossible to understand these regions in isolation from one another. Yet European Dutch politicians frequently conjure a situation of marginal and burdensome entanglement. They lament the financial "drain" wrought by the Caribbean territories and the problems stemming from the "generous" rights of the kingdom, including the (so far) unrestricted right of abode, even as growing numbers of European Dutch have moved to the Caribbean territories in the last decade.[34] The resonances between these attitudes and the colonial past that has bequeathed racialized understandings of citizenship is clear.

Born of an unwillingness to recognize the Caribbean as integral to Europe's social, economic, and cultural development, numerous proposals have sought to restrict rights for Caribbean Dutch citizens in the twenty-first century. In 2009, the Rijkswet Personenverkeer proposed to restrict residence for those born outside the European Union, ending the free settlement of citizens from the islands, which are designated as Overseas Countries and Territories of the EU. The Dutch parliament also approved a controversial measure to develop a database registering Caribbean-born citizens suspected of criminal behavior, which could be used to bar entry to the European Netherlands. Fiercely contested by Caribbean leaders and advocacy groups, both measures were ultimately abandoned after they were found to be in violation of constitutional protections and privacy laws.[35] Undaunted, in 2012 the European Dutch politician André Bosman of the Volkspartij voor Vrijheid en Democratie (VVD) proposed a bill that would require a residence permit for citizens from Aruba, Curaçao, and St. Maarten in the Netherlands. In addition to limiting rights of settlement (violation of which carried the penalty of imprisonment, expulsion, prohibition on reentry, and the suspension of social services), the proposed bill authorized police to stop and search individuals suspected of lacking the necessary permit. Human rights groups and advocacy organizations for Caribbean Dutch citizens denounced the bill's many injustices, including its legitimation of the already prevalent practice of racial profiling. Only after bitter protests by these organizations did Dutch parliamentarians reject the bill.[36] In 2021, Dutch Prime Minister Mark Rutte (VVD) and his cabinet resigned amid revelations that Dutch tax authorities had wrongfully accused over twenty-six thousand families of fraudulently collecting childcare allowances. The overwhelming majority were people of non-European ethnic origin, including thousands of citizens with a Caribbean background—a scandal anticipated by the racialization of welfare discussed in chapter 5.[37] While all this has occurred against a political backdrop of ascendant right-populism in the Netherlands, it is important to point out that these proposals have been designed and endorsed or else all too weakly refuted by liberal-centrist and progressive parties alike.

Undergirding these proposals is a staunch suppression of the intertwined histories linking Europe and the Caribbean and the racialization of citizenship itself.[38] Potent, too, is the assumption that the benefits of citizenship move only in one direction, with Caribbean Dutch citizens gaining from European largesse. This profound myopia obscures attention to the complex, extraterritorial entanglements that produced significant reward for many in Europe. The enormous profit reaped by the Royal Dutch Shell Group on Curaçao, which helped to launch the Netherlands as a major player in the energy field, is but one example. The consolidation of Aruba and Curaçao as offshore financial centers, prompted and promoted by Dutch initiatives and supported by Dutch foreign policy, serves as another. The wielding of Dutch sovereignty to carve out zones of exception in the spectacular accumulation of wealth helped to build the Netherlands into the prosperous financial hub it is today—a topic that deserves further scholarly consideration.[39]

In the twenty-first century, racial-sexual politics continue to play an important role in delimiting differential rights of citizenship in the transatlantic kingdom. The durable fear of Black sexuality in the Netherlands, continuously invoked in discussions of the "single mother" and the "pregnant teen," informs recurrent efforts to restrict the right of abode.[40] In recent years, however, racial-sexual stereotypes have assumed new forms alongside this abiding preoccupation with ostensibly improper heterosexuality. This is nowhere more evident than in the reformulation of kingdom ties after 2010, when the federation known as the Netherlands Antilles dissolved. Following a popular referendum, Curaçao and St. Maarten joined Aruba and the Netherlands as constituent countries of the kingdom. A first in kingdom history, the islands of Bonaire, Saba, and St. Eustatius became "special municipalities" of the European Dutch state. In a political climate where, since the 1990s, a wholly new consensus has emerged that sexual minorities and women should be defended vis-à-vis an imagined "immigrant" outsider (typically represented as Muslim), European Dutch politicians moved to ensure that the new Caribbean municipalities would receive Dutch same-sex marriage law.[41] While the islands were made fully "European" in the realm of same-sex marriage, they were denied equal belonging in the realm of social welfare. Residents of the overseas municipalities received reduced pensions, health care subsidies, and child stipends just as the cost of living rose precipitously. Though European Dutch politicians and media framed the tense exchanges resulting from these decisions as a dramatic culture clash between the presumably progressive Netherlands and its ostensibly conservative Caribbean territories (a framing that elided Caribbean contributions to sexual radicalism—including contemporary LGBTQ activism—and the recency of these values in the

Netherlands), discussions on same-sex marriage were not divisive for their moral content alone.[42] They raised unsettling reminders of the unfulfilled promise of Caribbean equality and the continuous creation of zones of exceptional legality at the very moment that such distinctions were to be effaced.

· · · · ·

Those thinking in and from the Caribbean have developed a rich conceptual vocabulary for understanding the region's uneven links to global power. Among these concepts, the offshore accounts for the archipelagoes of legal pluralism, extraterritoriality, and supposed exception forged by colonial powers and redefined in the context of contemporary capitalism to reproduce wealth. Even as these spaces appear as exceptions, they are, in fact, intimately imbricated in and make possible their seeming antitheses: the "normal" business of onshore capitalism and the sovereign nation-state.[43] These are not opposites of the offshore, but outcomes.

Esso's 1953 map tracing the global journeys of Aruban-refined petroleum, reproduced in the introduction to this book, offers a clear illustration of how the Dutch Caribbean islands stood at the center of the world that oil created, with the commodities produced there flowing away from San Nicolas and Willemstad and outward along the paths carved by foreign demand. We might reconceive of the substance and direction of the map's vectors to see in them multidirectional links hewed not by the circulation of petroleum products but by the movements of people who made them and the affections, longings, and hardships that they brought to bear in the process of their creation. Seen this way, the "offshore" might bespeak not only a problematic condition but a lived possibility. As the dictates of the energy economy fashioned zones of sexual exception to facilitate the export of wealth and to stanch the long, sobering effects of the industry's decline, Caribbean men and women made visible that which was so often concealed by the offshore economy. For themselves and their kin, they exploited the attachments that connected them, however unevenly, to the global oil economy and European metropole. Within, against, and in excess of those ties, they sought actively to shape the conditions of their labor, love, and belonging.

Acknowledgments

Much like the story contained in this book, the process of writing relied on the rigorous labor and devoted care of many people. At the CUNY Graduate Center, Dagmar Herzog's tireless feminist mentorship and ethically committed scholarship set the benchmarks to which I aspire. For her unflagging generosity and revelatory insight on sexuality in its lived intensity and messy political entanglement, I am so grateful. At crucial moments, Mary Roldán challenged me to draw connections between Aruba and Curaçao and the wider Americas and reminded me of my humanity. Joan W. Scott inspired me to read deeply into sources, highlighting contradictory messages not as problems to be resolved but as sites where meaning is made. Todd Shepard offered invaluable wisdom on sexuality, race, and empire in their local specificities and global resonances. Perceptive questions from Gary Wilder about oil and political economy helped to change the direction of this project. Herman Bennett nurtured a reverence for the writerly craft and introduced vital frameworks and methodologies in the study of the Black Atlantic.

I would not be a historian without the friendship and guidance of my undergraduate mentor, Robert Beachy, who illuminated a field and equipped me with the tools to find my place in it. When I briefly returned to my alma mater, Goucher College, as a contingent faculty member, Matt Hale, James Dator, and Evan Dawley shared insightful critique and pedagogical practices.

I knew the University of California, Irvine would be a fabulous intellectual home when Rachel O'Toole encouraged me during my interview to "let my freak flag fly." By this she meant it was fully okay, welcome even, to traverse regional containers and disciplinary boundaries. I am grateful to have colleagues in the History Department who share these commitments. Thanks to Kevan Aguilar, Houri Berberian, Sharon Block, Sarah Farmer, David Igler, Winston James, Felix Jean-Louis, Jessica Millward, Susan Morrissey, Rachel O'Toole, James Robertson, and Heidi Tinsman for sharing useful advice and commiserating. Emily Baum and David Fedman read drafts and offered unsparing encouragement. For their helpfulness and patience, I thank Marc Kanda, Cynthia Chen Bee, Michelle Spivey, and Sam Engler.

Writing about a company town while living in one heightened my appreciation for the solidarity and friendships forged even—and perhaps especially—in such deliberately depoliticizing spaces. Major gratitude to Samar Al-Bulushi, Tamara Beauchamp, Melanie Bowman, Long T. Bui, Ben Garceau, Sandra Harvey, Anneeth Kaur Hundle, George Lang, Ted Martin, Annie McClanahan, Liron Mor, and María Rebolleda-Gómez for support in many forms. I received an essential education on social reproduction, political economy, and Black study alongside individuals and collectives laboring to build a different world. For this and more, I thank comrades in the Political Education Committee, participants of the Abolition Politics Summer Reading Group, and friends and coconspirators, especially Yousuf Al-Bulushi, Nitin Goyal, Andrew Harrington, Nathan Hayden, Kavita Patel, and Diana Terreros.

A number of individuals read (and re-read) drafts and offered needed clarity. Megan Brown's sophisticated comments on the entire manuscript served as a foundational guide, her friendship a ballast. In every sense of the term, the sharp wit of Christopher Ewing sustained me in the long haul to completion and greatly improved multiple chapters. Kyle Francis took his inimitable red pen to an early version and gave me the courage to let it go. Margo Groenewoud has been an indispensable interlocutor; her comments on the entire manuscript and knowledge of Curaçaoan history edified my thinking and saved me from several mistakes. I am profusely grateful to Hannah Appel, Marc Matera, Lara Putnam, and Miguel Tinker Salas for offering detailed, transformative feedback on an earlier version of the manuscript and to Noah Patterson Hanohano Dolim for expanding my archipelagic imagination. Ian Beacock, Gianmaria Colpani, James Dator, Joan Flores-Villalobos, and Wigbertson Julian Isenia offered generous and generative comments on various chapters. Any remaining mistakes are, of course, my own.

I owe an immeasurable debt to the individuals whose intersectional studies of the Dutch Caribbean and its diasporas made possible this research. For sharing wisdom whether in brief or extended exchanges, I thank Rose Mary Allen, Luc Alofs, Gladys do Rego-Kuster, Margo Groenewoud, Francio Guadeloupe, Jeanne Henriquez, Rosemarijn Hoefte, Wigbertson Julian Isenia, Guno Jones, Lianne Leonora, Jacqueline (Jackie) Martis, Louis Philippe Römer, and Gloria Wekker.

The scholarship of Rose Mary Allen has been foundational, and few ideas in this book are untouched by its impact. Luc welcomed me to Aruba and offered an important orientation in the literature and sources. Gladys shared knowledge gained from a life of feminist activism that expanded my thought and praxis. I will not forget the generosity of Rosemarijn, who was quick to share her time and expertise at KITLV. Julian's steadfast and endlessly creative intellectual camaraderie is a gift; his innovative approach to the archive of sexuality and sovereignty inspires me as it no doubt will a coming generation of researchers. Lianne raised urgent, insightful questions about profits and power and helped me in locating critical sources. Jackie has been a fount of knowledge about sex work on Curaçao and conversations with her allowed me to grasp its racialization in new ways.

The opportunity to share this research in multiple venues shaped my ideas and contributed new ones. I am especially grateful to audiences at CUNY, the University of Curaçao, KITLV, the Universiteit van Amsterdam, Universiteit Utrecht, and participants of the 2015 and 2018 Association of Caribbean Historians meetings in The Bahamas and Barbados. In these and other settings, I received helpful input from Vanessa Agard-Jones, Neil Agarwal, Markus Balkenhol, Yarimar Bonilla, Esther Captain, Yannick Coenders, Gianmaria Colpani, Samuel Fury Childs-Daly, Robby Davidson, Bert de Graaff, Wannes Dupont, Jan Willem Duyvendak, Mohamad Junaid, Stacey Mac Donald, Anne Macpherson, Peter Meel, Gert Oostindie, Jessica Vance Roitman, Andrew D. J. Shield, Julie Skurski, Rachel Spronk, Fridus Steijlen, and Greg Zucker.

Many institutions and individuals made possible the research and writing of this book. I am grateful to the staff at the archives and libraries listed in the bibliography, including Nelson Thiel at the Archivo Nacional Aruba, Edwin Croes at the Biblioteca Nacional Aruba, and Nuzaira Scharbaai at the Nationaal Archief Curaçao. Precious time to research and write was supported by the Interim COVID-19 Research Recovery Program at UCI, the UC Humanities Research Institute (UCHRI), the Andrew W. Mellon Foundation, the Council on Library and Information Resources, a CUNY Dissertation Year Fellowship, and fellowships from the Advanced Research Collaborative, the Center for Latin American and Caribbean Studies, and Africana Studies at CUNY. Publication of this book was supported in part by a grant from the UCI Humanities Center.

Portions of chapter 2, 4, and 5 appeared in "'This is the Soul of Aruba Speaking': The 1951 Campo Alegre Protest and Insular Identity on Aruba," *New West Indian Guide* 90 (2016): 195–224; "Insurgent Intimacies: Sex, Socialism, and Black Power in the Dutch Atlantic," *Radical History Review* 136 (2020): 98–110; and "A Science of Reform and Retrenchment: Black Kinship Studies, Decolonisation and the Dutch Welfare State," *Contemporary European History* (forthcoming). I am grateful to the publishers for their permission to reprint pieces of these articles here.

At UC Press, I thank Kate Marshall for her vision and enthusiasm. Enrique Ochoa-Kaup and Chad Attenborough offered energetic assistance in preparing the manuscript. The three anonymous readers arranged by UC Press gifted me with incisive, actionable, and encouraging feedback for which I am deeply appreciative. Ben Pease made the beautiful maps and Catherine Osborne heroically copyedited the manuscript.

Friends and family have supported me since the first. Sarah Foster always picked up the tab when I was a graduate student and the constancy of her decades-long friendship has carried me through intense highs and lows. In the Netherlands, Janke Geertsma and Gauke Kooistra made me a member of their family, an act of love and generosity that changed me in innumerable ways. I am so grateful that Bodil Stelwagen, Reina Wouda, and Nienke McMurter took me under their wing then and have never failed to do so since. Tamara Beauchamp deserves a medal for indulging so many distractions and for being a good friend. The intellectual acuity of the Al-Bulushi/Horsley clan is matched only by their unceasing kindness. Thank you to Kathy, Mussa, and Samar for inspiring dinner conversation and for being such deeply principled and loving people. My aunt Gretchen fostered an appreciation for creative pursuits and showed me it was possible to build a life around them. Kristin, my sister, saved me from sending some awkward emails and together with my brother-in-law Casey offered a safe harbor during years of transience. The fact that they never took me too seriously injected levity and perspective into stressful situations. Norah and Quinn are lucky to have such cool and unflappable parents.

My parents, Tom and Jackie, have been my greatest teachers. My father's unblinking accounts of a childhood spent in tow of roving oil companies provided my first properly historical lessons about the world and oil. That he encouraged me from an early age to ask hard questions and to pursue answers was my most profound education, and the boundlessness of his support made everything possible. My mom had a proclivity for drawing out people's stories and was an unfailingly empathetic and attuned listener. Even in her absence, her way of being in the world remains a replenishing gift. With gratitude for the doors that they opened and with admiration for the limitlessness of their love, I dedicate this book to my parents.

In the simultaneously imaginative and challenging process of writing a book, I have leaned above all on the fierce brilliance and emotional succor of Yousuf Al-Bulushi. His joyful companionship and unerring moral conviction remind me each day that love is a revolutionary idea.

Notes

INTRODUCTION

1. Joost Jonker and Jan Luiten van Zanden, *A History of Royal Dutch Shell, Vol. 1: From Challenger to Joint Industry Leader, 1890–1939* (Oxford: Oxford University Press, 2007), 447, 449. Major oil corporations such as Standard Oil of New Jersey/Esso/ExxonMobil and The Royal Dutch Shell Group took on a dizzying array of corporate monikers and relied on numerous subsidiary companies to produce petroleum products. Because subsidiary company names often changed or were not widely used, this book employs the most recognizable company names throughout, including Shell or Isla for Curaçao's refinery and Standard Oil, Esso, or Lago for Aruba's refinery. When oil companies assumed new corporate identities, these changes are indicated in the text.

2. Wenzell Brown, *Angry Men—Laughing Men: The Caribbean Cauldron* (New York: Greenberg Publisher, 1947), 349–50.

3. Brown, *Angry Men*, 349.

4. On the limits of equating oil with wealth, see Hannah Appel, *The Licit Life of Capitalism: US Oil in Equatorial Guinea* (Durham, NC: Duke University Press, 2019), 32.

5. On race, labor, and oil production, see Robert Vitalis, *America's Kingdom: Mythmaking on the Saudi Oil Frontier* (Stanford, CA: Stanford University Press, 2007). On women's reproductive labor in oil camps, see Miguel Tinker Salas, *The Enduring Legacy: Oil, Culture, and Society in Venezuela* (Durham, NC: Duke

University Press, 2009), 66–67, 113–16, 148–51; Myrna Santiago, "Women of the Mexican Oil Fields: Class, Nationality, Economy, Culture, 1900–1938," *Journal of Women's History* 21, no. 1 (2009): 87–110. On representations of masculinity and oilmen, see Harvey Neptune, *Caliban and the Yankees: Trinidad and the United States Occupation* (Chapel Hill: University of North Carolina Press, 2007), 57–60; Myrna Santiago, *The Ecology of Oil: Environment, Labor, and the Mexican Revolution* (Cambridge: Cambridge University Press, 2014), 145–46, 227–30. On women's roles in oil-adjacent industries on Curaçao and Aruba, see Sonia Cuales, "Women, Reproduction and Foreign Capital in Curaçao," *Caraïbisch Forum* 1, no. 2 (1980): 75–86. My thinking on the profitability of women's reproductive labor is informed by Ann Laura Stoler, *Carnal Knowledge and Imperial Power: Race and the Intimate in Colonial Rule* (Berkeley: University of California Press, 2002), 47–55.

6. On gender and labor in Latin America and the Caribbean, see especially Lara Putnam, *The Company They Kept: Migrants and the Politics of Gender in Caribbean Costa Rica, 1870–1960* (Chapel Hill: University of North Carolina Press, 2002); Anne Macpherson, *From Colony to Nation: Women Activists and the Gendering of Politics in Belize, 1912–1982* (Lincoln: University of Nebraska Press, 2007); Thomas Miller Klubock, *Contested Communities: Class, Gender, and Politics in El Teniente Copper Mine, 1904–1951* (Durham, NC: Duke University Press, 1998); Ann Farnsworth-Alvear, *Dulcinea in the Factory: Myths, Morals, Men, and Women in Colombia's Industrial Experiment, 1905–1960* (Durham, NC: Duke University Press, 2000); Heidi Tinsman, *Partners in Conflict: The Politics of Gender, Sexuality, and Labor in Chilean Agricultural Reform, 1950–1973* (Durham, NC: Duke University Press, 2002).

7. On racial privilege and domestic arrangements in the oil industry, see Tinker Salas, *The Enduring Legacy*, chapter 5; Sarah Kunz, "A Business Empire and its Migrants: Royal Dutch Shell and the Management of Racial Capitalism," *Transactions of the Institute of British Geographers* 45, no. 2 (2019): 385–87.

8. Elizabeth Esch, *The Color Line and the Assembly Line: Managing Race in the Ford Empire* (Oakland: University of California Press, 2018), 2.

9. Sidney Mintz, "The Caribbean as a Socio-Cultural Area," *Cahiers d'histoire mondiale* 9, no. 1 (1965): 925. Drawing inspiration from this same passage, David Bond has suggested that in the Caribbean, the oil refinery was imagined less as an extension of the plantation than as a tool for its overcoming. See "Oil in the Caribbean: Refineries, Mangroves, and the Negative Ecologies of Crude Oil," *Comparative Studies in Society and History* 59, no. 3 (2017): 600–28.

10. This is a more contentious debate in the Netherlands, where for many years the prevailing view held that Atlantic slavery was not consequential to the accumulation of wealth in the Netherlands. This perspective has been powerfully challenged in recent scholarship; see for example Kwame Nimako and Glenn Willemsen, *The Dutch Atlantic: Slavery, Abolition, and Emancipation* (London:

Pluto Press, 2011); Matthias van Rossum and Karwan Fatah-Black, "Wat is winst? De economische impact van de Nederlandse trans-Atlantische slavenhandel," *Tijdschrift voor Sociale en Economische Geschiedenis* 9, no. 1 (2012): 3–29.

11. Oil and oil refineries are widely acknowledged in Caribbean historiography but seldom feature as the primary objects of historical analysis. For notable exceptions, see Jaap van Soest, *Olie als water. De Curaçaose economie in de eerste helft van de twintigste eeuw* (Zutphen: De Walburg Pers, 1977 [1976]); Tinker Salas, *The Enduring Legacy*; Fernando Coronil, *The Magical State: Nature, Money, and Modernity in Venezuela* (Chicago: University of Chicago Press, 1997); Bond, "Oil in the Caribbean."

12. For this argument, see especially van Soest, *Olie als water*; René Römer, *Een volk op weg, un pueblo na kaminda. Een sociologische studie van de Curaçaose samenleving* (Zutphen: De Walburg Pers, 1979); Jeroen J. H. Dekker, *Curaçao zonder/met Shell: Een bijdrage tot bestudering van demografische, economische en sociale processen in de periode 1900–1929* (Zutphen: De Walburg Pers, 1982). For classic accounts that deemphasize continuity with the preindustrial economy, see Harry Hoetink, *Het patroon van de oude Curaçaose samenleving. Een sociologische studie* (Assen: Van Gorcum, 1958); Johan Hartog, *Aruba Past and Present: From the Time of the Indians until Today*, trans. J. A. Verleun (Oranjestad: D. J. de Wit, 1961).

13. For a similar argument, see Bond, "Oil in the Caribbean," 603; Ryan Cecil Jobson, "Black Gold in El Dorado: Frontiers of Race and Oil in Guyana," *Items: Insights from SSRC*, January 8, 2019, https://items.ssrc.org/race-capitalism/black-gold-in-el-dorado-frontiers-of-race-and-oil-in-guyana. Caribbean theorists of the plantation economy emphasized structural continuity between the plantation and the development of export enclaves. See, for example, George L. Beckford, *Persistent Poverty: Underdevelopment in Plantation Economies of the Third World* (London: Oxford University Press, 1972); Lloyd Best and Kari Polanyi Levitt, *Essays on the Theory of Plantation Economy: A Historical and Institutional Approach to Caribbean Development* (Kingston: University of the West Indies Press, 2009). On the inadequacy of a tradition/modernity binary in the Caribbean, see Carla Freeman, *High Tech and High Heels in the Global Economy: Women, Work, and Pink-Collar Identities in the Caribbean* (Durham, NC: Duke University Press, 2000), 6.

14. Coronil, *The Magical State*, 70.

15. Jonker and van Zanden, *A History of Royal Dutch Shell*, 449.

16. Bennett H. Wall, *Growth in a Changing Environment: A History of Standard Oil Company (New Jersey) 1950–1972 and Exxon Corporation 1950–1975* (New York: McGraw-Hill Book Company, 1988), 389; *This is Lago*, 1949, UT, BCAH, EMHC, box 2.207/H20.

17. Esther Captain and Guno Jones, *Oorlogs erfgoed overzee. De erfenis van de tweede wereldoorlog van Aruba, Curaçao, Indonesië en Suriname* (Amsterdam:

Bert Bakker, 2010), 47; Rosemarijn Hoefte, *Suriname in the Long Twentieth Century: Domination, Contestation, Globalization* (Basingstoke: Palgrave Macmillan, 2014), 93–94.

18. Coronil, *The Magical State*, 107.

19. Trinidad and Tobago, where major deposits were found in the nineteenth century and one of the world's first oil wells drilled in 1866, is among the oldest oil-producing nations. See Bridget Brereton, *A History of Modern Trinidad, 1783–1962* (Kingston: Heinemann, 1981), chapter 11; David McDermott Hughes, *Energy Without Conscience: Oil, Climate Change, and Complicity* (Durham, NC: Duke University Press, 2017), 56. On the impending oil boom in Suriname, Guyana, and Cuba, see Hoefte, *Suriname in the Long Twentieth Century*, 191; Jobson, "Black Gold in El Dorado"; Nicole Fabricant and Bret Gustafson, "Revolutionary Oil? Offshore Drilling in Cuba," *NACLA Report on the Americas* 49, no. 4 (2017): 441–43.

20. Bond, "Oil in the Caribbean," 604.

21. Matthew T. Huber, *Lifeblood: Oil, Freedom, and the Forces of Capital* (Minneapolis: University of Minnesota Press, 2013), ix, 61; *Lago Highlights*, 1955, UT, BCAH, LCAC, box 2.207/M6.

22. Bond, "Oil in the Caribbean," 601–4.

23. David Kinley and Michele Salkin, "The Caribbean Export Refining Center," *NACLA's Latin America and Empire Report* 10, no. 8 (1976): 3.

24. Cara Daggett, "Petro-masculinity: Fossil Fuels and Authoritarian Desire," *Millennium: Journal of International Studies* 47, no. 1 (2018): 25–44; Huber, *Lifeblood*; Imre Szeman and Dominic Boyer, eds., *Energy Humanities: An Anthology* (Baltimore: Johns Hopkins University Press, 2017); Hannah Appel, Arthur Mason, and Michael Watts, eds., *Subterranean Estates: Life Worlds of Oil and Gas* (Ithaca, NY: Cornell University Press, 2015); Timothy Mitchell, *Carbon Democracy: Political Power in the Age of Oil* (London: Verso, 2011).

25. Huber, *Lifeblood*, 64.

26. Daggett, "Petro-masculinity," 35.

27. Dominic Boyer, "Energopower: An Introduction," *Anthropological Quarterly* 87, no. 2 (2014): 327. For an elaboration, see Cara Dagget, *The Birth of Energy: Fossil Fuels, Thermodynamics, and the Politics of Work* (Durham, NC: Duke University Press, 2019), 127–31.

28. Rosamond King, *Island Bodies: Transgressive Sexualities in the Caribbean Imagination* (Gainesville: University of Florida Press, 2014), 8.

29. Linda Rupert, *Creolization and Contraband: Curaçao in the Early Modern Atlantic World* (Athens: University of Georgia Press, 2012).

30. Rose Mary Allen, *Di ki manera? A Social History of Afro-Curaçaoans, 1863–1917* (Amsterdam: SWP, 2007), especially chapters 6 and 8.

31. Luc Alofs, "Onderhorigheid en separatisme: Koloniaal bestuur en lokale politiek op Aruba" (Ph.D. diss, Leiden University, 2011), 29–33.

32. On this constellation of issues in the Caribbean, see Juanita de Barros, *Reproducing the British Caribbean: Sex, Gender, and Population Politics after Slavery* (Chapel Hill: University of North Carolina Press, 2014); Laura Briggs, *Reproducing Empire: Race, Sex, Science, and U.S. Imperialism in Puerto Rico* (Berkeley: University of California Press, 2003); Brian Moore and Michelle Johnson, *Neither Led nor Driven: Contesting British Cultural Imperialism in Jamaica, 1865–1920* (Kingston: University of the West Indies Press, 2004), chapters 4–6. As industrial and political elites goaded local workers into allegedly depoliticizing marriages on Curaçao and Aruba, nationalist governments from Belize to The Bahamas launched similar efforts, hinging their legitimacy on the performance of sexual respectability and heteropatriarchy. See M. Jacqui Alexander, "Not Just Any(*body*) Can Be a Citizen: The Politics of Law, Sexuality and Postcoloniality in Trinidad and Tobago and the Bahamas," *Feminist Review* 48 (1994): 5–23; Macpherson, *From Colony to Nation*, 164.

33. Putnam, *The Company They Kept*, 92–93; Christel C. F. Antonius-Smits et al., "Gold and Commercial Sex: Exploring the Link between Small-Scale Gold Mining and Commercial Sex in the Rainforest of Suriname," in *Sun, Sex, and Gold: Tourism and Sex Work in the Caribbean*, ed. Kamala Kempadoo (Lanham: Rowman & Littlefield, 1999), 239; Michael Donoghue, *Borderland on the Isthmus: Race, Culture, and the Struggle for the Canal Zone* (Durham, NC: Duke University Press, 2014), 138–39.

34. Nicole Bourbonnais, *Birth Control in the Decolonizing Caribbean: Reproductive Politics and Practice on Four Islands, 1930–1970* (Cambridge: Cambridge University Press, 2016), 157; Briggs, *Reproducing Empire*, chapter 4.

35. For an insightful study of the omission of the Dutch Caribbean from Caribbean studies, see Margo Groenewoud, "Decolonization, Otherness, and the Neglect of the Dutch Caribbean in Caribbean Studies," *Small Axe* 64 (2021): 102–15. Other scholars have placed the Dutch Caribbean islands in regional circuits of exchange; see Rose Mary Allen, "Women Making Freedom: Locating Gender in Intra-Caribbean Migration from a Curaçaoan Perspective," *a/b: Auto/Biography Studies* 33, no. 3 (2018): 705–19; Rose Mary Allen, "'Learning to be a Man': Afro-Caribbean Seamen and Maritime Workers from Curaçao in the Beginning of the Twentieth Century," *Caribbean Studies* 39, no. 1 (2011): 43–64; Kamala Kempadoo, *Sexing the Caribbean: Gender, Race and Sexual Labor* (New York: Routledge, 2004); Francio Guadeloupe, *Chanting Down the New Jerusalem: Calypso, Christianity, and Capitalism in the Caribbean* (Berkeley: University of California Press, 2009), especially chapters 1–2; Vera Green, *Migrants in Aruba: Interethnic Integration* (Assen: Van Gorcum, 1974). On mobility in the circum-Caribbean region see especially Lara Putnam, *Radical Moves: Caribbean Migrants and the Politics of Race in the Jazz Age* (Chapel Hill: University of North Carolina Press, 2013); Lara Putnam, "Borderlands and Border Crossers: Migrants and Boundaries in the Greater Caribbean, 1840–1940," *Small Axe* 43

(2014): 7–21; Winston James, *Holding Aloft the Banner of Ethiopia: Caribbean Radicalism in Early Twentieth-Century America* (New York: Verso, 1998); Bonham C. Richardson, "Caribbean Migrations, 1838–1985," in *The Modern Caribbean*, ed. Franklin Knight and Colin Palmer (Chapel Hill: University of North Carolina Press, 1989), 203–28.

36. On migrant domestic workers in Curaçao and Aruba, see Ann E. Philipps, "De migratie van engelssprekende dienstboden naar Curaçao (1940–1960)," in *Mundu Yama Sinta Mira: Womanhood in Curaçao*, ed. Richenel Ansano et al. (Willemstad: Fundashon Publikashon Curaçao, 1992), 97–106; Rose Mary Allen, "An Intersectional Approach to Understanding the Social Life of Female, British Caribbean, Immigrant Domestic Workers in Twentieth Century Curaçao: Controlling Sexual Morality," in *Dissolving Disciplines: Tidal Shifts in the Study of Language, Literatures and Cultures of the Dutch Caribbean and Beyond*, ed. Nicholas Faraclas et al. (Curaçao and Puerto Rico: University of Curaçao and Universidad de Puerto Rico, 2018), 109–22; Paula Aymer, *Uprooted Women: Migrant Domestics in the Caribbean* (Westport, CT: Praeger, 1997).

37. Shaina Potts, "Offshore," in *Keywords in Radical Geography: Antipode at 50*, ed. *Antipode* Editorial Collective (Chichester: John Wiley & Sons Ltd., 2019); Appel, *The Licit Life of Capitalism*, 48–49; Ronen Palan, *The Offshore World: Sovereign Markets, Virtual Places, and Nomad Millionaires* (Ithaca, NY: Cornell University Press, 2006), chapter 4. On the history of the offshore, see Vanessa Ogle, "Archipelago Capitalism: Tax Havens, Offshore Money, and the State, 1950s–1970s," *American Historical Review* 122, no. 5 (2017): 1431–58. On exploitative financial practices before the "offshore" era, see Peter James Hudson, *Bankers and Empire: How Wall Street Colonized the Caribbean* (Chicago: University of Chicago Press, 2017).

38. Potts, "Offshore," 198.

39. These scholars analyze the role of sexuality in the symbolic ordering of states and global economic enterprises, such as tourism, while also inviting us to think beyond Caribbean sexuality as merely a fabrication of the European imaginary. See Alexander, "Not Just Any(*body*) Can Be a Citizen," 11–12; Kempadoo, *Sexing the Caribbean*, 7, 30; Faith Smith, "Introduction: Sexing the Citizen," in *Sex and the Citizen: Interrogating the Caribbean*, ed. Faith Smith (Charlottesville: University of Virginia Press, 2011), 7–9.

40. Bond, "Oil in the Caribbean," 605; Coronil, *The Magical State*, 107.

41. Kinley and Salkin, "The Caribbean Export Refining Center," 7.

42. Tijn van Beurden and Joost Jonker, "A Perfect Symbiosis: Curaçao, the Netherlands and Financial Offshore Services, 1951–2003," *Financial History Review* 28, no. 1 (2021): 73. In the mid-1980s, an international campaign against small offshore financial centers decimated the financial services industry in the Dutch islands; see Louis Philippe Römer, "Speaking Like a Sovereign Public: Talk Radio, Imperial Aftermaths, and Political Aspirations in Curaçao" (Ph.D.

diss, New York University, 2017), 30–35, 91. On the US and British Virgin Islands, see Tami Navarro, *Virgin Capital: Race, Gender, and Financialization in the US Virgin Islands* (Albany: SUNY Press, 2021), 17; Bill Maurer, *Recharting the Caribbean: Land, Law, and Citizenship in the British Virgin Islands* (Ann Arbor: University of Michigan Press, 1997).

43. Appel, *The Licit Life of Capitalism*, 49.

44. On women's role in the achievement of universal adult suffrage, see Rose Mary Allen, "Negotiating Gender, Citizenship, and Nationhood through Universal Adult Suffrage in Curaçao," *Caribbean Review of Gender Studies* 12 (2018): 299–318; Margo Groenewoud, "Les mobilisations féminines dans les Antilles néerlandaises (Curaçao et Aruba, 1946–1993)," *Clio. Femmes, Genre, Histoire* 50 (2019): 63–85.

45. Gert Oostindie and Inge Klinkers, *Decolonising the Caribbean: Dutch Policies in Comparative Perspective* (Amsterdam: Amsterdam University Press, 2003), 84–85.

46. This was the case until 2010 when the Netherlands Antilles dissolved and the islands acquired a new political status. Curaçao and St. Maarten became constituent countries of the kingdom, a status that Aruba achieved in 1986. As autonomous countries within the kingdom, residents of these islands do not vote in Dutch national elections. The islands of Bonaire, Saba, and St. Eustatius integrated into the Netherlands as "special municipalities." Residents of these islands now vote in Dutch national elections. Despite this tighter integration, other startling disparities remain, especially in social welfare. See Chelsea Schields, "Intimacy and Integration: The Ambivalent Achievement of Marriage Equality in the Dutch Caribbean, 2007–2012," in *Euro-Caribbean Societies in the 21st Century: Offshore Finance, Local Élites and Contentious Politics*, ed. Sébastien Chauvin, Peter Clegg, and Bruno Cousin (Abingdon, UK: Routledge, 2018), 180–81.

47. Yarimar Bonilla, *Non-Sovereign Futures: French Caribbean Politics in the Wake of Disenchantment* (Chicago: University of Chicago Press, 2015); Todd Shepard, *The Invention of Decolonization: The Algerian War and the Remaking of France* (Ithaca, NY: Cornell University Press, 2008); Frederick Cooper, *Citizenship between Empire and Nation: Remaking France and French Africa, 1945–1960* (Princeton, NJ: Princeton University Press, 2014); Marc Matera, *Black London: The Imperial Metropolis and Decolonization in the Twentieth Century* (Berkeley: University of California Press, 2015), 4; Adom Getachew, *Worldmaking after Empire: The Rise and Fall of Self-Determination* (Princeton, NJ: Princeton University Press, 2019).

48. On the panoply of these political arrangements, see Aarón Gamaliel Ramos and Ángel Israel Rivera Ortiz, eds., *Islands at the Crossroads: Politics in the Non-Independent Caribbean* (Kingston: Ian Randle Publishers, 2001); Lammert de Jong and Dirk Kruijt, eds., *Extended Statehood in the Caribbean:*

Paradoxes of Quasi Colonialism, Local Autonomy and Extended Statehood in the USA, French, Dutch and British Caribbean (Amsterdam: Rozenburg, 2005); Peter Clegg and Emilio Pantojas-García, eds., *Governance in the Non-Independent Caribbean: Challenges and Opportunities in the Twenty-First Century* (Kingston: Ian Randle Publishers, 2009).

49. Yarimar Bonilla, "Ordinary Sovereignty," *Small Axe* 13 (2014): 160–61. For a similar argument, see Palan, *The Offshore World*, 102.

50. On historical and contemporary sex worker migration in Curaçao, see Kempadoo, *Sexing the Caribbean*, chapter 4; Jacqueline Martis, "Tourism and the Sex Trade in St. Maarten and Curaçao, the Netherlands Antilles," in *Sun, Sex, and Gold: Tourism and Sex Work in the Caribbean*, ed. Kamala Kempadoo (Lanham: Rowman & Littlefield, 1999), 201–16.

51. I take inspiration from Sébastien Chauvin, Peter Clegg, and Bruno Cousin, "Introduction: Offshore Europe on the Move," in *Euro-Caribbean Societies in the 21st Century: Offshore Finance, Local Elites and Contentious Politics*, ed. Sébastien Chauvin, Peter Clegg, and Bruno Cousin (Abingdon, UK: Routledge, 2018), 8.

52. For a lucid meditation on historical and contemporary racial formations in Curaçao, see Angela Roe, "The Sound of Silence: Ideology of National Identity and Racial Inequality in Contemporary Curaçao" (Ph.D. diss, Florida International University, 2016).

53. Mimi Sheller, *Citizenship from Below: Erotic Agency and Caribbean Freedom* (Durham, NC: Duke University Press, 2012), 8.

54. On nonsovereignty as a potentially creative political formation and cultural practice to reimagine the world after empire, see Bonilla, *Non-Sovereign Futures*; Gary Wilder, *Freedom Time: Negritude, Decolonization, and the Future of the World* (Durham, NC: Duke University Press, 2015); Getachew, *Worldmaking after Empire*; Wigbertson Julian Isenia, "Queer Sovereignties: Cultural Practices of Sexual Citizenship in the Dutch Caribbean" (Ph.D. diss, Universiteit van Amsterdam, 2022); Yvon van der Pijl and Francio Guadeloupe, eds., *Equaliberty in the Dutch Caribbean: Ways of Being Non/Sovereign* (New Brunswick, NJ: Rutgers University Press, 2022).

55. Peter Hitchcock, "Velocity and Viscosity," in *Subterranean Estates: Life Worlds of Oil and Gas*, ed. Hannah Appel, Arthur Mason, and Michael Watts (Ithaca, NY: Cornell University Press, 2015), 45–46.

56. Shell received the opportunity to read van Soest's book prior to publication. See Ton de Jong, "De olie herbouwde Curaçao," *Antilliaans Dagblad*, January 31, 2014, https://antilliaansdagblad.com/nieuws-menu/curacao/publicaties/100-jaar-olie?limit=1&start=7. Van Soest's personal papers, housed at the Nationaal Archief Curaçao, were not open to researchers in October 2021 when I completed the research for this book. The data sets resulting from van Soest's exploration of corporate records are, however, digitally preserved and form an important source for this book.

57. This approach is informed by Black and Caribbean feminist scholarship. See among others Marisa Fuentes, *Dispossessed Lives: Enslaved Women, Violence, and the Archive* (Philadelphia: University of Pennsylvania Press, 2016); Saidiya Hartman, "Venus in Two Acts," *Small Axe* 26, no. 12 (2008): 1–14.

58. Lara Putnam, "The World in One Hot Sweaty Place: Migration, Family, and Global Transformation as Seen from Carúpano, Venezuela, 1860–1940," paper presented at the American Historical Association Annual Meeting, Atlanta, January 4–6, 2016.

59. Coronil, *The Magical State*, 18.

CHAPTER 1. CRUDE BARGAINS

1. Quoted in Jaap van Soest, *Olie als water. De Curaçaose economie in de eerste helft van de twintigste eeuw* (Zutphen: De Walburg Pers, 1977 [1976]), 523. See also Clendon H. Mason, *The Greatest of These* (St. Lucia: The Voice Publishing Co., 1953).

2. Hannah Appel, Arthur Mason, and Michael Watts, "Introduction: Oil Talk," in *Subterranean Estates: Life Worlds of Oil and Gas*, ed. Hannah Appel, Arthur Mason, and Michael Watts (Ithaca, NY: Cornell University Press, 2015), 17.

3. Kathi Weeks, *The Problem with Work: Feminism, Marxism, Antiwork Politics, and Postwork Imaginaries* (Durham, NC: Duke University Press, 2011), 9. Historians of Latin America have been especially attentive to gender performance and contestation in the workplace; see especially Thomas Miller Klubock, *Contested Communities: Class, Gender, and Politics in El Teniente Copper Mine, 1904–1951* (Durham, NC: Duke University Press, 1998); Ann Farnsworth-Alvear, *Dulcinea in the Factory: Myths, Morals, Men, and Women in Colombia's Industrial Experiment, 1905–1960* (Durham, NC: Duke University Press, 2000).

4. Jeroen J. H. Dekker, *Curaçao zonder/met Shell: Een bijdrage tot bestudering van demografische, economische en sociale processen in de periode 1900–1929* (Zutphen: De Walburg Pers, 1982), 56–57; "Bevolking totaal en per district, 1900–1960," Jaap van Soest Data Collection, University of Curaçao, accessed August 20, 2020, http://uoc.sobeklibrary.com/AA00000334/00001.

5. Quoted in van Soest, *Olie als water*, 199.

6. Charles P. do Rego, *The Portuguese Immigrant in Curaçao: Immigration, Participation, and Integration in the 20th Century* (Willemstad: Carib Publishing, 2012), 54–55, 60.

7. Carla Freeman, *High Tech and High Heels in the Global Economy: Women, Work, and Pink-Collar Identities in the Caribbean* (Durham, NC: Duke University Press, 2000), 105.

8. van Soest, *Olie als water*, 187.

9. van Soest, *Olie als water*, 199.

10. Rose Mary Allen, "Contesting Respectability and Sexual Politics in Post-Emancipation Curaçao," in *Archaeologies of Erasures and Silences: Recovering*

Othered Languages, Literatures and Cultures in the Dutch Caribbean and Beyond, ed. Nicholas Faraclas et al. (Curaçao and Puerto Rico: University of Curaçao and Universidad de Puerto Rico, 2017), 100.

11. Harry Hoetink, *Het patroon van de oude Curaçaose samenleving. Een sociologische studie* (Assen: Van Gorcum, 1958), 119–20; Saidiya Hartman, *Lose Your Mother: A Journey Along the Atlantic Slave Route* (New York: Farrar, Straus and Giroux, 2007), 80–83.

12. Kamala Kempadoo, *Sexing the Caribbean: Gender, Race and Sexual Labor* (New York: Routledge, 2004), 56. On intersecting gender and racial discrimination in Curaçao during slavery, see Nolda Römer-Kenepa, "Vrouwenleven op Curaçao: Laat achttiende eeuw en vroeg negentiende eeuw" (Master's thesis, Vrije Universiteit Amsterdam, 1980).

13. Rose Mary Allen, *Di ki manera? A Social History of Afro-Curaçaoans, 1863–1917* (Amsterdam: SWP, 2007), 90; Jessica Vance Roitman, "'A Mass of *Mestiezen, Castiezen*, and *Mulatten*': Contending with Color in the Netherlands Antilles," *Atlantic Studies* 14, no. 3 (2017): 401.

14. "Poenale Sanctie," *Amigoe di Curaçao*, December 13, 1924, 2.

15. "Openingsrede," *Amigoe di Curaçao*, May 16, 1925, 1; Recruiting workers from the territory Curaçao, 1936, NAC, Gouvernementsarchief [1934] 1938–1945 [1951], inv. nr. 2648.

16. On Caribbean labor migration, see Lara Putnam, *The Company They Kept: Migrants and the Politics of Gender in Caribbean Costa Rica, 1870–1960* (Chapel Hill: University of North Carolina Press, 2002); Aviva Chomsky, *West Indian Workers and the United Fruit Company in Costa Rica, 1870–1940* (Baton Rouge: Louisiana State University Press, 1996); Jorge L. Giovanetti, *Black British Migrants in Cuba: Race, Labor, and Empire in the Twentieth-Century Caribbean, 1898–1948* (Cambridge: Cambridge University Press, 2018); Matthew Casey, *Empire's Guestworkers: Haitian Migrants in Cuba during the Age of US Occupation* (Cambridge: Cambridge University Press, 2017). Curaçaoans also partook in these migrations; see Rose Mary Allen, "Emigración laboral de Curazao a Cuba a principios del siglo XX: Una experiencia," *Revista Mexicana del Caribe* 5, no. 9 (2000): 40–103.

17. van Soest, *Olie als water*, 243–45.

18. van Soest, *Olie als water*, 246; Charles P. do Rego, "Portuguese Labor Migration to Curaçao," *Caribbean Studies* 42, no. 2 (2014): 155–79.

19. Mason, *The Greatest of These*, 9–14, 17.

20. Shell began as the Koninklijke Nederlandsche Maatschappij tot Exploitatie van Petroleumbronnen in Nederlandsche Indië in Aceh/Atjeh in the former Dutch East Indies. See Joost Jonker and Jan Luiten van Zanden, *A History of Royal Dutch Shell, Vol. 1: From Challenger to Joint Industry Leader, 1890–1939* (Oxford: Oxford University Press, 2007), 16.

21. do Rego, *The Portuguese Immigrant in Curaçao*, 60.

22. Miguel Tinker Salas, *The Enduring Legacy: Oil, Culture, and Society in Venezuela* (Durham, NC: Duke University Press, 2009), 108.

23. This subsidiary company of Shell was first established in 1915 as the Bataafsche Petroleum Maatschappij. In 1917, this company was absorbed into the newly created Curaçaosche Petroleum Maatschappij and was renamed as the CPIM in 1925.

24. Rosemarijn Hoefte, *Suriname in the Long Twentieth Century: Domination, Contestation, Globalization* (Basingstoke: Palgrave Macmillan, 2014), 72–78; Margo Groenewoud, "Decolonization, Otherness, and the Neglect of the Dutch Caribbean in Caribbean Studies," *Small Axe* 64 (2021): 105.

25. do Rego, *The Portuguese Immigrant in Curaçao*, 58.

26. van Soest, *Olie als water*, 363; Report, July 19, 1922, NAC, Objectendossiers van de Gouvernementssecretarie, inv. nr. 25-17.

27. Rivka Jaffe, *Concrete Jungles: Urban Pollution and the Politics of Difference in the Caribbean* (Oxford: Oxford University Press, 2016), 36.

28. See, for instance, "Programa oficial dos festejos do primeiro do dezembro de 1949," December 1, 1949; "Programa de la celebración del 142 aniversário de la proclamación de la Independencia de Colombia," July 16, 1952; "Announcement of the Celebration of the French National Holiday," July 13, 1957, Mongui Maduro Library, Events Programs.

29. CPIM to governor of Curaçao, February 14, 1935; Governor of Curaçao to CPIM director, February 22, 1935, NAC, Gouvernementsarchief [1934] 1938–1945 [1951], inv. nr. 2647.

30. Bureau of Social and Economic Affairs to governor of Curaçao, October 9, 1943, NAC, Gouvernementsarchief [1934] 1938–1945 [1951], inv. nr. 2644.

31. "Contratos con los obreros colombianos en Curazao no se cumplen debidamente," *El Siglo*, October 28, 1944, NAC, Gouvernementsarchief [1934] 1938–1945 [1951], inv. nr. 2645.

32. Rose Mary Allen, "An Intersectional Approach to Understanding the Social Life of Female, British Caribbean, Immigrant Domestic Workers in Twentieth Century Curaçao: Controlling Sexual Morality," in *Dissolving Disciplines: Tidal Shifts in the Study of Language, Literatures and Cultures of the Dutch Caribbean and Beyond*, ed. Nicholas Faraclas et al. (Curaçao and Puerto Rico: University of Curaçao and Universidad de Puerto Rico, 2018), 116.

33. CPIM to attorney general, July 25, 1938, NAC, Gouvernementsarchief [1934] 1938–1945 [1951], inv. nr. 2647.

34. Allen, "An Intersectional Approach," 113.

35. Commander of military police to CPIM, August 22, 1938, NAC, Gouvernementsarchief [1934] 1938–1945 [1951], inv. nr. 2647.

36. Attorney general to governor of Curaçao, September 20, 1938, NAC, Gouvernementsarchief [1934] 1938–1945 [1951], inv. nr. 2647. On recruitment from Suriname and the British West Indies, see Ann E. Philipps, "De migratie van

engelssprekende dienstboden naar Curaçao (1940–1960)," in *Mundu Yama Sinta Mira: Womanhood in Curaçao*, ed. Richenel Ansano et al. (Willemstad: Fundashon Publikashon Curaçao, 1992), 99.

37. Paula Aymer, *Uprooted Women: Migrant Domestics in the Caribbean* (Westport, CT: Praeger, 1997), 56–57.

38. Philipps, "De migratie van engelssprekende dienstboden naar Curaçao," 99.

39. Joan Flores-Villalobos, "'Freak Letters': Tracing Gender, Race, and Diaspora in the Panama Canal Archive," *Small Axe* 59 (2019): 35.

40. On the organization of labor and company towns for political purposes, see J. Douglas Porteous, "Social Class in Atacama Company Towns," *Annals of the Association of American Geographers* 64, no. 3 (1974): 409–17. On the organization of oil camps, see Robert Vitalis, *America's Kingdom: Mythmaking on the Saudi Oil Frontier* (Stanford, CA: Stanford University Press, 2007), 92–93; Tinker Salas, *The Enduring Legacy*, 173; Myrna Santiago, *The Ecology of Oil: Environment, Labor, and the Mexican Revolution* (Cambridge: Cambridge University Press, 2014), 164–71; Arbella Bet-Shlimon, *City of Black Gold: Oil, Ethnicity, and the Making of Modern Kirkuk* (Stanford, CA: Stanford University Press, 2019), 114–15.

41. Hannah Appel, *The Licit Life of Capitalism: US Oil in Equatorial Guinea* (Durham, NC: Duke University Press, 2019), 103. Common practice in oil camps, the ethnic and racial division of labor also characterized other Caribbean enterprises such as commercial agriculture and bauxite mining. See Casey, *Empire's Guestworkers*, 108–10; Rosemarijn Hoefte with Anouk de Koning, "Bauxite Mining in Moengo: Remnants of the Past and Signs of Modernity," in *Suriname in the Long Twentieth Century*, 114, 116.

42. Guno Jones and Esther Captain, "Inversing Dependence: The Dutch Antilles, Suriname, and the Desperate Netherlands during World War II," in *World War II and the Caribbean*, ed. Karen Eccles and Debbie McCollin (Kingston: University of the West Indies Press, 2017), 77.

43. "Grote belangstelling voor Curaçao," *Amigoe di Curaçao*, March 21, 1942, 2; "Isla gaat Amerikanen bezighouden," *Amigoe di Curaçao*, June 10, 1942, 2.

44. In 1936, the Dutch governor ordered the deportation of foreign sex workers but this practice was soon resumed owing to an alleged increase in domestic prostitution. See Luc Alofs, "Publieke dames in een publiek debat: De geschiedenis van Campo Alegre op Aruba, 1950–1957," in *Cinco aña na caminda: Opstellen aangeboden ter gelegenheid van het eerste lustrum van de Universiteit van Aruba*, ed. G. F. M. Bussers, A. R. O. Ringeling, and M. Tratnik (Oranjestad: University of Aruba, 1993), 21.

45. Quoted in Henry Habibe, *Un herida biba ta: Een verkenning van het poëtisch oeuvre van Pierre Lauffer* (Curaçao: Self-published, 1994), 58.

46. For a parallel argument, see Richard Fogarty, "Race and Sex, Fear and Loathing in France during the Great War," in *Brutality and Desire: War and*

Sexuality in Europe's Twentieth Century, ed. Dagmar Herzog (Basingstoke: Palgrave Macmillan, 2009), 61.

47. Governor of Netherlands Antilles to minister of union affairs and overseas territories, November 17, 1949, NA, Ministerie van Koloniën en opvolgers: Dossierarchief, 2.10.51, inv. nr. 10284.

48. M. Gorsira to attorney general, n.d., ANA, BCAR, Bestrijding der Onzedelijkheid, inv. nr. 347, DS-13468.

49. General Situation Report No. 14, June 5, 1951, NA, Ministerie van Koloniën en opvolgers: Dossierarchief, 2.10.54, inv. nr. 10284.

50. Committee to Combat Prostitution and Venereal Disease, May 8, 1942, ANA, BCAR, Bestrijding der Onzedelijkheid, inv. nr. 544, DS-606-6.

51. Committee to Combat Prostitution and Venereal Disease, May 8, 1942, ANA, BCAR, Bestrijding der Onzedelijkheid, inv. nr. 544, DS-606-6.

52. Kempadoo, *Sexing the Caribbean*, 95. After 1966, Cuban women no longer came to Curaçao to sell sex, a subject explored in chapter 3 of this book. Venezuelan authorities also believed that the presence of Venezuelan sex workers in Curaçao damaged trade and business relations and forbade migration as a result (see Kempadoo, *Sexing the Caribbean*, 104).

53. I owe this formulation to Hannah Appel.

54. Documents related to diss. of Tjeerd de Reus (c. 1966), p. 2, NA, Collectie 420 P. Muntendam, 2.21.218, inv. nr. 2.

55. Harvey Neptune, *Caliban and the Yankees: Trinidad and the United States Occupation* (Chapel Hill: University of North Carolina Press, 2007), 161; van Soest, *Olie als water*, 469.

56. Documents related to diss. of Tjeerd de Reus (c. 1966), p. 2, NA, Collectie 420 P. Muntendam, 2.21.218, inv. nr. 2.

57. Attorney general to Dutch consul, December 31, 1943, NA, Nederlandse Consulaat te Santo Domingo, 2.05.336, inv. nr. 104.

58. Dutch consul to attorney general, July 18, 1947, NA, Nederlandse Consulaat te Santo Domingo, 2.05.336, inv. nr. 104. I have used pseudonyms to protect anonymity.

59. Dutch consul to attorney general, July 16, 1947, NA, Nederlandse Consulaat te Santo Domingo, 2.05.336, inv. nr. 104.

60. Kempadoo, *Sexing the Caribbean*, 94–95; Documents related to diss. of Tjeerd de Reus (c. 1966), p. 92, NA, Collectie 420 P. Muntendam, 2.21.218, inv. nr. 1.

61. Committee to Combat Prostitution and Venereal Disease, May 8, 1942, ANA, BCAR, Bestrijding der Onzedelijkheid, inv. nr. 544, DS-606-6.

62. Third meeting of the Committee to Study Prostitution, July 26, 1951, ANA, BCAR, Bestrijding der Onzedelijkheid, inv. nr. 544, DS-606-6.

63. Timothy Mitchell, *Carbon Democracy: Political Power in the Age of Oil* (London: Verso, 2011), 45.

64. Chelsea Schields, "'Combatting the Sensuality of the Youth': Youthful Sexuality and the Reformulation of Desire in the Dutch Vice Laws of 1911," *Gender & History* 31 (2019): 115–31.

65. Mariëlle Kleijn and Marlou Schrover, "The Dutch State as a Pimp: Policies Regarding a Brothel on Curaçao (1945–1956)," *Tijdschrift voor Sociale en Economische Geschiedenis* 10 (2013): 33–54.

66. Kleijn and Schrover, "The Dutch State as a Pimp," 49–50.

67. United Nations Economic and Social Council e/2548, February 26, 1954, NA, Ministerie van Koloniën en opvolgers: Dossierarchief, 2.10.54, inv. nr. 10284.

68. Kempadoo, *Sexing the Caribbean*, 95–96.

69. Lara Putnam, "Borderlands and Border Crossers: Migrants and Boundaries in the Greater Caribbean, 1840-1940," *Small Axe* 43 (2014): 16.

70. Myrna Santiago, "Women of the Mexican Oil Fields: Class, Nationality, Economy, Culture, 1900–1938," *Journal of Women's History* 21, no. 1 (2009): 103.

71. Jonker and van Zanden, *A History of Royal Dutch Shell*, 449.

72. van Soest, *Olie als water*, 464. For a parallel example, see Tinker Salas, *The Enduring Legacy*, 95.

73. Staten of Curaçao, 1942–43, Budget for 1943, UBL, KIT Collection.

74. Gert Oostindie and Inge Klinkers, *Decolonising the Caribbean: Dutch Policies in Comparative Perspective* (Amsterdam: Amsterdam University Press, 2003), 61. On late-colonial reform, see Frederick Cooper, "Modernizing Colonialism and the Limits of Empire," *Items & Issues: Social Science Research Council* 4, no. 4 (2003): 1–10.

75. Curaçao elected five members to the Staten while Aruba elected three. Bonaire elected one representative. Together, the three northeastern islands elected one member.

76. C. M. Grüning, J. L. Martina, and R. Winkel, eds., *50 jaar Staten van de Nederlandse Antillen* (Willemstad: Staten van de Nederlandse Antillen, 1988), 27.

77. Margo Groenewoud, "'Nou koest, nou kalm.' De ontwikkeling van de Curaçaose samenleving, 1915–1973: Van koloniaal en kerkelijk gezag naar zelfbestuur en burgerschap" (Ph.D. diss, Leiden University, 2017), 53.

78. Jaffe, *Concrete Jungles*, 36.

79. Minutes of the Staten of Curaçao, June 24, 1942, 27, UBL, KIT Collection.

80. Minutes of the Staten of Curaçao, April 6, 1943, 63, UBL, KIT Collection.

81. Minutes of the Staten of Curaçao, August 17, 1944, 37, UBL, KIT Collection.

82. Staten of Curaçao, 1944–45, Change of art. 706 and 709, Code of Civil Procedure, UBL, KIT Collection.

83. "Geen Verstekvonnissen meer op Curaçao," *Amigoe di Curaçao*, August 18, 1944, 2.

84. Staten of Curaçao, 1944–45, Change of art. 706 and 709, Code of Civil Procedure, Preliminary report, 2–3, UBL, KIT Collection.

85. "Staten Overzicht," *Amigoe di Curaçao*, August 18, 1944, 1.

86. In an obverse example, the liberalization of divorce law legitimized the United States military occupation of Puerto Rico after 1898; see Eileen Findlay, *Imposing Decency: The Politics of Sexuality and Race in Puerto Rico, 1870–1920* (Durham, NC: Duke University Press, 1999), 110–34.

87. Minutes of the Staten of Curaçao, April 4, 1944, 3, NAC.

88. "Erkenning van natuurlijke kinderen," *Amigoe di Curaçao*, August 17, 1944, 3. On coterminous campaigns in the Caribbean, see Tracy Robinson, "Mass Weddings in Jamaica and the Production of Academic Folk Knowledge," *Small Axe* 24, no. 3 (2020): 65–80.

89. Minutes of the Staten of Curaçao, April 4, 1944, 3, NAC.

90. Into the nineteenth century, members of Curaçao's Sephardic Jewish community were more likely than European Protestant men to inherit children born outside of formal marriage. Though generally not afforded the same status as children born within wedlock, these children might be integrated into the family business, entitled to some inheritance, and allowed to adopt the paternal surname. See Jessica Vance Roitman, "Mediating Multiculturalism: Jews, Blacks, and Curaçao, 1825–1970," in *The Sephardic Atlantic: Colonial Histories and Postcolonial Perspectives*, ed. Sina Rauschenbach and Jonathan Schorsch (Cham: Palgrave Macmillan, 2018), 94–95.

91. Evelyn Brooks Higginbotham, "African-American Women's History and the Metalanguage of Race," *Signs* 17, no. 2 (1992): 252. On post-abolition Curaçao, see Allen, *Di ki manera?*, chapters 6 and 8.

92. Yarimar Bonilla, *Non-Sovereign Futures: French Caribbean Politics in the Wake of Disenchantment* (Chicago: University of Chicago Press, 2015), 12–13.

93. Kristen Stromberg Childers, "Departmentalization, Migration, and the Politics of the Family in the Post-war French Caribbean," *History of the Family* 14 (2009): 177–90; Anne Macpherson, *From Colony to Nation: Women Activists and the Gendering of Politics in Belize, 1912–1982* (Lincoln: University of Nebraska Press, 2007), 160–61; Nicole Bourbonnais, *Birth Control in the Decolonizing Caribbean: Reproductive Politics and Practice on Four Islands, 1930–1970* (Cambridge: Cambridge University Press, 2016), 84–85; M. Jacqui Alexander, "Not Just Any(*body*) Can Be a Citizen: The Politics of Law, Sexuality and Postcoloniality in Trinidad and Tobago and the Bahamas," *Feminist Review* 48 (1994): 13–14.

94. Esther Captain and Guno Jones, *Oorlogs erfgoed overzee. De erfenis van de tweede wereldoorlog van Aruba, Curaçao, Indonesië en Suriname* (Amsterdam: Bert Bakker, 2010), 93–94.

95. Jennifer L. Foray, *Visions of Empire in the Nazi-Occupied Netherlands* (Cambridge: Cambridge University Press, 2013), 152–55.

96. Wilhelmina prinses der Nederlanden, *The Queen Looks at the Future: Important Statements of H. M. Queen Wilhelmina on War and Peace Aims* (New York: The Netherlands Information Bureau, 1943), 13. Here, Curaçao refers to "Curaçao and Dependencies," the six-island administrative grouping that, in 1948, was renamed the Netherlands Antilles.

97. Roitman, "Mediating Multiculturalism," 108.

98. Rose Mary Allen, "Contextualizing and Learning from Kas di Pueblo," in *Kas di pueblo: Kas ku un mishon . . . House with a mission*, ed. Rose Mary Allen and Maria Liberia-Peters (Curaçao: Fundashon Maria Liberia-Peters, 2019), 228–38.

99. Michael Collins, "Decolonisation and the 'Federal Moment,'" *Diplomacy and Statecraft* 24 (2013): 21–40. On ideas of commonwealth statehood in the Dutch, British, and French empires, see Foray, *Visions of Empire*; Frederick Cooper, *Citizenship between Empire and Nation: Remaking France and French Africa, 1945–1960* (Princeton, NJ: Princeton University Press, 2014); Eric D. Duke, *Building a Nation: Caribbean Federation in the Black Diaspora* (Gainesville: University Press of Florida, 2019).

100. Quoted in Groenewoud, "'Nou koest, nou kalm,'" 129.

101. Groenewoud, "'Nou koest, nou kalm,'" 134–36.

102. Stephen Howarth and Joost Jonker, *A History of Royal Dutch Shell, Vol. 2: Powering the Hydrocarbon Revolution, 1939–1973* (New York: Oxford University Press, 2007), 60, 103.

103. Nizaar Makdoembaks, *Killing Camp Suffisant: Brieven aan de Nederlandse regering rond een verhulde oorlogsmisdaad* (Curaçao: Stichting Eerherstel Oorlogsslachtoffers Curaçao, 2017).

104. Vitalis, *America's Kingdom*, 20–22.

105. Farnsworth-Alvear, *Dulcinea in the Factory*, 149–50. See also Anouk de Koning, "Shadows of the Plantation? A Social History of Suriname's Bauxite Town Moengo," *New West Indian Guide* 85, no. 3/4 (2011): 229; Klubock, *Contested Communities*, 56–58.

106. Governor of Curaçao to Troost, Office of Finances, CPIM, September 3, 1942, NAC, Gouvernementsarchief [1934] 1938–1945 [1951], inv. nr. 2634.

107. Translation of *Ahora*, October 13, 1943, NAC, Gouvernementsarchief [1934] 1938–1945 [1951], inv. nr. 2644.

108. Translation of *Diário de Notícias*, November 23, 1945, NAC, Gouvernementsarchief [1934] 1938–1945 [1951], inv. nr. 2646.

109. Attorney general to governor of Curaçao, March 7, 1946, NAC, Gouvernementsarchief [1934] 1938–1945 [1951], inv. nr. 2646.

110. Jaap van Soest, Curaçaose cijferreeksen 1828–1955, DANS, KNAW, 05.08.5 (28) Shell kampen en andere huisvesting voor gastarbeiders 1931–58, accessed October 19, 2021, https://easy.dans.knaw.nl/ui/datasets/id/easy-dataset:49962.

111. van Soest, *Olie als water*, 524.

112. "Verslag van de toespraak gehouden door de Voorzitter der Vereeniging van Geemployeerden der Koninklijke Shell," July 11, 1945, UBL, Collection Jan Carel van Essen (KITLV).

113. Eva Abraham-van der Mark, *Yu'i Mama. Enkele facetten van gezinsstructuur op Curaçao* (Assen: Van Gorcum, 1972), 18.

114. *De Passaat*, July 1947, 1, CPL, DN.

115. *De Passaat*, February 1947, 1, CPL, DN.

116. Abraham–van der Mark, *Yu'i Mama*, 17.

117. Births outside of wedlock were lowest in 1952 (23.9 percent) but rose steadily after mass layoffs resulting from mechanization at Isla in 1960 (27.9 percent), 1967 (34.9 percent), and 1970 (33.4 percent) (Abraham-van der Mark, *Yu'i Mama*, 19–21).

118. Nara Milanich, "Daddy Issues: 'Responsible Paternity' as Public Policy in Latin America," *World Policy Institute* XXXIV, no. 3 (2017): 10–11.

119. Historians who collaborated on the corporate history project have viewed regionalization as a positive sign of corporate adaptation. Other scholars have highlighted its lingering inequities. For the former argument, see Howarth and Jonker, *A History of the Royal Dutch Shell, Vol.* 2, 136; Keetie Sluyterman, "Decolonisation and the Organisation of the International Workforce: Dutch Multinationals in Indonesia, 1945–1967," *Business History* 62, no. 7 (2020): 1182–1201. For a critical take, see Sarah Kunz, "A Business Empire and its Migrants: Royal Dutch Shell and the Management of Racial Capitalism," *Transactions of the Institute of British Geographers* 45, no. 2 (2019): 381.

120. It was not until 1962 that Antillean staff outnumbered European staff. See van Soest, Curaçaose cijferreeksen 1828–1955, DANS, KNAW, 05.08.2 (30) Shell werkgelegenheid naar nationaliteit 1926–70, accessed October 19, 2021, https://easy.dans.knaw.nl/ui/datasets/id/easy-dataset:49962.

121. Howarth and Jonker, *A History of the Royal Dutch Shell, Vol.* 2, 125, 128.

122. Quoted in Anne Coles and Anne–Meike Fechter, *Gender and Family Among Transnational Professionals* (Abingdon, UK: Routledge, 2008), 31.

123. Frantz Fanon, *The Wretched of the Earth*, trans. Constance Farrington (New York: Grove Press, 1963), 28.

124. On the simultaneity of decolonization and the rise of corporate culture, see Kristin Ross, *Fast Cars, Clean Bodies: Decolonization and the Reordering of French Culture* (Boston: MIT Press, 1995), chapter 4.

125. Peter Hitchcock, "Velocity and Viscosity," in *Subterranean Estates: Life Worlds of Oil and Gas*, ed. Hannah Appel, Arthur Mason, and Michael Watts (Ithaca, NY: Cornell University Press, 2015), 46.

126. Appel, *The Licit Life of Capitalism*, 125.

127. Frederick Cooper, "Possibility and Constraint: African Independence in Historical Perspective," *The Journal of African History* 49, no. 2 (2009): 175.

CHAPTER 2. DIMINISHING RETURNS

1. "A Problem of Two Professions," *Time*, June 18, 1951, BNA, DAC, Kostbare Collectie (#619), scrapbook.

2. Accusations of political domination and racial antipathy have threatened multi-island or binational political ties in places such as St. Kitts and Anguilla, Trinidad and Tobago, the West Indies Federation, and Haiti and the Dominican

Republic. See, for instance, Richard Lee Turits, "A World Destroyed, A Nation Imposed: The 1937 Haitian Massacre in the Dominican Republic," *Hispanic American Historical Review* 82, no. 3 (2002): 589–635; Learie B. Luke, *Identity and Secession in the Caribbean: Tobago versus Trinidad, 1889–1980* (Kingston: University of the West Indies Press, 2007).

3. Luc Alofs, "Onderhorigheid en separatisme: Koloniaal bestuur en lokale politiek op Aruba" (Ph.D. diss, Leiden University, 2011), 153.

4. This analysis builds on scholarship that has viewed prostitution as a fulcrum for nationalist politics. See Donna Guy, *Sex and Danger in Buenos Aires: Prostitution, Family, and Nation in Argentina* (Cambridge: Cambridge University Press, 1991); Katherine Elaine Bliss, *Compromised Positions: Prostitution, Public Health, and Gender Politics in Revolutionary Mexico City* (University Park: Penn State University Press, 2002); Tiffany Sippial, *Prostitution, Modernity, and the Making of the Cuban Republic, 1840–1920* (Chapel Hill: University of North Carolina Press, 2013).

5. On elite and popular organizing around principles of domesticity, see Elizabeth Manley, *The Paradox of Paternalism: Women and the Politics of Authoritarianism in the Dominican Republic* (Gainesville: University Press of Florida, 2017), chapter 2.

6. Bridget Brereton, "Family Strategies, Gender, and the Shift to Wage Labour in the British Caribbean," in *The Colonial Caribbean in Transition: Essays on Postemancipation Social and Cultural History*, ed. Bridget Brereton and Kevin A. Yelvington (Gainesville: University Press of Florida, 1999), 77–107; William French, "Prostitutes and Guardian Angels: Women, Work, and the Family in Porfirian Mexico," *The Hispanic American Historical Review* 72 (1992): 531.

7. Miguel Tinker Salas, *The Enduring Legacy: Oil, Culture, and Society in Venezuela* (Durham, NC: Duke University Press, 2009), 55.

8. *This is Lago*, 1949, UT, BCAH, EMHC, box 2.207/H20.

9. Luc Alofs, "'Een vlek of dorp die men nergens anders aantreft': Savaneta en de dorpsvorming op het negentiende-eeuwse Aruba," in *Arubaans Akkord*, ed. Luc Alofs, W. Rutgers, and H. E. Coomans (Bloemendaal and The Hague: Kabinet van de Gevolmachtigde Minister van Aruba, 1997), 9.

10. Alofs, "Onderhorigheid en separatisme," 141–42.

11. Wenzell Brown, *Angry Men—Laughing Men: The Caribbean Cauldron* (New York: Greenberg Publisher, 1947), 351–52.

12. Brown, *Angry Men—Laughing Men*, 351–52.

13. Alofs, "Onderhorigheid en separatisme," 151.

14. Brown, *Angry Men—Laughing Men*, 351–52.

15. David Roediger, *The Wages of Whiteness: Race and the Making of the American Working Class* (London: Verso, 2007 [1991]), 12.

16. *This is Lago*, 1949, UT, BCAH, EMHC, box 2.207/H20.

17. Scrapbook of William Miller, "The Arubian [sic] Blues," 1930, UT, BCAH, LCAC, box 2.207/M11. I thank Kody Jackson for drawing my attention to this source.

18. Report on complaints of Dutch laborers on Aruba, 1934, NAC, Gouvernementsarchief [1934] 1938–1945 [1951], inv. nr. 2634.

19. Meeting of Employees' General Advisory Committee with plant management, September 29, 1934, NAC, Gouvernementsarchief [1934] 1938–1945 [1951], inv. nr. 2634.

20. Report on complaints of Dutch laborers on Aruba, 1934, NAC, Gouvernementsarchief [1934] 1938–1945 [1951], inv. nr. 2634.

21. Meeting of Employees' General Advisory Committee with plant management, September 29, 1934, NAC, Gouvernementsarchief [1934] 1938–1945 [1951], inv. nr. 2634.

22. Tinker Salas, *The Enduring Legacy*, 146–48.

23. General notice, August 7, 1934, NAC, Gouvernementsarchief [1934] 1938–1945 [1951], inv. nr. 2634.

24. Dawn S. Bowen, "In the Shadow of the Refinery: An American Oil Company Town on the Caribbean Island of Aruba," *Journal of Cultural Geography* 36, no. 1 (2019): 55–57.

25. "Aruban Annals," 1943, UT, BCAH, LCAC, box 2.207/M7.

26. Ray H. Burson, interview by Shaun Illingworth, David Fulvio, and Greg Flynn, May 15, 2008, transcript, 3, Rutgers Oral History Archives, https://oralhistory.rutgers.edu/images/PDFs/burson_ray.pdf.

27. Diary of Charlotte Life Warden, August 17, 1947, UT, BCAH, LCAC, box 2.207/M12. Warden's husband worked for a subcontractor of Lago, which amplified their social distance from Colony residents.

28. Paula Aymer, *Uprooted Women: Migrant Domestics in the Caribbean* (Westport, CT: Praeger, 1997), 126.

29. Aymer, *Uprooted Women*, 53.

30. Diary of Charlotte Life Warden, September 4, 1947, UT, BCAH, LCAC, box 2.207/M12.

31. Nicole Bourbonnais, *Birth Control in the Decolonizing Caribbean: Reproductive Politics and Practice on Four Islands, 1930–1970* (Cambridge: Cambridge University Press, 2016), 139, 148–49.

32. Diary of Charlotte Life Warden, September 11, 1947, UT, BCAH, LCAC, box 2.207/M12.

33. Diary of Charlotte Life Warden, February 1, 1948, UT, BCAH, LCAC, box 2.207/M12.

34. Diary of Charlotte Life Warden, August 24, 1947, UT, BCAH, LCAC, box 2.207/M12.

35. Tinker Salas, *The Enduring Legacy*, 171.

36. "The Island of Aruba: Information of Interest to Prospective Employees and Visitors," ca. 1940, UT, BCAH, LCAC, box 2.207/M8.

37. Johan Hartog, *Aruba Past and Present: From the Time of the Indians until Today*, trans. J. A. Verleun (Oranjestad: D. J. de Wit, 1961), 373. The original Dutch version appears as Johan Hartog, *Aruba: Zoals het was, zoals het werd* (Aruba: Gebroeders de Wit, 1953).

38. Matthew T. Huber, *Lifeblood: Oil, Freedom, and the Forces of Capital* (Minneapolis: University of Minnesota Press, 2013), 64.

39. Diary of Charlotte Life Warden, September 3, 1947, UT, BCAH, LCAC, box 2.207/M12.

40. Police report, March 18, 1943, NAC, Gouvernementsarchief [1934] 1938–1945 [1951], inv. nr. 2634.

41. Lieut. governor of Aruba to attorney general on Curaçao, March 26, 1943, NAC, Gouvernementsarchief [1934] 1938–1945 [1951], inv. nr. 2634.

42. Peter James Hudson, *Bankers and Empire: How Wall Street Colonized the Caribbean* (Chicago: University of Chicago Press, 2017), 14–15, 135–36.

43. *Club Comment*, August 13, 1931, UT, BCAH, LCAC, box 2.207/M5; "News and Views," *Aruba Esso News*, March 26, 1953, 8; "Fiesta Rotaria Attracts Over 600," *Aruba Esso News*, July 2, 1955, 6.

44. "FIESTA ROTARIA trekt overweldigende belangstelling," *Amigoe di Curaçao*, June 6, 1955, 5.

45. Brown, *Angry Men—Laughing Men*, 349.

46. *This is Lago*, 1949, UT, BCAH, EMHC, box 2.207/H20.

47. In January 1942, German forces began Operation *Paukenschlag* and U-boats attacked the Arend and Lago refineries on Aruba and Curaçao's Shell refinery. Arend was a small refinery developed in 1927. It ceased refining and transshipment operations in 1951 and 1953 respectively, serving thereafter as a local sales office for Shell. Because of its limited operation, Arend does not feature in this study. On Nazi attacks in the Caribbean, see Esther Captain and Guno Jones, *Oorlogs erfgoed overzee. De erfenis van de tweede wereldoorlog van Aruba, Curaçao, Indonesië en Suriname* (Amsterdam: Bert Bakker, 2010), 49.

48. E. R. Braithwaite, *To Sir, with Love* (New York: Open Roads, 1959), 207.

49. On the committee's deliberations, see Kamala Kempadoo, *Sexing the Caribbean: Gender, Race and Sexual Labor* (New York: Routledge, 2004), 92.

50. Luc Alofs, "Publieke dames in een publiek debat: De geschiedenis van Campo Alegre op Aruba, 1950–1957," in *Cinco aña na caminda: Opstellen aangeboden ter gelegenheid van het eerste lustrum van de Universiteit van Aruba*, ed. G. F. M. Bossers, A. R. O. Ringeling, and M. Tratnik (Oranjestad: University of Aruba, 1993), 21.

51. Braithwaite, *To Sir, With Love*, 208–9.

52. Dutch consul to lieut. governor of Aruba, December 3, 1943, NA, Nederlandse Consulaat te Santo Domingo, 2.05.336, inv. nr. 104.

53. Second meeting of the Committee to Study Prostitution, July 13, 1951, ANA, BCAR, Bestrijding der Onzedelijkheid, inv. nr. 544, DS-606-6.

54. Police report, June 4, 1948, ANA, BCAR, Bestrijding der Onzedelijkheid, inv. nr. 1.764, DS-65-5. At the request of the archive, I use pseudonyms for individuals appearing in police reports.

55. Second meeting of the Committee to Study Prostitution, July 13, 1951, ANA, BCAR, Bestrijding der Onzedelijkheid, inv. nr. 544, DS-606-6.

56. Police report, September 7, 1945, ANA, BCAR, Bestrijding der Onzedelijkheid, inv. nr. 1.764, DS-65-5.

57. Report by Police Commissioner Hendrik Cornelis Willemsen, May 12, 1955, ANA, BCAR, Bestrijding der Onzedelijkheid, inv. nr. 544, DS-606-6.

58. Request for hotel license by José María Debrot, June 4, 1949, ANA, BCAR, Bestrijding der Onzedelijkheid, inv. nr. 347, DS-13468.

59. J. M. Debrot to Mr. Pauw, September 17, 1949, ANA, BCAR, Bestrijding der Onzedelijkheid, inv. nr. 347, DS-13468.

60. "Chong Hong overleden," *Amigoe di Curaçao* April 7, 1975, 5.

61. Marriages between Aruban women and Chinese men were not uncommon in the 1940s, when primarily Chinese men migrated to the Caribbean. See Florence Kalm, "The Dispersive and Reintegrating Nature of Population Segments of a Third World Society: Aruba, Netherlands Antilles" (Ph.D. diss, City University of New York, 1975), 136–37.

62. Correspondence to lieut. governor, March 12, 1951, ANA, BCAR, Bestrijding der Onzedelijkheid, inv. nr. 347, DS-13474.

63. Documents concerning the diss. of Tjeerd de Reus (c. 1966), p. 20, NA, Collectie 420 P. Muntendam, 2.21.218, inv. nr. 2.

64. "Aruba's vrouwen zeggen: Wij willen geen buitenlandse prostitue's," *Amigoe di Curaçao*, November 13, 1951, 5. Ellipses are in the original.

65. Correspondence to lieut. governor, March 12, 1951, ANA, BCAR, Bestrijding der Onzedelijkheid, inv. nr. 347, DS-13474.

66. Report by Police Commissioner Hendrik Cornelis Willemsen, May 12, 1955, ANA, BCAR, Bestrijding der Onzedelijkheid, inv. nr. 544, DS-606-6.

67. Statistics quoted in Second meeting of the Committee to Study Prostitution, July 13, 1951, ANA, BCAR, Bestrijding der Onzedelijkheid, inv. nr. 544, DS-606-6. The statement on the absence of Aruban prostitutes is found in Report by Police Commissioner Hendrik Cornelis Willemsen, May 12, 1955, ANA, BCAR, Bestrijding der Onzedelijkheid, inv. nr. 544, DS-606-6.

68. Third meeting of the Committee to Study Prostitution, July 26, 1951, ANA, BCAR, Bestrijding der Onzedelijkheid, inv. nr. 544, DS-606-6.

69. "Aruba's vrouwen zeggen: Wij willen geen buitenlandse prostitue's," *Amigoe di Curaçao*, November 13, 1951, 5.

70. Eileen Findlay, *Imposing Decency: The Politics of Sexuality and Race in Puerto Rico, 1870–1920* (Durham, NC: Duke University Press, 1999), 71–74.

71. *Chuchubi*, July 30, 1952, ANA, BCAR, Bestrijding der Onzedelijkheid, inv. nr. 347, DS-13477-10.

72. Alofs, "Onderhorigheid en separatisme," 256.

73. Documents submitted during the conference, February 5–March 8, 1948, NA, Ronde Tafel Conferentie West, 2.10.24, inv. nr. 74.

74. Alofs, "Onderhorigheid en separatisme," 30.

75. Willem Koot and Anco Ringeling, *De Antillianen* (Muiderberg: Dick Coutinho, 1984), 29.

76. Alofs, "Onderhorigheid en separatisme," 40–41, 47.

77. Luc Alofs and Leontine Merkies, *Ken ta Arubiano? Sociale integratie en natievorming op Aruba* (Leiden: KITLV Press, 1990), 102–3; Jorge R. Ridderstaat, *The Lago Story: The Compelling Story of an Oil Company on the Island of Aruba* (Oranjestad, Aruba: Editorial Charuba, 2007), 82.

78. Alofs, "Onderhorigheid en separatisme," 229.

79. Fernando Coronil, *The Magical State: Nature, Money, and Modernity in Venezuela* (Chicago: University of Chicago Press, 1997), 16.

80. On the West Indies Federation, see Spencer Mawby, *Ordering Independence: The End of Empire in the Anglophone Caribbean, 1947–1969* (Basingstoke: Palgrave Macmillan, 2012); Colin Palmer, *Eric Williams and the Making of the Modern Caribbean* (Chapel Hill: University of North Carolina Press, 2009); Eric D. Duke, *Building a Nation: Caribbean Federation in the Black Diaspora* (Gainesville: University Press of Florida, 2019). On the Mali Federation, see Frederick Cooper, "Possibility and Constraint: African Independence in Historical Perspective," *The Journal of African History* 49, no. 2 (2009): 167–96.

81. Lara Putnam, *Radical Moves: Caribbean Migrants and the Politics of Race in the Jazz Age* (Chapel Hill: University of North Carolina Press, 2013), 97. On the gendered politics of populist projects in Latin America and the Caribbean, see Karen Kampwirth, ed., *Gender and Populism in Latin America: Passionate Politics* (University Park: Penn State University Press, 2010); Lauren Derby, *The Dictator's Seduction: Politics and the Popular Imagination in the Era of Trujillo* (Durham, NC: Duke University Press, 2004), especially chapters 3 and 5.

82. Adom Getachew, *Worldmaking after Empire: The Rise and Fall of Self-Determination* (Princeton, NJ: Princeton University Press, 2019), 141.

83. Gert Oostindie and Inge Klinkers, *Knellende Koninkrijksbanden. Het Nederlandse dekolonisatiebeleid in de Caraïben, 1940–2000* (Amsterdam: Amsterdam University Press, 2001), 116–17.

84. "KONINKLIJK BESLUIT van 3 Maart 1951, houdende de eilandenregeling Nederlandse Antillen," Overheid.nl, accessed March, 16, 2015, http://decentrale.regelgeving.overheid.nl/cvdr/XHTMLoutput/Historie/Nederlandse%20Antillen/7402/7402_1.html.

85. Oostindie and Klinkers, *Knellende Koninkrijksbanden*, 117–19.

86. National Decree, May 16, 1951, ANA, BCAR, Bestrijding der Onzedelijkheid, inv. nr. 347, DS-13468.

87. Telegram from Clarita Villalba and Marianita Chong to the governor of the Netherlands Antilles, May 30, 1951, BNA, DAC, Kostbare Collectie (#619), scrapbook.

88. Telegram from Clarita Villalba and Marianita Chong to Queen Juliana of the Netherlands, May 30, 1951, BNA, DAC, Kostbare Collectie (#619), scrapbook.

89. "Nog een overpeinzing over het Campo Alegre op Aruba," *Amigoe di Curaçao*, June 1, 1951, 3.

90. "Voorzetting Statenvergadering over Campo Alegre," *Amigoe di Curaçao*, June 2, 1951, 1.

91. "Nog een overpeinzing over het Campo Alegre op Aruba," *Amigoe di Curaçao*, June 1, 1951, 3.

92. "Politieke Overpeinzing," *Amigoe di Curaçao*, May 29, 1951, 3.

93. "Landsminister W. Lampe legt verklaring af inzake Campo Alegre," *Beurs- en Nieuwsberichten*, June 25, 1951.

94. "Bij Aruba begint de Victorie," *Amigoe di Curaçao*, June 20, 1951, 1.

95. "Het nieuws van vandaag," *Amigoe di Curaçao*, June 21, 1951, 1.

96. "Landsminister W. Lampe legt verklaring af inzake Campo Alegre," *Beurs- en Nieuwsberichten*, June 25, 1951.

97. "HBF Contracts Signed," *Aruba Esso News*, June 22, 1951, 1 and 7, https://dloc.com/CA03400001/00316. Alofs and Merkies, *Ken ta Arubiano?*, 103–4; Hartog, *Aruba, Past and Present*, 313.

98. *Aruba Esso News*, June 8, 1951, 4, https://dloc.com/CA03400001/00315.

99. Lago Training School Graduation Program, May 2, 1947, UT, BCAH, LCAC, box 2.207/M71.

100. Coronil, *The Magical State*, 107; Hartog, *Aruba, Past and Present*, 435. On the assertion of sovereign rights over natural resources, see Christopher Dietrich, *Oil Revolution: Anticolonial Elites, Sovereign Rights, and the Economic Culture of Decolonization* (Cambridge: Cambridge University Press, 2017).

101. Jaap van Soest, *Olie als water. De Curaçaose economie in de eerste helft van de twintigste eeuw* (Zutphen: De Walburg Pers, 1977 [1976]), 513.

102. "Lago Milestones (1924-1985)," *Aruba Esso News*, March 1985, 6, https://ufdc.ufl.edu/CA03400001/00205; Ridderstaat, *The Lago Story*, 97–98.

103. Employee Statistics, December 31, 1934–December 31, 1977, UT, BCAH, EMHC, box 2.207/H20.

104. Employee and Community Interests of Lago, 1952, UT, BCAH, EMHC, box 2.207/H20.

105. Charles P. do Rego, *The Portuguese Immigrant in Curaçao: Immigration, Participation, and Integration in the 20th Century* (Willemstad: Carib-Publishing, 2012), 115; Vera Green, *Migrants in Aruba: Interethnic Integration* (Assen: Van Gorcum, 1974), 29.

106. Papiamento is a creole language spoken by the majority of people on Aruba, while Papiamentu is spoken throughout Curaçao and Bonaire. The languages are mutually intelligible but have a separate orthography.

107. Protest poster, n.d., BNA, DAC, Kostbare Collectie (#619), scrapbook.

108. "Aruba: Verstoord gezins-geluk," *Amigoe di Curaçao*, May 17, 1957. Didactic accounts such as this often appeared in newspapers and novels on Curaçao and Aruba to accessibly communicate Catholic moral teachings. See Rose Mary Allen, *Di ki manera? A Social History of Afro-Curaçaoans, 1863–1917* (Amsterdam: SWP, 2007), 161.

109. "Carta abierta a las damas de Aruba," *Arubaanse Courant*, n.d., n.p.

110. "Arubaanse Kroniek," *Beurs- en Nieuwsberichten*, November 13, 1951, 4, BNA, DAC, Kostbare Collectie (#619), scrapbook.

111. First meeting of the Committee to Study Prostitution, July 4, 1951, ANA, BCAR, Bestrijding der Onzedelijkheid, inv. nr. 544, DS-606-6.

112. Interview with Dr. Maximiliaan Rudolf Willem Berkenveld, July 26, 1951, ANA, BCAR, Bestrijding der Onzedelijkheid, inv. nr. 544, DS-606-6.

113. See "Strike Over August 15," *Aruba Esso News*, August 24, 1951, 1-3, ANA, BCAR, Lago werkstaking, inv. nr. 527; Ridderstaat, *The Lago Story*, 87–89.

114. July 2, 1951; August 6, 1951; September 25, 1951, ANA, BCAR, Eilandsraad Notulen.

115. Curaçao also received the preponderance of seats in the Staten. Of the twenty-two seats in the Antillean parliament, voters on Curaçao elected twelve. In a major defeat to Aruban nationalist parties who desired parity, Aruban voters elected eight. The remaining two seats were chosen by Bonaire and by St. Maarten, St. Eustatius, and Saba collectively.

116. Attachments, Notes of the Island Council of Aruba, November 12, 1955, ANA, BCAR, Bestrijding der Onzedelijkheid, inv. nr. 1.764, DS-65-10.

117. Acting lieut. governor of Aruba to the minister of justice of the Netherlands Antilles, n.d., ANA, BCAR, Bestrijding der Onzedelijkheid, inv. nr. 1.764, DS-65-10. One researcher in 1969, however, observed a striking rapprochement. It appeared that some Aruban women valued foreign sex workers for the sexual outlet they provided men, which allowed wives to limit pregnancies without use of contraceptives. Because many (though not all) sex workers eventually left the island, Aruban women worried less about their spouses developing lasting relationships. See Florence Kalm, "The Two Faces of Antillean Prostitution," *Archives of Sexual Behavior* 14, no. 3 (1985): 213.

118. Report by the Children and Vice Squad, July 23, 1960; Attachments, Notes of the Island Council of Aruba, November 12, 1955, ANA, BCAR, Bestrijding der Onzedelijkheid, inv. nr. 1.764, DS-65-10.

CHAPTER 3. MANUFACTURING SURPLUS

1. Eva Abraham-van der Mark, "Continuity and Change in the Afro-Caribbean Family in Curaçao in the Twentieth Century," *Community, Work & Family* 6, no. 1 (2003): 83; William Anderson and Russell Dynes, *Social Movements,*

Violence, and Change: The May Movement in Curaçao (Columbus: Ohio State University Press, 1975), 55.

2. Scripts of Five Consecutive Radio Programmes of the Foundation for the Promotion of Responsible Parenthood, Program 4 [in English], NA, KabSNA, 2.10.41, inv. nr. 553.

3. Eva Abraham-van der Mark, *Yu'i Mama. Enkele facetten van gezinsstructuur op Curaçao* (Assen: Van Gorcum, 1972), 15.

4. Fernando Coronil, *The Magical State: Nature, Money, and Modernity in Venezuela* (Chicago: University of Chicago Press, 1997), 107; Stephen Howarth and Joost Jonker, *A History of Royal Dutch Shell, Vol. 2: Powering the Hydrocarbon Revolution, 1939–1973* (New York: Oxford University Press, 2007), 40–41.

5. Brian Hayes, "Automation on the Job," *American Scientist* 97, no. 1 (2009): 10.

6. Bonham C. Richardson, *The Caribbean in the Wider World, 1492–1992* (Cambridge: Cambridge University Press, 1992), 116.

7. David S. Painter, "The Marshall Plan and Oil," *Cold War History* 9, no. 2 (2009): 164, 167–68.

8. Howarth and Jonker, *A History of the Royal Dutch Shell, Vol. 2*, 263–65.

9. For a similar argument, see Raúl Necochea López, "Priests and Pills: Catholic Family Planning in Peru, 1967–1976," *Latin American Research Review* 43, no. 2 (2008): 34–56; Alana Harris, ed., *The Schism of '68: Catholicism, Contraception and Humanae Vitae in Europe, 1945–1975* (Cham: Palgrave Macmillan, 2018); Agata Ignaciuk and Laura Kelly, "Contraception and Catholicism in the Twentieth Century: Transnational Perspectives on Expert, Activist, and Intimate Practices," *Medical History* 64, no. 2 (2020): 163–72.

10. The plummeting price of sugar and other agricultural exports impacted economic prospects throughout the region. See O. Nigel Bolland, "Labor Protests, Rebellions, and the Rise of Nationalism during Depression and War," in *The Caribbean: A History of the Region and its Peoples*, ed. Stephan Palmié and Francisco A. Scarano (Chicago: University of Chicago Press, 2011), 463–64.

11. Deborah Thomas, "The Violence of Diaspora: Governmentality, Class Cultures, and Circulations," *Radical History Review* 103 (2009): 94.

12. Nicole Bourbonnais, *Birth Control in the Decolonizing Caribbean: Reproductive Politics and Practice on Four Islands, 1930–1970* (Cambridge: Cambridge University Press, 2016), 82.

13. Quoted in Charles Taussig, "A Four Power Program in the Caribbean," *Foreign Affairs* 24, no. 4 (1946): 701.

14. Frederick Cooper, "Writing the History of Development," *Journal of Modern European History* 8, no. 1 (2010): 9–12; Sara Lorenzini, *Development: A Cold War History* (Princeton, NJ: Princeton University Press, 2019), 9; Marc Matera, "An Empire of Development: Africa and the Caribbean in *God's Chillun*," *Twentieth Century British History* 23, no. 1 (2012): 17.

15. Paul Ehrlich, *The Population Bomb* (New York: Ballantine Books, 1968). The US author and founder of the Dixie Cup Corporation, Hugh Moore, coined the term in a popular 1954 pamphlet of the same title (Bourbonnais, *Birth Control in the Decolonizing Caribbean*, 174).

16. Matthew Connelly, *Fatal Misconception: The Struggle to Control World Population* (Cambridge: The Belknap Press of Harvard University Press, 2008), 121.

17. Abraham-van der Mark, "Continuity and Change," 83.

18. Governor Struycken to H. C. W. Moorman, August 12, 1953, NA, Collectie 417 Struycken, 2.21.217, inv. nr. 3.

19. Jaap van Soest, *Olie als water. De Curaçaose economie in de eerste helft van de twintigste eeuw* (Zutphen: De Walburg Pers, 1977 [1976]), 515.

20. Documented Paper on the Netherlands Antilles for the Conference on Demographic Problems of the Area Served by the Caribbean Commission, Port of Spain, Trinidad (July/August 1957), 25, UBL, KITLV Collection.

21. Jason Smith, *Smart Machines and Service Work: Automation in an Age of Stagnation* (London: Reaktion Books, 2020), 24–26.

22. Hayes, "Automation on the Job," 10.

23. van Soest, *Olie als water*, 514–16.

24. Anderson and Dynes, *Social Movements, Violence, and Change*, 55; Peter Verton, *Politieke dynamiek en dekolonisatie. De Nederlandse Antillen tussen autonomie en onafhankelijkheid* (Alphen aan den Rijn: Samsom, 1977), 61.

25. Anderson and Dynes, *Social Movements, Violence, and Change*, 55.

26. Documented Paper on the Netherlands Antilles, 43a.

27. Documented Paper on the Netherlands Antilles, 1–2.

28. Documented Paper on the Netherlands Antilles, 43a.

29. Documented Paper on the Netherlands Antilles, 43b.

30. Quoted in J. H. Westermann, "Demografische conferentie van de Caribische commissie, Trinidad, 1957," *Nieuw West Indische Gids* 38, no. 1 (1958): 142.

31. Bourbonnais, *Birth Control in the Decolonizing Caribbean*, 94–96, 173–74.

32. Documented Paper on the Netherlands Antilles, 47a.

33. Westermann, "Demografische conferentie," 133.

34. On the religious commitments of de la Try Ellis, see Margo Groenewoud, "'Nou koest, nou kalm.' De ontwikkeling van de Curaçaose samenleving, 1915–1973: Van koloniaal en kerkelijk gezag naar zelfbestuur en burgerschap" (Ph.D. diss, Leiden University, 2017), 116–17, 170–71.

35. Documented Paper on the Netherlands Antilles, Addendum V, 5.

36. Documented Paper on the Netherlands Antilles, 12.

37. Documented Paper on the Netherlands Antilles, 4. The report noted the decrease in "illegitimate" births that reached its lowest point when Shell implemented social programs in 1950 but did not connect these changes to industry practices (p. 16).

38. Chapter 5 explores these debates in greather depth. For an overview in the Caribbean context, see Christine Barrow, *Family in the Caribbean: Themes and Perspectives* (Kingston: Ian Randle Publishers, 1996), chapter 1.

39. Groenewoud, "'Nou koest, nou kalm,'" 16.

40. Dominican supervision remained in place from the creation of the Catholic mission in 1870 to 1973. During this period, no more than eight men of Netherlands Antillean origin were appointed as priests. The majority were sent from the Netherlands (Groenewoud, "'Nou koest, nou kalm,'" 28–30).

41. Rose Mary Allen, *Di ki manera? A Social History of Afro-Curaçaoans, 1863–1917* (Amsterdam: SWP, 2007), 158.

42. Jeannette van Ditzhuijzen, *Anyway . . . Sergio Leon, vrouwenarts en eilandskind* (Utrecht: LM Publishers, 2015), 47.

43. Marit Monteiro, *Gods predikers: Dominicanen in Nederland (1795–2000)* (Hilversum: Verloren, 2008), 561; Groenewoud, "'Nou koest, nou kalm,'" 176.

44. Monteiro, *Gods predikers*, 563.

45. Monteiro, *Gods predikers*, 274.

46. van der Marck to Provincial Father, June 30, 1959, 2, ENK, NPOD. I thank Margo Groenewoud for drawing my attention to these sources.

47. Report regarding the situation of the Dominicans in the Antilles, September 23, 1959, 1, ENK, NPOD.

48. van der Marck to Provincial Father, June 30, 1959, 2, ENK, NPOD. Emphasis in original.

49. Report on living situation in the Antilles, July 21, 1959, 8, ENK, NPOD.

50. This argument was reinforced in early sociological and anthropological studies of Afro-Curaçaoan kinship and receives extended treatment in chapter 5. See for example, Harry Hoetink, *Het patroon van de oude Curaçaose samenleving. Een sociologische studie* (Assen: Van Gorcum, 1958), 119–20.

51. Report on living situation in the Antilles, July 21, 1959, 8, ENK, NPOD. At this time, the term *geboorteregeling* could include so-called artificial means of contraception as well as periodic abstinence. It is unclear how van der Marck defined acceptable forms of birth control.

52. Wannes Dupont, "The Case for Contraception: Medicine, Morality, and Sexology at the Catholic University of Leuven (1930–1968)," *Histoire, médecine et santé* (2018): 55.

53. Chris Dols and Maarten van den Bos, "*Humanae Vitae*: Catholic Attitudes to Birth Control in the Netherlands and Transnational Church Politics, 1945–1975" in *The Schism of '68: Catholicism, Contraception and Humanae Vitae in Europe, 1945–1975*, ed. Alana Harris (Cham: Palgrave Macmillan, 2018), 24, 29.

54. Commentary on report by Lankveld, November 15, 1959, 1–2, ENK, NPOD.

55. Ditzhuijzen, *Anyway*, 79–80. This was not the only family planning initiative to have begun at Shell. An employee of Shell Oil in Trinidad opened the

island's first birth control clinic in 1956 (Bourbonnais, *Birth Control in the Decolonizing Caribbean*, 128).

56. Abraham-van der Mark, *Yu'i Mama*, 15.

57. Ditzhuijzen, *Anyway*, 79–80.

58. Quoted in Minister plenipotentiary of the Netherlands Antilles to deputy prime minister, April 1, 1968, NA, KabSNA, 2.10.41, inv. nr. 553.

59. In 1958, the apostolic vicariate of Willemstad was promoted in status and officially recognized as the Diocese of Willemstad (Groenewoud, "'Nou koest, nou kalm,'" 30). See Television program, "The Encyclical Letter and Family Planning," November 11, 1968 [in English], NA, KabSNA, 2.10.41, inv. nr. 553; van Ditzhuijzen, *Anyway*, 83–84. On the role of credit unions as a form of lay Catholic social work, see Monteiro, *Gods predikers*, 569; Groenewoud, "'Nou koest, nou kalm,'" 183–84.

60. General report of the foundation during the period Oct. 1, 1965–April 1, 1967, April 21, 1967; Annual report for the period April 1, 1968–April 1, 1969, April 17, 1969, NA, KabSNA, 2.10.41, inv. nr. 553.

61. Construction plan for a health center in Aruba, 1974–1975, NA, KabSNA, 2.10.41, inv. nr. 415.

62. Rotary Club of Aruba, October 6, 1958, UT, BCAH, LCAC, box 2.207/M5.

63. Florence Kalm, "The Dispersive and Reintegrating Nature of Population Segments of a Third World Society: Aruba, Netherlands Antilles" (Ph.D. diss, City University of New York, 1975), 225.

64. Paula Aymer, *Uprooted Women: Migrant Domestics in the Caribbean* (Westport, CT: Praeger, 1997), 111.

65. Kalm, "The Dispersive and Reintegrative Nature of Population Segments of a Third World Society," 226.

66. Maarten Kuitenbrouwer, *Dutch Scholarship in the Age of Empire and Beyond: KITLV—the Royal Netherlands Institute of Southeast Asian and Caribbean Studies, 1851–2011*, trans. Lorri Granger (Leiden: Brill, 2014), 177–79.

67. Gert Oostindie and Inge Klinkers, *Decolonising the Caribbean: Dutch Policies in Comparative Perspective* (Amsterdam: Amsterdam University Press, 2003), 158.

68. Minister plenipotentiary of the Netherlands Antilles to deputy prime minister, August 28, 1969; Minister of finances to deputy prime minister, September 8, 1969, NA, KabSNA, 2.10.41, inv. nr. 553.

69. Interdepartmental Workgroup on the Reception of Surinamese and Antilleans, 1967–1972; Mr. W. Duk on entry of Surinamese and Antilleans, January 2, 1963, NA, KabSNA, 2.10.41, inv nr, 1012.

70. Request of financial assistance for outpatient clinics in Suriname and Curaçao, 1971–1973, NA, KabSNA, 2.10.41, inv. nr. 412.

71. NVSH press release, October 2, 1967, IISG, NVSH.

72. These laws were based, respectively, on Articles 240bis, 451ter, and 251bis in the Dutch criminal code. On the introduction of anti-vice legislation in the Netherlands, see Chelsea Schields, "'Combatting the Sensuality of the Youth':

Youthful Sexuality and the Reformulation of Desire in the Dutch Vice Laws of 1911," *Gender & History* 31 (2019): 115–31.

73. Article 251bis, which criminalized abortion, was repealed in the Netherlands in 1980. For at least a decade prior to the decriminalization of abortion, many women had been able to undergo the procedure without tremendous fear of repercussion. See Henny Brandhorst, "From Neo-Malthusianism to Sexual Reform: The Dutch Section of the World League for Sexual Reform," *Journal of the History of Sexuality* 12 (2003): 38–67.

74. Minutes of the Staten of the Netherlands Antilles, 1967–68, Attachments, UBL, KIT Collection.

75. Abraham-van der Mark, "Continuity and Change," 82.

76. General report of the foundation during the period Oct. 1, 1965–April 1, 1967, April 21, 1967, NA, KabSNA, 2.10.41, inv. nr. 553.

77. Ditzhuijzen, *Anyway*, 86.

78. Scripts of Five Consecutive Radio Programmes of the Foundation for the Promotion of Responsible Parenthood [in English], NA, KabSNA, 2.10.41, inv. nr. 553.

79. Radio program, "Who is MY FATHER?????" [in English], NA, KabSNA, 2.10.41, inv. nr. 553.

80. Scripts of Seven Consecutive Television Programs of the Foundation for the Promotion of Responsible Parenthood, "Build a dam and wait for the rain," October 3, 1968 [in English], NA, KabSNA, 2.10.41, inv. nr. 553.

81. Scripts of Five Consecutive Radio Programmes of the Foundation for the Promotion of Responsible Parenthood [in English], Credit Union (3), NA, KabSNA, 2.10.41, inv. nr. 553.

82. Television program, "Mommy, Who is My Daddy" [in English], NA, KabSNA, 2.10.41, inv. nr. 553. The second two sets of ellipses are in the original.

83. Eva Abraham-van der Mark, "The Impact of Industrialization on Women: A Caribbean Case," in *Women, Men, and the International Division of Labor*, ed. June Nash and María P. Fernández-Kelly (Albany: SUNY Press, 1983), 380–81.

84. Michelle Murphy, *The Economization of Life* (Durham, NC: Duke University Press, 2017), 3–6, 12–13.

85. The term "single parent" referred to parents who raised children out of wedlock. But as Jeanne Henriquez notes, the term occludes the wider familial and intimate relations that participate in childrearing. See "Motherhood is a State of Mind: Testimonies of Single Curaçaoan Mothers," in *Mundu Yama Sinta Mira: Womanhood in Curaçao*, ed. Richenel Ansano, Joceline Clemencia, Jeanette Cook, and Eithel Martis (Willemstad: Fundashon Publikashon Curaçao, 1992), 90–92.

86. Rickie Solinger and Mie Nakachi, "Introduction," in *Reproductive States: Global Perspectives on the Invention and Implementation of Population Policy*, ed. Rickie Solinger and Mie Nakachi (Oxford: Oxford University Press, 2016), 4.

87. Dithuijzen, *Anyway*, 91.

88. Iris López, *Matters of Choice: Puerto Rican Women's Struggle for Reproductive Freedom* (New Brunswick, NJ: Rutgers University Press, 2008), 49–50.

89. Dithuijzen, *Anyway*, 95.

90. Television program, "Do You Wish to Put a Question?," November 4, 1968 [in English], NA, KabSNA, 2.10.41, inv. nr. 553.

91. Quoted in Dithuijzen, *Anyway*, 97. Ellipses in original.

92. Survey of Visits to the Family Planning Centers of the Foundation for the Promotion of Responsible Parenthood in the Year 1970, NA, KabSNA, 2.10.41, inv. nr. 553.

93. Dithuijzen, *Anyway*, 92.

94. Rebecca Kluchin, *Fit to be Tied: Sterilization and Reproductive Rights in America* (New Brunswick: Rutgers University Press, 2009), 90–94; Emma Tarlo, *Unsettling Memories: Narratives of the Emergency in Delhi* (Berkeley: University of California Press, 2003).

95. Bourbonnais, *Birth Control in the Decolonizing Caribbean*, 168–70; Laura Briggs, *Reproducing Empire: Race, Sex, Science, and U.S. Imperialism in Puerto Rico* (Berkeley: University of California Press, 2003), 156–58; López, *Matters of Choice*, 59.

96. Raúl Necochea López, *A History of Family Planning in Twentieth-Century Peru* (Chapel Hill: University of North Carolina Press, 2014), 89; Joanna Schoen, *Choice and Coercion: Birth Control, Sterilization, and Abortion in Public Health and Welfare* (Chapel Hill: University of North Carolina Press, 2005), 163.

97. López, *Matters of Choice*, xii–xix.

98. Famía Planiá's survey of visits in 1970—the only record of this kind that I have found—records six sterilization procedures that year. Survey of Visits to the Family Planning Centers of the Foundation for the Promotion of Responsible Parenthood in the Year 1970, NA, KabSNA, 2.10.41, inv. nr. 553.

99. Sonia Corrêa, "Reproductive Rights in Developing Nations," in *International Encyclopedia of the Social & Behavioral Sciences*, ed. Neil J. Smelser and Paul B. Baltes (Oxford: Pergamon, 2001), 13191.

100. Dorothy Roberts, *Killing the Black Body: Race, Reproduction, and the Meaning of Liberty* (New York: Vintage, 2017 [1997]), 21.

101. Ditzhuijzen, *Anyway*, 83.

102. Annette B. Ramírez de Arellano and Conrad Seipp, *Colonialism, Catholicism, and Contraception: A History of Birth Control in Puerto Rico* (Chapel Hill: University of North Carolina Press, 1983), ix. "Aggiornamento," a key term often invoked at and after the Second Vatican Council, is hard to translate but is usually given as "opening" or "updating" in English.

103. Wannes Dupont, "Of Human Love: Catholics Campaigning for Sexual Aggiornamento in Postwar Belgium," in *The Schism of '68: Catholicism, Contraception and Humanae Vitae in Europe, 1945-1975*, ed. Alana Harris (Cham: Palgrave Macmillan, 2018), 54–59.

104. Television program, "Do You Wish to Put a Question?," October 28, 1968 [in English], NA, KabSNA, 2.10.41, inv. nr. 553.

105. Television program, "The Encyclical Letter and Family Planning," November 11, 1968 [in English], NA, KabSNA, 2.10.41, inv. nr. 553.

106. Pamphlet, Katholiek Nationaal Bureau voor Geestelijke Gezondheidszorg, Utrecht, NA, KabSNA, 2.10.41, inv. nr. 553.

107. "INGEZONDEN Antwoord op vragen aan A. R.," *Amigoe di Curaçao,* January 17, 1972.

108. Not all progressive Catholics opposed family planning; in fact, liberation theology—with its focus on the experiences of marginalized communities—also opened new spiritual arguments for the use of contraception. In Peru and Colombia, for example, Catholics spearheaded family planning campaigns. See Mary Roldán, "Acción Cultural Popular, Responsible Procreation, and the Roots of Social Activism in Rural Colombia," *Latin American Research Review* 49 (2014): 28–29; Necochea López, "Priests and Pills," 37.

109. Groenewoud, "'Nou koest, nou kalm,'" 144.

110. Radio program, "Who is My Daddy?," October 21, 1968 [in English], NA, KabSNA, 2.10.41, inv. nr. 553.

111. Radio program, "Who is MY FATHER?????" [in English], NA, KabSNA, 2.10.41, inv. nr. 553.

112. Television program, "The Encyclical Letter and Family Planning," November 11, 1968 [in English], NA, KabSNA, 2.10.41, inv. nr. 553.

113. Abraham-van der Mark, *Yu'i Mama,* 23.

114. Ditzhuijzen, *Anyway,* 88. In 2012, the Curaçaoan government approved a paternity law. Leon criticized the efficacy of the law given that birth mothers needed to record the biological father's name in court and not at the time of birth, as is increasingly common in some Latin American countries. See Nara Milanich, "Daddy Issues: 'Responsible Paternity' as Public Policy in Latin America," *World Policy Institute* XXXIV, no. 3 (2017): 8–14.

115. Program One, August 14, 1968 [in English], NA, KabSNA, 2.10.41, inv. nr. 553.

116. "Curaçao [sic] scores TV and Radio Success," International Planned Parenthood Federation, February 1969, NA, KabSNA, 2.10.41, inv. nr. 553.

117. René Römer, *Een volk op weg, un pueblo na kaminda. Een sociologische studie van de Curaçaose samenleving* (Zutphen: De Walburg Pers, 1979), 111.

118. Carla Freeman, *Entrepreneurial Selves: Neoliberal Respectability and the Making of a Caribbean Middle Class* (Durham, NC: Duke University Press, 2014), 58.

CHAPTER 4. "SEXUALITY, YES! SLAVERY, NO!"

1. On January 1, 1967 Shell Curaçao assumed responsibility for sales and distribution previously overseen by CPIM.

2. Margo Groenewoud, "'Nou koest, nou kalm.' De ontwikkeling van de Curaçaose samenleving, 1915–1973: Van koloniaal en kerkelijk gezag naar zelfbestuur en burgerschap" (Ph.D. diss, Leiden University, 2017), 192; Gert Oostindie, "Black Power, Popular Revolt, and Decolonization in the Dutch Caribbean," in *Black Power in the Caribbean*, ed. Kate Quinn (Gainesville: University Press of Florida, 2014), 245.

3. Quoted in William Anderson and Russell Dynes, *Social Movements, Violence, and Change: The May Movement in Curaçao* (Columbus: Ohio State University Press, 1975), 82.

4. There are several book-length studies of May 30, 1969. In *Social Movements, Violence, and Change*, the US socialist scientists William Anderson and Russell Dynes analyzed May 30 through the lens of social movement theory, identifying different phases of the May Movement from its foundations in labor activism through to the "riot" and the "political phase" that manifested in concrete political demands. Gert Oostindie has emphasized the economic, (local) political, and social causes of the unrest and argued that the majority of people in the streets on May 30 lacked a concrete political program in "Woedend vuur: 'Trinta di mei,' dertig jaar later," in *Dromen en littekens. Dertig jaar na de Curaçaose revolte, 30 mei 1969*, ed. Gert Oostindie (Amsterdam: Amsterdam University Press, 1999), 13–20, 24–25. On the perspectives of participants and eyewitnesses, see Gert Oostindie, ed., *Curaçao, 30 mei 1969. Verhalen over de revolte* (Amsterdam: Amsterdam University Press, 1999).

5. Aisha Leer, "Muhé na Kandela (Women on Fire): Women's Role in the Revolt of 'Trinta di Mei,' 1969," paper presented at the Association of Caribbean Historians, Curaçao, May 26–30, 2019. On the overrepresentation of men, see Gert Oostindie, "De sprekers en hun verhalen," in *Curaçao, 30 mei 1969. Verhalen over de revolte*, ed. Gert Oostindie (Amsterdam: Amsterdam University Press, 1999), 8; Anderson and Dynes, *Social Movements, Violence, and Change*, 80. On women's radicalization, see Jeanne Henriquez, "'Black is Beautiful' is voor vrouwen heel belangrijk geweest," in *Curaçao, 30 mei 1969. Verhalen over de revolte*, ed. Gert Oostindie (Amsterdam: Amsterdam University Press, 1999), 45–47.

6. Rachel Hynson, "'Count, Capture, and Reeducate': The Campaign to Rehabilitate Cuba's Female Sex Workers, 1959–1966," *Journal of the History of Sexuality* 24, no. 1 (2015): 151.

7. Anne Macpherson, *From Colony to Nation: Women Activists and the Gendering of Politics in Belize, 1912–1982* (Lincoln: University of Nebraska Press, 2007), 257.

8. Todd Shepard, *Sex, France, and Arab Men, 1962–1978* (Chicago: University of Chicago Press, 2017), 16.

9. Christopher J. Lee, "Between a Movement and an Era: The Origins and Afterlives of Bandung," in *Making a World after Empire: The Bandung Moment*

and its Political Afterlives, ed. Christopher J. Lee (Athens: Ohio University Press, 2010), 25–26.

10. Another individual who occupied the role of prime minister, Moises Frumencio da Costa Gomez, was not routinely racialized as Afro-Curaçaoan because of his Jewish heritage.

11. Oostindie, "Woedend vuur," 30, 32.

12. Aruban officials also feared that Black Caribbean workers at the Lago refinery would follow suit and revolt. See Luc Alofs, "Revolte en afscheiding: Dertig mei en Aruba," in *Dromen en littekens. Dertig jaar na de Curaçaose revolte, 30 mei 1969*, ed. Gert Oostindie (Amsterdam: Amsterdam University Press, 1999), 163–76; Rosemarijn Hoefte, "The Difficulty of Getting it Right: Dutch Policy in the Caribbean," *Itinerario* 25, no. 2 (2001): 65.

13. Peter Verton, *Politieke dynamiek en dekolonisatie. De Nederlandse Antillen tussen autonomie en onafhankelijkheid* (Alphen aan den Rijn: Samsom, 1977), 63.

14. Verton, *Politieke dynamiek en dekolonisatie*, 68–69.

15. Hannah Appel, *The Licit Life of Capitalism: US Oil in Equatorial Guinea* (Durham, NC: Duke University Press, 2019), 181.

16. David Kinley and Michele Salkin, "The Caribbean Export Refining Center," *NACLA's Latin America and Empire Report* 10, no. 8 (1976): 7.

17. Verton, *Politieke dynamiek en dekolonisatie*, 63.

18. Jon Kutner, "Schlumberger," *Texas State Historical Association: Handbook of Texas*, accessed February 18, 2022, https://www.tshaonline.org/handbook/entries/schlumberger.

19. Tijn van Beurden and Joost Jonker, "A Perfect Symbiosis: Curaçao, the Netherlands and Financial Offshore Services, 1951–2003," *Financial History Review* 28, no. 1 (2021): 77.

20. Employment in the offshore sector peaked in the 1980s and was likely to have been smaller in the 1960s; see van Beurden and Jonker, "A Perfect Symbiosis," 80.

21. René Römer, "Labour Unions and Labour Conflict in Curaçao," *New West Indian Guide* 55, no. 3/4 (1981): 146.

22. Anderson and Dynes, *Social Movements, Violence, and Change*, 36–37.

23. Römer, "Labour Unions and Labour Conflict in Curaçao," 145.

24. Verton, *Politieke dynamiek en dekolonisatie*, 54; Anderson and Dynes, *Social Movements, Violence, and Change*, 37.

25. Anderson and Dynes, *Social Movements, Violence, and Change*, 59.

26. Quoted in Rose Mary Allen, "The Trinta di Mei Labor Revolt and Its Aftermath: Anticipating a Just and Equitable Curaçaoan Nation," in *Equaliberty in the Dutch Caribbean: Ways of Being Non/Sovereign*, ed. Yvon van der Pijl and Francio Guadeloupe (Newark, NJ: Rutgers University Press, 2022), 72. A similar pattern prevailed among return migrants in Suriname; see Rosemarijn Hoefte,

Suriname in the Long Twentieth Century: Domination, Contestation, Globalization (Basingstoke: Palgrave Macmillan, 2014), 71–72.

27. Anderson and Dynes, *Social Movements, Violence, and Change*, 71–73.

28. "Openingsrede," *Amigoe di Curaçao*, May 16, 1925, 1; "Recruiting workers from the territory Curaçao," 1936, NAC, Gouvernementsarchief [1934] 1938-1945 [1951], inv. nr. 2648.

29. René Römer, "Ik had nooit gedacht dat ons volk tot zo'n opstand in staat was," in *Curaçao, 30 mei 1969. Verhalen over de revolte*, ed. Gert Oostindie (Amsterdam: Amsterdam University Press, 1999), 110.

30. Rose Mary Allen, "Amador Paulo Nita: Writer, Labor Activist, and Politician," *Oxford African American Studies Center Database*, last modified May 31, 2017, https://doi.org/10.1093/acref/9780195301731.013.74671; Joceline Clemencia, "Katibu ta galiña: From Hidden to Open Protest in Curaçao," in *A History of Literature in the Caribbean, Vol. 2: English and Dutch Speaking Regions*, ed. A. James Arnold (Philadelphia: John Benjamins Publishing Co., 2001), 438–39.

31. Oostindie, "Black Power, Popular Revolt, and Decolonization in the Dutch Caribbean," 243. See also Andrew Daily, "Race, Citizenship, and Antillean Student Activism in Postwar France, 1946–1968," *French Historical Studies* 37, no. 2 (2014): 331–57.

32. Stanley Brown, editor-in-chief of the independent newspaper *Vitó*, described the Provo movement as a significant influence on his activism; see Stanley Brown, "Ik ben de Voltaire van dertig mei," in *Curaçao, 30 mei 1969. Verhalen over de revolte*, ed. Gert Oostindie (Amsterdam: Amsterdam University Press, 1999), 14. Harold Hollander of the progressive student group *Kambio* cited the "rebellious atmosphere" among Dutch students as a strong influence on him and other Antillean students; see Harold Hollander, "Er is van onze strijd niets terechtgekomen," in *Curaçao, 30 mei 1969. Verhalen over de revolte*, ed. Gert Oostindie (Amsterdam: Amsterdam University Press, 1999), 48–49. On the Provo movement, see Richard Kempton, *The Provos: Amsterdam's Anarchist Revolt* (New York: Autonomedia, 2007).

33. Willem Koot and Anco Ringeling, *De Antillianen* (Muiderberg: Dick Coutinho, 1984), 139.

34. "Kambio in druk op NA," *Amigoe di Curaçao*, September 30, 1966, 4.

35. "'Wij kunnen het de Nederlanders niet kwalijk nemen,'" *Amigoe di Curaçao*, October 21, 1965, 5.

36. "De student en zijn taak," *Kambio*, September 1966 2, no. 5, 1–3, IISG, Periodicals.

37. Anderson and Dynes, *Social Movements, Violence, and Change*, 51.

38. Oostindie, "Black Power, Popular Revolt, and Decolonization in the Dutch Caribbean," 245.

39. Stanley Brown to Provos, January 28, 1967, IISG, Archief Provo, box 14, folder 2.

40. On demonstrations at the Gomezplein, see German Gruber, Jr., dir., *HUMA: Trint'i Mei Lantamentu Anunsia* (NAAM Foundation, 2021), episode 2, 14:53 to 18:20.

41. "Gesprek met Brown," *Amigoe di Curaçao,* September 30, 1969, 11.

42. Anderson and Dynes, *Social Movements, Violence, and Change,* 65.

43. Circulation figures in Verton, *Politieke dynamiek en dekolonisatie,* 80. *Vitó* maintained a subscription swap with *Granma* in Cuba. See Brown, "Ik ben de Voltaire van dertig mei," 18.

44. "De 'protestmeisje' dat zich realiste noemt," *Amigoe di Curaçao*, April 4, 1970.

45. Gerald Bruins, "Hoe een gereformeerd meisje uit Friesland betrokken raakte bij een volksopstand op Curaçao," *Nederlands Dagblad*, June 1, 2019, https://www.nd.nl/nieuws/nederland/526862/hoe-een-gereformeerd-meisje-uit -friesland-betrokken-raakte-bij-een-volksopstand-op-curaao.

46. "Reportage di un diskushon tocante SEKSUALIDAD," *Vitó*, November 29, 1969, 4, IISG, Periodicals.

47. "30 Mei 1969: Rapport van de Commissie tot onderzoek van de achtergronden en oorzaken van de onlusten welke of 30 mei 1969 op Curaçao hebben plaatsgehad," Part II, 202, UBL, KITLV Collection.

48. Samir Amin, "Population Policies and Development Strategies: Underpopulated Africa" (Dakar, Senegal: UNESCO, 1971); Mahmood Mamdani, *The Myth of Population Control* (New York: Monthly Review Press, 1972).

49. "Lezing Ong-a-Kwie," *Amigoe di Curaçao*, October 26, 1967, 3.

50. Press release from the Curaçaose Federatie van Werknemers, May 20, 1970, NA, KabSNA, 2.10.41, inv. nr. 553.

51. "CFW voor eenheid Antillen met behoud secessierecht," *Amigoe di Curaçao*, May 27, 1974, 3.

52. "Karta abierta na hende muhe," *Vitó*, May 9, 1970, 1, IISG, Periodicals. Emphasis in original.

53. Matthew Connelly, *Fatal Misconception: The Struggle to Control World Population* (Cambridge: The Belknap Press of Harvard University Press, 2008), 121.

54. "Karta abierta na hende muhe," *Vitó*, May 9, 1970, 1, IISG, Periodicals.

55. "The Health System," *Kontakto Antiano*, December 1975, 12, IISG, Periodicals.

56. "Wetting, onwettig," *Kambio*, September 1965, 18, IISG, Periodicals.

57. Dagmar Herzog, *Sexuality in Europe: A Twentieth-Century History* (Cambridge: Cambridge University Press, 2011), 133.

58. "Veilig seksen," *Vitó* 3, no. 2 (1967), 8, IISG, Periodicals.

59. "Onze dubbele moraal," *Kambio*, May 1966, 5–6, IISG, Periodicals.

60. Herzog, *Sexuality in Europe*, 149.

61. *Vitó* 2, no. 7 (1967), 2, IISG, Periodicals.

62. "Karta abierta na hende muhe," *Vitó*, June 6, 1970, 2, IISG, Periodicals. Beginning in 1968, *Vitó* issued editions using the date of publication.

63. Translations of *Vitó*, "Buitenkinderen," December 19, 1970, NA, KabSNA, 2.10.41, inv. nr. 1287.

64. *Vitó* 2, no. 7 (1967), 8, IISG, Periodicals.

65. Charles P. do Rego, *The Portuguese Immigrant in Curaçao: Immigration, Participation, and Integration in the 20th Century* (Willemstad: CaribPublishing, 2012), 108–9.

66. Anderson and Dynes, *Social Movements, Violence, and Change*, 56.

67. Verton, *Politieke dynamiek en dekolonisatie*, 63–64.

68. Quoted in Verton, *Politieke dynamiek en dekolonisatie*, 83.

69. Hynson, "'Count, Capture, and Reeducate,'" 151.

70. Kamala Kempadoo, *Sexing the Caribbean: Gender, Race and Sexual Labor* (New York: Routledge, 2004), 104.

71. "Gangsters Go Home," *Kambio*, September 1967, 3, no. 5, IISG, Periodicals.

72. "Toerisme: Panacae of doos van Pandora?," *Kambio*, December 1967, 3, no. 7, IISG, Periodicals.

73. "Prostitutanan den cayanan di Willemstad," *Vitó*, January 9, 1971, IISG, Periodicals.

74. "Muher di bida den kayanan di Willemstad," *Vitó*, February 1, 1969, IISG, Periodicals.

75. Frank Martinus Arion, *Double Play*, trans. Paul Vincent (London: Faber and Faber Limited, 1998 [1973]), 179. Arion was personally involved in progressive activism, editing the critical magazine *Rukù* and promoting intellectual and cultural production in Papiamentu.

76. "Prostitusjon di mucha muhernan di pakus," *Vitó*, February 2, 1970, 2, IISG, Periodicals.

77. Michelle Chase and Isabella Cosse, "Revolutionary Positions: Sexuality and Gender in Cuba and Beyond," *Radical History Review* 136 (2020): 2.

78. Michelle Chase, *Revolution within the Revolution: Women and Gender Politics in Cuba, 1952–1962* (Chapel Hill: University of North Carolina Press, 2015), 46 and chapter 2 passim.

79. "Entrevista ku un HOMO-SEKSUAL," *Vitó*, April 5, 1969, IISG, Periodicals.

80. "Homosekswalidat . . . punta di akshon," *Kontakto Antiano*, March 1971, IISG, Periodicals.

81. For a nuanced take on these organizations, see Wigbertson Julian Isenia, "Queer Sovereignties: Cultural Practices of Sexual Citizenship in the Dutch Caribbean" (Ph.D. diss, Universiteit van Amsterdam, 2022), chapter 4. In subsequent decades, individuals from the Dutch Caribbean were involved in the creation of queer of color collectives in the Netherlands. See Chandra Frank, "Sister Outsider and Audre Lorde in the Netherlands: On Transnational Queer

Feminisms and Archival Methodological Practices," *Feminist Review* 121 (2019): 11–25; Gianmaria Colpani and Wigbertson Julian Isenia, "Strange Fruits: Queer of Color Intellectual Labor in the 1980s and 1990s," in *Postcolonial Intellectuals in Europe: Critics, Artists, Movements, and Their Publics*, ed. Sandra Ponzanesi and Adriano José Habed (Lanham, MD: Rowman & Littlefield International, 2018), 213–30.

82. Lillian Guerra, "Gender Policing, Homosexuality, and the New Patriarchy of the Cuban Revolution," *Social History* 35, no. 3 (2010): 268.

83. Pablo Ben and Santiago Joaquin Insausti, "Dictatorial Rule and Sexual Politics in Argentina: The Case of the Frente de Liberación Homosexual, 1967–1976," *Hispanic American Historical Review* 97, no. 2 (2017): 298. Nevertheless, others have identified a conservative, homophobic masculine ideal prevalent among the Latin American left in this same time period. See Florencia Mallon, "*Barbudos*, Warriors, and *Rotos*: The MIR, Masculinity, and Power in the Chilean Agrarian Reform, 1965–74," in *Changing Men and Masculinities in Latin America*, ed. Matthew C. Guttman (Durham, NC: Duke University Press, 2003), 182–83, 194.

84. The Young Lords developed a critique of patriarchy within nationalist struggles and had several prominent queer and gender nonconforming members. Like Antillean leftists, and in contrast to many other nationalist groups in this period, the Young Lords also emphasized feminism and reproductive rights. Despite the early condemnation of homosexuality by several leading members of the Black Panther Party, after 1970 cofounder Huey Newton pledged unequivocal support for the feminist and gay liberation movements. See Johanna Fernández, *The Young Lords: A Radical History* (Chapel Hill: University of North Carolina Press, 2019), 250-64; Laura Briggs, *Reproducing Empire: Race, Sex, Science, and U.S. Imperialism in Puerto Rico* (Berkeley: University of California Press, 2003), 19–20, 190; George Katsiaficas, "Organization and Movement: The Case of the Black Panther Party and the Revolutionary People's Constitutional Convention of 1970," in *Liberation, Imagination, and the Black Panther Party: A New Look at the Panthers and Their Legacy*, ed. Kathleen Cleaver and George Katsiaficas (New York: Routledge, 2001), 141–55; Lindsay Zafir, "Queer Connections: Jean Genet, the Black Panther Party, and the Coalition Politics of the Long 1960s," *GLQ: A Journal of Lesbian and Gay Studies* 27, no. 2 (2021): 253–79. On the assertion of normative desire in 1960s radical Caribbean movements, see Kate Quinn, "New Perspectives on Black Power in the Caribbean," in *Black Power in the Caribbean*, ed. Kate Quinn (Gainesville: University Press of Florida, 2014), 17.

85. On *kambrada*, see Wigbertson Julian Isenia, "Looking for *Kambrada*: Sexuality and Social Anxieties in the Dutch Colonial Archive," *Tijdschrift voor Genderstudies* 22, no. 2 (2019): 125–43. On *mati*, see Gloria Wekker, *The Politics of Passion: Women's Sexual Culture in the Afro-Surinamese Diaspora* (New York: Columbia University Press, 2006).

86. "Black Power," *Kambio*, September 1966, 2.5, 4, IISG, Periodicals.

87. Brown, "Ik ben de Voltaire van dertig mei," 16.

88. Brian Meeks, *Radical Caribbean: From Black Power to Abu Bakr* (Kingston: University of the West Indies Press, 1996), 1.

89. Oostindie, "Black Power, Popular Revolt, and Decolonization in the Dutch Caribbean," 249–50; Anderson and Dynes, *Social Movements, Violence, and Change*, 145.

90. "Di kon homber pretu ta prefera di drumi ku un muhe blanku riba un muhe pretu," *Vitó*, November 23, 1968, 3, IISG, Periodicals.

91. "Di kon homber pretu ta prefera di drumi ku un muhe blanku riba un muhe pretu."

92. "Segun 'Black Panthers,'" *Kontakto Antiano*, February 1970, IISG, Periodicals.

93. Interview by the author with Gladys do Rego-Kuster, Willemstad, Curaçao, August 1, 2016.

94. This was a recurring topic of discussion in UMA's radio program, *Bati Bleki*. See, among others, *Bati Bleki*, December 1, 1985; *Bati Bleki*, September 20, 1986, NAC, UMA—G. do Rego, inv. nr. 210, box 1.

95. Interview by the author with Gladys do Rego-Kuster, Willemstad, Curaçao, August 1, 2016. See also Henriquez, "'Black is Beautiful' is voor vrouwen heel belangrijk geweest," 45. On the history of feminism in Curaçao, see Sonia Cuales, "In Search of Our Memory: Gender in the Netherlands Antilles," *Feminist Review* 59 (1998): 86–100.

96. "Homber atraktivo," *Kontakto Antiano*, April 1970, IISG, Periodicals.

97. Guillermo Rosario, "Muhé Emansipa," *Kontakto Antiano*, April 1970, IISG, Periodicals.

98. Anthony Bogues, "The *Abeng* Newspaper and the Radical Politics of Postcolonial Blackness," in *Black Power in the Caribbean*, ed. Kate Quinn (Gainesville: University Press of Florida, 2014), 77.

99. Macpherson, *From Colony to Nation*, 257–63; Quito Swan, *Black Power in Bermuda: The Struggle for Decolonization* (Basingstoke: Palgrave Macmillan, 2009), 111.

100. Bogues, "The *Abeng* Newspaper and the Radical Politics of Postcolonial Blackness," 87.

101. Macpherson, *From Colony to Nation*, 257.

102. "Stanley Brown officieel uit Vito," *Amigoe di Curaçao*, October 2, 1969.

103. "Kwa di nos ta puta?," *Vitó*, June 20, 1970, IISG, Periodicals.

104. "Karta abierta na heude muhe," *Vitó*, May 9, 1970, IISG, Periodicals.

105. "Muhé Antiano: Usa bo sintí!" *Kontakto Antiano*, December 1971, 5, IISG, Periodicals; "Antilliaanse vrouwen: Gebruik je verstand," *Amigoe di Curaçao*, January 29, 1972, 9.

106. "Curaçao's Black God," *Vitó*, December 25, 1968, IISG, Periodicals.

107. Dagmar Herzog, *Sex after Fascism: Memory and Morality in Twentieth-Century Germany* (Princeton, NJ: Princeton University Press, 2005), chapter 4.

For a notable exception, see Todd Shepard's discussion of the Front homosexuel d'action révolutionnaire in Shepard, *Sex, France, and Arab Men*, 91–94.

108. Mimi Sheller, *Citizenship from Below: Erotic Agency and Caribbean Freedom* (Durham, NC: Duke University Press, 2012), 18. On "erotic autonomy," see M. Jacqui Alexander, *Pedagogies of Crossing: Meditations on Feminism, Sexual Politics, Memory, and the Sacred* (Durham, NC: Duke University Press, 2005), 21–22, 65.

109. Alexander, *Pedagogies of Crossing*, 23.

110. Translations of *Vitó*, NA, KabSNA, 2.10.41, inv. nr. 1287. See especially "Mafia op Antillen?" November 29, 1969; "Discriminatie bij Hilton," December 19, 1970; "Buitenkinderen," December 20, 1969; "Het leven in concubinaat gaat door," May 30, 1970.

111. "Constraints on Foreign Aid to National Family Planning Programs" by Mr. Wahren (SIDA), Organisation for Economic Cooperation and Development, July 26, 1971, NA, KabSNA, 2.10.41, inv. nr. 553.

112. Correspondence regarding visit of Prof. Haspels, April 25–May 20, 1969, NA, KabSNA, 2.10.41, inv. nr. 553.

113. "30 Mei 1969: Rapport van de Commissie tot onderzoek van de achtergronded en oorzaken van de onlusten welke of 30 mei 1969 op Curaçao hebben plaatsgehad," Part I, 179–84, UBL, KITLV Collection.

114. Prof. dr. A. A. Haspels, Report of a Visit to the Netherlands Antilles and Suriname, September 4–12, 1970 (Amsterdam: KIT, 1970), NA, KabSNA, 2.10.41, inv. nr. 553.

115. "Hulp?," *Amigoe di Curaçao*, July 23, 1971.

116. Anderson and Dynes, *Social Movements, Violence, and Change*, 85.

117. Anderson and Dynes, *Social Movements, Violence, and Change*, 100.

118. Anderson and Dynes, *Social Movements, Violence, and Change*, 109–12.

119. Anderson and Dynes, *Social Movements, Violence, and Change*, 99.

120. Anderson and Dynes, *Social Movements, Violence, and Change*, 80 and 83; Oostindie, "De sprekers en hun verhalen," 8.

121. Leer, "Muhé na Kandela."

122. Chase and Cosse, "Revolutionary Positions," 2.

123. Adaly Rodriguez, *The Rise of Women's Rights on Curaçao: The Potential of the Women's Convention to the Empowerment of Equal Rights of Women in Curaçao* (Amsterdam: Uitgeverij SWP, 2015), 100.

124. See Kaso Seru Fortuna; Kranten en tijdschriften, NAC, UMA—G. do Rego, inv. nr. 210, boxes 5 and 2.

125. Stanley Brown left the FOL following the split with Godett. Brown later established a party that sought to incorporate Curaçao as a province of the Netherlands. Godett, who remained active in the FOL, was later accused of corruption and fraud. Amador Nita was appointed as minister of social affairs in 1969 but died unexpectedly the following year. Members of the FOL suspected that he was poisoned by political opponents, but the Venezuelan and Cuban

doctors who conducted the autopsy concluded that the popular labor leader died of natural causes. See Oostindie, "Black Power, Popular Revolt, and Decolonization in the Dutch Caribbean," 256.

126. Interview by the author with Gladys do Rego-Kuster, Willemstad, Curaçao, August 1, 2016.

127. Henriquez, "'Black is Beautiful' is voor vrouwen heel belangrijk geweest," 45. Among Henriquez's many intellectual contributions is a volume documenting the life histories of seventy-five Curaçaoan women, including Gladys do Rego-Kuster and Emmy Henriquez. See Jeanne Henriquez, *Kòrsou su muhénan pionero* (Willemstad: Archivo Nashonal di Antia Hulandes, 2002).

128. Cuales, "In Search of Our Memory."

CHAPTER 5. DUTCH DISEASES

1. On economic cultures of decolonization, see Christopher Dietrich, *Oil Revolution: Anticolonial Elites, Sovereign Rights, and the Economic Culture of Decolonization* (Cambridge: Cambridge University Press, 2017); Giuliano Garavini, *The Rise and Fall of OPEC in the Twentieth Century* (Oxford: Oxford University Press, 2019).

2. Garavini, *The Rise and Fall of OPEC*, 193. Exxon replaced the name Esso in 1971.

3. Jose de Cordoba, "Aruba Braces for Loss of Refinery," *The Washington Post*, December 23, 1984, https://www.washingtonpost.com/archive/business/1984/12/23/aruba-braces-for-loss-of-refinery/e311cca4-3330-4c01-b4d0-65f35524cdf9.

4. Lara Putnam, *Radical Moves: Caribbean Migrants and the Politics of Race in the Jazz Age* (Chapel Hill: University of North Carolina Press, 2013), 18; Miguel Tinker Salas, *The Enduring Legacy: Oil, Culture, and Society in Venezuela* (Durham, NC: Duke University Press, 2009), 48; Rose Mary Allen, "Emigración laboral de Curazao a Cuba a principios del siglo XX: Una experiencia," *Revista Mexicana del Caribe* 5, no. 9 (2000): 40–103.

5. Sanneke Kuipers, *The Crisis Imperative: Crisis Rhetoric and Welfare State Reform in Belgium and the Netherlands in the Early 1990s* (Amsterdam: Amsterdam University Press, 2005), 119–21.

6. Fernando Coronil, *The Magical State: Nature, Money, and Modernity in Venezuela* (Chicago: University of Chicago Press, 1997), 7.

7. *Surinamers en Antillianen in Amsterdam: Verkorte versie van het onderzoeksverslag* (Amsterdam: Gemeentelijke Sociale Dienst, 1979), 3, UBL, KITLV Collection.

8. Katherine McKittrick, "Mathematics Black Life," *The Black Scholar* 44, no. 2 (2014): 19.

9. Roderick Ferguson, *Aberrations in Black: Toward a Queer of Color Critique* (Minneapolis: University of Minnesota Press, 2004), 87.

10. On the intersections of social science, decolonization, and the evolution of the welfare state in Britain and France, see Jordanna Bailkin, *The Afterlife of Empire* (Berkeley: University of California Press, 2013); Amelia Lyons, *The Civilizing Mission in the Metropole: Algerian Families and the French Welfare State during Decolonization* (Stanford, CA: Stanford University Press, 2013), chapter 2. On the postwar ascendance of social science and social work in the Netherlands, see Jan Rath, *Minorisiering. De sociale constructie van 'etnische minderheden'* (Amsterdam: Sua, 1991); Marja Gastelaars, *Een geregeld leven. Sociologie en sociale politiek in Nederland, 1925–1968* (Amsterdam: Sua, 1985).

11. D. Alissa Trotz, "Behind the Banner of Culture? Gender, 'Race,' and the Family in Guyana," *New West Indian Guide* 77, no. 1/2 (2003): 23.

12. Paul Scheffer, "De multiculturele drama," *NRC Handelsblad*, January 29, 2000, https://retro.nrc.nl/W2/Lab/Multicultureel/scheffer.html.

13. On the recruitment of Surinamese and Antillean laborers in the late 1950s and 1960s and the racial prejudice they encountered, see Guno Jones, "Tussen onderdanen, Rijksgenoten en Nederlanders: Nederlandse politici over burgers uit Oost en West en Nederland, 1945–2005" (Ph.D. diss., Vrije Universiteit Amsterdam, 2007), 203–17.

14. Jan Rath, "The Netherlands: A Reluctant Country of Immigration," *Tijdschrift voor economische en sociale geografie* 100, no. 5 (2009): 677.

15. Duco Hellema, Cees Wiebes, and Toby Witte, *The Netherlands and the Oil Crisis: Business as Usual* (Amsterdam: Amsterdam University Press, 2004), 27.

16. Hellema, Wiebes, and Witte, *The Netherlands and the Oil Crisis*, 99–100; Carola Hein, "Oil Spaces: The Global Petroleumscape in the Rotterdam/The Hague Area," *Journal of Urban History* 44, no. 5 (2018): 906–9, 914–20.

17. Timothy Mitchell, *Carbon Democracy: Political Power in the Age of Oil* (London: Verson, 2011), 184; Robert Vitalis, *Oilcraft: The Myths of Scarcity and Security That Haunt U.S. Energy Policy* (Stanford, CA: Stanford Univeristy Press, 2020), 67.

18. Hellema, Wiebes, and Witte, *The Netherlands and the Oil Crisis*, 52–62.

19. Garavini, *The Rise and Fall of OPEC*, 223.

20. Hans Vermeulen and Rinus Penninx, "Introduction," in *Immigrant Integration: The Dutch Case*, ed. Hans Vermeulen and Rinus Penninx (Amsterdam: Spinhuis, 2000), 6–7.

21. Documents concerning the eventual independence of the Netherlands Antilles, NAC, Kabinet van de Gouverneur van de Nederlandse Antillen 1949, 1951–1990, 2.3.1, inv. nr. 244.

22. Gert Oostindie and Inge Klinkers, *Decolonising the Caribbean: Dutch Policies in Comparative Perspective* (Amsterdam: Amsterdam University Press, 2003), 102.

23. Gert Oostindie, *Postcolonial Netherlands: Sixty-five Years of Forgetting, Commemorating, Silencing* (Amsterdam: Amsterdam University Press, 2010), 24.

24. Rosemarijn Hoefte, *Suriname in the Long Twentieth Century: Domination, Contestation, Globalization* (Basingstoke: Palgrave Macmillan, 2014), 133–43.

25. Anke van Dijk, Hans van Hulst, and Linda Terpstra, *Mama Soltera. De positie van 'alleenstaande' Curaçaose en Arubaanse moeders in Nederland* (The Hague: Warray, 1990), 3.

26. Cordoba, "Aruba Braces for Loss of Refinery."

27. William R. Long, "Aruba Hoping Suntan Oil Can Replace Crude Oil," *Los Angeles Times*, March 28, 1985, https://www.latimes.com/archives/la-xpm-1985 -03-28-fi-29238-story.html.

28. Cordoba, "Aruba Braces for Loss of Refinery."

29. Long, "Aruba Hoping Suntan Oil Can Replace Crude Oil."

30. Cordoba, "Aruba Braces for Loss of Refinery."

31. Summary of meeting between Aruba and ECCA/Lago negotiating teams, September 25, 1985, UT, BCAH, LCAC, box 2.207/M72.

32. Press release, November 20, 1985, UT, BCAH, LCAC, box 2.207/M25.

33. Hans van Hulst, "A Continuing Construction of Crisis: Antilleans, Especially Curaçaoans, in the Netherlands," in *Immigrant Integration: The Dutch Case*, ed. Hans Vermeulen and Rinus Penninx (Amsterdam: Spinhuis, 2000), 100.

34. Keetie Sluyterman, *A History of Royal Dutch Shell, Vol. 3: Keeping Competitive in Turbulent Markets* (Oxford: Oxford University Press, 2007), 76.

35. Ton de Jong, "Shell én PdVSA wilden de raffinaderij dicht hebben," *Antilliaans Dagblad*, May 4, 2015, https://antilliaansdagblad.com/nieuws-menu /curacao/publicaties/100-jaar-olie.

36. "Isla den nos bida," National Archaeological Anthropological Memory Management, accessed June 11, 2021, https://naam.cw/aktividat/isla-den-nos-bida /exhibition/after-1985.

37. Joseph B. Treaster, "Hard Times for Curaçao and Aruba," *New York Times*, March 15, 1985, https://www.nytimes.com/1985/03/15/business/no-headline -094002.html.

38. Tijn van Beurden and Joost Jonker, "A Perfect Symbiosis: Curaçao, the Netherlands and Financial Offshore Services, 1951–2003," *Financial History Review* 28, no. 1 (2021): 80.

39. Michael O. Sharpe, "Globalization and Migration: Post-Colonial Dutch Antillean and Aruban Immigrant Political Incorporation in the Netherlands," *Dialectical Anthropology* 29, no. 3/4 (2005). 219.

40. Memo: Prospectus of the Aruban Economy without Lago, 1981, UT, BCAH, LCAC, box 2.207/M71.

41. Announcement of refinery closure, October 31, 1984, UT, BCAH, LCAC, box 2.207/M22.

42. Margo Groenewoud, "Decolonization, Otherness, and the Neglect of the Dutch Caribbean in Caribbean Studies," *Small Axe* 64 (2021): 109. Important

criticisms were advanced already in the 1950s. Amador Nita wrote in 1952 about the urgency of creating economic equality across the kingdom, including welfare payments. See Rose Mary Allen, "The Trinta di Mei Labor Revolt and Its Aftermath: Anticipating a Just and Equitable Curaçaoan Nation," in *Equaliberty in the Dutch Caribbean: Ways of Being Non/Sovereign*, ed. Yvon van der Pijl and Francio Guadeloupe (Newark, NJ: Rutgers University Press, 2022), 74.

43. Inventory of problems created by the settlement of Surinamese and Antilleans in Amsterdam, 3, NA, KabSNA, 2.10.41, inv. nr. 1013.

44. Policy regarding Helpende Huizen and childcare for single parents, 1977–1980, SA, Archief van de Sociale Dienst, 30047, inv. nr. 889.

45. Markus Balkenhol, "Tracing Slavery: An Ethnography of Diaspora, Affect, and Cultural Heritage in Amsterdam" (Ph.D. diss., Vrije Universiteit Amsterdam, 2014), 64–65.

46. "Protest tegen discriminatie bij woning-toewijzing," *De Waarheid*, February 24, 1978, 7; Call for protest, January 30, 1978, SA, Archief van de Sociale Dienst, 30047, inv. nr. 845.

47. F. G. de Ruiter, "Leider Volksunie is trots op blank te zijn," *NRC Handelsbald*, May 24, 1974, 14.

48. *Kontakto Antiano*, January 1976, 30–31, IISG, Periodicals.

49. Letters to Amsterdam mayor and city council concerning the situation in hotels, March 15, 1977 and July 1977, SA, Archief van de Sociale Dienst, 30047, inv. nr. 837.

50. Agenda points for discussion with GDH/GDV/GDB/GSD, November 30, 1977, SA, Archief van de Sociale Dienst, 30047, inv. nr. 839.

51. Documents from the working group on very large families, SA, Archief van de Sociale Dienst, 30047, inv. nr. 837.

52. Report of the first meeting of the working group, May 25, 1979, SA, Archief van de Sociale Dienst, 30047, inv. nr. 837.

53. Sarah van Walsum, "Sex and the Regulation of Belonging: Dutch Family Migration Policies in the Context of Changing Family Norms," in *Gender, Generation and the Family in International Migration*, ed. Albert Kraler, Eleonore Kofman, Martin Kohli, and Camille Schmoll (Amsterdam: Amsterdam University Press, 2012), 60–61.

54. Jet Bussemaker et al., "Allenstaande moeders en sociaal beleid in Nederland: Van verzorgers naar kostwinners?," *Beleid en Maatschappij* 26, no. 1 (1996): 45.

55. Inventory of the problems created by the settlement of Surinamese and Antilleans in Amsterdam, p. 3, NA, KabSNA, 2.10.41, inv. nr. 1013.

56. Ineke Gooskens, *Surinaamse vrouwelijke gezinshoofden in Bijstand en W.W.V. te Amsterdam* (Amsterdam: Gemeentlijke Sociale Dienst, Afd. Beleidsvoorbereiding en Wetenschappelijke Onderzoek, 1975), UBL, KITLV Collection.

57. Report "Rijksgenoten in de bijstand en de WWV te Amsterdam," February 1972, SA, Archief van de Sociale Dienst, 30047, inv. nr. 3676. This report grouped welfare clients by the location of their birth.

58. Clients of the Municipal Social Service Department per April 1, 1972 and January 1, 1973, NA, LSWA, 2.19.01, inv. nr. 65.

59. Report "Rijksgenoten in de bijstand en de WWV te Amsterdam," February 1972, SA, Archief van de Sociale Dienst, 30047, inv. nr. 3676.

60. Philomena Essed and Kwame Nimako, "Designs and (Co)Incidents: Cultures of Scholarship and Public Policy on Immigrants/Minorities in the Netherlands," *International Journal of Comparative Sociology* 47, no. 3/4 (2006): 284.

61. van Walsum, "Sex and the Regulation of Belonging," 59-60; Gastelaars, *Een geregeld leven*, 180.

62. Rinus Penninx, *Wie betaalt, bepaalt? De ontwikkeling en programmering van onderzoek naar migranten, etnische minderheden en woonwagenbewoners 1955-1985, met speciale aandacht voor de rol van de overheid* (Amsterdam: Instituut voor Sociale Geographie, 1988), 25, 30.

63. Rinus Penninx, *Minderheidsvorming en emancipatie. Balans van kennisverwerving ten aanzien van immigranten en woonwagenbewoners, 1967-1987* (Alphen aan den Rijn: Samsom, 1988), 13.

64. Kuipers, *The Crisis Imperative*, 121, 135.

65. Kuipers, *The Crisis Imperative*, 122.

66. Penninx, *Wie betaalt, bepaalt?*, 25, 30.

67. On sociology and the family, see Alice O'Connor, *Poverty Knowledge: Social Science, Social Policy, and the Poor in Twentieth-Century US History* (Princeton, NJ: Princeton University Press, 2001), 74-77; Christine Barrow, *Family in the Caribbean: Themes and Perspectives* (Kingston: Ian Randle Publishers, 1996).

68. Deborah Thomas, "The Violence of Diaspora: Governmentality, Class Cultures, and Circulations," *Radical History Review* 103 (2009): 96.

69. On the debate between Frazier and Herskovits, see Jerry Gershenhorn, *Melville J. Herskovits and the Racial Politics of Knowledge* (Lincoln: University of Nebraska Press, 2004), 113-21; Daryl Michael Scott, *Contempt and Pity: Social Policy and the Image of the Damaged Black Psyche, 1880-1996* (Chapel Hill: University of North Carolina Press, 1997), 45-46. On the impact of this debate in African diaspora studies, see Sidney Mintz and Richard Price, *The Birth of African-American Culture: An Anthropological Perspective* (Boston: Beacon Press, 1992), 61-80.

70. Frazier's argument was, in fact, more complex. In his view, the mother-centered family was not inherently "disorganized" but became so in the process of rural to urban migration. This argument did not travel to the European Netherlands. See Scott, *Contempt and Pity*, 46-50.

71. Melville J. Herskovits, *The Myth of the Negro Past* (New York: Harper & Brothers Publishers, 1941), 167-84.

72. Oscar Lewis, *La Vida: A Puerto Rican Family in the Culture of Poverty* (New York: Random House, 1966). For this argument in Dutch research, see Daniëlle van 't Hoofd and Jolanda Westerlaken, "'Mi ta lóra koene': Een

onderzoek naar de leefsituatie van ongehuwde moeders met een onderstandsuit-kering op Curaçao" (Ph.D. diss, Katholieke Universiteit Brabant, 1988); Maria Lenders and Marjolein van Vlijmen-van de Rhoer, "Mijn God, hoe ga ik doen? De positie van Creoolse alleenstaande moeders in Amsterdam" (Ph.D. diss., Universiteit van Amsterdam, 1983).

73. See *Surinamers en Antillianen in Amsterdam*; W. D. van Hoorn, "Het kindertal van Surinamers en Antillianen in Nederland," *Maandstatistiek van de bevolking* 36, no. 1 (1988): 18–21; Hans van Leusden, "Indicators of Marriage and Marriage Dissolution of the Female Population of Curaçao, 1960–1962, 1970–1972, and 1980–1981: A Multidimensional Analysis," Working paper no. 66 (Voorburg: Netherlands Interuniversity Demographic Institute, 1985); Tulip Patricia Olton, *Minderheidsstatus of stijgingsdrang? Antilliaanse en Arubaanse vrouwen in Amsterdam en hun gezinsvorming* (Delft: Uitgeverij Eburon, 1994), 18–19.

74. Lenders and van Vlijmen-van de Rhoer, "Mijn God, hoe ga ik doen?," 17–18.

75. In 1986, the CBS published a two-part, nationwide report on Surinamese and Antilleans in the Netherlands: *De leefsituatie van Surinamers en Antillianen in Nederland 1985, Deel I en II* (The Hague: Staatsuitgeverij/CBS-Publikaties, 1986). After 1985, annual reports on the demographic development of Surinamese and Antillean populations in the Netherlands appeared in *Maandstatistiek van de bevolking* and *Statistisch magazine*.

76. Barrow, *Family in the Caribbean*, 8; Barbara Bush, "Colonial Research and the Social Sciences at the End of Empire: The West Indian Social Survey, 1944–57," *The Journal of Imperial and Commonwealth History* 41, no. 3 (2013): 451–74; Kristen Stromberg Childers, *Seeking Imperialism's Embrace: National Identity, Decolonization, and Assimilation in the French Caribbean* (Oxford: Oxford University Press, 2016), 156–57.

77. Laura Briggs, *Reproducing Empire: Race, Sex, Science, and U.S. Imperialism in Puerto Rico* (Berkeley: University of California Press, 2003), 164–65.

78. Daniel Patrick Moynihan, "The Negro Family: The Case for National Action" (Washington, DC: United States Department of Labor, 1965).

79. Harry Hoetink, *Caribbean Race Relations: A Study of Two Variants* (London: Institute of Race Relations, 1971). On Hoetink's impact on studies of race and ethnicity, see Gert Oostindie, ed., *Ethnicity in the Caribbean: Essays in Honor of Harry Hoetink* (Amsterdam: Amsterdam University Press, 2005).

80. Harry Hoetink, *Het patroon van de oude Curaçaose samenleving. Een sociologische studie* (Assen: Van Gorcum, 1958), 119–20.

81. Arnaud F. Marks, *Male and Female and the Afro-Curaçaoan Household*, trans. Maria J. L. van Yperen (The Hague: Martinus Nijhoff, 1976), 29; Eva Abraham-van der Mark, *Yu'i Mama. Enkele facetten van gezinsstructuur op Curaçao* (Assen: Van Gorcum, 1972), 10–11, 25–26. Curaçaoan scholar Alejandro F. Paula indicted the double standard that problematized "illegitimate" unions among Afro-Curaçaoans but not among the island's white elite in *From

Objective to Subjective Social Barriers: A Historico-Philosophical Analysis of Certain Negative Attitudes among the Negroid Population of Curaçao (Curaçao: Curaçao NV, 1972), 72.

82. Barrow, *Family in the Caribbean*, 48; Tracy Robinson, "The Properties of Citizens: A Caribbean Grammar of Conjugal Categories," *Du Bois Review* 10, no. 2 (2013): 425–46. The omission of same-sex relationships in municipally funded studies is especially pronounced given that some academics (including Herskovits) paid attention to erotic relationships among women in Suriname. See Willem F. L. Buschkens, *The Family System of the Paramaribo Creoles*, trans. Maria J. L. van Yperen (The Hague: Martinus Nijhoff, 1974), 248.

83. Robinson, "The Properties of Citizens," 426.

84. Jeanne Henriquez, "Motherhood is a State of Mind: Testimonies of Single Curaçaoan Mothers," in *Mundu Yama Sinta Mira: Womanhood in Curaçao*, ed. Richenel Ansano, Joceline Clemencia, Jeanette Cook, and Eithel Martis (Willemstad: Fundashon Publikashon Curaçao, 1992), 90–92.

85. *Surinamers en Antillianen in Amsterdam*, 9.

86. Hoefte, *Suriname in the Long Twentieth Century*, 9, 16–21.

87. *Surinamers en Antillianen in Amsterdam*, 8.

88. On the postwar disappearance of "race," see Gloria Wekker, *White Innocence: Paradoxes of Colonialism and Race* (Durham, NC: Duke University Press, 2016), 23; Kwame Nimako and Glenn Willemsen, *The Dutch Atlantic: Slavery, Abolition, and Emancipation* (London: Pluto Press, 2011), 187.

89. Étienne Balibar, "Is There a Neo-Racism?," in *Race, Nation, Class: Ambiguous Identities*, ed. Étienne Balibar and Immanuel Wallerstein (London: Verso, 1988), 22, 25.

90. On the global itinerancy of these ideas, see Françoise Vergès, *Monsters and Revolutionaries: Colonial Family Romance and Métissage* (Durham, NC: Duke University Press, 1999), 236–41.

91. R. A. de Moor, *Huwelijk en gezin. Wat is hun toekomst in West-Europa* (Baarn: Uitgeverij Ambo, 1985), 9.

92. *Surinamers en Antillianen in Amsterdam*, 37, 33.

93. van Walsum, "Sex and the Regulation of Belonging," 64.

94. Oostindie and Klinkers, *Decolonising the Caribbean*, 122; Rosemarijn Hoefte, "The Difficulty of Getting it Right: Dutch Policy in the Caribbean," *Itinerario* 25, no. 2 (2001): 65–66.

95. van Hulst, "A Continuing Construction of Crisis," 100.

96. In 1976, just prior to the end of the ten-year tax holiday, the company left Curaçao and laid off the entirety of its workforce. See Sonia Cuales, "Women, Reproduction and Foreign Capital in Curaçao," *Caraïbisch Forum* 1, no. 2 (1980): 75–86.

97. By one estimate, single mothers and their children comprised over 80 percent of the Antillean and Aruban population in the Netherlands by the late 1980s (van Dijke, van Hulst, and Terpstra, *Mama Soltera*, 3).

98. Eric H. Mielants, "From Periphery to the Core: A Case Study on the Migration and Incorporation of Recent Caribbean Immigrants in the Netherlands," in *Caribbean Migration to Western Europe and the United States: Essays on Incorporation, Identity, and Citizenship*, ed. Margarita Cervantes-Rodriguez, Ramón Grosfoguel, and Eric. H. Mielants (Philadelphia: Temple University Press, 2008), 76.

99. Anke van Dijke and Linda Terpstra, *Je kunt beter bij je moeder blijven* (Leiden: KITLV, 1987), 105.

100. Humphrey Lamur et al., *Caraïbische vrouwen en anticonceptie* (Delft: Uitgeverij Eburon, 1990), 13–14.

101. Lamur et al., *Caraïbische vrouwen en anticonceptie*, 75.

102. Adaly Rodriguez, *The Rise of Women's Rights on Curaçao: The Potential of the Women's Convention to the Empowerment of Equal Rights of Women in Curaçao* (Amsterdam: SWP, 2015), 244–45.

103. Anja van Heelsum, *Migranten organisaties in Nederland. Deel 2: Functioneren van de organisaties* (Utrecht: FORUM, Inst. voor Multiculturele Ontwikkeling, 2004), 77.

104. Jan Willem Duyvendak and P. W. A. Scholten, "Beyond the Dutch 'Multicultural Model,'" *Journal of International Migration and Integration* 12, no. 3 (2011): 338–39.

105. *Plataforma*, December 1983, 20, UBL, KITLV Collection.

106. Ulbe Bosma, *Terug uit de koloniën. Zestig jaar postkoloniale migranten en hun organisaties* (Amsterdam: Bert Bakker, 2009), 205; Duyvendak and Scholten, "Beyond the Dutch 'Multicultural Model,'" 332.

107. *Plataforma*, December 1983, 20, UBL, KITLV Collection.

108. POA, *Genoeg lippendienst, nu nog daadkracht! Aanzet voor een gericht beleid met betrekking tot Antilliaanse vrouwen in Nederland* (Utrecht: POA, 1986), 15, UBL, KITLV Collection.

109. *VSAW Bulletin: Orgaan van de Vereniging Surinaamse en Antilliaanse Welzijnwerk(st)ers* 3, no. 1 (May 1983): 9–10, UBL, KITLV Collection.

110. *VSAW Bulletin: Orgaan van de Vereniging Surinaamse en Antilliaanse Welzijnwerk(st)ers* 2, no. 4 (January 1983): 7–8, UBL, KITLV Collection.

111. Report of the workshop, "Van frustratie naar communicatie: Verslag themadag psycho-sociale hulpverlening aan Surinaamse en Antilliaanse vrouwen" (May 1989), June 28, 1988, 19, IISG.

112. *Plataforma*, April 1988, 19–20, UBL, KITLV Collection.

113. *VSAW Bulletin: Orgaan van de Vereniging Surinaamse en Antilliaanse Welzijnwerk(st)ers*, no. 3/4 (December 1983): 9, UBL, KITLV Collection.

114. Essed and Nimako, "Designs and (Co)Incidents," 285, 291. On attempts to strengthen research on race, especially within the field of gender studies, see Gloria Wekker and Helma Lutz, "Een hoogvlakte met koude winden. De geschiedenis van het gender- en etniciteitsdenken in Nederland," in *Caleidoscopische visies. De zwarte, migranten- en vluchtelingen-vrouwenbeweging in Nederland,*

ed. Maayke Botman and Nancy Jouwe (Amsterdam: Koninklijk Instituut voor de Tropen, 2001), 36–40.

115. Philomena Essed, *Alledaags Racisme* (Amsterdam: Feministische Uitgeverij Sara, 1984).

116. Philomena Essed, *Understanding Everyday Racism: An Interdisciplinary Theory* (London: Sage Publications, 1994), 20.

117. Penninx, *Minderheidsvorming en emancipatie*, 41.

118. *Plataforma*, April 1988, 20, UBL, KITLV Collection.

119. *Plataforma*, April 1988, 73, UBL, KITLV Collection.

120. Penninx, *Wie betaalt, bepaalt?*, 48.

121. Monique Haveman, *'Hier sta ik er alleen voor': Een inventariserend onderzoek onder Antilliaanse vrouwen* (Utrecht: Kibra Hacha, 1984), UBL, KITLV Collection.

122. Michael O. Sharpe argued that government subsidy had a neutralizing impact on social welfare organizations more generally, which created an allegiance to the government who supplied the funding and not the communities they were designed to serve. See *Postcolonial Citizens and Ethnic Migration: The Netherlands and Japan in the Age of Globalization* (Basingstoke: Palgrave Macmillan, 2014), 104–5.

123. van Dijke, Hulst, and Terpstra, *Mama Soltera*, 19, 23.

124. Mary Aitatus, *Union di Muhé: Ban Demonstrè* (1985), 28, UBL, KITLV Collection.

125. POA, *Genoeg lippendienst, nu nog daadkracht!*, 1, UBL, KITLV Collection.

126. R. A. Wong and J. Arends, *SAAM-groepen in de bijstand. Een exploratief onderzoek naar de financieel-materiële en uitstroomproblematiek van Surinamers, Antillianen, Arubanen en Molukkers in de bijstand* (The Hague: Ministerie van Sociale Zaken en Werkgelegenheid, 1992), 59.

127. Wong and Arends, *SAAM-groepen in de bijstand*, 74.

128. Anneke van Doorne-Huiskes and Laura den Dulk, "The Netherlands," in *Families and States in Western Europe*, ed. Quentin Skinner (Cambridge: Cambridge University Press, 2011), 136–37.

129. Frederick van der Ploeg, "The Political Economy of a Consensus Society: Experience from Behind the Dykes," *The Economic and Social Review* 28, no. 4 (1997): 307–32; Jelle Visser and Anton Hemerijck, *A Dutch Miracle: Job Growth, Welfare Reform and Corporatism in the Netherlands* (Amsterdam: University of Amsterdam Press, 1997).

130. Guno Jones and Betty de Hart, "(Not) Measuring Mixedness in the Netherlands," in *The Palgrave International Handbook of Mixed Racial and Ethnic Classification*, ed. Arine L. Rocha and Peter J. Apsinall (Cham: Palgrave Macmillan, 2020), 378. The fact that people from these kingdom territories were considered "migrants" in European Dutch research is another poignant example

of bifurcated citizenship, also evidenced in the official adoption in the mid-1990s of the categories of "autochtone" and "allochtone" to signify whether one was autochthonous in the Netherlands (that is, born within the territory of the European Netherlands) or born outside of it. In CBS research, these distinctions persisted for three generations and included in the "allochtonous" category even those with one grandparent born outside of the Netherlands.

131. Hazel Carby, *Imperial Intimacies: A Tale of Two Islands* (London: Verso, 2019), 65.

CONCLUSION

1. The surrounding city of San Nicolas remains home to a community of Arubans of African descent, many with ties to the former Lago plant. On notions of identity and self-understanding within this community, see Artwell Cain, *A Sense of Belonging. Multiple Narratives of English Speaking Arubans: Migration, Identification and Representation* (Edam: LM Publishers, 2017). On the influence of inter-Caribbean migration on Aruban culture, see G. T. E. Richardson, "Sweet Breakaway: An Ethnographic Study of Aruban Calypso Music and the Narratives of the One Happy Island" (Ph.D. diss., Vrije Universiteit Amsterdam, 2020), 61–62.

2. Mimi Sheller, *Island Futures: Caribbean Survival in the Anthropocene* (Durham, NC: Duke University Press, 2020), 10; Shaina Potts, "Offshore," in *Keywords in Radical Geography: Antipode at 50*, ed. *Antipode* Editorial Collective (Chichester: John Wiley & Sons Ltd., 2019), 200.

3. On the racial-sexual construction of the Caribbean as tourist "paradise," see M. Jacqui Alexander, *Pedagogies of Crossing: Meditations on Feminism, Sexual Politics, Memory, and the Sacred* (Durham, NC: Duke University Press, 2005), 54; Angelique V. Nixon, *Resisting Paradise: Tourism, Diaspora, and Sexuality in Caribbean Culture* (Jackson: University Press of Mississippi, 2015).

4. Ryan Cecil Jobson, "Black Gold in El Dorado: Frontiers of Race and Oil in Guyana," *Items: Insights from SSRC*, January 8, 2019, https://items.ssrc.org/race -capitalism/black-gold-in-el-dorado-frontiers-of-race-and-oil-in-guyana.

5. Robert Vitalis, *America's Kingdom: Mythmaking on the Saudi Oil Frontier* (Stanford, CA: Stanford University Press, 2007), xlll.

6. Lisa Lowe, *The Intimacies of Four Continents* (Durham, NC: Duke University Press, 2015), 18.

7. Hannah Appel, *The Licit Life of Capitalism: US Oil in Equatorial Guinea* (Durham, NC: Duke University Press, 2019), 97–99.

8. Linden Lewis, "Caribbean Masculinity at the *Fin de Siècle*," in *Interrogating Caribbean Masculinities: Theoretical and Empirical* Analyses, ed. Rhoda E. Reddock (Kingston: University of the West Indies Press, 2004), 255–56. As a

result of women's formal labor participation, fears of "male marginality" resonated across the region from the 1980s on. See Rhoda E. Reddock, "Interrogating Caribbean Masculinities: An Introduction," in *Interrogating Caribbean Masculinities: Theoretical and Empirical* Analyses, ed. Rhoda E. Reddock (Kingston: University of the West Indies Press, 2004), xvii.

9. Sonia Cuales, "Women, Reproduction and Foreign Capital in Curaçao," *Caraïbisch Forum* 1, no. 2 (1980): 77–80. The short-lived Texas Instruments assembly factory (1968–76) employed low-paid Curaçaoan women and abandoned the island just as union organizing increased and the company's ten-year tax holiday was set to expire.

10. Petrocultures Research Group, *After Oil* (Morgantown: West Virginia University Press, 2016), 24.

11. On migration as emancipatory practice, see Guno Jones, "Unequal Citizenship in the Netherlands: The Caribbean Dutch as Liminal Citizens," *Frame* 27, no. 2 (2014): 69–71.

12. Casey Williams, "Energy Humanities," *Energy Humanities*, October 6, 2020, https://www.energyhumanities.ca/news/energy-humanities-casey-williams.

13. Petrocultures Research Group, *After Oil*, 16, 19, 43.

14. Diary of Charlotte Life Warden, August 17, 1948, UT, BCAH, LCAC, box 2.207/M12.

15. "Coastal to Reopen Refinery in Aruba," *New York Times*, October 20, 1989, https://www.nytimes.com/1989/10/20/business/company-news-coastal-to -reopen-refinery-in-aruba.html.

16. "Valero buying Aruba refinery from El Paso," *Oil & Gas Journal*, February 5, 2004, https://www.ogj.com/general-interest/article/17292974/valero -buying-aruba-refinery-from-el-paso.

17. "De Lago en de Eagle: De olieindustrie op Aruba," Historia di Aruba, accessed July 31, 2022, http://www.historiadiaruba.aw/index.php?option=com _content&task=view&id=28&Itemid=42. In 2015, an Aruban state-run company assumed control of the refinery.

18. "Aruba delays refinery revamp amid US sanctions on Venezuela," *Oil & Gas Journal*, February 26, 2019, https://www.ogj.com/home/article/17222782 /aruba-delays-refinery-revamp-amid-us-sanctions-on-venezuela.

19. Patricia Garip and Canute James, "Caribbean aspires to reinvent downstream relics," *Argus*, July 8, 2021, https://www.argusmedia.com/en/news /2232378-caribbean-aspires-to-reinvent-downstream-relics; Luc Cohen, "Aruba looks towards long-Idled oil refinery, as tourism drop pummels economy," *Reuters*, April 19, 2021, https://www.reuters.com/world/americas/aruba-looks -towards-long-idled-oil-refinery-tourism-drop-pummels-economy-2021-04-19.

20. Patricia Garip, "Curaçao [sic] names another preferred refinery bidder," *Argus*, January 6, 2021, https://www.argusmedia.com/en/news/2174506-curacao -names-another-preferred-refinery-bidder.

21. "Curaçao sets talks with U.S.-Brazilian consortium to run island's oil refinery," *Reuters*, June 19, 2022, https://www.reuters.com/business/energy/curacao -sets-talks-with-us-brazilian-consortium-run-islands-oil-refinery-2022-06-20.

22. On legal disputes, see Ben Piven, "Curaçao [sic] oil refinery takeover: Good for jobs, bad for climate?" *Aljazeera*, December 29, 2019, https://www.aljazeera .com/economy/2019/12/27/curacao-oil-refinery-takeover-good-for-jobs-bad-for -climate. For research on atmospheric PAHs, see Erin L. Pulster et al., "Levels and Sources of Atmospheric Polycyclic Aromatic Hydrocarbons Surrounding an Oil Refinery in Curaçao," *Journal of Environmental Protection* 10 (2019): 431–51.

23. M. Crippa et al., *Fossil CO_2 and GHG Emissions of All World Countries* (Luxembourg: Publications Office of the European Union, 2019), 86.

24. Rivka Jaffe, *Concrete Jungles: Urban Pollution and the Politics of Difference in the Caribbean* (Oxford: Oxford University Press, 2016), 148–49. A similar attitude prevails in San Nicolas; see Richardson, "Sweet Breakaway," 64–65.

25. Irma was the first category five hurricane to reach the northeastern Caribbean islands of St. Maarten/St. Martin, Saba, and St. Eustatius. See Daphina Misiedjan, "Klimaat en het Koninkrijk: Waarom de internationale klimaatafspraken niet gelden voor de Caribische eilanden," *Nederlands Juristenblad* 25 (2022): 1683–88; Keston K. Perry, "Realising Climate Reparations: Towards a Global Climate Stabilization Fund and Resilience Fund Programme for Loss and Damage in Marginalised and Former Colonised Societies," *SSRN*, published March 1, 2020, https://ssrn.com/abstract=3561121. The island of Bonaire and Greenpeace began preparing a lawsuit against the Netherlands in 2022 to compel the country to address the devastating impact of climate change in this "overseas" municipality. See "Climate Change Could Have Devastating Impact on Bonaire," *Greenpeace*, September 28, 2022, https://www.greenpeace .org/nl/klimaatverandering/54574/bonaire-climare-research-lawsuit.

26. "Over Isla," Stichting SMOC, accessed July 31, 2022, https://www .stichtingsmoc.nl/over-isla/. According to an ExxonMobil-commissioned study, only 300,000 barrels of hydrocarbons were deemed recoverable. See Lago Phase II Environmental Assessment Report, 1985–6, UT, BCAH, LCAC, box 2.207/M23.

27. Misiedjan, "Klimaat en het Koninkrijk," 1686.

28. Yarimar Bonilla, "The Coloniality of Disaster: Race, Empire, and the Temporal Logics of Emergency in Puerto Rico, USA," *Political Geography* 78 (2020), https://doi.org/10.1016/j.polgeo.2020.102181. For examples of environmental harm caused by enclave refinery sites in the Caribbean, see Catalina M. de Onís, *Energy Islands: Metaphors of Power, Extractivism, and Justice in Puerto Rico* (Oakland: University of California Press, 2021), 45, 62–67; Matthew P. Johnson, "Black Gold of Paradise: Negotiating Oil Pollution in the US Virgin Islands, 1966–2012," *Environmental History* 24 (2019): 766–92; David Bond, "Oil in the Caribbean: Refineries, Mangroves, and the Negative Ecologies of Crude Oil," *Comparative Studies in Society and History* 59, no. 3 (2017): 600–28. On slow

violence, which accounts for accretive ecological devastation, see Rob Nixon, *Slow Violence and the Environmentalism of the Poor* (Cambridge: Harvard University Press, 2013).

29. On environmental damage and the body, see Linda Nash, *Inescapable Ecologies: A History of Disease, Environment, and Knowledge* (Berkeley: University of California Press, 2006); Vanessa Agard-Jones, "Bodies in the System," *Small Axe* 42 (2013): 182–92.

30. Cara Daggett, "Petro-masculinity: Fossil Fuels and Authoritarian Desire," *Millennium: Journal of International Studies* 47, no. 1 (2018): 31–32; Jaffe, *Concrete Jungles*, 136.

31. Kamala Kempadoo, *Sexing the Caribbean: Gender, Race and Sexual Labor* (New York: Routledge, 2004), 110.

32. On stereotypes of Latin American women, see Kempadoo, *Sexing the Caribbean*, 114, 105. On Venezuelan women's migration to Curaçao, see Jacqueline Martis, "Sun, Sex, and Not So Golden: 25 Years of Research on the Sex Trade in Curaçao," paper presented at the Society for Caribbean Studies, United Kingdom, July 6, 2022.

33. *Kontakto Antiano*, December 1971, 35, IISG, Periodicals; Tip Marugg, *The Roar of Morning*, trans. Paul Vincent (New Haven: Yale, 2015 [1988]), 106.

34. Gloria Wekker, *White Innocence: Paradoxes of Colonialism and Race* (Durham, NC: Duke University Press, 2016), 160–63. After 2010, when the islands of Bonaire, Saba, and St. Eustatius became "special municipalities" of the Netherlands, an increased number of European Dutch people relocated to the Caribbean Netherlands, especially to the island of Bonaire. This migration brings with it concerns about rising real estate costs and environmental degradation caused by coastal development. See Stacey Mac Donald, "Life in 'Paradise': A Social Psychological and Anthropological Study of Nature Conservation in the Caribbean Netherlands" (Ph.D. diss, Leiden University, 2022), prologue.

35. Michael O. Sharpe, *Postcolonial Citizens and Ethnic Migration: The Netherlands and Japan in the Age of Globalization* (Basingstoke: Palgrave Macmillan, 2014), 99–100; Gert Oostindie and Inge Klinkers, *Gedeeld Koninkrijk. De ontmanteling van de Nederlandse Antillen en de vernieuwing van de trans-Atlantische relaties* (Amsterdam: Amsterdam University Press, 2012), 80–81.

36. Jones, "Unequal Citizenship in the Netherlands."

37. Sam Jones, "Veel Caribische Nederlanders slachtoffer toeslagenaffaire," *Caribisch Netwerk*, February 1, 2021, https://caribischnetwerk.ntr.nl/2021/02/01/veel-caribische-nederlanders-slachtoffer-toeslagenaffaire/.

38. Wekker, *White Innocence*, 144–45; Philomena Essed and Isabel Hoving, "Innocence, Smug Ignorance, Resentment: An Introduction to Dutch Racism," in *Dutch Racism*, ed. Philemona Essed and Isabel Hoving (Leiden: Brill, 2014), 10–12.

39. Tijn van Beurden and Joost Jonker, "A Perfect Symbiosis: Curaçao, the Netherlands and Financial Offshore Services, 1951–2003," *Financial History*

Review 28, no. 1 (2021): 89–90. Conversations with Lianne Leonora shaped my thinking on this topic.

40. On this constellation of issues and the racialization of citizenship itself, see Egbert Alejandro Martina, "Policy and Intimacy," *Policy People*, accessed November 7, 2022, http://policy-people.com/egbert-alejandro-martina-policy-and-intimacy.

41. While antihomophobic and pro-feminist political movements have played an important part in Dutch political life since the 1960s, it is a relatively recent phenomenon for parties across the political spectrum to build consensus on issues like same-sex marriage, which developed concurrent to debates on immigration and citizenship. See Paul Mepschen and Jan Willem Duyvendak, "European Sexual Nationalisms: The Culturalization of Citizenship and the Sexual Politics of Belonging and Exclusion," *Perspectives on Europe* (2012): 70–76.

42. Chelsea Schields, "Intimacy and Integration: The Ambivalent Achievement of Marriage Equality in the Dutch Caribbean, 2007–2012," in *Euro-Caribbean Societies in the 21st Century: Offshore Finance, Local Élites and Contentious Politics*, ed. Sébastien Chauvin, Peter Clegg, and Bruno Cousin (Abingdon, UK: Routledge, 2018), 176–89. For an earlier debate on Aruba, see Omise'eke Natasha Tinsley, *Thiefing Sugar: Eroticism between Women in Caribbean Literature* (Durham, NC: Duke University Press, 2010), 30–32. Same-sex marriage is not legal in the autonomous countries of Aruba, Curaçao, and St. Maarten but island governments must recognize same-sex marriages performed elsewhere in the kingdom. See Wigbertson Julian Isenia, "Queer Sovereignties: Cultural Practices of Sexual Citizenship in the Dutch Caribbean" (Ph.D. diss, Universiteit van Amsterdam, 2022), 31.

43. Ronen Palan, *The Offshore World: Sovereign Markets, Virtual Places, and Nomad Millionaires* (Ithaca, NY: Cornell University Press, 2006), 11; Potts, "Offshore"; Yarimar Bonilla, "Ordinary Sovereignty," *Small Axe* 13 (2014): 152–65.

Bibliography

ARCHIVAL AND MANUSCRIPT SOURCES

Archivo Nacional Aruba (ANA), Oranjestad, Aruba
    Archief van het Bestuurscollege van het Eilandgebied Aruba, 1951–1961
        (BCAR)
        Bestrijding der Onzedelijkheid
        Eilandsraad Notulen
        Lago Werkstaking
Biblioteca Nacional Aruba (BNA), Oranjestad, Aruba
    Departamento Arubiana/Caribiana (DAC)
Curaçao Public Library (CPL), Willemstad, Curaçao
    Dokumento Nashonal (DN)
Erfgoedcentrum Nederlands Kloosterleven (ENK), St. Agatha, the Netherlands
    Nederlandse Provincie van de Order der Dominicanen (NPOD)
Internationaal Instituut voor Sociale Geschiedenis (IISG), Amsterdam, the
        Netherlands
    Archief Nederlandse Vereniging voor Seksuele Hervorming (NVSH)
    Archief Provo
    Periodicals
Mongui Maduro Library, Willemstad, Curaçao
    Antilliana Collection

Nationaal Archief Curaçao (NAC), Willemstad, Curaçao
  Gouvernementsarchief [1934] 1938–1945 [1951]
  Kabinet van de Gouverneur van de Nederlandse Antillen 1949, 1951–1990
  Objectendossiers van de Gouvernementssecretarie
  Staten van Curaçao
  Union di Muhé Antiano (UMA)—G. do Rego
Nationaal Archief van Nederland (NA), The Hague, the Netherlands
  Archief van het Kabinet van de Vice-Minister-President (1959–1972), Kabinet
      voor Surinaamse en Nederlands-Antilliaanse Zaken (KabSNA)
  Collectie 417 Struycken
  Collectie 420 P. Muntendam
  Landelijke Stichting Welzijn Antillianen (LSWA)
  Ministerie van Koloniën en opvolgers: Dossierarchief
  Nederlandse Consulaat te Santo Domingo
  Ronde Tafel Conferentie West
Stadsarchief Amsterdam (SA), Amsterdam, the Netherlands
  Archief van de Sociale Dienst
Universitaire Bibliotheken Leiden (UBL), Leiden, the Netherlands
  Koninklijk Instituut voor de Tropen Collection (KIT)
  Royal Netherlands Institute of Southeast Asian and Caribbean Studies/
      KITLV Collection
    Collection Jan Carel van Essen
University of Texas at Austin (UT), Dolph Briscoe Center for American History
      (BCAH), Austin, TX, United States
  ExxonMobil Historical Collection (EMHC)
  Lago Colony, Aruba Collection (LCAC)

SELECTED PERIODICALS AND JOURNALS

Amigoe di Curaçao (Curaçao)
Arubaanse Courant (Aruba)
Beurs- en Nieuwsberichten (Curaçao)
Kambio (Curaçao and the Netherlands)
Kontakto Antiano (the Netherlands)
Vitó (Curaçao)

ONLINE RESOURCES

Delpher, Koninklijke Bibliotheek, http://delpher.nl
Lago Oil and Transport Company Collection, Biblioteca Nacional Aruba,
  https://archive.org/details/lagocollection

Jaap van Soest, *Curaçaose cijferreeksen 1828–1955*, Data Archiving and Networking Services (DANS), Koninklijke Nederlandse Akademie van Wetenschappen (KNAW), https://easy.dans.knaw.nl/ui/datasets/id/easy-dataset:49962

Jaap van Soest Data Collection, Dutch Caribbean Digital Platform, University of Curaçao, http://uoc.sobeklibrary.com/jaapvansoest/all

Events Programs, Mongui Maduro Foundation, https://www.jstor.org/site/mongui-maduro-foundation/event-programs/

Aruba Esso News, Digital Library of the Caribbean, https://dloc.com/CA03400001/00315

PUBLISHED SOURCES

Abraham-van der Mark, Eva. "Continuity and Change in the Afro-Caribbean Family in Curaçao in the Twentieth Century." *Community, Work & Family* 6, no. 1 (2003): 77–88.

———. "The Impact of Industrialization on Women: A Caribbean Case." In *Women, Men, and the International Division of Labor*, edited by June Nash and María P. Fernández-Kelly, 374–86. Albany: SUNY Press, 1983.

———. *Yu'i Mama. Enkele facetten van gezinsstructuur op Curaçao*. Assen: Van Gorcum, 1972.

Agard-Jones, Vanessa. "Bodies in the System." *Small Axe* 42 (2013): 182–92.

Alexander, M. Jacqui. *Pedagogies of Crossing: Meditations on Feminism, Sexual Politics, Memory, and the Sacred*. Durham, NC: Duke University Press, 2005.

———. "Not Just Any(*body*) Can Be a Citizen: The Politics of Law, Sexuality and Postcoloniality in Trinidad and Tobago and the Bahamas." *Feminist Review* 48 (1994): 5–23.

Allen, Rose Mary. "Amador Paulo Nita: Writer, Labor Activist, and Politician." *Oxford African American Studies Center Database*. Last modified May 31, 2017. https://doi.org/10.1093/acref/9780195301731.013.74671.

———. *Di ki manera? A Social History of Afro-Curaçaoans, 1863–1917*. Amsterdam: SWP, 2007.

———. "Contesting Respectability and Sexual Politics in Post-Emancipation Curaçao." In *Archaeologies of Erasures and Silences: Recovering Othered Languages, Literatures and Cultures in the Dutch Caribbean and Beyond*, edited by Nicholas Faraclas, Ronald Severing, Christa Weijer, Elisabeth Echteld, Wim Rutgers, and Robert Dupey, 99–112. Curaçao and Puerto Rico: University of Curaçao and Universidad de Puerto Rico, 2017.

———. "Contextualizing and Learning from Kas di Pueblo." In *Kas di pueblo: Kas ku un mishon . . . House with a mission*, edited by Rose Mary Allen and Maria Liberia-Peters, 228–38. Curaçao: Fundashon Maria Liberia-Peters, 2019.

——. "Emigración laboral de Curazao a Cuba a principios del siglo XX: Una experiencia." *Revista Mexicana del Caribe* 5, no. 9 (2000): 40–103.

——. "An Intersectional Approach to Understanding the Social Life of Female, British Caribbean, Immigrant Domestic Workers in Twentieth Century Curaçao: Controlling Sexual Morality." In *Dissolving Disciplines: Tidal Shifts in the Study of Language, Literatures and Cultures of the Dutch Caribbean and Beyond*, edited by Nicholas Faraclas, Ronald Severing, Christa Weijer, Elisabeth Echteld, Wim Rutgers, and Sally Delgado, 109–22. Curaçao and Puerto Rico: University of Curaçao and Universidad de Puerto Rico, 2018.

——. "'Learning to be a Man': Afro-Caribbean Seamen and Maritime Workers from Curaçao in the Beginning of the Twentieth Century." *Caribbean Studies* 39, no. 1 (2011): 43–64.

——. "Negotiating Gender, Citizenship and Nationhood through Universal Adult Suffrage in Curaçao." *Caribbean Review of Gender Studies* 12 (2018): 299–318.

——. "Women Making Freedom: Locating Gender in Intra-Caribbean Migration from a Curaçaoan Perspective." *a/b: Auto/Biography Studies* 33, no. 3 (2018): 705–19.

——. "The Trinta di Mei Labor Revolt and Its Aftermath: Anticipating a Just and Equitable Curaçaoan Nation." In *Equaliberty in the Dutch Caribbean: Ways of Being Non/Sovereign*, edited by Yvon van der Pijl and Francio Guadeloupe, 69–84. Newark, NJ: Rutgers University Press, 2022.

Alofs, Luc. "'Een vlek of dorp die men nergens anders aantreft': Savaneta en de dorpsvorming op het negentiende-eeuwse Aruba." In *Arubaans Akkord*, edited by Luc Alofs, W. Rutgers, and H. E. Coomans, 1–11. Bloemendaal and The Hague: Kabinet van de Gevolmachtigde Minister van Aruba, 1997.

——. "Onderhorigheid en separatisme: Koloniaal bestuur en lokale politiek op Aruba." Ph.D. diss, Leiden University, 2011.

——. "Publieke dames in een publiek debat: De geschiedenis van Campo Alegre op Aruba, 1950–1957." In *Cinco aña na caminda: Opstellen aangeboden ter gelegenheid van het eerste lustrum van de Universiteit van Aruba*, edited by G. F. M. Bossers, A. R. O. Ringeling, and M. Tratnik, 21–32. Oranjestad: University of Aruba, 1993.

——. "Revolte en afscheiding: Dertig mei en Aruba." In *Dromen en littekens. Dertig jaar na de Curaçaose revolte, 30 mei 1969*, edited by Gert Oostindie, 163–76. Amsterdam: Amsterdam University Press, 1999.

Alofs, Luc, and Leontine Merkies. *Ken ta Arubiano? Sociale integratie en natievorming op Aruba*. Leiden: KITLV Press, 1990.

Amin, Samir. "Population Policies and Development Strategies: Underpopulated Africa." Dakar, Senegal: UNESCO, 1971.

Anderson, William, and Russell Dynes. *Social Movements, Violence, and Change: The May Movement in Curaçao*. Columbus: Ohio State University Press, 1975.

Antonius-Smits, Christel C. F., Juanita Altenberg, Teersa Burleson, Tania Taitt-Codrington, Muriel van Russel, Diana van der Leende, Deborah Hordijk, and Ruben F. Del Prado. "Gold and Commercial Sex: Exploring the Link between Small-Scale Gold Mining and Commercial Sex in the Rainforest of Suriname." In *Sun, Sex, and Gold: Tourism and Sex Work in the Caribbean*, edited by Kamala Kempadoo, 237–59. Lanham: Rowman & Littlefield, 1999.

Appel, Hannah. *The Licit Life of Capitalism: US Oil in Equatorial Guinea.* Durham, NC: Duke University Press, 2019.

Appel, Hannah, Arthur Mason, and Michael Watts. "Introduction: Oil Talk." In *Subterranean Estates: Life Worlds of Oil and Gas*, edited by Hannah Appel, Arthur Mason, and Michael Watts, 1–26. Ithaca, NY: Cornell University Press, 2015.

———, eds. *Subterranean Estates: Life Worlds of Oil and Gas.* Ithaca, NY: Cornell University Press, 2015.

Arion, Frank Martinus. *Double Play.* Translated by Paul Vincent. London: Farber and Farber, 1998 [1973].

Aymer, Paula. *Uprooted Women: Migrant Domestics in the Caribbean.* Westport, CT: Praeger, 1997.

Bailkin, Jordanna. *The Afterlife of Empire.* Berkeley: University of California Press, 2013.

Balibar, Étienne. "Is There a Neo-Racism?" In *Race, Nation, Class: Ambiguous Identities,* edited by Étienne Balibar and Immanuel Wallerstein, 17–28. London: Verso, 1988.

Balkenhol, Markus. "Tracing Slavery: An Ethnography of Diaspora, Affect, and Cultural Heritage in Amsterdam." Ph.D. diss., Vrije Universiteit Amsterdam, 2014.

Barrow, Christine. *Family in the Caribbean: Themes and Perspectives.* Kingston: Ian Randle Publishers, 1996.

Beckford, George. *Persistent Poverty: Underdevelopment in Plantation Economies of the Third World.* London: Oxford University Press, 1972.

Ben, Pablo, and Santiago Joaquin Insausti. "Dictatorial Rule and Sexual Politics in Argentina: The Case of the Frente de Liberación Homosexual, 1967–1976." *Hispanic American Historical Review* 97, no. 2 (2017): 297–325.

Best, Lloyd and Kari Polanyi Levitt. *Essays on the Theory of Plantation Economy: A Historical and Institutional Approach to Caribbean Development.* Kingston: University of the West Indies Press, 2009.

Bet-Shlimon, Arbella. *City of Black Gold: Oil, Ethnicity, and the Making of Modern Kirkuk.* Stanford, CA: Stanford University Press, 2019.

Bliss, Katherine Elaine. *Compromised Positions: Prostitution, Public Health, and Gender Politics in Revolutionary Mexico City.* University Park: Penn State University Press, 2002.

Bolland, O. Nigel. "Labor Protests, Rebellions, and the Rise of Nationalism during Depression and War." In *The Caribbean: A History of the Region and its Peoples*, edited by Stephan Palmié and Francisco A. Scarano, 459–74. Chicago: University of Chicago Press, 2011.

Bogues, Anthony. "The *Abeng* Newspaper and the Radical Politics of Postcolonial Blackness." In *Black Power in the Caribbean*, edited by Kate Quinn, 76–96. Gainesville: University Press of Florida, 2014.

Bond, David. "Oil in the Caribbean: Refineries, Mangroves, and the Negative Ecologies of Crude Oil." *Comparative Studies in Society and History* 59, no. 3 (2017): 600–28.

Bonilla, Yarimar. "The Coloniality of Disaster: Race, Empire, and the Temporal Logics of Emergency in Puerto Rico, USA." *Political Geography* 78 (2020). https://doi.org/10.1016/j.polgeo.2020.102181.

———. *Non-Sovereign Futures: French Caribbean Politics in the Wake of Disenchantment*. Chicago: University of Chicago Press, 2015.

———. "Ordinary Sovereignty." *Small Axe* 13 (2014): 152–65.

Bosma, Ulbe. *Terug uit de koloniën. Zestig jaar postkoloniale migranten en hun organisaties*. Amsterdam: Bert Bakker, 2009.

Bourbonnais, Nicole. *Birth Control in the Decolonizing Caribbean: Reproductive Politics and Practice on Four Islands, 1930–1970*. Cambridge: Cambridge University Press, 2016.

Bowen, Dawn S. "In the Shadow of the Refinery: An American Oil Company Town on the Caribbean Island of Aruba." *Journal of Cultural Geography* 36, no. 1 (2019): 49–77.

Boyer, Dominic. "Energopower: An Introduction." *Anthropological Quarterly* 87, no. 2 (2014): 309–34.

Braithwaite, E. R. *To Sir, with Love*. New York: Open Roads, 1959.

Brandhorst, Henny. "From Neo-Malthusianism to Sexual Reform: The Dutch Section of the World League for Sexual Reform." *Journal of the History of Sexuality* 12 (2003): 38–67.

Brereton, Bridget. "Family Strategies, Gender, and the Shift to Wage Labour in the British Caribbean." In *The Colonial Caribbean in Transition: Essays on Postemancipation Social and Cultural History*, edited by Bridget Brereton and Kevin A. Yelvington, 77–107. Gainesville: University Press of Florida, 1999.

———. *A History of Modern Trinidad, 1783–1962*. Kingston: Heinemann, 1981.

Briggs, Laura. *Reproducing Empire: Race, Sex, Science, and U.S. Imperialism in Puerto Rico*. Berkeley: University of California Press, 2003.

Brown, Stanley. "Ik ben de Voltaire van dertig mei." In *Curaçao, 30 mei 1969. Verhalen over de revolte*, edited by Gert Oostindie, 12–23. Amsterdam: Amsterdam University Press, 1999.

Brown, Wenzell. *Angry Men—Laughing Men: The Caribbean Cauldron*. New York: Greenberg, 1947.

Buschkens, Willem F. L. *The Family System of the Paramaribo Creoles*. Translated by Maria J. L. van Yperen. The Hague: Martinus Nijhoff, 1974.

Bush, Barbara. "Colonial Research and the Social Sciences at the End of
   Empire: The West Indian Social Survey, 1944–57." *The Journal of Imperial
   and Commonwealth History* 41, no. 3 (2013): 451–74.
Bussemaker, Jet, Annemiek van Drenth, Trudie Knijn, and Janneke Plantenga.
   "Allenstaande moeders en sociaal beleid in Nederland: Van verzorgers naar
   kostwinners?" *Beleid en Maatschappij* 26, no. 1 (1996): 41–51.
Cain, Artwell. *A Sense of Belonging. Multiple Narratives of English Speaking
   Arubans: Migration, Identification and Representation.* Edam: LM Pub-
   lishers, 2017.
Captain, Esther, and Guno Jones. "Inversing Dependence: The Dutch Antilles,
   Suriname and the Desperate Netherlands during World War II." In *World
   War II and the Caribbean*, edited by Karen Eccles and Debbie McCollin,
   71–91. Kingston: University of the West Indies Press, 2017.
———. *Oorlogs erfgoed overzee. De erfenis van de tweede wereldoorlog van
   Aruba, Curaçao, Indonesië en Suriname.* Amsterdam: Bert Bakker, 2010.
Carby, Hazel. *Imperial Intimacies: A Tale of Two Islands.* London: Verso, 2019.
Casey, Matthew. *Empire's Guestworkers: Haitian Migrants in Cuba during the
   Age of US Occupation.* Cambridge: Cambridge University Press, 2017.
Chase, Michelle. *Revolution within the Revolution: Women and Gender Politics
   in Cuba, 1952–1962.* Chapel Hill: University of North Carolina Press, 2015.
Chase, Michelle and Isabella Cosse. "Revolutionary Positions: Sexuality and
   Gender in Cuba and Beyond." *Radical History Review* 136 (2020): 1–10.
Chauvin, Sébastien, Peter Clegg, and Bruno Cousin. "Introduction: Offshore
   Europe on the Move." In *Euro-Caribbean Societies in the 21st Century:
   Offshore Finance, Local Elites and Contentious Politics*, edited by Sébastien
   Chauvin, Peter Clegg, and Bruno Cousin, 1–9. Abingdon, UK: Routledge, 2018.
Childers, Kristen Stromberg. "Departmentalization, Migration, and the Politics
   of the Family in the Post-war French Caribbean." *History of the Family* 14
   (2009): 177–90.
———. *Seeking Imperialism's Embrace: National Identity, Decolonization, and
   Assimilation in the French Caribbean.* Oxford: Oxford University Press, 2016.
Chomsky, Aviva. *West Indian Workers and the United Fruit Company in Costa
   Rica, 1870–1940.* Baton Rouge: Louisiana State University Press, 1996.
Clegg, Peter and Emilio Pantojas-García, eds. *Governance in the Non-
   Independent Caribbean: Challenges and Opportunities in the Twenty-First
   Century.* Kingston: Ian Randle Publishers, 2009.
Clemencia, Joceline. "Katibu ta galiña: From Hidden to Open Protest in
   Curaçao." In *A History of Literature in the Caribbean, Vol. 2: English and
   Dutch Speaking Regions*, edited by A. James Arnold, 433–42. Philadelphia:
   John Benjamins Publishing Co., 2001.
Coles, Anne, and Anne-Meike Fechter. *Gender and Family Among Trans-
   national Professionals.* Abingdon, UK: Routledge, 2008.

Collins, Michael. "Decolonisation and the 'Federal Moment.'" *Diplomacy and Statecraft* 24 (2013): 21–40.

Colpani, Gianmaria, and Wigbertson Julian Isenia. "Strange Fruits: Queer of Color Intellectual Labor in the 1980s and 1990s." In *Postcolonial Intellectuals in Europe: Critics, Artists, Movements, and Their Publics*, edited by Sandra Ponzanesi and Adriano José Habed, 213–30. Lanham, MD: Rowman & Littlefield International, 2018.

Connelly, Matthew. *Fatal Misconception: The Struggle to Control World Population*. Cambridge: The Belknap Press of Harvard University Press, 2008.

Cooper, Frederick. *Citizenship between Empire and Nation: Remaking France and French Africa, 1945–1960*. Princeton, NJ: Princeton University Press, 2014.

———. "Modernizing Colonialism and the Limits of Empire." *Items & Issues: Social Science Research Council* 4, no. 4 (2003): 1–10.

———. "Possibility and Constraint: African Independence in Historical Perspective." *The Journal of African History* 49, no. 2 (2009): 167–96.

———. "Writing the History of Development." *Journal of Modern European History* 8, no. 1 (2010): 9–12.

Coronil, Fernando. *The Magical State: Nature, Money, and Modernity in Venezuela*. Chicago: University of Chicago Press, 1997.

Corrêa, Sonia. "Reproductive Rights in Developing Nations." In *International Encyclopedia of the Social & Behavioral Sciences*, edited by Neil J. Smelser and Paul B. Baltes, 13188–193. Oxford: Pergamon, 2001.

Crippa, M., G. Oreggioni, D. Guizzardi, M. Muntean, E. Schaaf, E. Lo Vullo, E. Solazzo, F. Monforti-Ferrario, J. Olivier, and E. Vignati. *Fossil CO2 and GHG Emissions of All World Countries*. Luxembourg: Publications Office of the European Union, 2019.

Cuales, Sonia. "In Search of Our Memory: Gender in the Netherlands Antilles." *Feminist Review* 59 (1998): 86–100.

———. "Women, Reproduction and Foreign Capital in Curaçao." *Caraïbisch Forum* 1, no. 2 (1980): 75–86.

Dagget, Cara. *The Birth of Energy: Fossil Fuels, Thermodynamics, and the Politics of Work*. Durham, NC: Duke University Press, 2019.

———. "Petro-masculinity: Fossil Fuels and Authoritarian Desire." *Millennium: Journal of International Studies* 47, no. 1 (2018): 25–44.

Daily, Andrew. "Race, Citizenship, and Antillean Student Activism in Postwar France, 1946–1968." *French Historical Studies* 37, no. 2 (2014): 331–57.

de Barros, Juanita. *Reproducing the British Caribbean: Sex, Gender, and Population Politics after Slavery*. Chapel Hill: University of North Carolina Press, 2014.

de Jong, Lammert and Dirk Kruijt, eds. *Extended Statehood in the Caribbean: Paradoxes of Quasi Colonialism, Local Autonomy and Extended Statehood in the USA, French, Dutch and British Caribbean*. Amsterdam: Rozenburg, 2005.

de Koning, Anouk. "Shadows of the Plantation? A Social History of Suriname's Bauxite Town Moengo." *New West Indian Guide* 85, no. 3/4 (2011): 215–46.

De leefsituatie van Surinamers en Antillianen in Nederland 1985, Deel I en II. The Hague: Staatsuitgeverij/CBS-Publikaties, 1986.

de Moor, R. A. *Huwelijk en gezin. Wat is hun toekomst in West-Europa.* Baarn: Uitgeverij Ambo, 1985.

Dekker, Jeroen J. H. *Curaçao zonder/met Shell: Een bijdrage tot bestudering van demografische, economische en sociale processen in de periode 1900–1929.* Zutphen: De Walburg Pers, 1982.

Derby, Lauren. *The Dictator's Seduction: Politics and the Popular Imagination in the Era of Trujillo.* Durham, NC: Duke University Press, 2004.

Dietrich, Christopher. *Oil Revolution: Anticolonial Elites, Sovereign Rights, and the Economic Culture of Decolonization.* Cambridge: Cambridge University Press, 2017.

Dols, Chris, and Maarten van den Bos. "*Humanae Vitae*: Catholic Attitudes to Birth Control in the Netherlands and Transnational Church Politics, 1945–1975." In *The Schism of '68: Catholicism, Contraception and Humanae Vitae in Europe, 1945–1975,* edited by Alana Harris, 23–47. Cham: Palgrave Macmillan, 2018.

Donoghue, Michael E. *Borderland on the Isthmus: Race, Culture, and the Struggle for the Canal Zone.* Durham, NC: Duke University Press, 2014.

do Rego, Charles P. *The Portuguese Immigrant in Curaçao: Immigration, Participation, and Integration in the 20th Century.* Willemstad: Carib-Publishing, 2012.

———. "Portuguese Labor Migration to Curaçao." *Caribbean Studies* 42, no. 2 (2014): 155–79.

Duke, Eric D. *Building a Nation: Caribbean Federation in the Black Diaspora.* Gainesville: University Press of Florida, 2019.

Dupont, Wannes. "The Case for Contraception: Medicine, Morality, and Sexology at the Catholic University of Leuven (1930–1968)." *Histoire, médecine et santé* (2018): 49–65.

———. "Of Human Love: Catholics Campaigning for Sexual Aggiornamento in Postwar Belgium." In *The Schism of '68: Catholicism, Contraception and Humanae Vitae in Europe, 1945–1975,* edited by Alana Harris, 49–71. Cham: Palgrave Macmillan, 2018.

Duyvendak, Jan Willem and P. W. A. Scholten. "Beyond the Dutch 'Multicultural Model.'" *Journal of International Migration and Integration* 12, no. 3 (2011): 331–48.

Ehrlich, Paul. *The Population Bomb.* New York: Ballantine Books, 1968.

Esch, Elizabeth. *The Color Line and the Assembly Line: Managing Race in the Ford Empire.* Oakland: University of California Press, 2018.

Essed, Philomena. *Alledaags Racisme.* Amsterdam: Feministische Uitgeverij Sara, 1984.

———. *Understanding Everyday Racism: An Interdisciplinary Theory*. London: Sage Publications, 1994.

Essed, Philomena, and Isabel Hoving. "Innocence, Smug Ignorance, Resentment: An Introduction to Dutch Racism." In *Dutch Racism*, edited by Philemona Essed and Isabel Hoving, 9–29. Leiden: Brill, 2014.

Essed, Philomena, and Kwame Nimako. "Designs and (Co)Incidents: Cultures of Scholarship and Public Policy on Immigrants/Minorities in the Netherlands." *International Journal of Comparative Sociology* 47, no. 3/4 (2006): 281–312.

Fabricant, Nicole, and Bret Gustafson. "Revolutionary Oil? Offshore Drilling in Cuba." *NACLA Report on the Americas* 49, no. 4 (2017): 441–43.

Fanon, Frantz. *The Wretched of the Earth*. Translated by Constance Farrington. New York: Grove Press, 1963.

Farnsworth-Alvear, Ann. *Dulcinea in the Factory: Myths, Morals, Men, and Women in Colombia's Industrial Experiment, 1905–1960*. Durham, NC: Duke University Press, 2000.

Ferguson, Roderick. *Aberrations in Black: Toward a Queer of Color Critique*. Minneapolis: University of Minnesota Press, 2004.

Fernández, Johanna. *The Young Lords: A Radical History*. Chapel Hill: University of North Carolina Press, 2019.

Findlay, Eileen. *Imposing Decency: The Politics of Sexuality and Race in Puerto Rico, 1870–1920*. Durham, NC: Duke University Press, 1999.

Flores-Villalobos, Joan. "'Freak Letters': Tracing Gender, Race, and Diaspora in the Panama Canal Archive." *Small Axe* 59 (2019): 34–56.

Fogarty, Richard. "Race and Sex, Fear and Loathing in France during the Great War." In *Brutality and Desire: War and Sexuality in Europe's Twentieth Century*, edited by Dagmar Herzog, 59–90. Basingstoke: Palgrave Macmillan, 2009.

Foray, Jennifer L. *Visions of Empire in the Nazi-Occupied Netherlands*. Cambridge: Cambridge University Press, 2013.

Frank, Chandra. "Sister Outsider and Audre Lorde in the Netherlands: On Transnational Queer Feminisms and Archival Methodological Practices." *Feminist Review* 121 (2019): 11–25.

Freeman, Carla. *Entrepreneurial Selves: Neoliberal Respectability and the Making of a Caribbean Middle Class*. Durham, NC: Duke University Press, 2014.

———. *High Tech and High Heels in the Global Economy: Women, Work, and Pink-Collar Identities in the Caribbean*. Durham, NC: Duke University Press, 2000.

French, William. "Prostitutes and Guardian Angels: Women, Work, and the Family in Porfirian Mexico." *The Hispanic American Historical Review* 72 (1992): 529–53.

Fuentes, Marisa. *Dispossessed Lives: Enslaved Women, Violence, and the Archive*. Philadelphia: University of Pennsylvania Press, 2016.

Garavini, Giuliano. *The Rise and Fall of OPEC in the Twentieth Century.* Oxford: Oxford University Press, 2019.

Gastelaars, Marja. *Een geregeld leven. Sociologie en sociale politiek in Neder-land, 1925–1968.* Amsterdam: Sua, 1985.

Gershenhorn, Jerry. *Melville J. Herskovits and the Racial Politics of Knowledge.* Lincoln: University of Nebraska Press, 2004.

Getachew, Adom. *Worldmaking after Empire: The Rise and Fall of Self-Determination.* Princeton, NJ: Princeton University Press, 2019.

Giovanetti, Jorge L. *Black British Migrants in Cuba: Race, Labor, and Empire in the Twentieth-Century Caribbean, 1898–1948.* Cambridge: Cambridge University Press, 2018.

Gooskens, Ineke. *Surinaamse vrouwelijke gezinshoofden in Bijstand en W.W.V. te Amsterdam.* Amsterdam: Gemeentlijke Sociale Dienst, Afdeeling Beleidsvoorbereiding en Wetenschappelijke Onderzoek, 1975.

Green, Vera. *Migrants in Aruba: Interethnic Integration.* Assen: Van Gorcum, 1974.

Groenewoud, Margo. "Decolonization, Otherness, and the Neglect of the Dutch Caribbean in Caribbean Studies." *Small Axe* 64 (2021): 102–15.

——. "Les mobilisations féminines dans les Antilles néerlandaises (Curaçao et Aruba, 1946–1993)." *Clio. Femmes, Genre, Histoire* 50 (2019): 63–85.

——. "'Nou koest, nou kalm.' De ontwikkeling van de Curaçaose samenleving, 1915–1973: Van koloniaal en kerkelijk gezag naar zelfbestuur en burgerschap." Ph.D. diss, Leiden University, 2017.

Gruber, German, Jr. dir. *HUMA: Trint'i Mei Lantamentu Anunsia.* NAAM Foundation, 2021. https://www.youtube.com/watch?v=o_ZL6eQCXY8.

Grüning, C. M., J. L. Martina, and R. Winkel, eds. *50 jaar Staten van de Nederlandse Antillen.* Willemstad: Staten van de Nederlandse Antillen, 1988.

Guadeloupe, Francio. *Chanting Down the New Jerusalem: Calypso, Christianity, and Capitalism in the Caribbean.* Berkeley: University of California Press, 2009.

Guerra, Lillian. "Gender Policing, Homosexuality, and the New Patriarchy of the Cuban Revolution." *Social History* 35, no. 3 (2010): 268–89.

Guy, Donna. *Sex and Danger in Buenos Aires: Prostitution, Family, and Nation in Argentina.* Cambridge: Cambridge University Press, 1991.

Habibe, Henry. *Un herida biba ta: Een verkenning van het poëtisch oeuvre van Pierre Lauffer.* Curaçao: Self-published, 1994.

Harris, Alana, ed. *The Schism of '68: Catholicism, Contraception and Humanae Vitae in Europe, 1945–1975.* Cham: Palgrave Macmillan, 2018.

Hartman, Saidiya. *Lose Your Mother: A Journey Along the Atlantic Slave Route.* New York: Farrar, Straus and Giroux, 2007.

——. "Venus in Two Acts." *Small Axe* 26, no. 12 (2008): 1–14.

Hartog, Johan. *Aruba, Past and Present: From the Time of the Indians until Today*. Translated by J. A. Verleun. Oranjestad: D. J. de Wit, 1961.

———. *Aruba: Zoals het was, zoals het werd*. Oranjestad: Gebroeders de Wit, 1953.

Haveman, Monique. *'Hier sta ik er alleen voor': Een inventariserend onderzoek onder Antilliaanse vrouwen*. Utrecht: Kibra Hacha, 1984.

Hayes, Brian. "Automation on the Job." *American Scientist* 97, no. 1 (2009): 10–14.

Hein, Carola. "Oil Spaces: The Global Petroleumscape in the Rotterdam/The Hague Area." *Journal of Urban History* 44, no. 5 (2018): 887–929.

Hellema, Duco, Cees Wiebes, and Toby Witte. *The Netherlands and the Oil Crisis: Business as Usual*. Amsterdam: Amsterdam University Press, 2004.

Henriquez, Jeanne. "'Black is Beautiful' is voor vrouwen heel belangrijk geweest." In *Curaçao, 30 mei 1969. Verhalen over de revolte*, edited by Gert Oostindie, 42–47. Amsterdam: Amsterdam University Press, 1999.

———. *Kòrsou su muhénan pionero*. Willemstad: Archivo Nashonal di Antia Hulandes, 2002.

———. "Motherhood is a State of Mind: Testimonies of Single Curaçaoan Mothers." In *Mundu Yama Sinta Mira: Womanhood in Curaçao*, edited by Richenel Ansano, Joceline Clemencia, Jeanette Cook, and Eithel Martis, 81–96. Willemstad: Fundashon Publikashon Curaçao, 1992.

Herskovits, Melville J. *The Myth of the Negro Past*. New York: Harper & Brothers Publishers, 1941.

Herzog, Dagmar. *Sex after Fascism: Memory and Morality in Twentieth-Century Germany*. Princeton, NJ: Princeton University Press, 2005.

———. *Sexuality in Europe: A Twentieth-Century History*. Cambridge: Cambridge University Press, 2011.

Higginbotham, Evelyn Brooks. "African-American Women's History and the Metalanguage of Race." *Signs* 17, no. 2 (1992): 251–74.

Hitchcock, Peter. "Velocity and Viscosity." In *Subterranean Estates: Life Worlds of Oil and Gas*, edited by Hannah Appel, Arthur Mason, and Michael Watts, 45–60. Ithaca: Cornell University Press, 2015.

Hoefte, Rosemarijn. "The Difficulty of Getting it Right: Dutch Policy in the Caribbean." *Itinerario* 25, no. 2 (2001): 59–72.

———. *Suriname in the Long Twentieth Century: Domination, Contestation, Globalization*. Basingstoke: Palgrave Macmillan, 2014.

Hoefte, Rosemarijn, with Anouk de Koning. "Bauxite Mining in Moengo: Remnants of the Past and Signs of Modernity." In Hoefte, *Suriname in the Long Twentieth Century*, 113–32.

Hoetink, Harry. *Caribbean Race Relations: A Study of Two Variants*. London: Institute of Race Relations, 1971.

———. *Het patroon van de oude Curaçaose samenleving. Een sociologische studie*. Assen: Van Gorcum, 1958.

Hollander, Harold. "Er is van onze strijd niets terechtgekomen." In *Curaçao, 30 mei 1969: Verhalen over de revolte*, edited by Gert Oostindie, 48–53. Amsterdam: Amsterdam University Press, 1999.

Howarth, Stephen, and Joost Jonker. *A History of Royal Dutch Shell, Vol. 2: Powering the Hydrocarbon Revolution, 1939–1973*. New York: Oxford University Press, 2007.

Huber, Matthew. *Lifeblood: Oil, Freedom, and the Forces of Capital*. Minneapolis: University of Minnesota Press, 2013.

Hudson, Peter James. *Bankers and Empire: How Wall Street Colonized the Caribbean*. Chicago: University of Chicago Press, 2017.

Hughes, David McDermott. *Energy Without Conscience: Oil, Climate Change, and Complicity*. Durham, NC: Duke University Press, 2017.

Hynson, Rachel. "'Count, Capture, and Reeducate': The Campaign to Rehabilitate Cuba's Female Sex Workers, 1959–1966." *Journal of the History of Sexuality* 24, no. 1 (2015): 125–53.

Ignaciuk, Agata, and Laura Kelly. "Contraception and Catholicism in the Twentieth Century: Transnational Perspectives on Expert, Activist, and Intimate Practices." *Medical History* 64, no. 2 (2020): 163–72.

Isenia, Wigbertson Julian. "Looking for *Kambrada*: Sexuality and Social Anxieties in the Dutch Colonial Archive." *Tijdschrift voor Genderstudies* 22, no. 2 (2019): 125–43.

———. "Queer Sovereignties: Cultural Practices of Sexual Citizenship in the Dutch Caribbean." Ph.D. diss, Universiteit van Amsterdam, 2022.

Jaffe, Rivka. *Concrete Jungles: Urban Pollution and the Politics of Difference in the Caribbean*. Oxford: Oxford University Press, 2016.

James, Winston. *Holding Aloft the Banner of Ethiopia: Caribbean Radicalism in Early Twentieth-Century America*. New York: Verso, 1998.

Jobson, Ryan Cecil. "Black Gold in El Dorado: Frontiers of Race and Oil in Guyana." *Items: Insights from SSRC*. Published January 8, 2019. https://items.ssrc.org/race-capitalism/black-gold-in-el-dorado-frontiers-of-race-and-oil-in-guyana.

Johnson, Matthew P. "Black Gold of Paradise: Negotiating Oil Pollution in the US Virgin Islands, 1966-2012." *Environmental History* 24 (2019): 766–92.

Jones, Guno. "Tussen onderdanen, Rijksgenoten en Nederlanders: Nederlandse politici over burgers uit Oost en West en Nederland, 1945–2005." Ph.D. diss., Vrije Universiteit Amsterdam, 2007.

———. "Unequal Citizenship in the Netherlands: The Caribbean Dutch as Liminal Citizens." *Frame* 27, no. 2 (2014): 65–84.

Jones, Guno, and Betty de Hart. "(Not) Measuring Mixedness in the Netherlands." In *The Palgrave International Handbook of Mixed Racial and Ethnic Classification*, edited by Arine L. Rocha and Peter J. Apsinall, 367–87. Cham: Palgrave Macmillan, 2020.

Jonker, Joost, and Jan Luiten van Zanden. *A History of Royal Dutch Shell, Vol. 1: From Challenger to Joint Industry Leader, 1890–1939.* Oxford: Oxford University Press, 2007.

Kalm, Florence. "The Dispersive and Reintegrating Nature of Population Segments of a Third World Society: Aruba, Netherlands Antilles." Ph.D. diss, City University of New York, 1975.

———. "The Two Faces of Antillean Prostitution." *Archives of Sexual Behavior* 14, no. 3 (1985): 203–17.

Kampwirth, Karen, ed. *Gender and Populism in Latin America: Passionate Politics.* University Park: Penn State University Press, 2010.

Katsiaficas, George. "Organization and Movement: The Case of the Black Panther Party and the Revolutionary People's Constitutional Convention of 1970." In *Liberation, Imagination, and the Black Panther Party: A New Look at the Panthers and Their Legacy*, edited by Kathleen Cleaver and George Katsiaficas, 141–55. New York: Routledge, 2001.

Kempadoo, Kamala. *Sexing the Caribbean: Gender, Race and Sexual Labor.* New York: Routledge, 2004.

Kempton, Richard. *The Provos: Amsterdam's Anarchist Revolt.* New York: Autonomedia, 2007.

King, Rosamond. *Island Bodies: Transgressive Sexualities in the Caribbean Imagination.* Gainesville: University of Florida Press, 2014.

Kinley, David and Michele Salkin. "The Caribbean Export Refining Center." *NACLA's Latin America and Empire Report* 10, no. 8 (1976): 3–13.

Kleijn, Mariëlle, and Marlou Schrover. "The Dutch State as a Pimp: Policies Regarding a Brothel on Curaçao (1945–1956)." *Tijdschrift voor Sociale en Economische Geschiedenis* 10 (2013): 33–54.

Klubock, Thomas Miller. *Contested Communities: Class, Gender, and Politics in El Teniente Copper Mine, 1904–1951.* Durham, NC: Duke University Press, 1998.

Kluchin, Rebecca. *Fit to be Tied: Sterilization and Reproductive Rights in America.* New Brunswick, NJ: Rutgers University Press, 2009.

Koot, Willem, and Anco Ringeling. *De Antillianen.* Muiderberg: Dick Coutinho, 1984.

Kuipers, Sanneke. *The Crisis Imperative: Crisis Rhetoric and Welfare State Reform in Belgium and the Netherlands in the Early 1990s.* Amsterdam: Amsterdam University Press, 2005.

Kuitenbrouwer, Maarten. *Dutch Scholarship in the Age of Empire and Beyond: KITLV—the Royal Netherlands Institute of Southeast Asian and Caribbean Studies, 1851–2011.* Translated by Lorri Granger. Leiden: Brill, 2014.

Kunz, Sarah. "A Business Empire and its Migrants: Royal Dutch Shell and the Management of Racial Capitalism." *Transactions of the Institute of British Geographers* 45, no. 2 (2019): 377–91.

Kutner, Jon. "Schlumberger." *Texas State Historical Association: Handbook of Texas.* Accessed February 18, 2022. https://www.tshaonline.org/handbook /entries/schlumberger.

Lamur, Humphrey, Bina Makhan, Mariëlle Morsink, and Henny Reubsaet. *Caraïbische vrouwen en anticonceptie.* Delft: Uitgeverij Eburon, 1990.

Lee, Christopher J. "Between a Movement and an Era: The Origins and Afterlives of Bandung." In *Making a World after Empire: The Bandung Moment and its Political Afterlives,* edited by Christopher J. Lee, 1–42. Athens: Ohio University Press, 2010.

Leer, Aisha. "Muhé na Kandela (Women on Fire): Women's Role in the Revolt of 'Trinta di Mei,' 1969." Paper presented at the Association of Caribbean Historians, Curaçao, May 26–30, 2019.

Lenders, Maria, and Marjolein van Vlijmen-van de Rhoer. "Mijn God, hoe ga ik doen? De positie van Creoolse alleenstaande moeders in Amsterdam." Ph.D. diss., Universiteit van Amsterdam, 1983.

Lewis, Linden. "Caribbean Masculinity at the *Fin de Siècle.*" In *Interrogating Caribbean Masculinities: Theoretical and Empirical* Analyses, edited by Rhoda E. Reddock, 244–66. Kingston: University of the West Indies Press, 2004.

Lewis, Oscar. *La Vida: A Puerto Rican Family in the Culture of Poverty.* New York: Random House, 1966.

López, Iris. *Matters of Choice: Puerto Rican Women's Struggle for Reproductive Freedom.* New Brunswick, NJ: Rutgers University Press, 2008.

Lorenzini, Sara. *Development: A Cold War History.* Princeton, NJ: Princeton University Press, 2019.

Lowe, Lisa. *The Intimacies of Four Continents.* Durham, NC: Duke University Press, 2015.

Luke, Learie B. *Identity and Secession in the Caribbean: Tobago versus Trinidad, 1889–1980.* Kingston: University of the West Indies Press, 2007.

Lyons, Amelia. *The Civilizing Mission in the Metropole: Algerian Families and the French Welfare State during Decolonization.* Stanford, CA: Stanford University Press, 2013.

Mac Donald, Stacey. "Life in 'Paradise': A Social Psychological and Anthropological Study of Nature Conservation in the Caribbean Netherlands." Ph.D. diss, Leiden University, 2022.

Macpherson, Anne. *From Colony to Nation: Women Activists and the Gendering of Politics in Belize, 1912–1982.* Lincoln: University of Nebraska Press, 2007.

Makdoembaks, Nizaar. *Killing Camp Suffisant: Brieven aan de Nederlandse regering rond een verhulde oorlogsmisdaad.* Curaçao: Stichting Eerherstel Oorlogsslachtoffers Curaçao, 2017.

Mallon, Florencia. "*Barbudos*, Warriors, and *Rotos*: The MIR, Masculinity, and Power in the Chilean Agrarian Reform, 1965–74." In *Changing Men and*

Masculinities in Latin America, edited by Matthew C. Guttman, 179–215. Durham, NC: Duke University Press, 2003.

Mamdani, Mahmood. *The Myth of Population Control.* New York: Monthly Review Press, 1972.

Manley, Elizabeth. *The Paradox of Paternalism: Women and the Politics of Authoritarianism in the Dominican Republic.* Gainesville: University Press of Florida, 2017.

Marks, Arnaud F. *Male and Female and the Afro-Curaçaoan Household.* Translated by Maria J. L. van Yperen. The Hague: Martinus Nijhoff, 1976.

Martina, Egbert Alejandro. "Policy and Intimacy." *Policy People.* Accessed November 7, 2022. http://policy-people.com/egbert-alejandro-martina -policy-and-intimacy/.

Martis, Jacqueline. "Sun, Sex, and Not So Golden: 25 Years of Research on the Sex Trade in Curaçao." Paper presented at the Society for Caribbean Studies, United Kingdom, July 6, 2022.

———. "Tourism and the Sex Trade in St. Maarten and Curaçao, the Netherlands Antilles." In *Sun, Sex, and Gold: Tourism and Sex Work in the Caribbean,* edited by Kamala Kempadoo, 201–16. Lanham: Rowman & Littlefield, 1999.

Marugg, Tip. *The Roar of Morning.* Translated by Paul Vincent. New Haven: Yale, 2015 [1988].

Mason, Clendon H. *The Greatest of These.* St. Lucia: The Voice Publishing Co., 1953.

Matera, Marc. *Black London: The Imperial Metropolis and Decolonization in the Twentieth Century.* Berkeley: University of California Press, 2015.

———. "An Empire of Development: Africa and the Caribbean in *God's Chillun.*" *Twentieth Century British History* 23, no. 1 (2012): 12–37.

Maurer, Bill. *Recharting the Caribbean: Land, Law, and Citizenship in the British Virgin Islands.* Ann Arbor: University of Michigan Press, 1997.

Mawby, Spencer. *Ordering Independence: The End of Empire in the Anglophone Caribbean, 1947–1969.* Basingstoke: Palgrave Macmillan, 2012.

McKittrick, Katherine. "Mathematics Black Life." *The Black Scholar* 44, no. 2 (2014): 16–28.

Meeks, Brian. *Radical Caribbean: From Black Power to Abu Bakr.* Kingston: University of the West Indies Press, 1996.

Mepschen, Paul and Jan Willem Duyvendak. "European Sexual Nationalisms: The Culturalization of Citizenship and the Sexual Politics of Belonging and Exclusion." *Perspectives on Europe* (2012): 70–76.

Mielants, Eric H. "From Periphery to the Core: A Case Study on the Migration and Incorporation of Recent Caribbean Immigrants in the Netherlands." In *Caribbean Migration to Western Europe and the United States: Essays on Incorporation, Identity, and Citizenship,* edited by Margarita Cervantes-Rodriguez, Ramón Grosfoguel, and Eric. H. Mielants, 58–93. Philadelphia: Temple University Press, 2008.

Milanich, Nara. "Daddy Issues: 'Responsible Paternity' as Public Policy in Latin America." *World Policy Institute* XXXIV, no. 3 (2017): 8–14.

Mintz, Sidney. "The Caribbean as a Socio-Cultural Area." *Cahiers d'histoire mondiale* 9, no. 1 (1965): 912–37.

Mintz, Sidney, and Richard Price. *The Birth of African-American Culture: An Anthropological Perspective*. Boston: Beacon Press, 1992.

Misiedjan, Daphina. "Klimaat en het Koninkrijk: Waarom de internationale klimaatafspraken niet gelden voor de Caribische eilanden." *Nederlands Juristenblad* 25 (2022): 1683–88.

Mitchell, Timothy. *Carbon Democracy: Political Power in the Age of Oil*. London: Verso, 2011.

Monteiro, Marit. *Gods predikers: Dominicanen in Nederland (1795–2000)*. Hilversum: Verloren, 2008.

Moore, Brian, and Michelle Johnson. *Neither Led nor Driven: Contesting British Cultural Imperialism in Jamaica, 1865–1920*. Kingston: University of the West Indies Press, 2004.

Moynihan, Daniel Patrick. "The Negro Family: The Case for National Action." Washington, DC: United States Department of Labor, 1965.

Murphy, Michelle. *The Economization of Life*. Durham, NC: Duke University Press, 2017.

Nash, Linda. *Inescapable Ecologies: A History of Disease, Environment, and Knowledge*. Berkeley: University of California Press, 2006.

Navarro, Tami. *Virgin Capital: Race, Gender, and Financialization in the US Virgin Islands*. Albany: SUNY Press, 2021.

Necochea López, Raúl. *A History of Family Planning in Twentieth-Century Peru*. Chapel Hill: University of North Carolina Press, 2014.

———. "Priests and Pills: Catholic Family Planning in Peru, 1967–1976." *Latin American Research Review* 43, no. 2 (2008): 34–56.

Neptune, Harvey. *Caliban and the Yankees: Trinidad and the United States Occupation*. Chapel Hill: University of North Carolina Press, 2007.

Nimako, Kwame, and Glenn Willemsen. *The Dutch Atlantic: Slavery, Abolition and Emancipation*. London: Pluto Press, 2011.

Nixon, Angelique V. *Resisting Paradise: Tourism, Diaspora, and Sexuality in Caribbean Culture*. Jackson: University Press of Mississippi, 2015.

Nixon, Rob. *Slow Violence and the Environmentalism of the Poor*. Cambridge: Harvard University Press, 2013.

O'Connor, Alice. *Poverty Knowledge: Social Science, Social Policy, and the Poor in Twentieth-Century US History*. Princeton, NJ: Princeton University Press, 2001.

Ogle, Vanessa. "Archipelago Capitalism: Tax Havens, Offshore Money, and the State, 1950s–1970s." *American Historical Review* 122, no. 5 (2017): 1431–58.

Olton, Tulip Patricia. *Minderheidsstatus of stijgingsdrang? Antilliaanse en Arubaanse vrouwen in Amsterdam en hun gezinsvorming.* Delft: Uitgeverij Eburon, 1994.

de Onís, Catalina M. *Energy Islands: Metaphors of Power, Extractivism, and Justice in Puerto Rico.* Oakland: University of California Press, 2021.

Oostindie, Gert. "Black Power, Popular Revolt, and Decolonization in the Dutch Caribbean." In *Black Power in the Caribbean*, edited by Kate Quinn, 239–60. Gainesville: University Press of Florida, 2014.

——, ed. *Curaçao, 30 mei 1969. Verhalen over de revolte.* Amsterdam: Amsterdam University Press, 1999.

——. "De sprekers en hun verhalen." In *Curaçao, 30 mei 1969. Verhalen over de revolte*, edited by Gert Oostindie, 7–11. Amsterdam: Amsterdam University Press, 1999.

——, ed. *Ethnicity in the Caribbean: Essays in Honor of Harry Hoetink.* Amsterdam: Amsterdam University Press, 2005.

——. *Postcolonial Netherlands: Sixty-five Years of Forgetting, Commemorating, Silencing.* Amsterdam: Amsterdam University Press, 2010.

——. "Woedend vuur: 'Trinta di mei,' dertig jaar later." In *Dromen en littekens. Dertig jaar na de Curaçaose revolte, 30 mei 1969*, edited by Gert Oostindie, 9–39. Amsterdam: Amsterdam University Press, 1999.

Oostindie, Gert, and Inge Klinkers. *Decolonising the Caribbean: Dutch Policies in Comparative Perspective.* Amsterdam: Amsterdam University Press, 2003.

——. *Gedeeld Koninkrijk. De ontmanteling van de Nederlandse Antillen en de vernieuwing van de trans-Atlantische relaties.* Amsterdam: Amsterdam University Press, 2012.

——. *Knellende Koninkrijksbanden. Het Nederlandse dekolonisatiebeleid in de Caraïben, 1940–2000.* Amsterdam: Amsterdam University Press, 2001.

Painter, David S. "The Marshall Plan and Oil." *Cold War History* 9, no. 2 (2009): 159–75.

Palan, Ronen. *The Offshore World: Sovereign Markets, Virtual Places, and Nomad Millionaires.* Ithaca, NY: Cornell University Press, 2006.

Palmer, Colin. *Eric Williams and the Making of the Modern Caribbean.* Chapel Hill: University of North Carolina Press, 2009.

Paula, Alejandro F. *From Objective to Subjective Social Barriers: A Historico-Philosophical Analysis of Certain Negative Attitudes among the Negroid Population of Curaçao.* Curaçao: Curaçao NV, 1972.

Penninx, Rinus. *Minderheidsvorming en emancipatie. Balans van kennisverwerving ten aanzien van immigranten en woonwagenbewoners, 1967–1987.* Alphen aan den Rijn: Samsom, 1988.

——. *Wie betaalt, bepaalt? De ontwikkeling en programmering van onderzoek naar migranten, etnische minderheden en woonwagenbewoners 1955–1985, met speciale aandacht voor de rol van de overheid.* Amsterdam: Instituut voor Sociale Geographie, 1988.

Perry, Keston K. "Realising Climate Reparations: Towards a Global Climate Stabilization Fund and Resilience Fund Programme for Loss and Damage in Marginalised and Former Colonised Societies." *SSRN*. Published March 1, 2020. https://ssrn.com/abstract=3561121.

Petrocultures Research Group. *After Oil*. Morgantown: West Virginia University Press, 2016.

Philipps, Ann E. "De migratie van engelssprekende dienstboden naar Curaçao (1940–1960)." In *Mundu Yama Sinta Mira: Womanhood in Curaçao*, edited by Richenel Ansano, Joceline Clemencia, Jeanette Cook, and Eithel Martis, 97–106. Willemstad: Fundashon Publikashon Curaçao, 1992.

Porteous, J. Douglas. "Social Class in Atacama Company Towns." *Annals of the Association of American Geographers* 64, no. 3 (1974): 409–17.

Potts, Shaina. "Offshore." In *Keywords in Radical Geography: Antipode at 50*, edited by *Antipode* Editorial Collective, 198–201. Chichester: John Wiley & Sons Ltd., 2019.

Pulster, Erin L., Giffe Johnson, Dave Hollander, James McCluskey, and Raymond Harbison. "Levels and Sources of Atmospheric Polycyclic Aromatic Hydrocarbons Surrounding an Oil Refinery in Curaçao." *Journal of Environmental Protection* 10 (2019): 431–53.

Putnam, Lara. "Borderlands and Border Crossers: Migrants and Boundaries in the Greater Caribbean, 1840–1940." *Small Axe* 43 (2014): 7–21.

———. *The Company They Kept: Migrants and the Politics of Gender in Caribbean Costa Rica, 1870–1960*. Chapel Hill: University of North Carolina Press, 2002.

———. *Radical Moves: Caribbean Migrants and the Politics of Race in the Jazz Age*. Chapel Hill: University of North Carolina Press, 2013.

———. "The World in One Hot Sweaty Place: Migration, Family, and Global Transformation as Seen from Carúpano, Venezuela, 1860–1940." Paper presented at the American Historical Association Annual Meeting, Atlanta, January 4–6, 2016.

Quinn, Kate. "New Perspectives on Black Power in the Caribbean." In *Black Power in the Caribbean*, edited by Kate Quinn, 1–24. Gainesville: University Press of Florida, 2014.

Ramírez de Arellano, Annette B., and Conrad Seipp. *Colonialism, Catholicism and Contraception: A History of Birth Control in Puerto Rico*. Chapel Hill: University of North Carolina Press, 1983.

Ramos, Aarón Gamaliel, and Ángel Israel Rivera Ortiz, eds. *Islands at the Crossroads: Politics in the Non-Independent Caribbean*. Kingston: Ian Randle Publishers, 2001.

Rath, Jan. *Minorisiering. De sociale constructie van 'etnische minderheden.'* Amsterdam: Sua, 1991.

———. "The Netherlands: A Reluctant Country of Immigration." *Tijdschrift voor economische en sociale geografie* 100, no. 5 (2009): 674–81.

Reddock, Rhoda E. "Interrogating Caribbean Masculinities: An Introduction." In *Interrogating Caribbean Masculinities: Theoretical and Empirical Analyses*, edited by Rhoda E. Reddock, xiii–xxxiv. Kingston: University of the West Indies Press, 2004.

Richardson, G. T. E. "Sweet Breakaway: An Ethnographic Study of Aruban Calypso Music and the Narratives of the One Happy Island." Ph.D. diss., Vrije Universiteit Amsterdam, 2020.

Richardson, Bonham C. "Caribbean Migrations, 1838–1985." In *The Modern Caribbean*, edited by Franklin Knight and Colin Palmer, 203–28. Chapel Hill: University of North Carolina Press, 1989.

———. *The Caribbean in the Wider World, 1492–1992*. Cambridge: Cambridge University Press, 1992.

Ridderstaat, Jorge R. *The Lago Story: The Compelling Story of an Oil Company on the Island of Aruba*. Oranjestad: Editorial Charuba, 2007.

Roberts, Dorothy. *Killing the Black Body: Race, Reproduction, and the Meaning of Liberty*. New York: Vintage, 2017 [1997].

Robinson, Tracy. "Mass Weddings in Jamaica and the Production of Academic Folk Knowledge." *Small Axe* 24, no. 3 (2020): 65–80.

———. "The Properties of Citizens: A Caribbean Grammar of Conjugal Categories." *Du Bois Review* 10, no. 2 (2013): 425–46.

Rodriguez, Adaly. *The Rise of Women's Rights on Curaçao: The Potential of the Women's Convention to the Empowerment of Equal Rights of Women in Curaçao*. Amsterdam: SWP, 2015.

Roe, Angela. "The Sound of Silence: Ideology of National Identity and Racial Inequality in Contemporary Curaçao." Ph.D. diss, Florida International University, 2016.

Roediger, David. *The Wages of Whiteness: Race and the Making of the American Working Class*. London: Verso, 2007 [1991].

Roitman, Jessica Vance. "'A Mass of *Mestiezen, Castiezen*, and *Mulatten*': Contending with Color in the Netherlands Antilles." *Atlantic Studies* 14, no. 3 (2017): 399–417.

———. "Mediating Multiculturalism: Jews, Blacks, and Curaçao." In *The Sephardic Atlantic: Colonial Histories and Postcolonial Perspectives*, edited by Sina Rauschenbach and Jonathan Schorsch, 85–111. Cham: Palgrave Macmillan, 2018.

Roldán, Mary. "Acción Cultural Popular, Responsible Procreation, and the Roots of Social Activism in Rural Colombia." *Latin American Research Review* 49 (2014): 27–44.

Römer, Louis Philippe. "Speaking Like a Sovereign Public: Talk Radio, Imperial Aftermaths, and Political Aspirations in Curaçao." Ph.D. diss, New York University, 2017.

Römer, René. *Een volk op weg, un pueblo na kaminda. Een sociologische studie van de Curaçaose samenleving*. Zutphen: De Walburg Pers, 1979.

———. "Ik had nooit gedacht dat ons volk tot zo'n opstand in staat was." In *Curaçao, 30 mei 1969. Verhalen over de revolte*, edited by Gert Oostindie, 108–15. Amsterdam: Amsterdam University Press, 1999.

———. "Labour Unions and Labour Conflict in Curaçao." *New West Indian Guide* 55, no. 3/4 (1981): 138–53.

Römer-Kenepa, Nolda. "Vrouwenleven op Curaçao: Laat achttiende eeuw en vroeg negentiende eeuw." Master's thesis, Vrije Universiteit Amsterdam, 1980.

Ross, Kristin. *Fast Cars, Clean Bodies: Decolonization and the Reordering of French Culture*. Boston: MIT Press, 1995.

Rupert, Linda. *Creolization and Contraband: Curaçao in the Early Modern Atlantic World*. Athens: University of Georgia Press, 2012.

Santiago, Myrna. *The Ecology of Oil: Environment, Labor, and the Mexican Revolution*. Cambridge: Cambridge University Press, 2014.

———. "Women of the Mexican Oil Fields: Class, Nationality, Economy, Culture, 1900–1938." *Journal of Women's History* 21, no. 1 (2009): 87–110.

Schields, Chelsea. "'Combatting the Sensuality of the Youth': Youthful Sexuality and the Reformulation of Desire in the Dutch Vice Laws of 1911." *Gender & History* 31 (2019): 115–31.

———. "Intimacy and Integration: The Ambivalent Achievement of Marriage Equality in the Dutch Caribbean, 2007–2012." In *Euro-Caribbean Societies in the 21st Century: Offshore Finance, Local Élites and Contentious Politics*, edited by Sébastien Chauvin, Peter Clegg, and Bruno Cousin, 176–89. Abingdon, UK: Routledge, 2018.

Schoen, Joanna. *Choice and Coercion: Birth Control, Sterilization, and Abortion in Public Health and Welfare*. Chapel Hill: University of North Carolina Press, 2005.

Scott, Daryl Michael. *Contempt and Pity: Social Policy and the Image of the Damaged Black Psyche, 1880–1996*. Chapel Hill: University of North Carolina Press, 1997.

Sharpe, Michael O. "Globalization and Migration: Post-Colonial Dutch Antillean and Aruban Immigrant Political Incorporation in the Netherlands." *Dialectical Anthropology* 29, no. 3/4 (2005): 291–314.

———. *Postcolonial Citizens and Ethnic Migration: The Netherlands and Japan in the Age of Globalization*. Basingstoke: Palgrave Macmillan, 2014.

Sheller, Mimi. *Citizenship from Below: Erotic Agency and Caribbean Freedom*. Durham, NC: Duke University Press, 2012.

———. *Island Futures: Caribbean Survival in the Anthropocene*. Durham, NC: Duke University Press, 2020.

Shepard, Todd. *The Invention of Decolonization: The Algerian War and the Remaking of France*. Ithaca, NY: Cornell University Press, 2008.

———. *Sex, France, and Arab Men, 1962–1978*. Chicago: University of Chicago Press, 2017.

Sippial, Tiffany. *Prostitution, Modernity, and the Making of the Cuban Republic, 1840–1920.* Chapel Hill: University of North Carolina Press, 2013.

Sluyterman, Keetie. "Decolonisation and the Organisation of the International Workforce: Dutch Multinationals in Indonesia, 1945–1967." *Business History* 62, no. 7 (2020): 1182–1201.

———. *A History of Royal Dutch Shell, Vol. 3: Keeping Competitive in Turbulent Markets.* Oxford: Oxford University Press, 2007.

Smith, Faith. "Introduction: Sexing the Citizen." In *Sex and the Citizen: Interrogating the Caribbean*, edited by Faith Smith, 1–17. Charlottesville: University of Virginia Press, 2011.

Smith, Jason. *Smart Machines and Service Work: Automation in an Age of Stagnation.* London: Reaktion Books, 2020.

Solinger, Rickie, and Mie Nakachi. "Introduction." In *Reproductive States: Global Perspectives on the Invention and Implementation of Population Policy*, edited by Rickie Solinger and Mie Nakachi, 1–32. Oxford: Oxford University Press, 2016.

Stoler, Ann Laura. *Carnal Knowledge and Imperial Power: Race and the Intimate in Colonial Rule.* Berkeley: University of California Press, 2002.

Surinamers en Antillianen in Amsterdam: Verkorte versie van het onderzoeksverslag. Amsterdam: Gemeentelijke Sociale Dienst, 1979.

Swan, Quito. *Black Power in Bermuda: The Struggle for Decolonization.* Basingstoke: Palgrave Macmillan, 2009.

Szeman, Imre, and Dominic Boyer, eds. *Energy Humanities: An Anthology.* Baltimore: Johns Hopkins University Press, 2017.

Tarlo, Emma. *Unsettling Memories: Narratives of the Emergency in Delhi.* Berkeley: University of California Press, 2003.

Taussig, Charles. "A Four Power Program in the Caribbean." *Foreign Affairs* 24, no. 4 (1946): 699–710.

Thomas, Deborah. "The Violence of Diaspora: Governmentality, Class Cultures, and Circulations." *Radical History Review* 103 (2009): 83–104.

Tinker Salas, Miguel. *The Enduring Legacy: Oil, Culture, and Society in Venezuela.* Durham, NC: Duke University Press, 2009.

Tinsley, Omise'eke Natasha. *Thiefing Sugar: Eroticism between Women in Caribbean Literature.* Durham, NC: Duke University Press, 2010.

Tinsman, Heidi. *Partners in Conflict: The Politics of Gender, Sexuality, and Labor in Chilean Agricultural Reform, 1950–1973.* Durham, NC: Duke University Press, 2002.

Trotz, D. Alissa. "Behind the Banner of Culture? Gender, 'Race,' and the Family in Guyana." *New West Indian Guide* 77, no. 1/2 (2003): 5–29.

Turits, Richard Lee. "A World Destroyed, A Nation Imposed: The 1937 Haitian Massacre in the Dominican Republic." *Hispanic American Historical Review* 82, no. 3 (2002): 589–635.

van Beurden, Tijn, and Joost Jonker. "A Perfect Symbiosis: Curaçao, the Netherlands and Financial Offshore Services, 1951–2003." *Financial History Review* 28, no. 1 (2021): 67–95.

van der Pijl, Yvon, and Francio Guadeloupe, eds. *Equaliberty in the Dutch Caribbean: Ways of Being Non/Sovereign*. New Brunswick, NJ: Rutgers University Press, 2022.

van der Ploeg, Frederick. "The Political Economy of a Consensus Society: Experience from Behind the Dykes." *The Economic and Social Review* 28, no. 4 (1997): 307–32.

van Dijk, Anke, Hans van Hulst, and Linda Terpstra. *Mama Soltera. De positie van 'alleenstaande' Curaçaose en Arubaanse moeders in Nederland*. The Hague: Warray, 1990.

van Dijke, Anke, and Linda Terpstra. *Je kunt beter bij je moeder blijven*. Leiden: KITLV, 1987.

van Ditzhuijzen, Jeannette. *Anyway . . . Sergio Leon, vrouwenarts en eilandskind*. Utrecht: LM Publishers, 2015.

van Doorne-Huiskes, Anneke, and Laura den Dulk. "The Netherlands." In *Families and States in Western Europe*, edited by Quentin Skinner, 129–45. Cambridge: Cambridge University Press, 2011.

van Heelsum, Anja. *Migranten organisaties in Nederland. Deel 2: Functioneren van de organisaties*. Utrecht: FORUM, Instituut voor Multiculturele Ontwikkeling, 2004.

van Hoorn, W. D. "Het kindertal van Surinamers en Antillianen in Nederland." *Maandstatistiek van de bevolking* 36, no. 1 (1988): 18–21.

van Hulst, Hans. "A Continuing Construction of Crisis: Antilleans, Especially Curaçaoans, in the Netherlands." In *Immigrant Integration: The Dutch Case*, edited by Hans Vermeulen and Rinus Penninx, 93–122. Amsterdam: Spinhuis, 2000.

van Leusden, Hans. "Indicators of Marriage and Marriage Dissolution of the Female Population of Curaçao, 1960–1962, 1970–1972, and 1980–1981: A Multidimensional Analysis." Working paper no. 66. Voorburg: Netherlands Interuniversity Demographic Institute, 1985.

van Rossum, Matthias, and Karwan Fatah-Black. "Wat is winst? De economische impact van de Nederlandse trans-Atlantische slavenhandel." *Tijdschrift voor Sociale en Economische Geschiedenis* 9, no. 1 (2012): 3–29.

van Soest, Jaap. *Olie als water. De Curaçaose economie in de eerste helft van de twintigste eeuw*. Zutphen: De Walburg Pers, 1977 [1976].

van 't Hoofd, Danielle, and Jolanda Westerlaken. "'Mi ta lóra koene': Een onderzoek naar de leefsituatie van ongehuwde moeders met een onderstandsuitkering op Curaçao." Ph.D. diss, Katholieke Universiteit Brabant, 1988.

van Walsum, Sarah. "Sex and the Regulation of Belonging: Dutch Family Migration Policies in the Context of Changing Family Norms." In *Gender,*

Generation and the Family in International Migration, edited by Albert Kraler, Eleonore Kofman, Martin Kohli, and Camille Schmoll, 43–58. Amsterdam: Amsterdam University Press, 2012.

Vergès, Françoise. *Monsters and Revolutionaries: Colonial Family Romance and Métissage.* Durham, NC: Duke University Press, 1999.

Vermeulen, Hans and Rinus Penninx. "Introduction." In *Immigrant Integration: The Dutch Case*, edited by Hans Vermeulen and Rinus Penninx, 1–35. Amsterdam: Spinhuis, 2000.

Verton, Peter. *Politieke dynamiek en dekolonisatie. De Nederlandse Antillen tussen autonomie en onafhankelijkheid.* Alphen aan den Rijn: Samsom, 1977.

Visser, Jelle, and Anton Hemerijck. *A Dutch Miracle: Job Growth, Welfare Reform and Corporatism in the Netherlands.* Amsterdam: University of Amsterdam Press, 1997.

Vitalis, Robert. *America's Kingdom: Mythmaking on the Saudi Oil Frontier.* Stanford, CA: Stanford University Press, 2007.

Vitalis, Robert. *Oilcraft: The Myths of Scarcity and Security That Haunt U.S. Energy Policy.* Stanford, CA: Stanford Univeristy Press, 2020.

Wall, Bennett H. *Growth in a Changing Environment: A History of Standard Oil Company (New Jersey) 1950–1972 and Exxon Corporation 1950–1975.* New York: McGraw-Hill Book Company, 1988.

Weeks, Kathi. *The Problem with Work: Feminism, Marxism, Antiwork Politics, and Postwork Imaginaries.* Durham, NC: Duke University Press, 2011.

Wekker, Gloria. *The Politics of Passion: Women's Sexual Culture in the Afro-Surinamese Diaspora.* New York: Columbia University Press, 2006.

———. *White Innocence: Paradoxes of Colonialism and Race.* Durham, NC: Duke University Press, 2016.

Wekker, Gloria, and Helma Lutz. "Een hoogvlakte met koude winden. De geschiedenis van het gender- en etniciteitsdenken in Nederland." In *Caleidoscopische visies. De zwarte, migranten- en vluchtelingen-vrouwenbeweging in Nederland*, edited by Maayke Botman and Nancy Jouwe, 25–49. Amsterdam: Koninklijk Instituut voor de Tropen, 2001.

Westermann, J. H. "Demografische conferentie van de Caribische commissie, Trinidad, 1957." *Nieuw West Indische Gids* 38, no. 1 (1958): 129–48.

Wilder, Gary. *Freedom Time: Negritude, Decolonization, and the Future of the World.* Durham, NC: Duke University Press, 2015.

Wilhelmina prinses der Nederlanden. *The Queen Looks at the Future: Important Statements of H. M. Queen Wilhelmina on War and Peace Aims.* New York: The Netherlands Information Bureau, 1943.

Williams, Casey. "Energy Humanities." *Energy Humanities.* Published October 6, 2020. https://www.energyhumanities.ca/news/energy-humanities-casey-williams.

Wong, R. A., and J. Arends. *SAAM-groepen in de bijstand. Een exploratief onderzoek naar de financieel-materiële en uitstroomproblematiek van Surinamers, Antillianen, Arubanen en Molukkers in de bijstand.* The Hague: Ministerie van Sociale Zaken en Werkgelegenheid, 1992.

Zafir, Lindsay. "Queer Connections: Jean Genet, the Black Panther Party, and the Coalition Politics of the Long 1960s." *GLQ: A Journal of Lesbian and Gay Studies* 27, no. 2 (2021): 253–79.

Index

abortion, 104–5, 133, 173; arguments for decriminalization of, 133; laws criminalizing, 110, 227n73

Abraham-van der Mark, Eva, 47–48, 105

Aceh, 25, 208n20

Afro-Curaçaoans, 22–23, 24, 38, 95, 98, 117, 168, 243–44n81; laborers, 11, 25, 37, 45, 50, 121; mobilization of, 44; racial-sexual subjection of, 10, 23–24, 39, 95

Afro-Curaçaoan women, 27, 28, 88; attempts to regulate fertility of, 88, 109–10; economic practices, 28–29. *See also* sex workers, Afro-Curaçaoan

Aitatus, Mary, 175

Alexander, M. Jacqui, 146

Algemene Bijstandswet (ABW), 162–63, 179–80

Algemene Haven Unie (AHU), 124

Algeria, 151

Alkema, Yellie, 128–29

American Federation of Labor and Congress of Industrial Organizations (AFL-CIO), 123

Amigoe di Curaçao, 69, 82

Amin, Samir, 130

Amsterdam, 124–25, 128, 160, 161, 162, 163, 169

Antillean criminal code, 31, 35, 65, 75; distinction from Dutch law, 40, 105

anti-imperialism, 151

anti-vice legislation (Dutch), 75, 104–5

Apostel, E. S., 49*fig.*

Arend refinery, 218n47

Arends, Harold, 125

Arends, J., 178

Arion, Frank Martinus, 137, 234n75

Aruba, 1, 13, 51, 102, 151, 152, 158, 170, 192; African presence in preindustrial Aruba, 10–11, 71; aversion of to the pursuit of national sovereignty, 72–73, 172; Chinese migration to, 67; and claims to whiteness, 57–59, 68, 72; complaints concerning the treatment of Aruban workers, 58–59; economic boom of the 1930s to 1950s, 3, 12, 55–56; economic bust of and the shuttering of oil refineries on, 3, 12, 80–81, 157–58; family planning campaign on, 14–15, 102–3; migrants to, 56–57, 67; nonsovereign political status of, 73; nostalgia in for the age of oil, 7; oil and political aspirations in, 53; racial antagonism as a management strategy in, 58; recruitment of sex workers to, 2, 3; and regulation of prostitution, 64–66; role of in fueling interconnection, 7, 8–9*fig.*; and separation from the Netherlands Antilles or "status

Founded in 1893,
UNIVERSITY OF CALIFORNIA PRESS
publishes bold, progressive books and journals
on topics in the arts, humanities, social sciences,
and natural sciences—with a focus on social
justice issues—that inspire thought and action
among readers worldwide.

The UC PRESS FOUNDATION
raises funds to uphold the press's vital role
as an independent, nonprofit publisher, and
receives philanthropic support from a wide
range of individuals and institutions—and from
committed readers like you. To learn more, visit
ucpress.edu/supportus.